Also by John Kelly

Three on the Edge

The Great Mortality

The
GRAVES
ARE WALKING

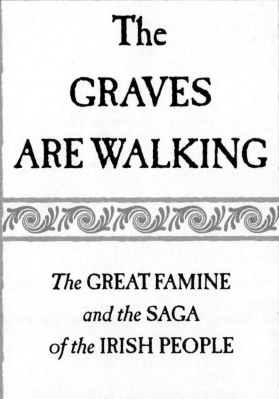

The
GRAVES
ARE WALKING

The GREAT FAMINE
and the SAGA
of the IRISH PEOPLE

JOHN KELLY

Henry Holt and Company   New York

Henry Holt and Company, LLC
Publishers since 1866
175 Fifth Avenue
New York, New York 10010
www.henryholt.com

Henry Holt® and Ⓜ® are registered trademarks of Henry Holt and Company, LLC.

Library of Congress Cataloging-in-Publication Data

Kelly, John, 1945–
  The graves are walking : the great famine and the saga of the Irish people / John
Kelly.—1st ed.
      p. cm.
  Includes bibliographical references and index.
  ISBN 978-0-8050-9184-7
  1. Ireland—History—Famine, 1845–1852. 2. Irish—Migrations—
History—19th century. 3. Ireland—Emigration and immigration—History—
19th century. 4. Famines—Ireland—History—19th century. I. Title.
II. Title: Great famine and the saga of the Irish people.
  DA950.7.K45 2012
  941.5081—dc23   2012011493

Henry Holt books are available for special promotions and premiums.
For details contact: Director, Special Markets.

First Edition 2012

Designed by Meryl Sussman Levavi

Printed in the United States of America

1 3 5 7 9 10 8 6 4 2

For Tim Malloy

They say that now the land is famine struck
The graves are walking.
. . . Two nights ago, at [a] churchyard,
A herdsman met a man who had no mouth,
Nor eyes, nor ears; his face a wall of flesh;
He saw him plainly by the light of the moon,
. . . What is the good of praying?

    —From scene 1, *The Countess Cathleen*,
    a verse drama by William Butler Yeats

Contents

The
GRAVES
ARE WALKING

Introduction

On a January morning in 1847, a carriage halted in front of a cabin outside Skibbereen, a market town in southwest Cork. The driver picked up the box on the carriage seat and handed it to the cabin owner, a small farmer, who had come out to greet him. "My dog brought it home last night," the driver said, apologetically. After he left, the farmer removed the mutilated head from the box, took it into the cabin, and wrapped it in a cloth. Tomorrow, he would return his wife's decapitated head to her grave.

By early 1847, "sights that . . . poison life til life is done" had become commonplace in Ireland. In the countryside, packs of feral dogs dug up the graves of the famine dead. In the cities, shoeless pauper women, with dead infants in their arms, stood on street corners, begging; along the coasts, men and women scaled three-hundred-foot cliffs in winter cold and wind in search of seagull eggs, or scoured the January tideline for seaweed. In the pestilential hospitals and workhouses, the weekly death rate rose into the thousands; in the crowded port towns, emigrants fought each other for space on the teeming docks. After more than two years of famine, people were no were longer leaving Ireland; they were fleeing, the way a crowd flees a burning building—heedlessly, recklessly—on ships that had no business on any ocean, let alone a January ocean, and often they fled in defiance of the family bonds for which the Irish were justly famous. In the overpowering desire to get out, husbands deserted wives, parents, children, brothers, sisters, sisters, brothers.

"The emigrants of this year are not like those of former years," the *Cork Examiner* declared in March 1847. "They are now actually *running away*." Ask an emigrant his destination that March, and he would have replied, "anywhere that wasn't Ireland." Among those too old, too young, too poor, sick, or frightened to leave, the ubiquity of death had compressed life to two simple wishes: an unmolested grave and a coffin to be buried in.

〄

Terry Eagleton, a former professor of literature at Oxford, has called the Irish famine "the greatest social disaster of 19th century Europe—an event with something of the characteristics of a low-level nuclear attack." In terms of the famine's impact on Irish demography, that is a fair assessment. Between 1845 and 1855—the period that encompasses the crisis years of 1845 to 1847 and their immediate aftermath—the Irish population of almost 8.2 million shrank by a third. Starvation and disease killed 1.1 million; emigration claimed another 2 million. On an absolute basis, the numbers pale in comparison to the 30 million Chinese who died in the Great Leap Forward famine of the early 1960s, and the 7 million who perished in the Ukrainian famine of the early 1930s; but Mao Zedong's China and Joseph Stalin's Soviet Union were large, populous nations able to sustain catastrophic mortalities. Ireland was not. At the end of the famine, one out of every three people was gone, and the survivors felt as stunned and bewildered by the scale of the loss as the Italian poet Petrarch did after the Black Death:

> Where are our dear friends now? What lightning bolt devoured them, what earthquake toppled them? What tempest drowned them? . . . There was a crowd of us, now we are almost alone.

What made the famine so devastating?

The role of simple bad luck cannot be ignored. Had the potato failed two generations earlier, when Ireland had a lower rate of potato dependency—or two generations later, when the economy was on a sounder footing, the demographic impact might have been less severe. But the potato failed in the mid-1840s, when a generation-long collapse in peasant living standards had made the bottom two-thirds of the nation solely, or almost solely, reliant on the potato, and Ireland had not yet developed the physical, commercial, and human infrastructure needed to cope with a major catastrophe. There were not enough food stores in rural areas to feed the suddenly potato-less peasantry, not enough mills to process the hundreds of thousands of tons of provisions that had to be imported to replace the lost potatoes, not enough physicians to cope with the historic pestilence that broke out in the midst of the famine, and not enough engineers, administrators, or other trained personnel to organize and manage an efficient relief effort. A modern example of the difference such resources can make in a national crisis is the contrasting experiences of Haiti, a country with an undeveloped infrastructure, where in 2010 an earthquake of magnitude 7.0 killed as many as 85,000, and Japan, a sophisticated and resource-rich country, where in 2011 an earthquake, of 9.0 magnitude, a tsunami, and a nuclear meltdown, produced a death toll of under 25,000. In 1845, when *Phytophthora infestans*, the fungus that caused the crop failures, appeared for the first time, Ireland was Haiti.

However, bad luck, a primitive infrastructure, and a poverty bordering on immiseration can only explain so much of the one-third population loss. British policy makers also bore much responsibility for what happened. The accusation is not new, of course, but the modern brief against Britain contains a different set of accusations. The old Irish nationalist charge that London pursued a deliberate policy of genocide in Ireland has been discredited; modern research has also tempered another old charge. With the exception of one critical period in late 1846 and early 1847, famine Ireland imported more food than she exported. What turned a natural disaster into a human disaster was the determination of senior British officials to use relief policy as an instrument of nation building in one of the most impoverished and turbulent parts of the Empire. In particular, Whitehall and Westminister were eager to modernize the Irish agricultural economy, which was widely viewed as the principal source of Ireland's poverty and chronic violence, and to improve the Irish character, which exhibited an alarming "dependence on government" and was utterly lacking in the virtues of the new industrial age, such as self-discipline and initiative. The result was a relief program that, in its particulars, was more concerned with fostering change than with saving lives. Thus, to facilitate agricultural modernization, London demanded that the inefficient small farmer, surrender his two- or three-acre plot in order to qualify for relief; and to promote self-reliance, Parliament passed the Poor Law Extension Act, which transferred the entire cost of relief to Ireland. The Extension Act proved a great boon for Irish tax collectors, whose numbers increased by 222.5 percent during the famine—and for Irish coffin makers, whose numbers increased by 187.6 percent—but not for the Irish peasantry, who were doing most of the dying. With saving lives reduced to a second order priority, the death toll continued its relentless march upward toward 1.1 million, carrying the headless mothers under one arm and the starving children under the other.

In *The Last Conquest of Ireland*, John Mitchel, a founding father of modern Irish nationalism, depicted the British officials who presided over the famine as genocidal gargoyles. They were not. In the main, they were wakeful-minded, God-fearing, and—by their own lights—well-intentioned men, and that is what makes them so depressing. If the famine has any enduring lesson to teach, it is about the harm that even the best are capable of when they lose their way and allow religion and political ideology to traduce reason and humanity.

CHAPTER ONE

The Savage Shore:
Three Englishmen in Ireland

L ate on a September afternoon in 1845, when the sky was low and the wind close, a horseman with a rooster's plume of red hair and an indefinable air of Englishness about him stood on a road in Donegal, surveying the empty landscape. Near Lough Derg, the rider had passed two dirty peasant children selling "rudely carved wooden crucifixes" and a peeling window poster proclaiming "the Sacred beauty of Jesus," and near Ballyshannon, a knot of half clad, shoeless peasant women lifting panniers of turf onto the back of an ancient ass. Then, the wind died, the ubiquitous castle ruins—palimpsests of conquest and loss—vanished from the landscape and the rider passed from human to geological time. Savage rock and cold mountain surrounded him now, and the only sound to be heard in the perfect stillness of the afternoon was the gravel crunching under the weight of his horse.

Out over the Atlantic, silos of angry black storm clouds were billowing skyward over a white-capped sea. By the time the rider arrived in Gweedore, it would be raining again. Even for Ireland, the weather had been unusually mutinous of late. "Heat, rain, cold and sunshine succeed each other at a confusing rate," the *Dublin Evening Post* had complained the other day. "Monday last was extremely wet, Tuesday was beautifully dry; yesterday . . . both wet and dry, and to-day again is equally

variable." During harvest season, the weather was always a major preoccupation in Ireland, but this season the news from Europe had made the preoccupation all-consuming. In June, a mysterious potato disease had appeared in Flanders; by the end of July, scarcely a sound potato was left between Silesia and Normandy; then, in early August, the Channel Islands and England were infected. Now there were rumors that the disease had appeared here.

In a country where two thirds of the population lived by the aphorism

Potatoes in the morning
Potatoes at night
And if I got up at midnight
It would still be potatoes.

the appearance of the new disease could be catastrophic. The rider was unworried, though. In Dungloe, he had passed fields "heavy" with healthy-looking potatoes, and last week, in County Fermanagh, the "luxuriant" potato fields had stretched all the way to the horizon. The Irish were an excitable people. The news from Europe, and the weather, had them on edge.

Mr. Thomas Campbell Foster's journey to Ireland had begun with a summons. Earlier in the year, he had been called to Printing House Square, home of his former employer, *The Times of London*, and offered a challenging assignment. In the forty-four years since the formation of the Anglo-Irish Union, Britain had grown steadily wealthier and mightier, while her partner, Ireland, had grown steadily poorer and more disorderly. The editors of *The Times* wanted Mr. Thomas Campbell Foster to cross the Irish Sea and answer a question that had eluded the best efforts of one hundred and fourteen government commissions, sixty-one special committees, and fifty years of study by almost every leading political economist of the age:

Why was Ireland collapsing?

It was now several months later, and as Mr. Foster made his way northwest to Donegal, he found himself thinking what a sad, poor country Ireland was. Every road crowded with paupers entombed in rags and filth; every field crowded with slatternly little farms, undrained bogs, roofless barns, broken fences, and mud cabins that defied every architectural principle Mr. Foster was aware of: smoke poured out through a hole in the front of the cabin where the door ought to be, rain poured in through the roof, and wind whistled through cracks in the mud walls. In front of almost every dwelling sat a pig in a puddle and a pile of dung, and behind many dwellings, a line of somber, untreed hills. The Irish hill was one of the most forlorn things Mr. Foster had ever seen.

In the 1830s and early 1840s, Ireland occupied the same place in the western mind that Haiti, the Congo, and Somalia occupy today. The very long parade of Irish experts that Mr. Foster joined the morning he accepted the *Times* assignment included not only government commissioners, members of Parliament, and political economists, but also some of the most famously enlightened personalities of the Victorian age, among them Alexis de Tocqueville, Sir Walter Scott, William Makepeace Thackeray, Anthony Trollope, Thomas Carlyle, and the well-known German travel writer Johann Kohl. On visits to Ireland, the celebrity experts would poke and probe every facet of the Irish economy, the Irish mind, the Irish family, the Irish work ethic, the Irish agricultural system, the Irish procreation rate, then return home in despair and write a book explaining why Ireland was the worst place in the world. "I used to pity the poor Letts of Livonia," declared the German Kohl. "Well, pardon my ignorance, now, I have seen Ireland." The Scot Carlyle came back to London proclaiming that he had seen hell: "The earth disowns it. Heaven is against it. Ireland should be burnt into a black unpeopled field rather than this should last."

Most contemporary analysis of Irish poverty began with Irish demography. In the late eighteenth and early nineteenth century, population growth accelerated everywhere in Europe but nowhere so sharply as in Ireland. Between about 1745 and 1800, the population doubled, from two and a half million to five million; then, between 1800 and 1845, it almost doubled again, from five million to nearly 8.2 million. During the French Wars—1793 to 1815—British demand for Irish foodstuffs and manufactures provided enough revenue to support the expanding population. In the early 1800s, the better sort of Irish farmer often lived nearly as well as his English counterpart. There was a sturdy two-story stone house, a wife and daughters dressed in imported clothes, and a cupboard full of tea, tobacco, and other luxury items. For a few decades, the smooth glide of history even made the life of the eternally poor Irish peasant more tolerable. With the country awash in British money, the peasant could afford to supplement his traditional bowl of potatoes with "extras" like buttermilk, meat, and herring. The official who called Napoleon the best friend the Irish farmer ever had exaggerated—but not greatly.

Waterloo brought an end to the happy time. In the postwar years, British demand for Irish goods weakened, agricultural prices fell, and the domestic economy contracted. In the 1820s, when tariffs between the Union partners were lifted, the contraction intensified. An influx of cheap machine-made goods from the mills of Lancaster devastated the Irish textile industry outside Ulster. Thousands were thrown out of work, and, in the pockets of southern Ireland where the industry survived, wages fell precipitously. In 1800, at the height of the wartime boom, a weaver in Drogheda, a town north of Dublin, earned between 14 shillings and 21 shillings (£1.1) per week. A generation later, a Drogheda weaver earned a quarter to a half of what his father had: 4 shillings per week for plain goods and 8 shillings for fancy goods. In Limerick, John Geary, a physician, told a visiting English commission about his recent encounter with a former textile worker; the man was lying in bed next to his wife, who had typhus. "I begged him to get up," said Geary, "and I shall never forget so long as I live his answer to me, 'Ah sir, if I get up and breathe the air and walk about I will get an appetite . . . and I have nothing to eat and not a penny to buy anything.'"

Between 1821 and 1841, shipbuilding, glass making, and other domestic industries followed textile manufacture into oblivion, and the portion of the Irish workforce employed in manufacturing plummeted from 43 percent to 28 percent. At a trade show in Dublin in the early 1850s, almost all the machinery on exhibit was British. "A net for confining sheep on pasture" was one of the few examples of Irish technology.

The industrial collapse pushed people onto the already crowded land. In the 1820s and 1830s, Irish agriculture went where Irish agriculture had never gone before—up mountainsides, down to the thin sandy soils of the seashore, out onto wild, windswept cliffs. For a time, Irish rents also went where Irish rents had never gone before, and although they stablilized in the years before 1845, the Irish farmer was slow to feel the stabilization. "People are forced from want to promise any rent," a land agent in Galway observed. "I know a man named Laughlin, who outbid his own brother and took a farm for more than it ever was or ever will be worth."

The intense land hunger produced a granular subdivision of the Irish countryside. Unable to make the rent, the four-acre farmer would sublet two acres to another farmer, who would rent half an acre of potato ground to an agricultural laborer. By 1841, 45 percent of the agricultural holdings in Ireland were under five acres, and as subsistence farming grew, living standards fell. Milk disappeared from the peasant diet or became bull's milk—unsifted oats fermented in water. Meat, eggs, butter, herring also vanished. And the cow that had formerly attended the peasant's cabin was replaced by the pig, less expensive and easier to convert into rent money. Asked why he allowed his pig to sleep in the family cabin, one peasant replied, "It's him that pays the rent, ain't it."

Peasant dress also grew meaner; clothing was mended, remended, then mended a third, fourth, and fifth time. The kaleidoscope of patched elbows, knees, and bottoms in peasant Ireland astonished the German traveler Kohl. The Irish look like a nation of "broken down dance masters," he declared. As living standards fell, the potato became an even more irresistible economic proposition for the small subsistence farmer and for the agricultural laborer, who was often unemployed half the year.

A single acre of potato ground produced up to six tons of food, enough to feed a family of six for up to a year, and the potato's high nutritional content ensured that every member of the family enjoyed rude good health.

The robust appearance of the Irish peasantry gave much of the contemporary writing about prefamine Ireland a slightly schizophrenic quality. In one sentence the author would be decrying the wretched state of Irish dress, in the next, praising the athleticism of the men and the beauty of the women. Adam Smith, of all people, was among the first to notice this Irish paradox and he was quick to credit the potato for it. In London, noted the economist, the strongest men and most beautiful women were largely drawn from the "lowest rank of people in Ireland, who are fed on this root." The Halls, an English couple, who visited Ireland in the early 1840s went even further than Smith, crediting the potato with producing the hardiest peasantry in the world. And, indeed, on metrics of physical well-being like height and strength, the early-nineteenth-century Irishman was a wonder. Half an inch taller than the Englishman and an inch taller than the Belgian, the Irishman was stronger than both. On a Victorian contraption called a dynamometer, the average physical strength of the Irishman was 432 lb. compared to 403 lb. for the Englishman and 339 lb. for the Belgian.

Nonetheless, the fact remained, the profound nature of Irish poverty made the Irish peasant acutely vulnerable to the potato's failure, and, in the years following the French Wars, the potato had become almost reliably unreliable. In the 1830s, scarcely a year passed without a regional crop failure somewhere in Ireland. A general failure would deprive as many as five million people of their dietary mainstay, and, too poor to purchase an alternate food, most of them would immediately plunge into starvation. Thomas Malthus's work on poverty, rapid population growth, and demographic disaster suggested what would happen next. There would be death, and death not in the thousands or tens of thousands, but in the hundreds of thousands, perhaps millions.

In 1841, when new census data indicated a slowing in the growth of the Irish birth rate, the Malthusian threat seemed to recede, but the data were misleading. The subsistence farmers and landless agricultural laborers, who accounted for 70 percent of the population of rural Ireland, were still having six or seven children, and those children were growing up to become laborers and subsistence farmers who led lives at least as brutal and desperate as their parents'. In 1837, when residents of Tullagh-obegly, Donegal, submitted a memorial—a petition for assistance—to the lord lieutenant, the chief British official in Ireland, the introductory page included a description of life in Tullaghobegly by the local teacher, Patrick M'Kye:

> I have traveled a part of England and Scotland, together with part of British America. . . . , I have likewise perambulated 2,253 miles in seven United States and never witnessed [a] tenth of such hunger, hardships and nakedness [as here]. . . . More than one half of both men and women cannot afford shoes to their feet, nor can many of them afford a second bed, . . . whole families of sons and daughters of mature age [lie] indiscriminately together with their parents in the bare buff. . . . None of the women can afford more than one shift . . . [and the] children are crying and fainting with hunger.

Donegal was one of the poorest counties in the poorest region of Ireland. When British officials had nightmares about all the things that could go wrong in Ireland, the nightmares were usually set in the west, in Donegal, Kerry, Mayo, and Galway. The region had the highest rate of population growth and the largest number of subsistence farms; 64 percent of the agricultural holdings in the west were under five acres (the national average was 45 percent). However, by 1845, immiseration, the deepest form of poverty, had spread to parts of the (relatively) prosperous east and north. At the end of the national cattle show in Dublin, the Scottish writer Henry Inglis was astonished to see paupers slip into the exhibition ring and fill their pockets with the half-eaten turnips discarded by the animal contestants. In Londonderry, an Ulster "boomtown" of six thousand, "people regularly [pawned] their Sunday clothes on Monday morning and release[d] them on . . . Saturday night," after Friday payday. In County Wicklow, another "prosperous" region, a traveler saw a young mother pick up a gooseberry seed spat out by a passerby, lick it clean with her tongue, and feed it to her baby. Asenath Nicholson, an American visitor, described the Irish pauper as "a hunger-armed assassin."

⟶⬥⟵

Visiting Cavan, an Ulster market town, Mr. Foster encountered another aspect of Irish life that troubled British officials as much as the poverty. In high summer, Cavan usually bustled with traders and tinkers and broad-shouldered countrymen in from the surrounding farms, but the day Mr. Foster passed through on his way to Donegal, Cavan had the look of an armed camp. Thick metal locks hung from the doors of the public houses and municipal buildings, and notices covered the walls near the town square. Some offered rewards "for private information relative to the secret society commonly called . . . [the] Molly Maguires"; others ordered the arrest "of all vagrants and suspicious persons." Except for a contingent of red-jacketed Royal Dragoons and a handful of Irish Constabulary officers, almost as glamorous looking in olive-green coatees and white duck trousers, the streets were empty. Upon inquiry, Mr. Foster learned that Cavan had been "proclaimed"—put under martial law—in late June, after the assassination of a local magistrate, a Mr. Bell-Booth, who had been murdered one Sunday morning while driving his children home from church. As the magistrate lay slumped across the carriage seat, dying, an old man, himself too feeble to assist, had shouted to the crowd around the carriage: "For God's sake, someone help the man!" No one moved.

The economic malaise of the 1820s and 1830s had also inflamed Ireland's bitter class and sectarian divisions. Public officials, landowners, land agents, large farmers—almost every member of the gentry, Protestant or Catholic—lived in fear of the "midnight legislators," the Molly Maguires, the Whiteboys, and the other secret societies that defended the interests of the subsistence farmer and agricultural laborer. The proprietor, or large farmer—the fifty- to hundred-acre man—who rack-rented (charged an exorbitant rent) or evicted a tenant could find his cattle "cliffed" (driven over the edge of a cliff), his hunting dogs clubbed to death, or his horses immolated in a fire. In Galway, the "midnight legislators" dug up the corpse of a landlord who had evicted 108 families and placed a gallows over his body. The bitter historic emnity between the Catholic majority—eighty percent of the population—and the Protestant Anglo-Irish ruling class both exacerbated and made the violence hard to control. The day Mr. Foster visited Cavan, the municipal authorities were grappling with a problem familiar to Irish officials. All the Catholic witnesses to the Bell-Booth murder refused to come forward because the assailant was a Catholic, and the one Protestant witness, the magistrate's sister-in-law, was afraid to testify for fear of assassination. Visiting Ireland in 1835, Alexis de Tocqueville wondered how long Britain could maintain order in a nation where the disaffected majority refused to acknowledge the legitimacy of the legal system.

In 1843, the Devon Commission was established to examine what most experts believed to be the principal source of Irish poverty and violence, the Irish landholding system. In testimony, commission witnesses described the Irish landowner as often indebted and improvident, frequently exploitative and only occasionally interested in agricultural investment, while the small Irish tenant farmer was depicted as living on the edge of immiseration and unwilling to make even minimal agricultural improvements as he held his land "at will," without a lease, and could be evicted "at will" by the landlord.

"Are the small tenantry improving in their condition or otherwise?" the Commission asked John Duke, a County Leitrim surgeon.

Duke: "They are fifty percent worse than they were twenty years ago."

Commission: "What is the cause of their being so wretched?"

Duke: "They are not able to pay their rents and are lying naked in such a state, it would hardly be believed."

※

Very little of surgeon Duke's testimony or that of his fellow witnesses ended up in the Commission's policy recommendations. The Earl of Devon, the chairman, was a political ally of the current prime minister, Sir Robert Peel, and Peel wanted a report that appeared to do something without actually doing anything. Eager to oblige, Devon and his colleagues produced a set of policy recommendations most notable for an octopuslike ability to embrace every side of every question. Thus, the Commission saw "unequivocal symptoms of improvement" in Ireland except when it did not see them: "We regret . . . that the agricultural laborer . . . continues to suffer the greatest deprivations and hardships." The Commission likewise expressed a fervent desire to bring an end to the inhumane practice of mass evictions, except in instances where mass evictions were useful. "When it is seen . . . how minute . . . holdings are frequently found to be, it cannot be denied that such a step is, in many cases, absolutely necessary." The commission also supported tenant leases, except when it opposed tenant leases as an infringement on the property rights of the proprietor. "We cannot recommend any direct interference by the Legislature." The Devon Commission's report was published in February 1845 and concluded with a rousing defense of the Irish landlord. "There has been much exaggeration and misstatement in the sweeping charges which have been directed against Irish landlords," declared the commissioners, all Irish landlords themselves.

A uniformly "unreadable," unfailingly "ponderous" "cartload of cross examinations," erupted *The Times*. John Delane, the paper's ambitious young editor, decided the moment had come for *The Times* to send its own man to Ireland. A *Times* commissioner would be appointed to conduct an inquiry into "the mischief which prevails" in that country, "lay out the simple, basic facts" of the Irish situation, and suggest remedies. "Whatever the success of our present inquiry," *The Times* told its readers, ". . . we have this consolation . . . every other method has failed."

A Leeds man and a journalist's son, Mr. Thomas Campbell Foster was not the most obvious choice for the post. Only thirty-two, he possessed no special knowledge of Ireland, and had left journalism to study for the bar at Middle Temple. If his name sounded familiar to *Times* readers, it was because Foster had done some enterprising reporting during the Rebecca Riots, a worker uprising in Wales. Entrusting the prestige of the most influential newspaper in the world to a young man of such thin experience was not without risk; but Mr. Foster was intelligent, intrepid, resourceful, a fast, facile writer, possessed of all the unearned confidence of youth, and had a big personality—an important asset in a small island full of big personalities.

In Whitehall and Westminster, the Foster appointment was greeted with loud harrumphs: *The Times* was engaging in another publicity stunt. And so it was. Still, there was historical precedent for the Foster mission. Twice before at a critical moment in Irish history, a man with a plan had appeared, and, like Mr. Foster, he was English.

The Poet

One day in 1582, in a hillside cottage heavy with the smell of men who had walked a distance in the morning sun, a group of literary-minded friends gathered to hear Lodowick Bryskett, a retired civil servant, read from his current work in progress, *Discourse of Civill Life*. The guests were mostly military men, though a few of Bryskett's fellow civil servants were also present, among them a young man whose physical glamour put a colleague in mind of an "Italianate signor." Edmund Spenser was an aide to Lord Grey de Wilton, the British governor in Ireland, and an aspiring poet. He was in Ireland for the same reason as the other guests. In the 1580s, Ireland was one of the few places in the Elizabethan world where a young man of humble origins and large ambitions could hope to make a mark, and Spenser was both humbly born and hugely ambitious. Within fifteen years, the cloth-maker's son would change the course of English literature with a poem, *The Faerie Queene*, and the course of Irish history with a book, *A View of the Present State of Ireland*.

In 1582, Spenser had been in the country for only two years—not long, but long enough to come to one conclusion: Ireland was in a state of savage primitiveness. Even on the most rudimentary measure of "civilized" development, a knowledge of the national geography, the Irish were lacking. While the country's four provinces—Connaught in the west, Munster in the south, Ulster in the north, and Leinster in the east—had been delineated, within each province many regions remained unshired (that is, they had not been divided into counties) and unmapped. A century after Columbus sailed to the Americas, exactly where the coast of Donegal began and ended remained a mystery. This inattention to marking and ordering extended into the Irish agricultural system. The lack of hedges and fences made it difficult to tell where an Irish farm or pasture began or ended, and the lack of common measurements like the acre made it difficult to determine the farm's size. Ask an Irish farmer how much land he held and he would reply, "A cow's grass," meaning the amount of land required to feed a cow. Except for coastal settlements like Galway and Dublin, the country had nothing an Englishman would call a town, and except for fortified redoubts and churches, it had few stone buildings. About the Irish national character, Spenser was in accord with the medieval Welsh monk Giraldus Cambrensis, who declared the natives to be "a race of savages, I say again, a race of utter savages."

For Irish backwardness, the poet blamed the "Old English," the country's nominal rulers. Instead of anglicizing the natives, the natives had celticized the conquerors. Beyond the pale of settlement, a thin strip of land around Dublin, England barely existed, even as an idea. Celtic law, language, manners, and customs dominated the rhythms and activities of daily life for both the "Old English," descendants of the twelfth-century Anglo-Norman conquerors, and the Irish. As Spenser contemplated these facts, he reached a second momentous conclusion: Ireland would have to be reconquered and forcibly anglicized and modernized. Irish and Old English lords who resisted the reestablishment of English rule, law, and culture would be summarily executed; those suspected of resisting, imprisoned. The bearers of Celtic culture—the bards and storytellers—would also be physically eliminated. In the final stages of the reconquest, the lands of the domestic aristocracy would be seized and transferred to Protestant settlers from England and Scotland, who would anglicize the Irish and the Old English remnant through personal example.

In the early 1580s, a war with Spain loomed, and Queen Elizabeth was loath to provoke her Irish subjects with talk of reconquest and plantation, but a decade later, when Ulster rose in rebellion, the Spanish Armada was at the bottom of the English Channel, and royal patience with the tumultuous Irish was at a nadir. For Old English and Celtic chieftains, rebellion was almost a form of sport; the Ulster uprising was at least the fourth in as many decades but it possessed two particularly menacing characteristics. It spread quickly to the rest of the island and the leaders, the enigmatic Earl of Tyrone and that wickedly handsome Braveheart, Red Hugh O'Donnell, had Spanish backing. Having failed to batter down England's front door, Spain was now using the Ulster warlords to pick the lock on her back door. Upon defeat of the rebellion, the Crown ordered the lands of Tyrone, O'Donnell, and their lieutenants seized and transferred to English settlers. Within a few generations, Ulster, formerly the most Celtic of the four Irish provinces, became the most British region of the country. A rebellion by Old English and native Irish in the 1640s set the stage for the reconquest of the rest of the country. On August 15, 1649, Oliver Cromwell arrived in Ireland with an army of eight thousand foot and four thousand on horse, and "lightening passed through the land." Three years later, as many as 400,000 people out of a population of a little over a million were dead, and British settlers—"planters"—were pouring into the country.

In 1600, a year after Spenser's death, Ireland was 2 percent British; in 1700, after the Cromwellian reconquest and the victory of the Protestant armies of William of Orange at the Battle of the Boyne in 1690, Ireland was 27 percent British. By 1750, English and Scottish settlers controlled 95 percent of the land and held all social, political, and economic power. After the Penal Laws stripped Catholics of the right to practice their religion freely, to own firearms, to purchase or inherit estates, to own a horse, or to lease land beyond a certain value, some of the Celtic and Old English elite fled abroad, some converted to Protestantism, and some became tenant farmers. The Irish language and Irish culture went into exile in the cabins of the peasantry.

The Protestant Ascendancy had begun.

The Agriculturalist

On a late June morning in 1776, a Suffolk man with flaring black eyebrows, a lively expression, and the callused hands of a farmer sat in a harbor station on the eastern shore of the Irish Sea, awaiting his packet, the *Claremont*. For millennia, Holyhead in Wales had been the departure point for the Ireland-bound, but the eighteenth-century traveler remained as much at the mercy of wind, tide, and the vagaries of the Welsh weather as his prehistoric counterpart.

> *Here I sit in Holyhead*
> *With muddy ale and moldy bread.*
> *For want of matter swears and frets*
> *Are forced to read the old gazettes*

wrote one long-suffering traveler, the Irish cleric Jonathan Swift.

This morning wind and tide favored the Dublin-bound. Twenty-two uneventful but tedious hours later, the traveler, Arthur Young, was surprised to find himself in a handsome Anglo-Irish city of broad streets, well-tended parks, sun-dappled squares, gracious Georgian homes, and "magnificent" public buildings. On the banks of the River Liffey, the sons and daughters of the Ascendancy had torn down Spenser's dark, savage Ireland and erected a sparkling monument of cut stone and brick to themselves. Dublin has "much exceeded my expectations," declared Young, author of two renowned books on agriculture, *A Six Weeks Tour Through the Southern Counties of England and Wales* and *A Six Months Tour Through the North of England*.

Dublin's resemblance to a national capital was not a matter of happenstance. In the generations after the plantations, the descendants of the colonists, like their counterparts in North America, had grown restive under English rule, and for many of the same reasons: unfair imperial tax and trade policies, and a colonial nationalism born of economic achievement. Between the 1720s and the 1770s, Irish per capita income may have doubled. The morning Young arrived—June 20, 1776—in Dublin, as in Philadelphia, the talk was all of independence. In the corridors of the "spacious, elegant" new Parliament building, there were discussions about an Irish navy, Irish ambassadors, and the proper accent for the new Irish nation. Spenser's vision of an anglicized Ireland was dead; the new vision was of a semi-autonomous Anglo-Irish state. Ireland and England would remain linked together under the Crown, but an independent Irish legislature would be free to act in Irish interests.

Young's role in the formation of the new state, though more indirect than Spenser's, was, nonetheless, foundational. In *A Tour in Ireland*, he provided the first comprehensive look at the agricultural system that had evolved out of the plantation period and that would still be in place seventy years later when Mr. Foster visited. For the patriots in Dublin who were relying on the agricultural economy to support the new Anglo-Irish state, *Tour* made sober reading.

✳

On the surface, the Irish landholding system resembled the English. At the top was a small elite of eight thousand to ten thousand landowning families, almost all descendants of the Protestant planters; below the landowners was a large group of tenant farmers with holdings of various sizes, and below the farmers, an even larger group of landless laborers. However, the peculiarities of Irish history had produced singularities at every point in the system, beginning at the top. Almost every foreign expert who visited Ireland, from Young in 1776 to the Frenchman Gustave de Beaumont in 1835, believed Irish poverty was rooted in the unproductive use of the land. The experts also agreed that the low quality of Irish agriculture was rooted in the peculiar character of the Irish landowning class. Between 20 percent and 30 percent of the land was held by absentee owners, men whose families had acquired Irish land during the plantations, and who lived in England or elsewhere in Ireland and rarely visited their nonresidential properties. "My father saw [the estate] but once, when he drove along the mail coach road that skirts it," recalled William Bence Jones, an English absentee. With notable exceptions, the goal of the absentee landowner was to extract the maximum amount of wealth from his holdings with the minimum investment of time and money.

Resident landowners had their own singularity: a preference for conspicuous consumption over agricultural investment. Memorable examples of the Irish landowners' tropism for unnecessary fabulousness included Lord Baltimore's touring entourage of eight mistresses and a black eunuch; the £20,000 Lord Muskerry spent on a home he never bothered to finish; and the almost million acres of Irish deer parks and gardens. "Our great farming Landlords . . . are lost in admiration [for] the wonderful effects of their abilities on 100 acres . . . altogether neglecting the

ten, fifty or hundred thousand acres . . . beyond the little boundary en-
closing themselves." John Pitt Kennedy, a leading Irish agriculturalist,
was right. Often, the landlord's hundred acres of lawn and garden was
surrounded by miles of broken fences, slouching cabins, rudely cultivated fields, and treeless hills. In Spenser's time, woodland had covered
an eighth of the Irish land surface; by Young's time, ruthless commercial
deforestation had reduced the tree cover to a scattered series of redoubts.
If "you would hang all the landlords . . . who destroy trees without planting, you would lay your axe to the root of the evil," Young declared.

The power the Irish proprietor exercised over his tenants was, with
the exception of the American South, also singular. "A landlord in Ireland can scarcely invent an order which a servant laborer . . . refuses to
execute," noted Young. "Nothing satisfies him but an unlimited submis-
siveness. Disrespect or anything tending toward sauciness he may punish
with his cane or his horsewhip." On some estates, proprietors also demanded sexual services. When one "landlord of consequence" defended
the practice, asserting that many "cottars [poor laborers] . . . think themselves honored to have their wives and daughters sent to the bed of their
master," Young was outraged. Sexual exploitation is "a mark of slavery,"
he declared.

Tour also included examples of humane, wakeful-minded proprietors, but about the middleman, another singularity of the Irish landholding system, Young found nothing good to say. Typically, a middleman
leased several hundred acres from a proprietor and divided the land into
rental plots. The members of this class were famous largely for "screwing
up the rent to the highest farthing," for commandeering their tenants'
horses and carts at harvest time to take in their crops, and for a love of
strong drink and fast hounds. "These men, very generally [are] the masters of packs of hounds, with which they waste their time and money
and . . . are the hardest drinkers in Ireland."

Below the middlemen were the tenants. Large farmers, some descendants of old Catholic gentry, typically held fifty to a hundred acres; middling farmers, between ten and forty acres; and small farmers, four, five
or six acres. The bottom of the landholding system was home to two types
of laborers: the cottier, who bartered his labor in return for a cabin and a
potato plot, and the spalpeen, the itinerant laborer, who survived on day

work and rented a conacre, a small plot of potato ground from a local farmer, usually on an eleven-month lease. Demographically, the largest segment of the population, the agricultural peasantry, was also the class most resistant to anglicization. In the cabins of the small farmer and laborer, ancient Celtic culture continued to dominate the rhythms of life. In this "Hidden Ireland," Irish remained the first language; myth and legend attached itself to every feature of the landscape; the storyteller and the poet remained revered figures; and the great old Irish families—the dispossessed "ancient race"—were remembered and honored. "Oh sir," joked a nervous Ulsterman about a rumored list of confiscated Catholic estates, "there is a map . . . [that] would singe your eyebrows but to smell the fiery fragment . . . ; you would bless yourself to peruse the hideous, barbaric names with which it abounds. . . . Published sir . . . for the sole purpose of reminding herdsmen and ditchers of what great folks their grandmas were."

For all the hardships of peasant life, Young believed contemporary accounts of Irish poverty were somewhat overstated. True, the roadside cabins of the spalpeens—"a few sticks, furze, and fern" propped up against a rise—had the ephemeral look of a Bedouin encampment, the townland, the closest thing Hidden Ireland had to a village, contained no shops, no paved roads, no church steeples, and no monetary economy to speak of; in Hidden Ireland the primary unit of exchange remained the barter of land and labor for goods. Still, the shoeless feet, the straw bedding, the meanness of the economic system, had to be set against the livestock that often attended even the lowest hovels and against the superb physical condition of the peasantry, which Young, like Smith, attributed to the potato. Observing the cottages swarming with pink-cheeked children, the great black eyebrows flared, and England's leading agriculturalist exclaimed, "Vive la pomme de Terre."

Except for the robust condition of the peasantry, however, Young's *Tour in Ireland*, published in 1780, contained little good news for the Anglo-Irish patriots in Dublin. Irish barns and fences were in short supply; farmers bound the feet of their turkeys and chickens to keep them out of the cow pastures; crops were improperly rotated, which kept yields low; the lack of agricultural tools reduced productivity; and inadequate capital investment by landowners allowed tens of thousands of acres of potentially valuable farmland to go to waste. On almost every metric associated with national prosperity, Irish agriculture failed.

Young could think of only one solution: a massive influx of English investment capital. No one including, probably, Young, expected the recommendation to be adopted.

⊰⊕⊱

A few years after *Tour* was published, the dream of an Anglo-Irish state died in the hills of Wexford and Mayo. Upon the outbreak of the French Wars in 1793, the French began to dream the old Spanish dream: an attack on England through disaffected Ireland. In November 1796, a French invasion fleet appeared off Bantry Bay. A "Protestant wind" drove the invasion force away, but ambitious Frenchmen and disaffected Irishmen continued to conspire. In May 1798, the Catholic peasantry of Wexford rose and slaughtered the local Protestant gentry, and in August a French invasion force of a thousand and a band of Mayo peasants, whose martial ardor exceeded their military skills, attacked the market town of Castlebar. A British army of twenty thousand took the field and the glen hollows, and what remained of the "goodly woods" filled with "anatomies of death." As many as thirty thousand rebels and loyalists may have died.

In a postmortem on the uprising, London concluded that a semi-autonomous Irish state was economically untenable and strategically dangerous. On January 1, 1801, Great Britain and Ireland were joined in Union. "Yesterday morning," the *Belfast News Letter* declared on the second, "the Union flag was hoisted at the Market House, and at one o'clock a Royal salute was fired by the Royal Artillery."

The Irish Parliament building, constructed at a cost of £95,000, almost enough to fund Young's investment scheme, became a bank.

The *Times* Commissioner

On the morning of September 3, 1845, a homesick Mr. Foster sat at a window in the Gweedore Inn. Except for the mountains off toward the sea, he might have been in England. Four days later, *The Times* published the commissioner's first column from Gweedore. "I date my letter from the center of the hills in the north of Donegal, where ten years ago, there was not a road—where scarcely anything but bogs and heather and rock were to be seen for miles—where the people held the land in rundale [a form of communal farming], paid no rent and lived on potatoes. . . . Yet I now write from an inn as comfortable as any in England. . . . Luxuriant crops surround the inn; industry; industriousness and cleanliness begin to mark the people; each man has . . . a decent cottage and there are good roads." All this is to be attributed to "the . . . individual and personal exertions of the present noble owner."

The "noble owner," Lord George Hill, was "a gravely handsome" former army major with a national reputation as a wakeful-minded agriculturalist. In the 1830s, when Hill purchased a 23,000-acre estate in Gweedore, the local people were still tail plowing (attaching the horse to the plow by tying it to the animal's tail), measuring land by the cow's grass, and practiced rundale farming, an ancient and unproductive form of communal agriculture in a which a group of small farmers worked a jointly held field. By 1845, Hill's modernization efforts, recounted in an influential pamphlet, "Facts from Gweedore," had made him a symbol of the latest scheme to modernize Ireland: English-style commercial farming.

Early in the nineteenth century, Malthus, the first man to propose the idea, argued that commercial farming would restrain Irish population growth because the wage-earning laborer on a commercial farm would have to purchase his food: that necessity would make him more alive to the consequences of unrestrained procreation. In the 1830s and early 1840s, with the British permanent garrison numbering between 15,000 and 25,000, advocates of commercial farming advanced a new rationale: anglicizing the landholding system would help reduce Irish poverty and violence and undermine the assault on the Anglo-Irish Union by the Catholic leader Daniel O'Connell.

※

One day, not long after the American Revolution, nine-year-old Daniel O'Connell turned to his uncle, "Hunting Cap," and announced, "I'll make a stir in the world yet." And so the boy would. Kerry handsome and honey voiced, O'Connell's personality was large enough to encompass all manner of contradictions—statesman and ward pol, idealist and rogue, charmer and deceiver. In the 1820s, during the campaign for

Catholic Emancipation, O'Connell acted upon Catholic Ireland as a lit match acts upon an oil slick. When the emancipation campaign ended in 1829, Catholics had won the right to sit in Parliament and serve in the military (rights promised thirty years earlier when the Union was formed), O'Connell had a new name, the Liberator, and Ireland had two power centers: Dublin Castle, the ancient seat of British rule in Ireland—and the man from Kerry.

In the 1830s, London introduced a series of reforms in an attempt to weaken O'Connell's hold on Catholic Ireland, including an Education Act, which created the first national school system, and a Poor Law, which created the first national welfare system, a network of 130 workhouses dedicated to the care of the indigent poor. But the reforms were overshadowed by an ever lengthening litany of peasant miseries. In the decade before the famine, the potato grew more unreliable, plots smaller, landlords meaner, and shoes and leases rarer. "Worse than we are, we cannot be," an Irish countryman told a group of visiting English commissioners.

England has given us rags and misery, declared O'Connell. Repeal the Union! By August 1843, the Liberator's Repeal Association had grown into the most powerful political organization in Ireland and his almost weekly anti-Union rallies were the talk of Europe. No one could remember the last politician who was able to routinely turn out crowds of a hundred thousand or more. By September 1843, anxious British politicians were consulting their calendars. O'Connell's next "monster" rally was scheduled for October 8 in Clontarf, a Dublin suburb. At 3:30 on the afternoon of October 7, Dublin Castle issued a proclamation banning the meeting. Fearing a bloody clash with the army, O'Connell, dedicated to non-violent resistance, observed the ban. The next morning, the rally field was empty except for a detachment of the 60th Rifles and 5th Dragoons. A few days later, London ordered the flotilla of warships stationed in Dublin harbor back to Britain.

The anti-Union agitation led to the creation of the Devon Commission, and the witness testimony it collected—as opposed to its recommendations—led many British officials to conclude that the Irish peasantry would never reconcile themselves to the Union or forswear violence until they were released from an agricultural system that provided only a subsistence living and not always even that. By the time the

Devon Commission published its report in February 1845, there was a consensus that the Irish landholding system, unchanged since Young's time, would have to be restructured. But in what way?

Prime Minister Peel and Lord John Russell, leader of the opposition Whig party, eminent political economists like Nassau Senior and Robert Torrens, and the *Times* commissioner believed that the best answer to the question was Malthus's old answer. The modern English commercial farm, structured around an owner, a few large tenant farmers, and a proletariat of wage-earning laborers, would extract far more wealth from the soil than would improvident and absentee landowners and three- and four-acre farmers who were about half as productive as their English counterparts.

Theories about the origins of the Irish peasant's low productivity abounded. The potato's ease of cultivation had fostered a culture of laziness, said some critics. Others blamed Irish history. Two centuries of oppression had deprived the peasant of ambition and a sense of agency. "It is because the poor Celt is content to put up with bad fare and worse clothing . . . that he is made to put up with them," wrote a visiting Englishman. Peasant culture, which put a high premium on leisure activities, also came in for blame. "If there be a market to attend, a fair or funeral, a horse race or fight, the peasant forgets all else," complained George Nicholls, a British official. More thoughtful critics recognized that the Irish landowning class also played a role in the productivity gap; the typical proprietor was far more interested in prompt rent payment than in providing tenants with modern farm implements or schooling them in the techniques of modern agriculture. Nonetheless, the fact remained that the Irish peasant was poor because he was unproductive and he was unproductive because his work ethic was wanting.

In the 1830s, a canny Scot textile magnate named Buchanan demonstrated one way to improve the Irish work ethic: hire children "almost naked . . . off the streets" and put them into the structured environment of a factory where they could be taught industriousness, self-discipline, initiative, and personal responsibility. Advocates of commercial farming believed that the modern agricultural enterprise, which operated not unlike the modern factory, could also be used to inculcate the values of the new industrial age into the "aboriginal" Irish—to use a favorite term of the period.

Proponents also pointed to other ancillary benefits of the new agricultural system. During the transition to commercial farming, weak landowners—those who lacked sufficient capital and technical expertise—would fall or be pushed to the wayside, making room for a new class of solvent, industrious, business-minded proprietors like Lord Hill. In addition, the new system would promote commercial development. The wage-earning laborer would need to purchase food, and that would give rise to a network of provision shops in rural Ireland; as commercial food proliferated, dependency on the increasingly undependable potato would decline—and with it, the traditional barter economy of the countryside, which would be replaced by a modern economy.

However, before the plan could be implemented, a way had to be found to dispose of the hundreds of thousands of small farms and potato plots that presently cluttered the countryside, and to remove the incompetent landlords who had allowed the proliferation to occur. No one, including the most enthusiastic proponents of commercial farming, expected that to be easy. The Irish landowner was protected by history and by tightly written deeds, and the Irish peasant was unlikely to give up his two or three acres on the vague promise of a better life at some distant date in the future. Lord Hill's first attempts at modernization in Gweedore had been met with uprooted fences, damaged barns, and other acts of vandalism. Like Spenser's plantation scheme, the transition to commercial farming could best be accomplished in the plastic atmosphere of a crisis—a rebellion or natural disaster that destabilized the established order.

On September 9, 1845, two days after Mr. Foster's Gweedore column appeared in *The Times,* the *Dublin Evening Post* carried an interview with David Moore, the chief curator at the National Botanic Gardens in Dublin. Mr. Moore, who had recently examined several samples from the new potato crop, told the *Post* that the samples contained "only too convincing proof of the rapid progress this alarming disease is making."

"This alarming disease" was *Phytophthora infestans,* the mysterious ailment that had destroyed the continental potato crop earlier in the summer.

CHAPTER TWO

The News from Ireland

Across most of western Europe, the early summer of 1845 was unseasonably cool and wet. Almost daily, sheets of pelting rain lashed trees, swelled rivers, pummeled fields, and washed away roads. In mud-soaked pastures, livestock huddled together, eyes shut against wind and rain; in farmhouses, men stood in doorways, listening to the crackle and boom of thunder and praying for the rain to end. The summer of 1816 had begun like this—persistent rain and cold—and ended in continent-wide crop failure, starvation, and death. Heavy summer rains always brought ill tidings; 1845 would be no exception. In June, potato farmers in Flanders noticed a powerful stench in the air. Men put on greatcoats and boots and went out into the muddy fields to investigate. Fresh white spots had formed on the leaves of the potato plants; the next day the spots had turned brown and gangrenous, and the potato stalks were wilting and blackening; the day after that, the tubers in the wet earth beneath the stalks were dead. Variations on this pattern occurred. Some potato fields died in the space of a single night; some potatoes grew no larger than a walnut, others were full-sized but a slimy residue had formed on their grotesquely pockmarked jackets. Pluck such a potato from the ground and it would slip from the hand; cut it open and a putrid, oozing mass of red-brown mucus spilled out. One element of the pattern never varied: the violent odor of decay. Even the rains could not wash it away.

Dread seized Flanders. Once a single tuber displayed symptoms of infection, the entire potato field was often doomed. In the cheerless June of 1845, Flemish barns were transformed into triage centers; amid the smell of livestock and damp wood, women and children worked deep into the summer evenings, cutting away the blighted portions of infected tubers. Surgical intervention proved useless. The disease quickly reappeared and the salvaged portion of the potato died. Even tubers healthy when harvested frequently turned bad in storage. No one had ever seen a potato die-off quite like this before. Flemish farmers stood in town halls and beer halls and debated the cause. Was it due to the degeneration of the potato's "vital forces"? A prominent school of scientific opinion held that the tuber's recent vulnerability to disease had its genesis in the constant inbreeding that made midgets and dwarfs common in certain royal lines. Was it the weather? Across Flanders that June, men who had lost everything stood in the ruined fields cursing God and the rains. Though largely ignored, there was another explanation for the mystery.

In 1843, the same year the Provincial Council of Flanders attempted to strengthen the "degenerate" local strain of potato by cross-breeding it with a sturdy republican strain of American tubers, a new potato disease appeared in the United States. By the autumn of 1843, hardly a sound potato was left between Maryland and Massachusetts. The following year, 1844, the disease reappeared, and this time its reach extended northward into Canada and westward into the Great Lakes region. In the summer of 1845, weather and geography allowed the mysterious disease to move across the European plain even more swiftly. By early July, the Flemish potato crop was all but destroyed, and farmers in neighboring Holland were awakening to a foul odor in the morning air. France and Germany were infected next. A satellite photo of western Europe in mid-August 1845 would have shown great black swaths of ruin crisscrossing thousands of neatly squared gold and green fields. Some of the swaths would have been capriciously shaped, beginning here and ending there; others would be composed of telegraph-like dots and dashes; still others would extend in a monstrous unbroken line for a hundred miles or more.

To the east, the black lines would sweep past Sedan and halt abruptly in front of the high forest of the Ardennes; others would pivot around the forest in the direction of the German heartland. To the west, the ruined swaths would extend from Paris to Normandy, break up in the dense bocage country behind the Norman coast, halt at the waterline, then re-appear on the Isle of Wight, disturbing the domestic prettiness of the local market gardens.

The *Gardener's Chronicle and Horticultural Gazette* was the first publication to announce the arrival of the new disease on British soil. In the August 16 issue, the *Chronicle* warned that "a blight of unusual char-acter" had infected the potato gardens on the Isle of wight. The paper's intelligence was about two weeks behind the disease, which had already ravaged the island's potato crop and was now on the British mainland. Five days before the *Chronicle* announcement, one Mr. Parker, an En-glish potato dealer, told the Home Office that the potato fields in Kent, a channel county, and in East Ham and West Ham in Essex were exhibit-ing signs of infection. In the final weeks of August, English farmers learned what Flemish farmers had learned in June: even if a potato field looked healthy, a heavy odor in the air meant the field would die. The August 23 issue of the *Chronicle* offered a fuller description of the blight, and this time the editors did not hide their alarm. "We are visited by a great calamity. . . . Should we have fine weather, the disease will probably disappear; should rain and cold continue, it will spread." The *Chronicle's* readers were well advised to pray for fine weather. "As to cure for this distemper," the editors declared, "there is none."

By early September, *The Times of London*, *The Manchester Guardian*, *Le Moniteur Belge*, the *Journal des Débats*, and the *Journal de Bruxelles*— major national publications—were giving the blight extensive coverage. Specialty publications soon followed suit. *The Mark Lane Express*, a busi-ness paper, and *Banker's Circular* wrote about the disease's likely effect on grain prices and credit, while *The Dublin Medical Press* worried about the effect on physicians' incomes if the government used the famine threat to pass a "medical charities bill." In London, *The Medical Times* declared war on "the Giessen-bitten boys," the chemists who ascribed the die-off to chemical changes in the potato. Watching the coverage from America, *The Monthly Journal of Agriculture* complained that the

British press had lost interest in everything except the potato distemper and the bubble in railway stocks.

✳

For the past hundred years, the potato—high yielding, reliable, and inexpensive—had been a major engine of European growth. Both the dramatic rise in population—from 140 million in 1750 to 266 million in 1850—and the industrialization that allowed Europe to feed its growing working class from a shrinking agricultural base owed much to the potato; it produced two to four times more calories per acre than grain and was cheaper and easier to prepare than bread. By August, the dietary mainstay of the European industrial worker and the agricultural laborer was in the midst of a massive die off. Belgium had lost 87 percent of its potato crop (in Flanders, 92 percent); in Germany and France, the disease claimed 20 percent of the potato crop; in Holland, 70 percent. One Dutch newspaper, *De Leidsche Courant*, reported that "many and among them fairly well to do people . . . live on the herbs of the field . . . on stinging nettles, wild elder and such plants." Toward September, the prospect of a hungry, violent winter began to agitate the European mind. "The whole of the [potato] crops . . . [are] rapidly perishing from the rot," *The Economist* wrote on September 6. "With the grain crop damaged by the summer rains and the international food supply depleted by the blight, the question [of] how people are to be fed is becoming urgent." *The Morning Chronicle*, a large London daily, painted an even more vivid picture of the threat facing Europe. "In Poland, there is such a dearth that the people are making sudden eruptions into the neighboring parts of Prussia. . . . The north of Russia is in a state of famine. . . . The Ottoman Court . . . has issued a decree prohibiting the export of grain. . . . France has, during the whole summer, been importing wheat. . . . [I]n Belgium and Holland the potato crop is a complete failure. . . . [The] surplus of food . . . is becoming less and less."

✳

On August 20, as the blight slithered through the potato fields of West Ham, a letter from Charles Morren, a professor of botany at the University of Liège, appeared on the front page of *L'Indépendent Belge*, a large

Brussels paper. Brilliant and vainglorious, Morren dismissed the current theories about the blight with a rhetorical wave of the hand. The true cause of the disease, he declared, was a fungus of the *Botrytis* genus. Two weeks later, on September 4, a letter of historic importance appeared in the *Gardener's Chronicle*. An observant reader named Matthew Moggridge, who lived near a smelting factory, had noticed an interesting correlation. The nearer a potato garden was to the factory chimney, which puffed out copper smoke, the less likely the garden was to be infected. Gardens within two hundred feet of the chimney were completely free of disease. Neither man had all the details right. Nonetheless, a month before the destruction of the main Irish potato crop, the cause and cure of the blight had been identified. Habits of mind, vanity, ambition, jealousy, stubbornness, stupidity—all the usual suspects—would prevent the information from being put to a useful purpose.

The blight divided the European scientific community into three hostile camps. The botanists, who gathered under the flag of meteorology, held the wet, cold summer of 1845 responsible for the disease. Besides the advantage of defending the conventional wisdom, the meteorological camp also had a formidable leader, Dr. John Lindley, editor of *Gardener's Chronicle* and the first professor of botany at the University of London. Urbane, intelligent, with a core of toughness, Lindley was the botanist as imperial viceroy. In early September, he set out the meteorological case with forceful authority. "During the present season . . . the Potatoes have been compelled to absorb an unusual quantity of water [due to the rain]; the lowness of the temperature has prevented them from digesting it."

A second group of scientists assembled under the flag of degeneracy. The "degenerists," who included botanists, pamphleteers, and the "Gissenbitten boys" (chemists), also had a claim on the conventional wisdom and a plausible theory of the case. They held that the blight was simply another manifestation of the biological corruption produced by "the repeated cultivation of the same stock."

The third group, the fungalists, had neither conventional wisdom nor public opinion on their side, as well as a highly idiosyncratic membership: a self-taught lady botanist; a former French army surgeon, Jean Montagne; an abbot; several mycologists (students of fungi); and the group's two leaders: Charles Morren, the flamboyant Belgian botanist, who spoke only in exclamation marks, and the Reverend Miles Joseph Berkeley, an English vicar, who barely spoke at all.

Through sheer force of personality, Morren dominated the causation debate through August and early September. His articles on the fungal theory appeared in France, Belgium, and North America. In Paris, the *Journal des Débats*, the official government paper, printed a Morren article on the front page. Then, a Brussels municipal body warned that the fungalists were destroying the potato market, and the tide began to turn. One former colleague denounced Morren as an "armchair scientist!" a "controversialist!" an "egotist!" "The sun will soon dispose of M. Morren's ... microscopic fabrications," predicted another former associate. And, indeed, by mid-September the sun had begun to set on Morren. All that bravado! All that vainglory! Even supporters found the swaggering Belgian exhausting. Meanwhile, Jean Montagne, the army surgeon, had deserted to the anti-fungal camp.

Montagne life's dream was to become a member of the French Academy of Sciences, and as the controversy over the blight intensified, he could see the doors of the academy shutting in his face. When Morren had a public temper tantrum and called his critics "harebrained" and "full of evil passions," the fate of the fungal theory fell into the tremulous hands of the Reverend Miles Joseph Berkeley, vicar of Kings Cliffe in Northamptonshire and "a gentleman eminent in the habits of fungi." In between tending to church duties and his fifteen children, Berkeley had written two classic monographs: *Notices of British Fungi* (with C. E. Broome) and *Outlines of British Fungology*. Despite his professional association with fungi, for most of the summer Berkeley had stood shoulder to shoulder with Lindley in the meteorology camp. Only when the blight arrived in Northamptonshire and the opportunity arose to observe the disease firsthand did the clergyman change his mind. After Morren retreated to his laboratory to sulk, Berkeley became the only member of the fungal camp with the scientific prestige to make a credible defense of the theory, and by late autumn the theory badly needed a defender. Most scientists were now persuaded that the fungus, evident on infected potatoes, was a byproduct of other diseases and/or physical insults, not a cause of the blight. During the annual meeting of the British

Association for the Advancement of Science, the fungalists could be counted on the fingers of one hand. The fungal theory "ha[s] lost ground latterly, very materially," noted the prominent Dr. E. Solly. At a moment in the debate when a shout was urgently needed, the Reverend Berkeley chose to whisper again. In a paper in the *Journal of the Horticultural Society of London*, he offered this tepid declaration:

> After an attentive consideration of the progress of the disease and of almost everything of value that has been written on the subject and after duly weighing the peculiar difficulties with which it is attended, I must candidly confess, that . . . I believe the fungal theory to be the true one.

When the Royal Agricultural Society conducted an essay contest on the origins of the blight, the first, second, and third prizes went to contestants who subscribed to the meteorological theory.

Sixteen years would pass before the fungal origins of the blight were recognized. The Frenchman who established its legitimacy, Anton de Bary, also had a genius for names. He called the fungus *Phytophthora infestans*. *Phytophthora* means "plant destroyer"; *infestans*, "infective." Neither word overstates the case; between them, they also provide a good description of how the fungus works. The spores of *P. infestans* settle on the leaf of a plant, where they generate tubular filaments; the tubes penetrate the "tightly packed palisade cells" near the surface of the leaf and invade the interior, where the business of plant life is conducted, where nutrients and gases are processed into food, and from which waste products, such as water vapor, are emitted. Using the interior tissue as an energy source, the fungus manufactures new spore-bearing filaments. The terrible odor associated with *P. infestans* is the smell of a living thing being eaten from the inside out. Upon maturing, the filaments push their way through the decaying plant interior to the stomata (the plant pores) and eject spores into the atmosphere; the spores land on a nearby potato plant, and the process of invasion, corruption, and death repeats itself. The meteorologists were right about one aspect of the disease: weather plays an important role in the transmission of *P. infestans*. Wind spreads the spores from plant to plant, while moisture fosters spore reproduction and enhances the spore's ability to move across a leaf and penetrate the surface. Moisture is also essential in the second mode of infection. Grotesquely misshapen potatoes are infected not from the stem but from spores that are washed off the leaves by rain and penetrate the wet, loose soil to reach the tubers beneath.

Moggridge's observation about copper took even longer to verify. Not until the 1880s did another French scientist, Pierre-Marie-Alexis Millardet, demonstrate why famine-era experiments with copper solutions had failed. Following the example of wheat farmers, early experimenters bathed potatoes in a copper solution. Two generations later, botanists discovered that what works for wheat does not work for potatoes. To protect a tuber, the solution must be applied directly to the leaves.

✖

Over the summer of 1845, events in Europe intruded on Irish life, though not deeply enough to take people's minds off the weather. Not even the elderly could remember a June as hot and dry. Grass parched, streams evaporated, sweat stained shirt collars and hat brims. Then, in early July, the skies darkened, the air acquired an edge, and everyone said, Can you remember a July so cool and wet? "As much rain has fallen [in] the last fortnight . . . as during the previous four months," the *Athlone Sentinel* reported on the sixteenth. Traveling through County Down three days later, a *Belfast Penny Journal* correspondent passed row upon row of cabins "oozing . . . liquid filth." August was wetter still. For three weeks, howling rains rattled windows, flooded hollows, collapsed mud walls, and stung exposed skin. On the hillsides of Kerry and Donegal, the shivering sheep looked like cotton balls afloat on a teal-colored sea.

Occasionally, a blight report from England or the continent produced a ripple of anxiety, but then people went back to complaining about the weather. In mid-August, while the *Gardener's Chronicle* was warning readers that "a fearful malady has broken out among the potato crop," in County Wicklow, Elizabeth Smith, the wife of a prominent local landlord, was complaining to her diary: "So little is there to write about here, . . . [this] journal stands very little chance of filling rapidly." On September 17, four days after the *Gardener's Chronicle* stopped the presses to announce "with very great regret . . . that the potato Murrain has un-equivocally declared itself in Ireland," the talk of the Royal Horticultural Society exhibition in Dublin was of grapes, melons, plums, and peaches, and of "plants never [so] numerous and evidenc[ing] very superior man-agement."

The final weeks of that last Irish summer before the famine had a soft, valedictory glow, which the *Dublin Evening Post*'s interview with Dr. Moore of the Dublin Botanical Gardens did little to disturb. After the interview appeared on September 9, press accounts of the potato dis-ease began to appear more frequently, but the notices—small, qualified, and full of reasons why readers should not worry—continued to be over-shadowed by the other news of the day. A suspect—a man named Heany—had been arrested in the murder of Mr. Bell-Booth, the Cavan magistrate; and Daniel O'Connell and Mr. Foster, the *Times* commis-sioner, had become embroiled in an amusing and very noisy public quar-rel over the quality of Irish beauty. "No race [is] . . . more perfectly developed than the Irish," declared the Liberator. "A stunted people," re-sponded the *Times* commissioner.

In London, summer ended on a more anxious note. The arrival of the blight in Ireland was causing deep concern in the Home Office, the department responsible for the internal affairs of the United Kingdom. In England, a crop failure would produce hardship, but factory workers and agricultural laborers earned a cash wage and English shops were stocked with food. In rural Ireland, where provision shops and cash wages were scarce, more than half the population depended entirely or mostly on home-grown potatoes for food. "If [the potato] fail[s] . . . fam-ine becomes a fatal certainty," declared Sir James Graham, the home secretary.

At fifty-three, Sir James had had a more than normally interesting ca-reer. Formerly the handsomest man in England—"a very Apollo"—he was now a stout, balding, middle-aged politician; formerly a Whig, he was now a Tory; formerly an MP for Carlisle, Pembroke, and Dorchester, he was now MP for Ripon; formerly an Anglican, he was now a Providentialist. Prime Minister Peel, himself a man of twists and turns, pierced through the change-abouts, through the reputation for ruthlessness and the "ter-rifyingly logical mind," and saw what nearly every other colleague of

A scene of an Irish jig

Graham had missed. Sir James had the makings of a perfect number two man: loyal, efficient, competent, and, when the occasion demanded, prepared to be ruthless on behalf of his prime minister. When Peel came to power in 1841, one of his first acts was to send Graham to the Home Office.

In mid-September, Sir James, though concerned, remained hopeful that a disaster could be avoided in Ireland. Reports from the Irish Constabulary, which had officers in the field monitoring the progress of the blight, indicated that the disease was confined to a few counties in the east; moreover, it was progressing in a checkerboard pattern: an infected field here, a healthy field there. The great swaths of ruin characteristic of a general disease metastasis had not developed. Intelligence from the Coast Guard and the Bank of Ireland, which also had people in the field, painted a similarly reassuring picture. On the twenty-fifth, Robert Murray, an official of the Provincial Bank of Ireland, pronounced the failure of the potato crop "very greatly exaggerated," and on the twenty-eighth the Constabulary informed the government that a larger than normal potato crop had been planted in the spring. The extra planting would provide a food reserve if the blight did spread. A few days later, a report from Ulster described the oat crop as "the best . . . , in quantity and quality, we have had for ten years past." There was also a reassuring crop report from Mayo, one of the most potato-dependent regions of the country. Images of harrowing affliction began to recede from the home secretary's mind. At the end of September, Graham told Peel, "I am willing now to hope that the . . . supply [of potatoes in Ireland] will not . . . be much below average."

The Freeman's Journal, a leading voice of Catholic Ireland, was more pessimistic. "Up to the hour," the paper wrote on September 17, "the accounts we continue to receive as to the prevalence of the blight . . . [are] discouraging." Still, the *Journal* was careful to avoid alarmism: "In all probability, we are better off than England or the continental countries." In late September, almost every Irish paper provided its readers with some version of that reassurance, and there was a legitimate reason for the optimism: the reports from Europe indicated that wet harvest weather hastened the spread of the blight, and Ireland had had a dry, sunny September.

In early October, when heavy rains brought the clement weather to an end, public anxiety rose. The late crop, the main potato crop, was about to be taken out of the ground. On the eighth, with the Dublin streets full of dripping black umbrellas, the Bank of Ireland warned that a failure of the potato was now likely in many districts. A week later, the Constabulary reported that the disease had regained momentum. The blight was either advancing, intensifying, or appearing for the first time in Antrim and Armagh in the northeast and in Bantry, Brandon, and Kinsale in the south. A negative report from Lord Heytesbury, the Irish viceroy, made a particularly deep impression in Downing Street. In the main, London distrusted reports from Irish officials; the same lively Hibernian imagination that saw imaginary fairies could also see imaginary crop failures. Heytesbury was a levelheaded Englishman. If he said there was reason for concern, there was. On October 13, Graham, ever the loyal subordinate, attempted to reassure his prime minister. I am "willing still to hope," he told Peel.

In Ireland, the late harvest was just beginning. A half century later—in Liverpool, London, Glasgow, Brooklyn, Montreal, Sydney, San Francisco, and Boston—men and women too old to remember anything else would still remember October 1845. The way the watery afternoon light fled up the hillsides, the dense blue fog that settled over the puddled potato fields, the odor of decay in the air, the "terrible stillness" that would descend on a field when the wind and rain died away, the heaving of the heavy October seas against the tide line. Irish folk memory also recalled the shock and terror that attended the 1845 harvest. In Cork, men wept openly as half-ruined potatoes were lifted from the ground. In Limerick, shovels dropped and laborers soaked through to the skin with rain filed out of the fields like mourners. In County Sligo, the howl of one bereft peasant awoke the entire town of Moytirra. In Castlederg, a farmer named Robert Verner plunged a bayonet into the chest of his son John during an argument over the family potato ground. Men sprinkled holy water on their potatoes; they buried them with religious medallions and pictures of Christ and the Virgin Mother. Nothing worked. God had turned away.

In mid-October a new set of Constabulary reports indicated that the area of infection was widening in the east and new areas of infection were appearing in the west. In Inishowen, Donegal, a region of low mountains and dense bogland, Michael Loughrey, a local landowner, instructed his bailiff to inform the tenantry that he would "demand no rent at present; and that should any of the tenants be obliged to sell any part of their crop for other purposes, he will give them the highest price." As the bailiff made his rounds, the hills above Inishowen flared red with celebratory bonfires.

On October 25, James Prendergast, of Milltown, County Kerry, described the events of the past few weeks to his children in "Boston, America" (in a letter written by the town scrivener):

> The beginning of the Harvest was very promising, the Crops . . . had a very rich appearance. And it was generally expected that [the] season would be very plentiful. But within the last few days, the greatest alarm prevails throughout the Kingdom. . . . A disease has seized the potato crop . . . the

standing food of the country. The Potatoes which were good and healthy a few days since are now rotten in the Ground, even some which were . . . stored in pits seem to be affected with the same blight. The Newspapers teem with alarming accounts of the same disease throughout the Kingdom.

. . . [I]t is dreaded that nothing less than a famine must prevail.

In England, the crop failure quickly turned into a political crisis, ushering in a radical new phase in the thirty years' war over the Corn Laws. In 1815, when Parliament passed the Corn Laws, which imposed tariffs on foreign grain ("corn" is the European name for cereal grains, such as wheat and oats), proponents predicted an era of prosperity and tranquillity. Instead, a generation of bitter class warfare followed. The aristocracy, whose estates provided most of Britain's grain, benefited greatly from the legislation, which protected them from competiton with cheap foreign grain. But high grain prices beggared factory workers, clerks, and tradesmen, the foot soldiers and quartermasters of the industrial revolution.

In 1842, agitation by industrialists, financiers, and merchants—who believed cheap food for the laboring classes was essential to Britain's industrial growth—forced the government to amend the Corn Laws. When the crop failed in 1845, the Anti–Corn Law League, the most powerful free-trade organization in the United Kingdom, eschewed compromise and demanded complete repeal of the laws. In pamphlets and mass demonstrations, league members warned that the combination of food tariffs and the failure of the potato, an important food for poor Britons, would impose terrible suffering on the industrial classes during the coming winter. The aristocracy also put out the battle flags. In London, the Duchess of Richmond placed a half dozen stuffed rats under a glass cover, decorated the cover with pictures of prominent free-trade proponents, and placed it on her dining table. The government braced for a season of civil disorder. Food tariffs had the power to transform perfectly decent butter merchants, greengrocers, and aristocratic ladies into lunatics who screamed "Murderer!" at opponents and chained themselves to fences.

In Ireland, too, the food crisis quickly erupted into a political crisis. Protestants blamed the blight on Catholics, Catholics on Protestants; Daniel O'Connell, always alert to political opportunity, blamed the Anglo-Irish Union. At a "monster" rally in Tipperary in October, O'Connell denounced the Union under a banner inscribed "England has given us ignorance and bigotry, starvation and rags." The theft of firearms rose—portent of a violent winter on the horizon. In Dublin, there was talk of a British plan to reinforce every regiment in the country with a reserve battalion. In Limerick, gangs of "armed banditti" roamed the nighttime countryside, terrorizing farmers, bailiffs, and other local officials. Christopher Bunton, a well-off farmer, was dragged from his bed in the middle of the night and beaten severely about the head. Thomas Coghlan, John Hogan, and dozens of other prominent local men also fell victim to the "banditti." In Irish country houses, fears grew about the export crops, a major source of revenue for the landowning gentry. Rumor had it that "violent priests" were "advising laborers not to thresh the corn or allow it to go to market at Limerick—as strangers will be eating it in England."

Images of affliction again began to crowd the home secretary's mind.

❦

On the afternoon of October 18, four men gathered in a Yorkshire country house, Drayton Manor, to discuss the crop crisis. William Buckland was an eminent geologist, Josiah Parkes an expert in agricultural drainage; Lyon Playfair was the twenty-seven-year-old wunderkind of British chemistry. The fourth man was the prime minister of Great Britain, the fifty-seven-year-old Sir Robert Peel. A French diplomat who met Peel around this time described him as a man in "the full flower of his powers . . . [his] thick hair an auburn hue, [his] complexion blond, . . . [his] constitution well calculated to endure the fatigues and trials of public life."

The gifted first son of a wealthy textile industrialist, the prime minister had impressed from the very beginning. "We all had great hopes for Peel, masters and scholars alike," recalled Lord Byron, a schoolmate at Harrow. Praise and high expectations followed the future prime minister through Oxford and later through a political apprenticeship that included learning how to write thank-you notes for George III and how to cut orders for a certain Captain Bligh, after the captain had become stranded in the South Seas by a mutiny on his ship, the *Bounty*. On a visit to Ireland with the Duke of Wellington, the young apprentice politician also got a first glimpse into the private lives of the good and great. "Wellington . . . stayed in the house of a Mr. Dickson, a shoemaker," Peel wrote a friend. "Mrs. Dickson had a son, who by some accident or other bore a much stronger resemblance to Lord Wellington than Mr. Dickson." In Ireland, Peel also displayed his executive abilities for the first time. During a crop failure in 1816, the young chief secretary organized a model relief program. As secretary of the Home Office in the 1820s, he scored a further triumph: the creation of the Metropolitan Police—the "Bobbies," the first modern police force in the world.

By the mid-1840s, Peel had become an icon to the strivers of provincial Britain, though not to his colleagues in the House of Commons. The cheerless Peel manner was italicized by a lifeless smile that one parliamentarian likened to "a silver platter on a coffin." There was also the odd foppishness: the "perfumed handkerchiefs," the fashionably "thin shoes." Peel "looks more like a dapper shopkeeper than a Prime Minister," complained the political diarist Charles Greville. And even the prime minister's most sympathetic biographer described his country house, Drayton Manor—a whirligig of "dull cupolas," monkey-puzzle trees, and winged cherubs—as "one of the first great examples of the disintegration of taste" in the Victorian era.

Fellow MPs also had more substantive complaints about the prime minister. Young Benjamin Disraeli accused Peel of stealing other people's ideas: "There is no statesman who has committed political larceny on so great a scale." Peel's frequent changes of mind also inspired distrust. "Altered circumstances," the prime minister explained when he changed his mind about the gold standard, and again when he changed his mind about Catholic Emancipation. More recently, Peel had appeared to change his mind about Ireland. As Irish chief secretary, the prime minister had been such an ardent supporter of Anglo-Ireland that O'Connell christened him "Orange Peel." (Orange was the signature color of Protestant Ireland.) Now, Orange Peel was courting Catholic Ireland with promises of educational reform. Underneath the patina of English solidity lay a complex, enigmatic personality.

Peel had summoned Playfair, Parkes, and Buckland to Drayton

Sir Robert Peel

Manor for advice on a scientific problem. In Ireland, healthy potatoes were turning bad in storage. Could anything be done to prevent the spoilage? Dr. Playfair thought a chemical treatment might solve the problem. That night, in a letter to Graham, the prime minister sounded almost optimistic: "Dr. Lyon Playfair, Buckland and Josiah Parkes are here. . . . They are impressed with the belief that it may be possible to mitigate the evil of the potato disease by some chemical application and by the issue of practical instructions for . . . treatment." The next day, Playfair returned to London with orders to begin experimenting on chemical treatments immediately.

⬧

Over the next week, the news from Ireland worsened. Lord Monteagle, a prominent Limerick landlord, told Peel he could not "recall a former . . . calamitous failure being anything near so great." Mr. Bueller, the secretary of the Royal Agricultural Society of Ireland, believed "the entire crop [was] . . . affected in all parts of the country." Though the situation was clearly serious, a small but persistent stream of favorable reports suggested there still might be reason for optimism. In Galway, the local potato crop was said to be "abundant"; in Tralee (County Kerry), the blight had not even appeared; and in Athlone (County Roscommon), it had caused only minor damage. "There is nothing like a fact," the prime minister believed, but the current set of "facts" had the spongy feel of rumor and innuendo. Peel decided to appoint a Scientific Commission to assess "the real character and extent of the evil."

The Times immediately gave the three-member commission a snappy name, "Potato Triumvirate," and hailed the scientific prowess of its members. The paper would come to deeply regret its haste. One member, Dr. Lindley, though an accomplished scientist, was a leading proponent of the meteorological theory, while Dr. Playfair knew more about fatty acids and atomic volume than potatoes. Moreover, he owed his scientific reputation as much to his skills as a courtier (he was a gentleman usher in the household of Prince Albert) as to his acumen in the laboratory. The Irish member of the commission, the ubiquitous Dr. Robert Kane, did know Ireland and potatoes; but Kane had been the token Irish Catholic on so many royal commissions he was in danger of appearing like the product of an imperial affirmative action policy.

The Dublin that the two English members of the commission visited in late October maintained an air of normalcy. In the harbor, shouting, shoving porters pressed the charms of local hotels and lodging houses on arriving visitors. The shops along Grafton Street were as "busy as beehives"; the parks and squares packed with "swirling crowds"; and, to at least one visitor's eye, the city's fashionable women looked "the equal of Frenchwomen in good taste" and far superior to the "vulgar, shewy English." The Dublin press, however, was anxious. The autumn crop was the main source of food for the peasantry from October until May, and even out of the ground the 1845 crop was continuing to shrink. Many seemingly healthy potatoes were dying in the underground pits the peasants dug to store tubers. One man buried sixty barrels of potatoes and walked away from his pit, thinking he had a five-month food supply for his family. A few weeks later, not enough edible potatoes were left to fill a single barrel. Toward the end of the month, a Dublin market report warned that even "with the greatest care, the [current] crop will be all out by the end of January . . . as the tendency to decay, even in the best, is evident."

In a six-county tour of the east and Irish Midlands, the Potato Triumvirate found little to contradict the pessimistic press accounts. Blackened stalks hugging the roads; diseased tubers scattered across watery fields; dazed laborers and cottiers standing idle in the rain; children eating turnip tops: almost every district presented the same bleak picture of want. In January and February, the fields would be crowded with men and women down on their hands and knees in the snow, digging for nettles and grass. The commissioners returned to Dublin in a fume of despair. "At a low estimate," half the 1845 crop had been lost, and that did not account for the eighth of the good crop that would have to be set aside as seed for the 1846 planting, or for the losses in the storage pits. When it was learned that only three-eighths of the 1845 crop could be salvaged, the public-spirited stepped forward with suggestions to counter the famine threat. Lord Kenyon, an astute Yorkshire man, urged the government to pay the Irish peasant a bounty for every fish he caught and make "a special public acknowledgement of . . . God's mercy." The Duke of Norfolk recommended curry powder. Imported curry powder would not materially increase the Irish food supply, said Norfolk, but it would make hunger more tolerable. "When a man came home and . . . had nothing better [to eat], this [curry powder] would make him warm in his stomach and he could go to bed better and more comfortable."

On October 26, the chemist Playfair urged that British consular officials in the blight-free parts of southern Europe—northern Spain, Portugal, Italy—inquire into the availability of potato exports in their region. "Pray aid us," Playfair pleaded to Peel. A few days later, James MacEnvoy, a parish priest, stood on a road in County Meath, watching fifty drays (carts) of meal moving on to Drogheda. From Drogheda, most of the grain would go to London, which was importing 16,000 quarters (a quarter equals 480 pounds) of Irish grain a week in October 1845. That night, MacEnvoy thought of the difference the fifty drays would make to his parishioners. "Self preservation is the first law of nature," he wrote in a letter to a Dublin paper. "The right of the starving to . . . sustain existence is far and away paramount to every right property confers." In early November, Dr. Lindley, the most influential member of the commission, returned to England, depressed. A good part of the 1845 crop was gone, he told Peel, and the rest was likely to go in the next few weeks, unless the new storage pit guidelines that the commission had issued were implemented; Lindley thought that unlikely. For the unpopularity of the guidelines, he blamed "want of means," "landlord tenant disputes," the "wet climate"—everything except the guidelines themselves. Pity the poor parish priest or land agent who had to explain "Advice Concerning the Potato Crop," a pamphlet on storage pit construction, to thirty or forty illiterate laborers:

> Mark out on the ground a space six feet wide and as long as you please. Dig a shallow trench two feet wide all around and throw the mould upon the space; then level it and cover it with a floor of turf sods, set on their edges. On this sift or spread very thinly, the dry mixtures, or any of the dry materials described below and which you may call the packing stuff. Also get some dry slack lime, and dust all the potatoes with it as well as you can. Then put one row of turf sods, laid flat, on the top of the floor, all around the sides, so as to form a broad edge, and within this, spread the dry potatoes, mixed well with the packing stuff, so as not to touch one another. When you have covered the floor in this manner, up to the top of the sods, lay another row of sods all around the first.

Those able to faithfully follow the instructions in "Advice," quickly discovered the commissioners didn't know what they were talking about. Even a dry, ventilated trench offered little protection against *P. infestans*.

Another pamphlet, "How to Save the Value of Every Bad Potato," did little to restore the commissioners' reputations for scientific acuity. To extract edible food from a diseased potato, the reader was advised to equip himself with a grater, which he could purchase for five shillings, more than a week's wages for an Irish countryman—or he could make his own grater, by punching holes in a sheet of tin. The conversion process also required "a hair sieve or hand sieve or lining cloth, . . . a griddle and two tubs or pails of water." Implements at the ready, the reader was instructed to rasp the diseased tubers into one of the tubs, wash the pulp, strain, and dry. Repeated enough times, the process eventually produced pulp for the griddle, and starch for soup and pies and bread. "There will of course be a great deal of trouble doing everything that we have recommended," the pamphlet admitted. "But we are confident that all true Irishmen will exert themselves and never let it be said that in Ireland the inhabitants lacked courage to meet difficulties against which other nations are successfully struggling."

Arguably, the Scientific Commission's only real achievement was to produce a rare instance of Anglo-Irish accord. "Vain" in its researches, "idle in its suggestions," and "unsatisfactory" in its information, sneered a disillusioned *Times*. *The Freeman's Journal* agreed: "[The] Commissioners have satisfactorily proved, [that] they know nothing whatever about the cause of, or remedies for, the disease." The criticism was deserved. Besides burying Ireland in a blizzard of useless pamphlets, Lindley, Playfair, and Kane had also miscalculated the extent of the crop losses, in part because they failed to include the increased size of the 1845 planting, which was about 6 percent above average.*

⚬

On the afternoon of November 3, a train of carriages passed through the main gates of Phoenix Park in Dublin and disappeared into a landscape of mist, wood, and lawn. Near an ancient tower of beaten stone the caravan halted, black-coated footmen appeared, carriage doors were flung open, collapsible steps popped from the bottom lip of the carriage doors, and Daniel O'Connell, Lord Cloncurry, John O'Neill, John Arabin, the lord mayor of Dublin, and a host of other dignitaries stepped onto the lawn of the Viceregal Lodge, the private residence of the English viceroy.† Inside, the very sour current viceroy, Lord Heytesbury, awaited the party in a large reception room. As the visitors disappeared into the lodge, a *Morning Chronicle* reporter on the lawn checked the time: almost exactly three P.M.

The atmosphere in the reception room was chilly as the lord mayor read aloud the emergency relief program prepared by the Dublin Corpo-

---

*Some scholors believe the 1845 crop was as much as 30 percent larger than the typical crop.
†The lord lieutenant of Ireland was also commonly called the viceroy.

ration, the municipal government of the capital. The six points in the plan included a ban on food exports (a common measure after crop failures and one already taken by Belgium, Holland, and Russia); a ban on the use of grain in the distillation of alcohol; a suspension of food tariffs; the establishment of a network of government food depots; and a national program of public works to put food money into the pockets of the peasantry. After the mayor finished, a "very cold" Heytesbury praised British vigilance and concern for Ireland—"the state of the potato crop ... [occupies] the anxious attention of the Government"—and hailed the efforts of the Potato Triumvirate. A few minutes later, the dignitaries were back on the lawn waiting for their carriages to come up from the carriage park.

"They may starve!" *The Freeman's Journal* shouted the next morning. "Such in spirit, if not in words, was the reply given yesterday by the English viceroy to the memorial of the deputation." Reading the press accounts, Heytesbury must have felt aggrieved. Twice in the past few weeks he had petitioned Peel to close the ports (to food exports), and twice Peel had refused. The prime minister had quietly drawn up his own plan for "averting disaster" in Ireland, and in one respect it was far more radical than the Dublin Corporation's. Along with a public works program and the creation of a Dublin-based relief commission to coordinate the efforts of national and local officials, the plan included a proposal to abolish the Corn Laws, not temporarily but once and for all and in every part of the United Kingdom. On November 1, at a cabinet meeting in his London home in Whitehall Gardens, the gout-stricken prime minister laid out his reasoning: it would be impossible to suspend food tariffs in Ireland without also suspending food tariffs in England. Moreover, given the current state of Anti–Corn Law League agitation, tariffs, once suspended, would be difficult if not impossible to reimpose after the scarcity. With a few notable exceptions, cabinet reaction to the proposal was sharply negative. Some ministers argued that Corn Law reform would ignite a bitter and distracting legislative battle, impairing the government's ability to respond to the emergency in Ireland; others, that repeal would damage the economic interests of the landed classes—the base of the Tory party—and produce a new round of class warfare.

Already, *The Economist*, a radical laissez-faire publication, was attacking the British landowner as a selfish and reactionary class warrior. "The aristocracy," the paper had declared in a recent editorial, "are struggling against . . . the prayers of the manufacturing classes; they are struggling against the supplications of the people for food . . . they are struggling against common sense and against the irresistible progress of society."

Peel could not be dissuaded by his ministers. Ireland, he insisted, would benefit from Corn Law reform. Perhaps. But how was hard to see. Ireland was not in the midst of an industrial revolution and thus not in need of cheap food for her factory workers to sustain the revolution. England, of course, was.

As they drove home through the November night, the gas lamps on the other side of the Thames twinkling in the darkness, some of the cabinet ministers must have wondered what the prime minister was up to. Ireland was on the edge of famine; why tie her relief to an issue as politically volatile as the Corn Law reform? One thing was certain. If the prime minister persisted in his campaign to abolish the Corn Laws, the Tory party would break in two over the issue.

CHAPTER THREE

"The Irish Can Live on Anything"

On a damp afternoon toward the middle of November, a large, walrus-shaped Englishman of cheerful disposition and steady habit arrived at the Salt Hill Hotel outside Dublin, a favorite gathering place for visiting British officials and the capital's large population of super-annuated colonels, who spent the long damp autumn afternoons sipping whiskeys and reading three-day-old copies of *The Times* in between gold-plated spittoons and potted palms in the lobby. Some of the old soldiers may have recognized the new guest from Waterloo, others as that quartermaster fellow who only married Frenchwomen. (Twice!) But most of the early imbibers would have recognized Sir Randolph Isham Routh—Dorset born, Newfoundland raised, old Etonian—as the senior officer in the Commissariat, the British army's quartermaster corps. In November 1845, everything England knew about feeding large groups of people in a crisis was encapsulated in the brain of sixty-three-year-old Commissary General Routh. Throughout the British government, the author of *Observations on the Commissariat Field Service and Home Defence* was regarded as a logistical thinker of great depth and subtlety. The official who wanted to know the spoilage rate of grain, the weight-bearing capacity of a Spanish dray, or why the No. 2 sack was the pick of the litter of packing sacks, would invariably be told, "See Sir Randolph."

The only black mark on Routh's otherwise stellar record was an occasional tendency "to lead the government into unnecessary expense," but that almost cost him appointment to the government's new Irish Relief Commission. The last thing Home Secretary Graham wanted was a commissioner inclined to "make relief attractive." For a week, the Routh appointment loitered in the Home Office's "maybe" tray; then, some wakeful mind in Whitehall remembered that Sir Randolph was the man who had fed the thin red line at Waterloo and helped suppress an 1837 rebellion in Canada that could have cost Britain her other North American colony. Upon reconsideration, Graham ruled that "on the present occasion . . . the objection that Routh indulges in *large* views [on finance] ought not . . . to prevail." The home secretary also hesitated over the appointment of Edward Lucas, a prominent Irish landlord. During a partial crop failure in 1842, then–Irish Undersecretary Lucas had also displayed a tendency to "lead the government into unnecessary expenditure." Again, practicality trumped doubt. Peel intended to limit British involvement in the crop failure to organizational support, loans, and some supplies. A Treasury memo was quite explicit about who would play the lead role in relief. "The [Irish] landlords and other rate payers are the parties . . . both legally and morally responsible for affording the relief to the destitute poor." As an influential member of the Irish gentry, Lucas seemed the perfect person to tell his fellow landlords that they were going to have to pick up most of the cost of relief. Graham made Lucas chairman of the commission. The other appointees were Colonel Harry Jones, a royal engineer and chairman of the Irish Board of Works; Colonel Duncan McGregor, inspector general of the Irish Constabulary; Sir James Dombrain, inspector general of the Coast Guard; John Pitt Kennedy, author of a popular pamphlet on the Irish peasantry ("Instruct: Employ: Don't Hang Them"); and Dr. Robert Kane, late of the Potato Triumvirate. "He has gained some practical knowledge on other commissions . . . he has written on the industrial resources of Ireland. But mainly he is Roman Catholic," noted Prime Minister Peel. The appointment of Edward Twisleton, director of the Irish Poor Law system, was not controversial, but it was surprising. During the two most recent crop failures, in 1839 and 1842, the Poor Law workhouses had refused to participate in the emergency relief effort.

✳

Public poor relief, a tradition in England since Elizabethan times, was slow in coming to Ireland: 2.3 million people in chronic destitution, perhaps an equal number destitute for part of each year—every time British officials looked at the numbers they shook their heads. Funding an Irish poor relief system would be prohibitively expensive. Many officials also feared that public assistance would deepen what most of them regarded as the Irish national affliction, "dependence on government." Then, there was Dr. Malthus. In *An Essay on the Principle of Population*, Malthus had drawn a harrowing picture of the connection between public relief and the high birthrate of the poor. And Malthus had been writing about the English poor!

By the early 1830s, however, a consensus had emerged on one aspect of Irish poverty: it had become so terrible, it was draining the Irish people morally as well as physically. The peasantry have "an appearance of apathy and depression. This is seen in their mode of living, in their dress, in the dress of their children. . . . They seem to have no pride, no emulation." George Nicholls, the author of those words, knew poverty better than most men. For most of his adult life, Nicholls had worked with the English poor; but even in the wretched hovels of industrial-age Manchester, he had only occasionally encountered horrors equal to those he witnessed during a nine-week tour of Ireland. An English Poor Law commissioner, Nicholls owed his presence in Ireland to the recently disbanded Whately Commission. Created in 1833 to devise a public assistance program for Ireland, the commission came up with a program so comprehensive in scope and enormous in cost, almost no one was pleased with it except the commission's chairman, Richard Whately, (Protestant) Archbishop of Dublin and professor of political economy at Oxford. In 1836, Nicholls was rushed over to Ireland with instructions to create a relief system that was small, inexpensive, and resistant to abuse—and create it quickly enough to make everyone forget the Whately Commission. In large measure, Nicholls succeeded.

The Irish Poor Law system was small—130 workhouses with a total capacity of 100,000 beds—and unlike the English system it offered no right to relief. When the last workhouse bed was taken, the right to assistance ended. Besides the workhouse itself, the signature feature of the Irish system was the Poor Law Union, the geographical unit each workhouse served. Every landholder in the Union who held property valued at £4 or more was liable for a tax called the poor rate, which was set by the "guardians"—the workhouse administrators—and used to clothe and feed inmates. Like its English model, the Irish system was less interested in alleviating suffering than in promoting behavioral change. Sometime in the

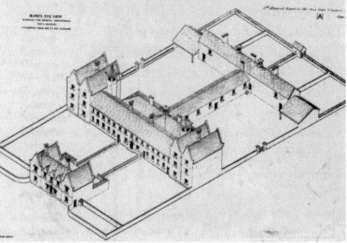

Two views of an Irish workhouse

eighteenth century, the definition of poverty changed. It ceased to be viewed as a natural aspect of the human condition like illness and war and became a badge of moral turpitude. People were poor, not because, as scripture says, "ye have the poor always with you" but because the poor were morally weak and in their weakness they succumbed to indolence, irresponsibility, promiscuity, and bibulousness. The task of the Irish (and English) workhouse was to rehabilitate the afflicted by further afflicting them—by making poverty so unendurable, its victims would embrace the virtues of the saved: industry, self-reliance, and personal discipline. The Irish system executed this mission with unfailing energy and imagination. The relief applicant who managed to remain unintimidated by the forbidding architecture of the workhouse—the high walls, the bleak grassless courtyard, the narrow windows like gun slits—had to endure an admissions process that included procedures "disgusting to the Celtic mind," including a "fearful ordeal by water." He was also required to bring his family into the workhouse with him, to dress in penal-like garb, to wear shoes that pointed straight ahead rather than left and right, and to engage in heavy manual labor. By September 1845, the frightful reputation of the Irish workhouse was having the desired effect. The occupancy rate in the 118 completed workhouses was under 50 percent. The system was also designed to change the behavior of the Irish landlord by tying his poor rate to his eviction rate: the more tenants he threw onto the roads, the higher his poor rate. However, this part of the rehabilitation theory failed. In 1843, the British army and Irish Constabulary had to virtually invade Mayo and Galway to collect the poor rate.

In November 1845, when his fellow commissioners began pestering Mr. Twisleton about the use of his half-empty workhouses, he stood his ground. The Poor Law system was created to rehabilitate the poor, not to feed the victims of a crop failure. Moreover, emergency relief was administered outdoors in a soup kitchen or similar facility, and Irish workhouses were strictly forbidden from providing outdoor relief in any form and under any circumstance.

※

On November 20, when the Relief Commission met for the first time, the only settled issue before its members was the mode of relief. With the

Poor Law workhouses off limits, the commission would have to follow the 1842 precedent and create a network of local relief committees to distribute food to blight victims. Every other issue before the commission ended in a question mark, including the extent of the crop losses. If the estimates of Playfair and Lindley were correct, serious want could appear as early as January; if 1846 was like 1822 (another year of crop failure), the potato supply would last until April. The absence of accurate crop-loss data also made it difficult to determine how to allocate relief resources. An impoverished district with a 30 percent crop loss might require more assistance than a relatively prosperous district with a 50 percent loss. The commission also had no information on food prices, which were certain to rise soon, or on the size of the food reserve held in military depots in England. With little information about the food supply, the commission was also unable to assess the fever risk. In Ireland, major crop failures were often followed by major fever epidemics, like the epidemic of 1816–1819, which killed 65,000 people. About one thing the commissioners were certain: it would be impossible to mount a major relief operation before May 1846. Provision orders had to be placed with export houses in North America, the Mediterranean basin, and the Black Sea; transport fleets had to be mobilized and the Commissariat mustered for duty in Ireland; a network of local relief committees had to be formed. With that thought in mind, the commissioners turned their attention to the plan Peel had drawn up for Ireland.

In broad outline, the scheme resembled the relief plans employed in the 1839 and 1842 crop failures: food would be imported to cover the potato losses, local relief committees created to purchase the imports and sell them at cost to potato-less peasants, and public works projects established to permit the peasant, who normally bartered his labor for food, to earn a cash wage. Private enterprise, not the British government, would provide most of the imports. In *The Wealth of Nations*, Adam Smith had created an imaginary pin factory to illustrate how dozens of individuals, each pursuing his own private interest, served the common good. In May and June 1846, in Dungannon, in Ennis, in Belmullet, in Skibbereen, and in ten thousand places in between, the British government would transform Smith's theory into reality. The fate of millions would hang on the ability of the small, still flame of human self-interest to animate exporters in New Orleans, Alexandria, and Odessa; importers in Liverpool, London, and Cork city; stevedores in New York and Panama; ship captains in Newburyport and Cornwall; food merchants in Galway; and millers in Kerry.

However, Peel was not prepared to let human self-interest loose on four million hungry peasants without checks. In early November he asked Baring Bros., a large London financial house, to purchase £100,000 worth of American maize. That was enough food to feed a million people for forty days, but Peel intended to use the corn primarily as a price control mechanism. When merchants threatened to drive food prices to unaffordable levels, the government would throw a supply of cheap maize on the market to force prices down again. Essentially, Baring's role in the corn purchase was that of front man. If agents of the British government began making large buys in the international markets, prices would spike instantly, and the private merchants the government was relying on to provision Ireland would flee, frightened by the prospect of competing against cheap Crown food.

※

Maize—or Indian corn, as it was often called—had many attractions as a government food. It was inexpensive, relatively familiar in Ireland— maize had been used during several previous scarcities—and unlikely to provoke accusations of "Government interference!" from the private trade. Except in periods of dearth, no one in Ireland ate Indian corn, so the government would not be intruding on a lucrative private market. In selecting maize, Peel was also thinking about the future. As early as 1822, the Horticultural Society of London had warned that, because of its increasing unreliability, the potato was no longer suited to serve as a major crop. "Wherever [the potato] shall . . . become the chief or sole support of a county, [it] must inevitably lead to all the misery of famine." The Irish loved their potatoes, but several generations of major and minor crop failures may have made the people receptive to the introduction of a new dietary staple and, as the potato's successor, Indian corn had much to recommend it.

Maize had a short growing season and a high yield, and could play an important role in the plan to modernize Ireland. The Victorians, who saw diet and character as interrelated, believed that grains, such as maize, promoted character development, while "lower" foods, such as the potato, retarded it. According to the *Edinburgh Review*, a leading journal of the Victorian age, many of the flaws in the Irish character had their genesis in potato dependency. Why did the Irish have "domestic habits . . . of the lowest and most degrading kind"? Why did they "encourage . . . pigs and poultry [to] become . . . inmates of the cabin"? Why was their "mode of life more akin to the South Seas . . . than [to] the great civilized communities of the ancient world"? Potato dependency! *The Economist* put the case against the potato succinctly:

> *Food for the contented slave.*
> *Not the hardy and the brave.*

William Wilde, a leading Irish medical man (and, later, the father of Oscar Wilde), held the potato responsible for placing the Irish somewhere between the "Greenlander and the Esquimaux" in moral and cultural development. In a magazine article, Wilde drew a memorable word picture of the Irish cabin at dinnertime: the turf fire burning, the thatched roof dripping soot, and the peasant and his family gathered around a three-legged stool, enjoying "potatoes and point"—potatoes dipped in a herring garnish. "Each party (barring the pig) removes the fine outer rind of the lumper . . . [then] flavors the esculent by a dip into the saucer of point."

In different ways, William Wilde, the *Edinburgh Review*, and *The Economist* were expressing the fundamental British complaint about the potato. Its ease of cultivation—only a few months of intermittent labor were required to produce a year's supply of food—produced habits and values incompatible with the swift winds of change blowing through the nineteenth century. Routh, who imagined himself a student of the Irish character, told a colleague: "The little industry called for to rear the potato, and its prolific growth leave the people to indolence and vice." Routh was certain a maize diet would lead to the "regeneration" of Ireland; the *Edinburgh Review* agreed. Indian corn was a grain, and the grain eater, noted the *Review*, was characterized by "thrift," "energy," and "a vast accumulation of capital." The nation-builders in Britain thought maize had another important virtue: it could not be grown in the wet Irish climate. Therefore, it would have to be purchased, which would help inaugurate a virtuous cycle of economic development. Store-bought food required hard currency, which would make the small peasant farmer more amenable to employment as a salaried laborer on a commercial farm. As the number of salaried laborers grew, a consumer society would develop in rural areas, and shops, warehouses, transportation systems, and a money economy would arise to serve it.

By early January 1846, American ports were filled with ships taking on Yankee corn, and Mr. Thomas Ward, Baring Bros. agent in the United States, was feeling quite pleased with himself. Normally, large purchases moved market prices, but Mr. Ward, a clever and discreet Bostonian, had made his buys so quietly, the markets had barely noticed.

⬦

If the maize purchase was the strongest part of Peel's relief plan, the weakest part was its reliance on the Irish landed classes. The traditional European model of relief assigned the landed classes an important role. In periods of crisis, the gentry in a district were expected to fund employment and food schemes for the local poor. But in Ireland the model had rarely worked well. During a scarcity in 1839, Captain Chads, a Royal Navy man seconded to relief duty, was shocked at the way the hungry were left to save themselves. "[T]he poor ... [had to] part with everything to obtain food, even their crops in the ground. All these evils ... must have been seen by [those] possessing property in the country; ... yet with a few honourable exceptions, no steps were taken to avert them. Thus, there [are] vast numbers of poor with large families, tenants of large landed proprietors, almost in a state of starvation. ... [Such is] the indifference and coldness of many of the Irish landlords." Gustave de Beaumont, who visited Ireland with his friend Alexis de Tocqueville in 1835, believed this indifference to peasant suffering was a byproduct of the plantations. The Irish "landlord, though he touches the soil, rarely takes root in it ... Ireland is not the country to which he believes that his cares and sacrifices are due."

The Peel plan also required a modern commercial infrastructure to work effectively. There had to be merchants who knew how to order food

from the Ukraine, Egypt, and the Ohio Valley, and how to arrange shipping with an agent in Liverpool or London. There also had to be a milling industry to process the maize. Outside of Dublin, Cork city, and
Belfast, such men and resources were rare; indeed, they were uncommon
even in the big metropolitan areas. The plan also ignored the primitive
nature of the Irish distribution system. Unlike Britain and France, rural
Ireland did not have a network of village provision shops. Volunteer relief committees formed from the local gentry would plug some of the
gaps in the distribution system, but in many back places, there was no
resident gentry. The more Routh thought about the distribution problem,
the more his mind turned to Mr. Twisleton's half-empty workhouses.
The houses would extend the Relief Commission's reach into remote areas and, the poor rate was a more secure source of relief funding than
landlord donations, the traditional source. It was time to have another
talk with "the little Cockney Poor Law King."

In December, Routh supported a proposal that would permit Irish
workhouses to establish poor rate–funded soup kitchens or provide some
other form of outdoor relief. The British Poor Law system permitted outdoor relief in periods of national emergency; why not the Irish? Mr.
Twisleton was dismayed by the proposal, Home Secretary Graham
horrified. Ireland was not England. Once the ban on outdoor relief was
lifted, reimposing it would be impossible. There would be marches, protests, riots, and God knows how many inflammatory speeches by Daniel
O'Connell. At the end of the scarcity, a nation with 2.3 million chronic
paupers—a quarter of the population—would be burdened with a ruinous new welfare entitlement: outdoor relief. Instead of being employed to
modernize their agricultural operations, the landowners' capital would
be swallowed up by a confiscatory poor rate. Ireland would become a
"giant workhouse presided over by the Prime Minister of Great Britain."
Every Irish child would imbibe "dependency on government" with his
mother's milk. The home secretary saw the future, and it was frighten-
ing. "The locusts will devour the land."

On November 22, readers of *The Morning Chronicle* opened the paper expecting to find the news of the day and instead were treated to a
personal confession by one of the leading men in British public life, Lord
John Russell, head of the Whig party and a member of one of the most

storied of English families. For four hundred years, the Russells had tumbled down through English history like the notes of a particularly sparkling tune. There had been Russell dukes and baronets, Russell soldiers and diplomats, Russell rebels and courtiers, and one Russell wine merchant—the founder of the dynasty. One day in 1506, the commoner John Russell plucked a shipwrecked Hapsburg archduke out of a storm-tossed Channel sea. The grateful duke was delivered to London; the pleased king activated the royal spigot; grants and titles flowed out; Mr. Russell closed his wine shop; and, as one biographer noted, "the family never looked back."

The current John Russell stood five feet, four inches tall, had a statesman's noble head, an undersized body, a nervous temperament, a foxlike quickness, a good if sometimes indecisive mind, and an older brother

Lord John Russell

who persisted in calling him "little Johnny" well into middle age. He also had a history of achievement unusual even in a family as distinguished as the Russells. In the early 1830s Lord John had been a leader of the Reform Movement (the campaign to extend the franchise), and as home secretary in the mid-1830s, he had sent Mr. Nicholls to Ireland to create a Poor Law system. Like most members of his class, Russell had also been a protectionist. No more, though. In the *Morning Chronicle* confession, he proclaimed himself a born-again free-market man. "I used to be of the opinion that corn [grain] was the exception to the general rules of political economy; but observation and experience have convinced me that we ought to abstain from all interference with the supply of food." Despite the measured tone, the confession was a naked political ploy. Lord John wanted to be prime minister, and the crop failures in England and Ireland had transformed the Anti–Corn Law movement into a powerful political force. Why stand in front of the train when he could ride it into 10 Downing Street? On November 25, while Peel was managing the Irish crisis and the Corn Law crisis, Lord John was enjoying the praise of a grateful press. "A bold man," declared *The Illustrated London News*; a paragon of "straightforward manliness," said *The Morning Chronicle*. Both papers were now referring to the Russell confession as the Edinburgh Letter. St. Paul received his revelation on the road to Damascus; John Russell his during a visit to Edinburgh.

For Peel, the Edinburgh Letter was only the latest woe in a month heavy with woes. Many of the predictions made at the Whitehall Gardens meeting in November had come to pass. His cabinet was deadlocked over the Corn Law issue. The Tory party had split into protectionist and free-trade wings; and the protectionists had appropriated the Irish crisis as a weapon. In speeches and pamphlets, they portrayed the crop failure as a hoax, an invention of "Slippery Eel," who had inflated a routine crop failure into a national emergency in order to repeal the tariffs on food. In an address to the Leicester Agricultural Society, the Duke of Cambridge, a leading protectionist and Queen Victoria's uncle, listed three reasons why talk of a famine in Ireland was rubbish. First, said Cambridge, "Ireland was in a very comfortable situation compared with the statements made concerning her in the newspapers." Second, he had been told by "the professors [Lindley and Playfair] that rotten sea weed and grass, or even grass properly mixed, afforded a very wholesome and nutritious food." And third, "Irishmen can live on anything."

The free-trade movement had also turned the Irish crisis to its purposes. Evangelical Protestant members of the movement who believed free trade to be a natural law—that is, a law of God—began arguing that the Irish crop failure was not a natural disaster; it was a Visitation of Providence. God had destroyed the potato crop to punish man for violating His laws on food tariffs. Why the Almighty would deprive the Irish peasant of his potatoes to spite the Duke of Cambridge was a mystery as deep as the virgin birth. But the Corn Law debate had long since slipped the surly bonds of reason. "It is awful to observe how the Almighty humbles the pride of nations," declared the home secretary, who had long ago abandoned the tranquil, sunlit uplands of Anglicanism for the volcanic fields of Providentialism.

On December 5, with Britain torn apart by the Corn Law controversy, the Peel government fell; on the eighteenth, Lord John agreed to form a government. He had to withdraw the offer on the nineteenth because of divisions in the Whig party, and Peel became prime minister again on the twentieth. This French farce ended with Russell embarrassed, Peel vindicated, the British public in a state of vertigo, and the Irish crisis all but forgotten, except in the speeches of the protectionist and evangelical free-traders. Reading the skimpy press coverage from Ireland, the average Briton would never have guessed she was sliding toward the abyss, but she was.

CHAPTER FOUR

Want

In the midst of comings and goings in London, a party of bailiffs, Irish Constabulary officers, and a work crew arrived unannounced in Tullycrine, a townland in western Clare. It was winter now, and the Constabulary officers dispersing around the townland were careful to take up positions that offered protection against the wind coming up from the sea below Kilmore. A bailiff removed a piece of paper from his pocket, examined it, then gave the work crew a name. The crew—mostly ex-military men, with hard, closed faces—picked up their crowbars and sledgehammers and marched down the narrow lanes of Tullycrine, behind a pack of dogs. When the strangers reached Thomas Walters's cabin, they halted. Walters had a wife, ten children, a few acres of farmland, and no hope of ever having anything more. Curses and threats were exchanged, children roused, possessions tossed into the lanes, cabin walls smashed, and a squealing pig confiscated. Next, the work crew visited the cabin of an old widow with seven children and four acres. After the widow's cabin had been demolished, the chief bailiff examined the eviction list again. Simon Kean and his brother John were next, then Connor Crelan. By late afternoon there was not a structure standing on the winter landscape, and the only sound to be heard was the sound of wind coming up over the hills from the unseen sea. In a letter to *The Nation*, a

Dublin-based nationalist paper, Martin Meehan, the priest in Tullycrine, wrote that "there is one particular circumstance which cannot be passed over. . . . [The people] were turned out immediately before the joyous festival of Christmas—they were all people of the best character; their rents in every case, paid up. . . . There was no crime against them. . . . If Ireland agitating is [Peel's] great difficulty, Ireland starving will surely be his monster difficulty."

A few days later, Mr. Edward Moloney, a County Roscommon bailiff whose duties included rent collection, was beaten about the face and stomach by a group of masked intruders. When one intruder pulled out a knife, Mrs. Moloney flung herself across her husband's body and begged mercy for "the father of her children." Before vanishing back into the night, the intruders warned Moloney "on his life, not to serve or post any notices to pay rent and . . . [to] return whatever rents he had received." On January 6, 1846, the *New York Tribune* correspondent in Dublin reported that "the excitement here is daily growing more intense and the time is not distant when a terrific outbreak must be a consequence."

A week or so later, cresting a hill in Limerick, a mixed detachment of constabulary and dragoons were confronted by a large crowd armed with pitchforks, hurley sticks, shovels, rocks, and whiskey. Alarmed by rumors of mass evictions in the neighborhood, the local people had taken up positions on the hill, which straddled the detachment's route of march. Riding forward, a dragoons officer ordered the crowd to disperse. "We would die before we would allow any ejectments," a man shouted. After this exchange, said the *Limerick Chronicle*, "the police and military advanced . . . in a show of force and the crowd broke and fled." The *Chronicle* had the end of the story right, but had neglected the dramatic middle scene. In a secret report on the confrontation, Major Hasting Doyle, the commander of the detachment, reported that the crowd had to be ordered to disperse three times—not once—and that the third time a dragoons officer ordered the hill cleared, the crowd picked up their pitchforks, spades, pikes, and stones and hurtled down the slope toward Doyle and his men. A mounted detachment of Constabulary surged forward and a ferocious mêlée ensued. Curses and cries echoed across the valley as clubbed peasants fell to the ground. "Steady boys, keep your places," one man shouted to his fellow insurgents. Major Doyle knew determined men when he saw them. In his report on the incident, Doyle warned that fear was making the people hard in a way he had not seen before. "I cannot help thinking . . . that from the determined spirit evidenced by the assembled mass . . . if a process [eviction notice] had been served, they [the crowd] would have resisted, notwithstanding the imposing force brought against them."

Around mid-January, the hunger began. In Sligo and Waterford, thousands were "compelled by dire necessity to eat . . . diseased potatoes." In Dungarvan, Waterford, "upwards of 5,000 human beings [were] . . . in a state of want and wretchedness requiring immediate assistance from the government." In the Limerick market town of Kilfinane, each of the 3,182 residents had roughly 180 pounds of potatoes to live on until August, when the early potato crop would be harvested; in Ballagh, Tipperary, the people had no "more than a week's provisions"; in nearby Borrisoleigh, parents were going without in order to feed their children. In Kilglass, Roscommon, "eighty families [had] . . . provisions for one to four weeks"; and in Clare, the population in one district was "eating food from which so putrid and offensive effluvia issued that in consuming it they were obliged to leave the doors of their cabins open."

In January, food prices also began to rise noticeably. This time last year, a stone of potatoes (14 pounds) cost 3 pence in Belfast. Now, it cost more than twice that sum, 6½ pence. In Galway, potato prices were up by 50 percent; in Howth, a town near Dublin, by nearly 40 percent. Pigs were the only commodity falling in price. To raise food money, farmers and laborers were dumping their one liquid asset onto the market. "Pigs that averaged 43 to 44 shillings per cwt [hundredweight] a fortnight back could not bring 35 shillings at the fair at Taghmon on Wednesday," a Wexford paper reported. "With potatoes at their present prices," one woman calculated, "it would take nine shillings a week to buy sufficient [food] for the laborer's family; [but the laborer] can earn at best but six shillings and there are all his other necessities—house, rent, clothes, fuel, milk." Edward Shannon, a Wexford laborer, did everything he could to raise food money. He "worked until quite unfit. . . . He sublet his land for firing wood, he sold his cow to pay his debts, and now here he is," noted a neighbor, "with six children, five of them girls and one an idiot." In

Clare, Edward Barry, a local priest, burst into tears as he described "the distress and wretchedness" in his parish; he had to be helped to a chair.

A poem in *The Nation* gave voice to the growing sense of panic in the country:

> *Striding nearer every day,*
> *Like a wolf in search of prey,*
> *Comes the Famine on his way.*

With "want moaning down the highways," public attention turned to the oat and wheat crops and the larders of butter and sides of beef leaving the country on every tide. On a winter morning, when the wharves of Galway city were piled high with grain and a Union Jack flew above almost every ship in the bay, a new poster appeared on the walls of the city: "Merchants stores will be broken up by the people if any further exportation of corn were attempted." Alarmed, Dublin Castle ordered the 13th Light Dragoons into Galway from the nearby village of Gort and placed two companies of the 30th Dragoons in reserve. The next evening, as the remains of the day bled into the Atlantic sky, the British war steamer *Stromboli* entered Galway Bay. The following morning, when the townspeople awoke, the streets were occupied by dragoons, and the *Stromboli*'s guns were trained on the harbor. Of Lord Lieutenant Heytesbury, who had ordered these military measures, the *Cork Examiner* wrote: "What cares this English official . . . for the starving people? . . . What sympathy could he have for their misery—what fellow feeling in their distress? 'Tis a heartless mockery, this creating Englishmen and Scotchmen into . . . [viceroys]; . . . giving them jurisdiction and sway over a warm-hearted people in whose elevation they take no interest, for whose prosperity they are not proud, and for whose afflictions they do not grieve."

A few weeks later, in Parliament, Daniel O'Connell read a list of the provisions Ireland had exported to Britain during the scarcity year of 1845: two hundred thousand head of livestock, two million quarters of grain, and several hundred million pounds of flour. Should Britain fail to display generosity in the present circumstance, said O'Connell, her failure would become eternally lodged in the deepest ventricle of Irish

memory. "There are five millions of people . . . on the verge of starvation . . .
and I am speaking from the depth of my conviction when I [say] that . . .
I believe the result of neglect . . . in the present instance will be death to
an enormous amount."

In Milltown, Kerry, James Prendergast sat down at his kitchen table,
and, with the help of the town scrivener, recounted the tumultuous events
of the past few months to his children in "Boston, America":

> The state of the country . . . is very uncertain. . . . The public
> papers teem with accts. of the [potato] loss in Various parts
> of this Kingdom. Government sent out Commissioners to
> discover the cause & means to prevent . . . [the blight] but all
> in Vain. . . . Petitions crowded in from all parts . . . Praying
> that Government would open the Ports and grant a free
> Trade. The Cabinet Council disagreed & resigned. . . . No
> scarcity appears in our part of the Country yet thank God.
> But the spring and summer, it is dreaded will be very dear,
> as great quantities of Potatoes have been lost in every part of
> the Country.

Despite the growing fear of famine, a new Constabulary report indicated that the food situation was not as desperate as Prendergrast thought
and many Irish papers were suggesting. The blight had claimed between
a quarter and a third of the potato crop, not the potato commissioners'
five-eighths. Moreover, even allowing for exports, there was still a substantial supply of beef and grain in the country. By some estimates, the
combined value of the 1845 crops was £26.8 million and the combined
value of the livestock £15.9 million: large sums in the mid-nineteenth
century. If there was a famine in the spring, it would occur for the same
reason people were already starving in Kilfinane, Kilglass, Ballagh, and
Borrisoleigh: not absolute scarcity, but high food prices and an inadequate distribution system.

Present plans called for the creation of a two-tier system to distribute
the government corn. Commissariat depots would provision populated
areas; a string of Coast Guard subdepots, the back places of the west and
the Irish Midlands. Everywhere else, London was relying on the market

to provide provisions and the local relief committees to distribute them. The committees would offer the poor cheap prices—a penny a pound for maize—but to fund their own food purchases, the committees needed donations from the local gentry, and even with London offering matching grants of up to a pound for every pound raised in contributions, not many donations were coming forward. On January 10, a group of County Clare proprietors announced that in light of their "present difficulties and in apprehension of those that may come in the spring, they [could] neither advance funds now, nor [could] they offer any sufficient security for the payment of installments hereafter." A few days later, a second group of Clare proprietors announced that they could "see no way the want can be supplied, but by . . . the . . . Government." The Peel government, aware of the history of the Irish landed classes, was prepared for such a reaction. Recalcitrant landlords were warned that they could find their names published in the press; as a further stir to conscience, grants to "distressed" districts were made contingent on the level of local charitable contributions.

These "inducements" failed to materially increase the flow of donations.

On January 20, in a sharply worded memo, Edward Lucas, the chairman of the Relief Commission, warned London that no measures in use, being planned, or even contemplated were adequate to the looming crisis. Unless things changed, and quickly, said Lucas, the likely result would be "death from famine." The next day, in a second report, coauthored by Routh, he asserted that the landlords could not be relied on to "any considerable extent," and he requested government funding in the amount of £500,000—ten times the £50,000 London had promised Lord Lieutenant Heytesbury.

Home Secretary Graham dismissed Lucas and reduced the commission to three members: Dr. Kane, Mr. Twisleton, and Routh, who replaced Lucas as chairman.

What Graham—and Peel—did not do was impose a temporary tax on the gentry to provide the relief program with a secure source of funding. The prime minister, who had been abandoned by two-thirds of the Conservative party during the last vote on the Corn Law repeal bill, needed the support of Irish MPs.

On December 23, 1845, an envelope bearing the seal of the British Treasury arrived at the Southampton residence of Mr. William Hewetson, an obscure half-pay Commissariat officer. Inside was an early Christmas present. After the holidays, Mr. Hewetson was to report forthwith "to Commissary General Sir R. Routh for the purpose of superintending, under the instruction of that officer, arrangements for disposing . . . of the Indian corn and meal shortly expected to arrive" from America. For Mr. Hewetson, the half-pay officer's life of long walks and shabby gentlemen's hotels was over; he had received one of the premier commands in the relief program. The American corn was to be milled and sacked in Cork city, then delivered to the Commissariat depots which would sell it to the local relief committees at cost. Mr. Hewetson was to command milling operations in Cork. For this, he had the old-boy network at Whitehall and his own inflamed imagination to thank. On November 5, he had sent an unsolicited letter to Peel in which he described himself as an authority on Indian corn by virtue of his "long residence in North America as a public officer," and urged the prime minister to purchase a quantity of maize for relief operations in Ireland. An acquaintance at Treasury passed the letter on to Downing Street, and a week later Mr. Hewetson's day was brightened by a personal thank-you note from the prime minister: "Sir Robert Peel presents his compliments . . . and is much obliged by the communication."

Two months later, Mr. Hewetson was standing on a harbor street in Cork. A year from now, the city would be as steeped in sorrows as the hills of Jerusalem, but before the armies of dreamless dead descended, Cork was enjoying a final season of normalcy. Carriages bustled over the broad municipal thoroughfares, drays lined up in front of the Ballincollig Royal Gunpowder Mills, and the banks of the Lee, the river that intersects the city, were empty except for the occasional gull, perched on a rotting ship carcass. The harbor, though full, was not as full as it had been in Cork's golden age. During the French Wars, when ships of every shape and size lay at anchor in the harbor, and the city's factories produced a cask of such incomparable quality, one visitor proclaimed, it "holds the pickle better than any cask made elsewhere." Today, January 10, 1846, Mr.

Hewetson planned to begin his search for a mill; with Peel's maize purchase still a state secret, he was under orders not to reveal the purpose of his visit. On the January mornings to come, gulls making a dawn circle over the harbor would see a top-hatted English gentleman wandering the empty lanes near the water. Of indeterminate age and vaguely military bearing, the gentleman would stop here and there to peer though the darkened window of a deserted mill, and whenever someone stopped and asked him his business he would reply: "I am a gentleman traveling on [my] own affairs."

"The good people of Cork have not the slightest idea of the measures the Government has in progress," Mr. Hewetson assured Routh shortly after his arrival.

A few hundred yards from Anderson's Wharf, the former half-pay officer found what he was looking for. The Lee Mills had a storage capacity of eighteen thousand barrels; fifteen pairs of grinding stones; two drying kilns, each measuring six hundred square feet; a bag and flour store capable of grinding and dressing eight hundred to a thousand barrels of grain per week; and a miller's house and office. Mr. Hewetson could scarcely believe his good fortune. The Lee facility was "twice the size of the Home Office and the Board of Trade." However, in his excitement, Mr. Hewetson apparently misheard the rent. The owners of the Lee facility had asked for £600 per month. Mr. Hewetson told Routh the mill could be had for £500 a month. When the first American ships arrived in Cork, other difficulties arose.

In early January, an American consular official in Brussels warned London that the flinty maize kernel was so difficult to grind, in the American South, maize was processed in steel mills. How many grinding stones would be required to duplicate the effects of a Carolina steel mill? Mr. Hewetson had no idea. What type of grinding stone should be employed: the French buhr, or a sturdy English stone? Another mystery. How quickly or slowly should the stones move during grinding? The mysteries multiplied. The experts were called in. Captain Maconochie, a former superintendent of the convict establishment on Norfolk Island, had little to offer except sympathy. Mr. Robertson, the American consul at Bremen, seemed to favor the French buhr, while Messrs. Grinnell, Minturn & Co., a New York export house, were more interested in knowing if the firm would be held liable for any corn spoilage on their ships. The canvassing, which included discussions with Cork merchants, did produce several dozen corn recipes, including one for johnnycake and another for *tortillas gordas* (the contribution of the American consul in Brussels), and instructions for a milling procedure that was adopted despite its fiendish complexity. It began with eight hours of kiln drying (to prevent the corn from spoiling), followed by forty-eight hours of cooling. Grinding, the next step, was followed by a second cooling period of forty-eight hours, then sacking. After a third cooling period of a day or two, the corn could safely be shipped to the network of Commissariat depots in the east (Dublin, Waterford, Dundalk, and Athy), the Midlands (Longford, Kilrush, and Banagher), and the west (Galway, Kilrush, Sligo, and Westport).

In early February, Mr. Hewetson reported that "Indian corn . . . cannot be turned out so quickly as wheat, not only from the larger size of the grain, but from it being necessary that the stones be kept wider apart and not driven too rapidly." Finding the right sacks for corn also proved difficult. The Ordnance Department sent several sample types down to Cork, but the clerk who sent the sacks forgot to put identification tags on them. "I chose four," Mr. Hewetson told Treasury, "but as they had no mark I cannot identify them." A series of strikes by the millers at the Lee facility produced further delay.

On February 12, Hewetson informed Routh that the Lee mill had fallen seriously behind schedule. "You will have observed that in my previous reports these mills are estimated to turn out from 800 to 1,000 barrels of grain per week. . . . I will now estimate [the mill's] capability at 600 barrels . . . per week." Mr. Hewetson saved the worst news for last: two hundred and thirty thousand bushels of American corn were due to arrive in the next few weeks; the Lee facility would only be able to process a small fraction of the delivery—thirty thousand bushels—by May, when the deepest want was expected to begin.

The Hewetson announcement coincided with another piece of bad news. A few days earlier, Routh again revisited the outdoor relief question with Mr. Twisleton, and again been told no; but this time little Mr. Twisleton's no had steel in it. On February 10, in a forceful memo, he reminded Routh that the workhouses were "not entitled to levy rates for outdoor relief."

*Yankee corn dealer displaying his international reputation for
avariciousness, from* Yankee Doodle, *1846*

Routh suppressed his disappointment and pressed forward. An
abundant supply of grain was still available in places like County Sligo.
Why not purchase the grain to bolster the small government food reserve in Ireland? Treasury, which had placed a ban on government food
purchases in Ireland, was wary. Domestic food prices were already rising. Large government buys in the Dublin and Cork food markets could

make them rise even more sharply. After energetic lobbying by Routh, Treasury agreed to a grudging compromise. "The rules laid down . . . regarding the purchase of provisions . . . ought not to be departed from without satisfactory reason. . . . Even then, the departure . . . should be as slight as possible . . . [and] the principle of instruction [no food purchases in Ireland] should be observed even when the letter . . . is deviated from."

Routh turned to the military depots in England and Ireland. The Relief Commission had been given access to the provisions in the depots, but a thorough search of the stock produced only one item of unambiguous value—biscuits—and on biscuits Treasury refused to compromise. Biscuits are "costly and may be needed for the troops." On February 20, *The Times* had more bad news for Routh. The private importers were doing very little importing for Ireland. "The grain markets have continued in the same dull state," the paper reported. Until the Corn Law issue was resolved, the mercantile community was reluctant to act.

The commercial shippers and the weather were also causing difficulties. Even in good weather, the west coast of Ireland is a navigator's nightmare: towering cliffs, leaping whitecaps, ever shifting winds, and a catacomb of treacherous inlets; and in February 1846, the weather in the west was not good. Up and down the coast, there were treacherous gales and high seas. In the shipping houses of Liverpool and London, nervous fingers ran down the map of the coast. It was like running a finger across a jagged piece of glass—the Bloody Foreland in Donegal could produce a bad nick, and Broadhaven in Mayo another. By the time a man got down to Kerry, he would be lucky to have any finger at all. The commercial shippers demanded a special premium to deliver government provisions to districts in the west.

The Admiralty stepped in and offered two ships, though after inspecting the *Alban* and *Dee*, Routh huffed, not two very good ships. The Navy offered two more ships. They were worse. One was unseaworthy and had to be removed from service; the other only made four miles per hour, even slower than the "proverbially slow Dee." When Routh examined a map of the west coast, he saw more than treacherous inlets and dangerous passages; he saw the hand of God. The lack of good natural harbors proved it: "Providence had never intended Ireland to be a great nation."

CHAPTER FIVE

The Hanging of Bryan Serry

On a Friday morning not long after Valentine's Day 1846, elements of the 11th Light Dragoons, the 8th Hussars, and the 6th Foot assembled in a square in Mullingar, a market town in the Irish Midlands. Behind the soldiers, a lost Dublin butter merchant was searching vainly for directions to the Mullingar butter market. How odd, the merchant thought: a fume of spring in the air and not a soul in the square except the soldiers. Earl Street, the local high street, was also deserted. The paupers in the doorways would get to sleep late this morning. The Earl Street merchants, like the rest of Mullingar, were staying home today in protest. Just past the shuttered chemist's shop at the far end of the street, a mail carriage was heading north to pick up the Galway road. It would be halfway up to Robinstown by the time of the hanging.

At a quarter to twelve, the bark of a sergeant major brought the soldiers in the square to attention. Chin straps were adjusted, boots and buttons inspected a final time, and helmets straightened. Then, like a painting composing itself, row upon row of red, blue, and gray jackets, striped trousers, and gold braids fell into line in front of a jerrybuilt wooden platform. At the 11th Hussars, the line sagged slightly (a light cavalry formation, the hussars had not a single trooper over five feet, eight inches tall); then rose again at the 8th Dragoons, an Irish unit, imposing in foot-high brown bearskin caps. A few minutes after noon, Bryan Serry, sentenced to death for an attempt on the life of Sir Francis Hopkins, a prominent local man, arrived in the square in chains. He was accompanied by a troop of Constabulary officers and his confessor, Father Savage, a politically astute cleric who had turned the anonymous laborer Serry into a nationalist martyr.

The drum line struck up a tattoo.

Standing beneath the hangman's noose, "the ill-fated, . . . universally-believed-to-be-innocent Bryan Serry" stepped forward and proclaimed his innocence a final time: "Before my God, I had neither act, hand, part or knowledge in the crime for which I am going to die here." A moment later, the floor under Serry dropped away; his lower body disappeared into a hole; his neck broke, his spine was severed, and a general paralysis seized his muscular laborer's body. A murmur of "Lord, have mercy on him" echoed down the British line. The half-dead body twitched at the end of the rope for several moments; then, said a *Times* reporter in the square, "the unhappy man was launched into eternity."

On the "Dismissed!" command, a sigh of relief went up in the ranks. Sir Guy Campbell, the official overseeing the execution, had kept the soldiers in the square an extra hour. For the last few days, rumors of a pardon had circulated, and Campbell had delayed the execution until the late morning coach arrived from Dublin. The mail pouch carried the latest edition of the Dublin papers and a packet of letters, but no reprieve from Dublin Castle. Crimes against persons and property had risen almost 100 percent during the scarcity year of 1845—from 3,103 offenses in 1844 to 5,281. The execution of Bryan Serry provided the castle an opportunity to show resolve on the crime issue.

"It is melancholy . . . to contemplate the lawless, disorganized state of rural districts where no respectable family is safe from aggression," the *Limerick Chronicle* lamented a few days later. "The industrious farmer with a patch of five or ten acres, the country gentleman who holds 100 [acres] . . . and the laborious, peaceable cottier, who strives to support his poor family on an acre of potato garden [are all targets] of intimidation and violence." The *Chronicle* did not say that the violence was also becoming more brutal, but it was. There were the Tuthills, a Cork couple, whose home was broken into: the husband beaten senseless, the wife stripped naked and thrown backward across a bed of burning coals. There was a young Antrim girl named McElhill, half her head blown away in an assassination attempt on her mother; the aged Mrs. Bennett of Tipperary, pistol-whipped on her way to church; and Mrs. Gallagher of Cavan, who dropped dead upon hearing that her husband and son had been killed. The dead woman's fifteen-year-old-daughter, the only surviving member of the family, was said to be "quite out of her mind."

On February 23, the House of Lords addressed the lawless condition of Ireland. Lord Lansdowne, a prominent Whig politician and Irish landowner, described the state of the country as "horrible"; the Earl St. German, a former Irish chief secretary, said Ireland was in "a state of terror"; while the aged Lord Brougham told the House that Britain's union partner was no longer "a habitable country."

In the 1830s, Catholic resistance to the tithe, the tax that funded the Church of Ireland, had set the countryside ablaze for nearly a decade; now, British officials feared want would once again mobilize the forces of disorder and violence. Recently, John Mitchel, a radical Ulster nationalist, had proposed sabotaging the new Irish railway system to disrupt British troop movements. "The military uses (and abuses) of the railway are tolerably well understood," declared Mitchel, "but it might be useful to promulgate through the country . . . a few short, easy rules as to the mode of dealing with railways in the case of any enemy daring to make hostile use of them."

By late February 1846, the incidence of disease, another common byproduct of disorder and want, was also rising. Infected potatoes wreak havoc on the stomach and bowels, and, despite the Relief Commission's prediction that the supply of sound potatoes would last until April, tens of thousands of peasant families were already living on blighted tubers. On February 17, R. M. Tagard, a Donegal medical officer, reported a rise in gastrointestinal and bowel disorders, "violent and painful." The infirmary in Markethill, County Cavan, also reported a sharp increase in abdominal complaints, nausea and diarrhea. In London, William Smith O'Brien, the MP for Limerick, told the House of Commons that "whole families [are] . . . sitting down to a meal of potatoes [that an Englishman] would be sorry to offer his hogs." However, blighted potatoes rarely killed. For Josh Lynn, chief medical officer at Markethill, as for most of the Irish medical community, the great threat was famine fever. Between 1816 and 1817, a period of deep scarcity, 1.5 million people had been infected with the disease and 65,000 had died. Even if the current scarcity produced a pestilence of only half that magnitude, the small Irish medical system would be overwhelmed. There were only 101 fever hospitals in the country. Under an 1843 law, the Poor Law workhouses were authorized to provide fever care, either by establishing a special ward—renting a house for fever cases—or by arranging treatment with a local hospital; but compliance would entail an increase in the hated poor rate, and workhouse guardians knew from experience how unhappy that would make ratepayers.

In September 1845, when the blight first appeared, only forty-two workhouses had made arrangements to treat fever cases. In December and then again in January, the Relief Commission had sent urgent reminders to noncomplying workhouses. On February 17, while the commission was awaiting replies, a serious fever outbreak occurred, at the Ballyhooly dispensary in County Cork. "Daily [admissions] . . . , formerly at eight to ten, has latterly increased to fifty or sixty," reported J. P. Edgar, a physician at the dispensary. Now, fever was raging in Fermoy, another Cork municipality. "Increase in fever [is] so alarming . . . a special meeting . . . to be called for its consideration," reported Charles Murphy, a hospital official. In County Cavan, James Adams, a physician in a local infirmary, looked south to Cork, then made a prediction: famine fever would arrive in Cavan in "April or sooner."

⊰⊕⊱

On February 24, after a day of listening to stories of tenant hardship, Elizabeth Smith, the County Wicklow woman, sat down at her bedroom desk and wrote, "Potatoes are now 5 [pence] a stone. . . . This spring will be one of deep distress." In Erris, a sunless peninsula on the edge of Mayo, spring arrived early. In late February, the only provisions in Erris was the cornmeal in the local subdepot, and the officer in charge of the depot was under orders to keep his doors closed until May. After several desperate pleas, the Relief Commission relented and allowed him to open early. Between January 10, when Killarty, a hamlet outside Limerick city, received an emergency £15 food grant, and February 10, a total of ninety localities joined Erris on the list of "distressed districts," including Skull, Baltimore, Berehaven, Crookhaven, and almost every other market town of any consequence in southwest Cork.

The news that almost a hundred localities in Ireland were already nearing the "final extremity"—frank famine—was greeted calmly in London. In general, reports from the western side of the Irish Sea were regarded more as interesting examples of the fanciful Celtic mind at work than as sources of intelligence. There must be food in Ireland, officials in Whitehall told one another. Generations of crop failure had taught the Irish peasant to set aside provisions for periods of scarcity. An instruction was drawn up and sent to British relief officers in Ireland. "The resources within . . . reach of the community must first be applied to [its] wants." The memo was an example of the fanciful Anglo-Saxon mind at work.

It was getting toward March now; in most cabins, the last of the 1845 crop was gone or almost gone, and the hunger so deep in some places men were sacrificing whatever dignity they had left to feed their families. A Tipperary farmer who caught a peasant foraging in his fields asked, "Why do you come by night to take what I would have gladly given you by day?" The thief replied, "I was too ashamed to let anyone know I was in such want." In areas devastated by the blight, scenes familiar from a thousand years of Irish hunger reappeared: men in early-morning fields, sucking blood from the neck of a living cow, seaweed on the boil; grass-stained mouths and hands; women running an anxious hand over a sleeping child to see if she still breathed. With food available only in shops, and the barter economy unable to produce wage-paying employment, potato-less peasants sold shirts, pants, shoes—anything of value—in order to purchase provisions. For the gombeen men, the only source of food loans in many parts of rural Ireland, February 1846 was a happy time. Business was brisk, and there was nothing to fear from the local relief committees.

As of mid-February, not a single committee had been formed. "Even if we had food land on our shores, there is no machinery for its satisfactory distribution," the *Belfast Vindicator* declared on the fourth. "If things are left as they are, ravenous hunger [will] drive the distracted millions to disregard the rights of property."

Under pressure from Routh, on February 20 Treasury announced that "the time has arrived for the authoritative promulgation of the plans of the Government." A few weeks later, hundreds of magistrates, Constabulary officers, and clergymen spread out across the Irish countryside to distribute copies of "Instructions to Committees of Relief Districts," a how-to guide on establishing a relief committee. Then the thing Routh most feared would happen did: nothing. Even in the districts with relief committees, donations flowed in with the speed of a dripping faucet. "Where are these private subscriptions?" asked *The Morning Chronicle* on March 10. "In what banker's hands is the money lodged?" In Limerick city, a major metropolitan area, the local committee received a total of £500 in donations, enough to buy fifty tons of corn at £10 a ton, or thirty-three tons of oatmeal at £15 a ton. To the east, in County Waterford, the Lismore relief committee received £169 in contributions; in Woodford, Galway, donations amounted to £100; on the Aran Islands, where the hunger had shocked Mr. Foster of *The Times,* £71. In Clare, the response was little short of appalling; in a county of more than 300,000 people— most of them desperately poor—donations amounted to £417. Like Mr. Micawber, Sir Lucius O'Brien, the county lieutenant (the chief Crown officer in Clare), was sure something would turn up. Don't worry, he told Routh. "The event was coming, but not come." Indeed, with a little luck and a spell of dry weather—who knows? said Sir Lucius, "[the scarcity] might not come at all." The spring sowing season was only a month or so away, and sowing would provide employment and wages for "a large proportion of the indigent population." "In some parts of Clare . . . there seems to be a determination to subscribe [donate] nothing," Routh sighed.

The Relief Commission was especially worried by the failure of commercial towns to form committees. In a remote district like Erris, where an absolute absence of food existed, the cry, "Want among plenty!" was an abstraction; in places like Clonmel, a transport hub in Tipperary, the cry was both an observable reality and a standing incitement to violence. Every day, the starving townfolk passed store windows full of baked goods and dodged drays lumbering down the lanes toward the wharves on the River Suir. In a few weeks, the Tipperary grain on the drays would end up on dining tables in Essex, Suffolk, and Devon. While the grain did provide export earnings, and the earnings would help pay for the maize en route from Odessa and the Ohio Valley, that kind of economics was hard to explain to a countrywoman with four hungry children.

On March 27, the Clonmel authorities received a warning from the Relief Commission: either form a relief committee "or take . . . steps to preserve the good order." The authorities did neither; grain from the farms of Tipperary continued to flow into Clonmel; hunger deepened, anger rose—until finally the townspeople found the situation intolerable. "You have no idea of the state this town is in," a Clonmel resident wrote. "We have cannon at either end of the town and the streets are full of army and police. This morning the mob broke into every baker's shop in town and . . . also into some of the stores and took flour . . . and 50 tons of oatmeal." Watching the emaciated rioters swarm through the rubble and cannon smoke, one observer thought: here is what the armies of the dead would look like "risen from their shrouds."

William Dobree, a young Commissariat officer recently transferred to Ireland, feared that 1846 was becoming a repetition of 1839. "It is evident that those persons on whom . . . responsibility is . . . vested"—the landed classes—"are doing nothing more than thinking upon what the government is going to do."

<hr />

From the crop failure onward, nationalist and Catholic politicians had given no end of speeches about the wickedness and irresponsibility of the Anglo-Irish landed classes. Thus far, though, fine phrases were almost all the domestic political class had contributed to the crisis. In March 1846, as in December 1845, no subject engaged the Repeal club-houses more than the deepening rift between the seventy-one-year-old Daniel O'Connell and the rising star of the Repeal movement, forty-three-year-old William Smith O'Brien, a Limerick landowner descended from the medieval Irish high king Brian Boru. Smith O'Brien led his own faction within the Repeal movement Young Ireland, a group of mostly well-born, high-minded youngish gentlemen like himself.

While not entirely devoid of ego, the conflict between O'Connell and Smith O'Brien was rooted in principled differences. The Liberator, a happy opportunist on most issues, was resolute in his commitment to nonviolent, constitutional struggle; Smith O'Brien believed physical force justified in certain circumstances. The two men also disagreed about engaging British politicians. O'Connell was prepared to deal with almost anyone, including the devil (provided the devil was not Robert Peel; in 1815, the two had come very close to fighting a duel). Smith O'Brien, a more pristine character, viewed cooperation with the two great English parties, the Tories and the Whigs, as tantamount to collaboration. From time to time, the two rivals still worked together. They joined forces in the spring of 1846 to oppose the Protection of Life Act, Peel's response to the rising Irish crime rate. Even for a Tory government, whose aristocratic members had a special affinity for their Irish counterparts, the act was a particularly nasty piece of business. It punished curfew violations with fifteen years' transportation to Australia. Preoccupied by the crime bill, O'Connell and Smith O'Brien had not given much serious thought to the famine threat. The Liberator's solution to the crisis amounted to little more than ousting Peel from office; Smith O'Brien's, to securing a four-month window of duty-free grain for Ireland.

With the Irish political class preoccupied by internal divisions, predatory landlords began to move against the small tenant farmers, the three- and four-acre men, whose plots were viewed as an obstacle to agricultural modernization. One morning toward the Ides of March 1846, a road near the Roscommon-Galway border echoed with the heaving of men marching in quick step. Several companies of the 49th Regiment, elements of the 13th Regiment, a "heavy body" of Constabulary officers, and a party of bailiffs were marching toward Ballinglass, a village of 270 residents and 61 dwellings on the Galway side of the border. Ever since Irish beef had begun bringing a better price than Irish grain in the Liverpool and London markets, the proprietress of Ballinglass, a Mrs. Gerrard, had contemplated converting the village into pastureland. About a mile from Mount Bellew, the column swung off the main road. Past a mist-shrouded field, the cottages of Ballinglass—whitewashed and surrounded by "neat kitchen gardens"—were just visible in the distance. In the village, it was the waking hour. Half-dressed men stood in cottage doorways, lighting a first pipe of the day; women in shawls and capes gathered cooking water from a stream near a half-cleared bog. Here and there, the face of a sleepy child appeared in a cabin door.

Suddenly, the village dogs began to yelp; the heavy thud of running boots echoed down the road, then a flying column of soldiers and police burst out of the mist, and a confusion of sights and sounds followed: "the screaming of children, the wild wailing of mothers . . . roofs and walls tumbling down"; squealing pigs running between the cottages, soldiers cursing; the howling of a boy trapped under a collapsed cabin wall; the pleas of mercy from an elderly couple in fever. Above the mêlée, the barking of the dogs continued. "Such bawling and screaming . . . I never heard," said a resident. "You'd think the brutes [the dogs] knew what it was all about . . . they howled away until all the houses were down and . . . one wouldn't leave [his master's cottage] for anyone."

By late afternoon not a cottage stood in Ballinglass, except that of the fever couple. At nightfall, a soft rain began to fall, and word filtered through the glens and hollows where the evicted residents had taken refuge that "some of the [cabin] walls were left standing." In parties of two, three, and four, the villagers began to slip back into Ballinglass to "throw up hippeens" (shacks made of sticks). The next morning, the villagers collected dung from the fields and erected a manure barrier at the entrance to the village. For most of the morning the Roscommon-Galway road remained empty. There was just the silent silhouette of Mount Bellew, off in the "wet, drizzling" distance. Then, toward afternoon, several drays filled with armed men appeared on the road. At the cutoff, the drays turned in toward Ballinglass. "Well, God forgive her [Mrs. Gerrard]," said an eyewitness. "She ordered her bailiffs to root up the foundations to prevent the wretches—its wretches . . . they were called—from going there any more. I saw one . . . woman with a child on her breast hunted from three places by the bailiffs."

Driven from Ballinglass a second time, the villagers took shelter in the ditches along the corduroy track that led up to the road. The bailiffs went into the ditches with clubs and cleared them. Over the next few weeks, the evicted fled from one neighboring townland to the next, Mrs. Gerrard's bailiffs in pursuit. At each townland, a bailiff would leap from his mount and announce that, should any tenant be found sheltering the Ballinglass evictees, they "would [be] served [evicted] in the same way."

On March 17, four days after the Gerrard evictions, the elegant

A "scalpeen" at Dunmore, from Illustrated London News, *1848*

figure of a lone horseman appeared in the upper gate of Dublin Castle. Lieutenant General Sir Edward Blakeney—slim, high-foreheaded, and dressed in a heavily braided uniform—cantered into the cobblestone courtyard on a black charger amid "prodigious" cheers from a crowd of Dublin notables and off-duty clerks, junior officials, and policemen. Blakeney was followed by a company of Queen's Bays marching under gold-trimmed pennants and wearing bright green shamrocks; the rear was brought up by a military band playing Irish airs. The crowd burst into song, the soldiers positioned themselves around the courtyard, and a waving Viceroy Heytesbury appeared on a castle balcony. On most days, the Viceroy's face was a maw of stern countenance. Not this day, though. Heytesbury was wearing a smile as wide as London Bridge and a shamrock so large, the ubiquitous *Times* man in Ireland described it as "monstrous." Toward evening, an armada of carriages sailed into the courtyard under a rough March wind. Nine hundred guests attended the St. Patrick's Day Ball. There were two orchestras, footmen in white wigs, beakers of champagne, naked shoulders, flirtatious glances, clinking china, gleaming silver, and toasts: hurrahs were offered for the queen and the lord lieutenant; for the departing chief secretary, Mr. Freemantle; for the "gallant" General Blakeney, commander of the British garrison in Ireland; and for the British army of India, which had recently won a splendid victory over a much larger Sikh force in the Punjab.

A few days after the fête, Daniel O'Connell rose from his seat in the Commons to call attention to an overlooked aspect of the victory over the Sikhs. Upon examining "the returns from the . . . glorious battles lately fought in India," declared O'Connell, "I have found a great number of names in the [casualty] list exactly resembling the names of the cottagers dispossessed by Mrs. Gerrard."

✂

"Oh, Heaven!" exclaimed a Dublin paper as the Corn Law debate entered its fourth month. "Do these men know what potatoes are—what famishing men are? Have they any conception . . . that there may soon be millions of human beings in Ireland who have nothing to eat?" John Mansfield, a Kilkenny man, already had no food. During the final weeks of winter, Mansfield, a small tenant farmer with just enough education to read and write, had fed his family from the proceeds of the pawnshop and the gombeen man. Now, with both sources exhausted, Mansfield had turned to his clergyman. "Reverend Sir," he wrote, "pardon me for letting you [know] my great distress. I did not earn one Shilling This 3 weeks. I had not one Bite for my family since yesterday morning to eat. And I am applying to you as a good charitable gentle man to lend me a little Reliefe."

While hunger, like the blight, was spreading in a checkerboard pattern—deep in some areas, shallow in others—the March distress reports suggested that small farmers like Mansfield were falling into destitution more quickly than expected. The geographic pattern of distress was also troubling. A relatively prosperous county like Wicklow should not be reporting a "great mass of people consuming unfit food," or Westmeath, another relatively prosperous county, "pressing and urgent" want. In parts of the impoverished west, the news was also worse than expected. Galway was reporting "thousands out of provisions"; Clare, "much suffering from want." Officials were perplexed. Was the crisis breaking earlier than expected, or was pauper Ireland, the country's permanent reservoir of 2.3 million indigent poor, inflating the distress numbers?

Months of scarcity had made it difficult to distinguish between small farmers like Mansfield, who had lost their potato crop and were eligible for emergency relief, and the pauper hordes, who, having had no potatoes to lose, were not.

Edward Pine Coffin, a senior Commissariat officer, decided to make a personal assessment of the want. Sixty-two, nearly as old as Routh, and his match in experience and ability, Pine Coffin returned from a tour of the west alarmed. The Relief Commission's timetable would have to be altered. Present plans called for the Commissariat to put Peel's Yankee corn on sale in May, when the deep want was expected to begin. In a letter to Routh, Pine Coffin admitted that releasing the corn earlier would create "a great risk of our stores being exhausted"; nonetheless, he felt the risk necessary. Some districts had reached the "final extremity," and relief could not be deferred "in all cases, to so late a date as May."

Just before St. Patrick's Day, a group of angry paupers burst into the courtyard of a Tipperary workhouse to demand outdoor relief; refusing, the administrator summoned the Constabulary to clear the courtyard. A few days later, "a group of 100 laborers of the lowest orders" marched to the door of a workhouse in Kilkenny, chanting, "We have not eaten for two days." When Mr. R. Sullivan, the local justice of the peace, appeared on the steps of the facility, the marchers threatened to riot "unless . . . afforded relief." Mr. Sullivan scolded the men for "impropriety," then announced that "as many [demonstrators] as wished would be admitted into the Poor House." Mr. Sullivan could afford to be magnanimous. In March, the Poor Law workhouses, which had a hundred-thousand-bed capacity, held only 47,403 inmates, and rising agricultural prices had produced a bonanza in Poor Law tax revenues: £260,000, a substantial sum. Outside the workhouses, the hunger was deep, and violence pervasive; inside, there were two beds for every inmate, and in many institutions, oatmeal instead of the usual potatoes. However, inside there were also procedures "disgusting to the Celtic mind," and shoes with no left and right. As Mr. Sullivan undoubtedly knew, even a starving pauper's desperation had limits.

Not a single man accepted his offer.

On March 23, John Smith, a Galway man, reported what may have been the first starvation death of the scarcity. Smith told the Relief Commission in Dublin that it was his "melancholy task to relate that the first victim . . . has fallen . . . a father of five children. . . . The government was awfully to blame."

In many places, a stone of sound potatoes (fourteen pounds) cost half again what a stone had cost in the spring of 1845: 4½ pence versus 3 pence. And the relief committee system, intended to provide the peasantry with convenient access to affordable food, remained very much a work in progress.

Somewhere between the Relief Commission offices in Dublin, the Irish Board of Works, the local pub, and the local courthouse, hundreds—perhaps thousands—of copies of the "Instructions on Relief Committees" had gotten lost. At the end of March, some districts were without a committee because no one in the district had any idea how to form one. Recruitment difficulties also slowed committee formation. The government wanted men of standing to serve: magistrates, clergymen, Board of Works officers, the chairman of the local Poor Law Union, workhouse guardians, the county lieutenant. But in a country plagued by sectarian and political conflict, sharp differences often divided local men of standing. Protestant members sometimes blocked the appointment of a Catholic priest, fearing he would pack the relief rolls with parishioners, while Catholic committee members might object to the appointment of a Church of Ireland vicar, fearing he would deny Catholic peasants relief. The demanding nature of committee work also made it unattractive. Members had to compile "minute reports" of the circumstances of each relief applicant and keep a record of every applicant who qualified for a food ticket, the certificate that entitled the bearer to purchase committee food at cost or, if the bearer lacked money, to purchase it by performing a task of "public improvement." Denial further shrank the pool of potential committee members. "I believe that the wealthy inhabitants of this locality will not admit that distress . . . exists to any great extent," an Ulster man told the *Belfast Vindicator*.

Persistent bad weather also slowed implementation of the government relief plan. In mid-March, it took the *Alban* a fortnight to transport a shipment of corn from Cork to the Limerick depot; and the captain told Mr. Pine Coffin he counted himself fortunate to have arrived in Limerick in one piece. A few weeks later the American transport *Harriet Rockwell*, laden with Indian corn, got caught in a gale off Cork and was blown north to Waterford. With want deepening, land transportation had also become dangerous.

In Mitchelstown, Cork, a crowd of a women and children attacked a supply convoy. Sacks were slashed open and pockets, hats, and shawls stuffed full of government corn. On the River Fergus, an angry mob seized a barge laden with corn and flour. In Westmeath, a British soldier shot a man dead on the back of a dray as he slung a sack of meal over his shoulder. Seconds earlier, another British soldier had fired his rifle into the air rather than kill the looter. "Irishmen!" declared a mock proclamation in *The Nation*, the newspaper of Young Ireland. "We, your English governors, have provisions, purchased with your money and stored in your towns; we have soldiery—Foot, Dragoons, Artillery—to keep them there. You are starving. Very well, you may starve until it is our pleasure to give you a morsel.

"In the meantime, go to . . . Mrs. Gerrard, who [is], you know, notorious for charity."

In Cork city, where a stone of potatoes sold for eleven pence, more than twice the national average, the Relief Committee of the Gentlemen of Cork, under intense public pressure, agreed to open its food depots for a single day, March 28. The committee set the price of its corn low to make it affordable; but even a penny a pound was too high for many buyers. In an *Illustrated London News* sketch of the opening, a ragged peasant woman sits crumpled in despair on a sidewalk in front of a crowded depot, while her young son stands next to her, shoeless and coatless in the March cold. The *News* described the twenty-eighth as a "turbulent" day; *The Times* (ever the voice of optimism) called it "tremendous." By any definition, the twenty-ninth was more tremendous still. The announcement that the depots would not open for a second day caused "considerable excitement," and violence might easily have ensued had not Cork's mayor possessed a gift for duplicity remarkable even in a politician. As angry crowds poured into the streets, the mayor issued a proclamation: the depots were empty, but a new shipment of corn "was daily expected"—a promise as hopeful yet vague as the date of the Second

Coming. In several other districts, pressing want also forced the authorities to open the depots early, though, as in Cork, food was dispensed under tight restrictions.

Meanwhile, in London, the politicians were becoming impatient. Peel complained to Viceroy Heytesbury that only a "trifling amount" of progress was being made in establishing the relief apparatus. The viceroy ordered an immediate investigation. Clerks were summoned, records scrutinized, officials interviewed, members of the Relief Commission and the Irish Board of Works interrogated, a report compiled and sent to London. The report stated that the delay was due to "secret and underhanded instructions to individuals in this country from subordinate authorities in London." The "subordinate authorities" were unidentified, but the prime minister did not need a name. It was that "consummate fool" Trevelyan again.

CHAPTER SIX

The Lord of Providence

T here are two iconic images of Charles Edward Trevelyan.

The first, a portrait from the famine era, shows the assistant secretary of the British Treasury in his prime. Preternaturally self-assured, pantherlike in his sleek physical glamour, this Trevelyan could be a symbol of Britain in the high noon of imperial glory. The second iconic image dates from the 1870s and presents the Trevelyan of history: a scowling, abrasive, ravaged old man, who looks like the Ghost of Christmas Past; this Trevelyan has survived war, ridicule, and controversy to emerge as the greatest British civil servant of his generation. Neither image, however, possesses the psychological power of the family memorial in the Northumberland church where Trevelyan worshipped. Along a wall of the nave, the bane of prime ministers, chancellors of the Exchequer, newspaper editors, and Indian undersecretaries bestrides a stained-glass window, dressed in the gold armor of an archangel. A royal blue sash inscribed "Veritas" adorns the Trevelyan chest; above his head, a dovelike Holy Ghost hovers protectively; and under a golden-booted foot is the epithet of a man who never knew moral doubt: "I have fought the good fight. I have finished my course."

The Trevelyan family history presents the familiar English story of an "old" "good family" doing progressively better by itself as the empire

Sir Charles Edward Trevelyan as a young man and as a middle-aged man

expands. Modest beginnings in Cornwall are followed by the establishment of two family seats, Nettlesome Court in Somerset and Walling-
ford in Northumberland, and a baker's dozen of baronets and battalions
of soldiers and vicars. Younger sons are washed through the army and
the church like the family's inferior linen. For a time, Archdeacon George
Trevelyan entertained hopes that the fourth of his nine children, Charles
Edward, would follow him into the church, though Charles would first
have to learn to control his zeal, an unattractive trait in an Anglican
churchman. Instead, the East India Company got Charles. At seventeen,
Trevelyan became a student at the company training college in Here-
fordshire, where he won a prize in Greek, formed a lifelong attachment
to the works of Adam Smith and Edmund Burke, and occasionally encountered the college's most eminent faculty member out on walks: a
beak-nosed, bent old gentleman the students called "Pop" Malthus.

In India, where he arrived in 1826 as a twenty-one-year-old East India
clerk, Trevelyan enthralled, annoyed, and perplexed. In short order, he

displayed great courage in exposing the corruption of Sir Edward Cole-brooke, a senior colonial official; appalled James Mill, an East India col-league, with a plan to Christianize the subcontinent by replacing Sanskrit with the Roman alphabet; and exasperated Thomas Babington Macau-lay, an aide to the governor general. Macaulay had never seen a man quite like the handsome young clerk. The fellow courted his sister with talk of railway construction and road improvement. It was all most extraordinary! Trevelyan "has no small talk," marveled Macaulay. "His mind is full of schemes of moral and political improvement and his zeal boils over." Upon Trevelyan's departure from the subcontinent, the re-lieved viceroy, William Bentinck, declared, "That man is almost always on the right side in every question and it is well that he is so, for he gives the most confounded amount of trouble when he takes the wrong one."

Upon his return to England, Trevelyan joined the Treasury depart-ment, where he soon attracted notice by launching an investigation into the distribution of free prayer books in the House of Commons. The nov-elist Anthony Trollope, a man with a good eye for the absurd, made Trev-elyan the model for Sir Gregory Hardlines, the passionately parsimonious civil servant in his novel *The Three Clerks*. As the years passed, Trevelyan's reputation grew more complex. People still spoke of the unbending moral rectitude, the personal intensity, and the thrusting personality, yet in the drawing rooms and clubs of the imperial capital one now heard more and more about Trevelyan the ruthless political operative. Mr. Trevelyan, said one observer, would "use whatever tool came to hand—debate, hyperbole, caricature, ridicule, intrigue, personal contacts, manipulation of the press."

To the Irish crisis, Trevelyan brought a first-rate mind, superior or-ganizational skills, a conviction that the ultimate answer to the Irish quagmire was agricultural modernization and anglicization, and a com-plex set of religious, political, and economic beliefs that deeply influ-enced his decisions on relief policy. Politically, Trevelyan was a Whig, and the Whigs, in the main, were more hostile to the Irish landed classes than the Tories. In this the party reflected British public opinion, which viewed Ireland as an international embarrassment—and the Anglo-Irish, the way a proper family views a slightly mad second cousin. In economic matters, Trevelyan was a passionate laissez-faire man; in religious mat-ters, he was an adherent of Moralism, an evangelical sect that preached a passionate gospel of self-help. Moralists opposed public assistance on the grounds that relief deprived the poor of the incentive to change the behaviors that had made them poor—alcoholism, sloth, indolence, sexual promiscuity. Relieve the poor man, warned Thomas Chalmers, the leading Moralist thinker of the Victorian age, and you deprive him of the impetus to become self-reliant, self-disciplined, industrious, sober, and chaste.

Chalmers's thinking resonated in one of Trevelyan's first recorded remarks about relief policy. He told a colleague God had "sent the calamity to teach the Irish a lesson . . . [and it] must not be too much mitigated." However, in the early months of the scarcity, no one much cared what Trevelyan thought about Ireland. In 1843, he had leaked secret government information to *The Morning Chronicle*, greatly irritating Peel: "how a man . . . could think it consistent to reveal . . . to the world all he told us is passing strange." The deepening crisis in Ireland and the gravitational pull of the government organization charts restored Trevelyan's position. Treasury controlled the Commissariat and relief funding, which made it almost impossible to do anything in Ireland without going through Trevelyan. By mid-March 1846, he had oversight over the relief committees, the food depots, and the public works program. Soon Mr. Trevelyan would again preoccupy the prime minister's thoughts.

✄

The public works program, enacted by Parliament on March 5, 1846, was designed to put food money into the pocket of the peasant. Districts would borrow money from the government to fund employment projects, and the local peasants would use their earnings to purchase food from the local relief committee or a private merchant. In November 1845, when the public works program was first discussed, Peel said he wanted the program to build harbors, fisheries, canals—projects that contributed to Irish modernization. Generations of road building, the traditional form of relief employment, had left nothing behind but decapitated hills and an ugly tangle of unfinished roads that made the once-lovely Irish landscape look like it had been strip-mined. But somewhere between Peel's November pronouncement and the March law, the incentives in the loan program became confused. Loans for harbors, for canals, and other infrastructure improvements had to be repaid in full, loans for road building did not. A district that borrowed £10,000 for road construction had to repay only £5,000; the government treated the outstanding £5,000 as a grant. By March 11, six days after Parliament enacted the public works legislation, one Clare district had submitted ninety-two applications for half-grant loans; another Clare district submitted 113 applications within a few weeks. Lord George Hill, the author of "Facts from Gweedore," made a personal call on Trevelyan to request a half-grant loan. Trevelyan said maybe; Hill told the Irish Board of Works, the agency overseeing the public works program, Trevelyan had said yes. Sir John Bourke, another prominent landlord, all but threatened to back up a cart to the Bank of England. Sir John complained to Routh that "in the last scarcity, he did not get his fair share of the booty and . . . he [was] taking precautions not [to] commit the same error on this occasion." Applying Sir John's logic, a district in Limerick requested £20,000 for road work; a district in Mayo, £15,000. Galway wanted £17,922, as well as a £4,000 grant for a military barracks to aid "the health and comfort of the troops" and to act as a guarantor of "the security of the country." A program originally budgeted at £50,000 attracted somewhere between £800,000 and £1 million in loan applications. Worse, it soon became clear that many of the applicants intended to use the government money to fund projects that personally benefited them and their friends, not the local poor. Mr. Trevelyan was outraged. "Instead *of a real test of distress we have* [created] *a bounty on exaggerated interest.*"

On March 8, in a blistering memo, Trevelyan warned that "the machinery which has been set by the government *for the special object of the relief of the people from famine* is being, to a great extent, worked by the proprietors with a view to *the execution of works of local* [private] *interest of various kinds.*" On April 4, Trevelyan issued another dictate. Acting on his own authority, he declared that, henceforth, every loan application would be subject to four criteria: Would the loan create an employment project in a district already in distress or in imminent danger of distress? Would the proposed project employ the laboring poor or only artisans? (The presence of artisans was often a sign the loan money would be used to fund a private improvement.) Would a particular landowner or group of landowners benefit in a special way, and if so, would the beneficiaries contribute to the project's cost? To signal that the days of easy government money were over, Trevelyan canceled several previously approved public works projects.

Home Secretary Graham was aghast. Thus far only £70,000 had been approved for the public works schemes, and the heavy spring rains had delayed the start of the sowing season, a traditional source of wage employment for the peasantry in April and May. The Trevelyan criteria would slow job creation further, and in a country where relief provisions were sold and those at risk had no means of earning money nothing could prevent famine. There was an obvious way to avert the threat—give away food—but London was unprepared to do that in a nation where "dependency on government" was already a "moral plague." On a gray April morning, residents of Carrick-on-Suir awoke to shouts of "Work!" "Work!" Outside in the streets, hundreds of men and women were milling about. On the outer edge of the crowd, Constabulary officers with carbines were taking up positions in doorways. By midmorning, the chant of "Work!" had become deafening, the crowd menacing; in the doorways, nervous fingers curled around triggers. Only intervention by municipal officials, who promised to provide temporary employment, prevented the protest from turning bloody. A few days later, in Dublin, a party of laborers burst into a sitting of the Petty Session, a minor local court, shouting, "Employment!" "Wages!" In early May, the agitation for work spread to Dundalk, a town midway between Dublin and Belfast. The local Church of Ireland vicar, the Reverend Elias Thackeray, a cousin of the novelist, was deeply affected by the demonstration. Reverend Thackeray had lived through 1798; he knew how fragile the bonds of society were in Ireland. Employment, the people need employment, he wrote in a letter to Dublin.

Pulsating with hunger and fear, the unemployed sacked food shops, stole livestock, attacked food convoys. By mid-April, the thirteen miles of river between the trading centers of Carrick-on-Suir and Clonmel had become among the most dangerous stretches of water in Ireland. Grain barges traveling between the two towns were escorted by "two warships and 50 cavalry and 80 infantry." Soldiers marched ahead of the barges, clearing the riverbank of ambushers. "Today," wrote a correspondent traveling with a convoy, "we go down river . . . with guns and every kind of combustible." Dublin Castle blamed the newspapers, not the deepening hunger and lack of work, for the convoy attacks. "The people are excited by the . . . press," declared Lord Heytesbury. "They believe they have the right to call on the government for employment . . . and for the supply of a better description of food." *The Freeman's Journal* responded to the viceroy's accusation in a sharp editorial: "There is but one way of curbing [the] wayward violence. *Feed the people.*"

In April, for the first time since the beginning of the scarcity, emigration spiked noticeably. The numbers leaving concerned the authorities less than the caliber of the leave-takers. They were not the impoverished and illiterate, the Irish-speaking peasants from the backplaces of Donegal, Clare, and Kerry who peeled their potatoes with a fingernail and "whose departure might . . . be a blessing to themselves and the country." The emigrants were the bone and marrow of Ireland—the young, energetic, and relatively prosperous. Of the "thousand human beings . . . taking their departure from here," wrote a resident of Sligo town, "a great majority are well-dressed and comfortable-looking farmers and the better class of peasantry, who are carrying away with them no inconsiderable share of the wealth of the country." People who still had faith in their own futures had lost faith in Ireland's. The cry "Old Ireland is dying!" had yet to reach down to the chimneyless cabins of the peasantry, but in the fine stone houses of the large farmers and in the shops of the tradesmen, it had become the anthem of a hard, wet spring.

⬥

On March 23, Henry Pelham-Clinton—the future fifth Duke of Newcastle, the current twelfth Earl of Lincoln, and the former British commissioner of woods and forests—arrived in Dublin to assume the office of Irish chief secretary amid a swirl of rumor and innuendo. There were stories about Lincoln's father, the fourth Duke of Newcastle, a man of historic unpleasantness; about Lincoln's wife, a woman of perpetual unfaithfulness; and about Lincoln himself, a man with a reputation for unmitigated mediocrity. What! Lincoln, Irish chief secretary? How could that be? incredulous colleagues asked when the appointment was announced. According to the most credible rumor, Lincoln owed his appointment to a process of elimination: Peel and Graham had turned to him in desperation after every more qualified man had turned the Irish post down. The prime minister and home secretary wanted the Trevelyan "undercurrent" checked and the pace of job creation quickened, even if it meant tolerating a certain amount of fraud and abuse. Better that than starvation, violence, and mass death.

"Be bold," Graham told Lincoln. The new chief secretary would have to be more than bold. Trevelyan was a castle in a forest. He enjoyed the support and protection of his immediate superior, Henry Goulburn, Chancellor of the Exchequer; as permanent undersecretary of the Treasury, he had control of the Commissariat and all monies dispensed for relief funding, including for public works; and he had a loyal cadre of subordinates in Ireland, who—beholden to him for promotions, postings, and pay raises—were attentive to his wishes. To everyone's surprise, including perhaps his own, Lincoln was able to check, if not abolish, the Trevelyan "undercurrent." When Trevelyan vetoed a Routh request to lift the ban on Irish food purchases, Lincoln overruled the veto. "I'll probably get a good rap on the knuckles from Trevelyan," he joked. Nonetheless, his veto stood. A measure of Lincoln's success was the contrite memo Trevelyan was made to write to Routh: "The chief responsible authority in Ireland is the Lord Lieutenant. . . . [Y]ou are to obey [his] instructions . . . even if they should differ from the instructions . . . from this office [Treasury]."

Even with Trevelyan subdued, however, there was still the Irish Board of Works. Prior to the scarcity, the Board had juggled an odd combination of housekeeping and administrative tasks from a warren of offices in the Dublin Custom House. Under windows illuminated by a dull municipal sun, and walls decorated by the good and great of Anglo-Ireland, the board's workday proceeded with the deliberateness of a Cycle of Cathay (500 years). Each morning, supplicants would arrive for interminable interviews about drainage and road projects that only intermittently came to fruition.

This stately routine ended abruptly in March, when the board was placed at the center of the public works program. Districts, groups, and individuals seeking loans for employment projects had to submit plans to the understaffed, overworked board for review. "I am without hope of ever reaping either satisfaction or credit from this appointment beyond that negative satisfaction of having toiled from . . . morning . . . until after *seven* in the evening," wrote one exhausted board officer. The heavy agency workload was made all the heavier by a requirement that, prior to approval, each work project be personally inspected by a board officer, who was also required to determine whether the distress in the surrounding district was related to the crop failure. Where would the small board find the hundreds of trained men needed to conduct the personal inspections? After exhausting Ireland's small pool of engineers and surveyors, the agency began hiring the semi-proficient and non-proficient. Even with the help of "Enclosure C," a board pamphlet that explained every aspect of road building, including how to lay out a road (find "the shortest line between two points"), many of the new recruits remained confused. Should that lovely hedge be torn down to make way for a road? The wrong answer was given often enough to provoke public outrage. "We have many . . . [objections that our] roads are . . . destroying ornamental and highly cultivated lands," a board official reported. There were also complaints about the poor quality of board roads and about incompetent planning. Not uncommonly, board work crews in adjoining districts would fail to coordinate their projects; as a result, instead of joining at the boundary between the districts, one road would end up north, south, east, or west of the other. "We have people . . . who are [ignorant] of rules and regulations *and their places cannot be supplied if you dismiss them*," complained a veteran agency official.

It was the stated policy of the Peel administration to make public works the centerpiece of the relief program, but even after the influence of Mr. Trevelyan had been (temporarily) checked and some of the board's problems sorted out, job creation remained slow. Employment projects were subject not only to Board of Works review but also had to be sanctioned by the viceroy and by the Treasury in London. At Routh's suggestion fifty officers from the Ordnance Survey and six officers from the Royal Engineers were transferred to the Board of Works for emergency duty. The manpower shortage eased, though not enough to make a material difference in the board's efficiency.

In late April, with rain still postponing the sowing season, the only hope a man had of earning a wage was as a replacement for a laborer who fell ill at an operational work site. On wet, chilly spring mornings, dozens of unemployed laborers would gather at work sites across the country to wait. "There might be one hundred men sitting on the boundary to see if any man would drop out," a peasant woman named Brigid Keane recalled. One waiting man in Clare, James Carrig, heard the ganger (foreman) call his name. Carrig made eight pence that day. Another day's work and he would have enough money to purchase a stone of potatoes in Ennis. The next morning, though, the ganger called another man when a laborer fell from the line. The trip into Ennis would have to await a luckier day. At another Clare work site, the hopeful lost patience; a hundred and fifty men pushed past the police and gangers, seized shovels, and dared anyone to turn them out. In early May, when the weather cleared and hiring for the spring sowing season began, the waiting laborers disappeared, but board officials knew they would be back when the season ended.

Meanwhile, in London, Mr. Trevelyan, checked but undaunted, was still in close contact with his subordinates in Ireland. One day Mr. Pine Coffin, the director of the Limerick food depot, received a gift from Mr. Trevelyan, a copy of Edmund Burke's "Thoughts and Details on Scarcity." Reading the first sentence—"Of all things, an indiscreet tampering with the trade of provisions is the most dangerous"—Mr. Pine Coffin must have wondered: Was Mr. Trevelyan planning an intrusion into the food program?

⚯

On May 13, two days before the official opening of the government food depots, Mr. Pine Coffin sat in his Limerick office counting fully provisioned depots. There was one: Mr. Hewetson's facility in Cork city. In a letter to Routh, Pine Coffin urged that the depot openings be postponed. On May 14, Routh sat in his office, counting ships. London had recently requisitioned one of his transports, the *Rhadamanthus*, to carry the 93rd Regiment from Liverpool to Cork, and had transferred another, the converted war steamer *Stromboli*, to the Dublin station, where she would be available for troop transport in an emergency. A third vessel, the *Crocodile*, was in Plymouth, and a fourth, the *Waterwitch*, "*hors de combat*."

May 15 dawned bright and sunny, a welcome relief from the furies of

March and April when the skies had been low and dark, the fields wet and empty, and every conversation seemed to end with the same lament: "[The] curse of God is upon the land." As the sky above the hill line brightened, large parties of agricultural laborers gathered in the fields. The sowing season was now in full swing. Around the fields, the roads teemed with the expectant, the resolute, the desperate, and the destitute. Up with the day, the crowds were all animated by the same thought: "Government corn!" For the past few weeks, officials in England and Ireland had made an energetic effort to lower Irish expectations about the food program. Mr. Pine Coffin repeatedly told visiting relief committees that the purpose of the government corn was to "maintain an equilibrium of prices," not to feed the people.

On April 17, in a Commons speech, Prime Minister Peel had been blunter. "It is quite impossible for the government to feed four million people. It is utterly impossible for us to adopt the means of preventing cases of individual misery in the wilds of Galway, Donegal or Mayo." But in the wilds of Galway, Donegal, and Mayo, hardly anyone had heard of Robert Peel, but everyone had heard about the government corn. By midmorning of the fifteenth, long lines of drays surrounded the depots. Under the Relief Commission plan, depot purchases were restricted to local relief committees, who were permitted to buy from five to twenty tons. Individuals were allowed to buy from one to seven pounds from a relief committee at a penny a pound. Penny a pound? Some buyers were shocked. Wasn't the government supposed to give away food for free? Even so, the Yankee meal was too good a thing to pass up. In Dungarvan, on opening day, "500 to 600 . . . fishermen entered the . . . yard [of a local committee] and . . . squatted . . . on the cold ground. . . . As you cast your eyes on [them]," said a visitor, ". . . want and famine looked you forcefully in the face." In Cork, a witness was struck by "the hue of death" upon the faces of the men and women who had gathered to buy meal. In Longford, people walked ten miles to purchase meal. In Mayo, a farmer too proud to publicly admit to destitution walked twelve miles to buy food in a locality where no one knew him. In Galway, one relief seeker, a young woman "near the end of her confinement," was pulled aside and interrogated by a member of the relief committee.

What are your circumstances? the committee man asked.

The woman said that she and her husband had been without food for two days.

Well then, why is your husband not here with you?

A priest named Peter Daly intervened. The woman's husband was "now too ill through starvation" to walk, he told the committee man.

Daly had been at the committee's office since early morning and was in despair. "Hundreds of his parishioners were in the same condition as [the young woman], and he had no means of helping them." The press accounts of opening day, while uniformly heartrending, were not uniformly complete. A noticeable number of first-day purchasers were reasonably well fed, while others were landless paupers, who had managed to scrape together a penny or two. Technically, both groups were forbidden from purchasing government corn. But for reasons ranging from pity to fear of retribution to patronage, many relief committees chose not to inquire into "the minute circumstance" of a relief applicant before issuing a meal ticket.

Within days of the depot openings, Providence performed a small miracle: the British government became popular in Ireland. In Tipperary, a priest told a relief official, "We know not what we [would] do for the poor, if these supplies were not in existence." In Cork, Father Theobald Mathew, the charismatic leader of the Irish temperance movement, personally thanked Mr. Trevelyan. "A frightful famine has been warded off. . . . [T]he wise and generous measure[s] adopted by the Government . . . [are a] complete success." In Banagher, a town in the Irish Midlands, a young army captain named Pole, impressed by the rush of contributions from the landed classes, hailed the relief program as a triumph of Irish self-help. "The State [has] established within the minds of the people that great and true maxim: The owners of property and other ratepayers are the parties both legally and morally responsible for affording due relief to the destitute poor." In Limerick, Mr. Pine Coffin—older, more experienced, and more cynical—attributed the rush of gentry contributions to the April riots in Clonmel and Carrick-on-Suir. "The motive of self preservation [is strong] among all those who have anything to lose by the effect of popular tumult."

Here and there, a number of first-time corn eaters complained of abdominal cramps and bowel distress. That was to be expected—and,

God knows, given Indian corn's history in Ireland, the reaction could have been a lot worse. Though maize had been imported during earlier scarcities, its effect on the human digestive system did not become fully apparent until the emergency depot openings in March and early April, when everyone who ate it seemed to develop diarrhea or some other gastrointestinal complaint. Thereafter, maize became universally known as Peel's brimstone, and a "strong prejudice" developed against it. In April, inmates at a workhouse in Mallow, Cork, "not only refused to eat [maize], but rose *en masse*, denouncing all who had had any hand in its introduction." Routh, who incorrectly believed Indian corn more nutritious than the potato—it is less nutritious—correctly identified the source of the gastrointestinal complaints. Two grindings were required to make the hard corn kernel digestible, and Mr. Hewetson was only grinding his corn once. Mr. Trevelyan, always alert to examples of misguided humanity, resisted Routh's pleas for a second grinding. "We must not aim at making the corn anything more than comfortable . . . it would do permanent harm to make dependence on charity an agreeable mode of life." After repeated entreaties, Routh prevailed.

The second grinding helped to wear down "the strong prejudice" against maize, as did its low price and a new serving formulation—three parts cornmeal, one part oatmeal. The government also issued a new booklet of easy-to-follow corn recipes, including a recipe for a corn biscuit devised by the renowned Dublin baker O'Brien. The O'Brien biscuit, pronounced "splendid" by the prime minister of Great Britain, won its creator a medal for his services to the Crown.

As May drew to a close, almost the only unhappy group in Ireland were the importers, and they were very unhappy. Despite Peel's repeated pledges to the contrary, the government was feeding the people—or, at least, enough of them to put pricing pressure on the mercantile men. Since November, the government corn supply had grown from eight thousand tons to almost twenty thousand tons. In Mayo, a miller and small-time trader who had carefully built up a corn reserve of ten tons over the winter, expecting to make a killing in the spring, was forced to sell his reserve at the government price, a penny a pound. When a (false) rumor surfaced that the government planned to reduce the price of its meal further, Mr. Hewetson dispatched an immediate warning to London: "You will alarm the importers. They are indeed already alarmed."

On June 3, in an attempt to suppress demand for government food, Mr. Trevelyan ordered Routh to raise the price of depot meal. Ten days later, he declined an offer to purchase a further supply of corn. "No steps whatever should be taken to replace the meal" in the depots. (An exception was made for districts in extreme distress.) In late June, when the sowing season ended and thousands of unemployed agricultural laborers applied for assistance, the food supply came under heavy pressure. On the twentieth, Routh reported, "All Donegal and county Mayo are crying out [for provisions]. . . . Limerick must be kept up. . . . Westport has been almost exhausted and Sligo, too. . . . We have deputations from Clare and Kilkenny who are in great alarm." Parts of the country appeared to be approaching the "final extremity." In Kilkenny, the populace was "staggering through the streets with hunger." In Clifden, Galway, "people were in tears for want of food." In County Wicklow, Mrs. Smith, the landlord's wife, watched "a ragged, frightened boy" collect the shakings of a picnicker's tablecloth on a stone, "piling up crusts of bread with one hand and holding bare bones in his mouth with the other."

The hungry pawned their clothing and livestock to raise food money, but in many places there was no meal to be bought. Cork had only five thousand bushels of ground corn left (about 280,000 pounds), and the Limerick depot had been issuing five hundred tons of meal a week (one million pounds). On June 22, Routh sent Trevelyan another alarming report. "The whole district of Connemara (Galway) is crying out . . . [and] we shall require at Cork an additional thousand tons [of corn]." That same day Captain Perceval, the director of the big government depot in Westport, County Mayo, reported: "Our issues are . . . very rapid . . . and I am sorry to say that the starvation and suffering is . . . very urgent in some of the localities on the coast." Perceval's dispatch included a report from the commander of the revenue cutter *Eliza*. "He tells me that on his last trip to the Killeries [a remote Mayo coastal district] . . . a boat . . . pulled alongside, . . . [A man on this boat] was stretched out half dead and . . . unable to eat the bread given him." Sir James Dombrain, the inspector general of the Coast Guard, immediately ordered a food transport to the Killeries; Dombrain was severely reprimanded for his initiative. On the twenty-fourth, Mrs. Smith received a letter from a Dublin friend who said that there was not a single sack of corn left in the capital. But "for the Government meal," Mr. Pine Coffin wrote that same day, "thousands would now be dying by the roadside." On June 25, Trevelyan again told Routh to raise food prices. "An unduly low price . . . prematurely exhausts our depots by bringing the whole country upon them. *No addition we can make to our stock could stand a demand arising from such a cause.*"

Indignant, Routh replied, "I am . . . quite certain that I have not erred in fixing [the] price." An increase would produce "a strong expression of feeling in the country." In the next exchange of letters, Trevelyan again demanded "an early revision of prices"; Routh again refused. The country "cannot by any possible means bear a higher price"—and then he cut the letter short. "I cannot write more as I am an invalid today."

"We have no time to be ill," Trevelyan wrote in his next letter.

At the end of June, Trevelyan instructed Routh to begin "closing down our present service." The ghost of Edmund Burke hung over the order—"Of all things, an indiscreet tampering with the trade of provisions is the most dangerous"—and so, perhaps, did rumors about a reappearance of the blight. However, the state of the 1846 crop would not be known till August. If the disease did reappear, the relief program would have to be closed and restructured to meet the new crisis.

Meanwhile, there was the public works program to worry about. In April, Trevelyan had warned about the dangers of making public works employment attractive. By June, events had proven him correct. The average agricultural laborer earned 4 to 6 pence per day (plus meals); the average public works laborer 10 pence to a shilling. Moreover, whether he broke two, five, or ten rocks a day, the public works laborer was paid 10 pence to a shilling. And while working conditions were harsh at some sites—road gangs labored to the rhythmic crack of the ganger's whip or dug ditches in waist-high water—elsewhere conditions were more than tolerable. Under the eye of a lax overseer, a man could earn his 10 pence to a shilling a day for "talking or smoking tobacco," drinking, or telling tall tales. Traveling through Kerry, a foreign visitor came across two idle workers sitting by a roadside; the men were dressed like a *Punch* version of Irishmen, in swallow-tailed coats, very dirty and much patched; threadbare breeches; and battered bowler hats.

"Your honor," said one of the laborers, rising to greet the stranger, "you won't believe my stories about the fairies, but I'd lay wager that there are many among us here who have experienced their wonder." Then he offered the traveler the happy example of his companion.

"See sir, here is Tom Sullivan, son of Patrick O'Sullivan, son of Phelm Fad. Until Tom was thirty, he had not touched the bag pipes. Then, one night in his sleep, he was visited by the fairies, who played him the most beautiful tunes in the world. Now, Tom is the finest piper in these parts. That's a fact, your honor."

"It is?" the skeptical traveler asked Tom.

"It is just so," a smiling Tom replied, "and very nice little people they were, sir."

The pleasant conditions at many sites quickly turned the public works program into a magnet. First came the agricultural laborers, finished with the spring planting, and the small tenant farmers; then came workers from the Shannon River project, where the toil was hard (the laborers were draining the river) and the pay by the hated piece-rate system (that is, by the amount of labor performed); then came the sixty thousand migrant laborers, the men who usually traveled to England for the summer harvest. After the migrant laborers came the tenants of influential landlords, the parishioners of influential priests, and the sons of influential large tenant farmers. Ireland's large pool of chronically destitute were also as well represented in the work gangs as in the food lines. "It may be anticipated that the Government will be expected to provide [work] for every laboring man in the country": that warning was not far from the mark. For one brief period in August, the public works labor force, which had averaged from 70,000 to 100,000 for most of the summer, rose to 560,000.

Years after the famine, the surgeon William Wilde recalled the summer of 1846 in an image that evoked *Waiting for Godot*. Each morning, wrote Wilde, "ghosts of men [would] travel several miles" through an untreed landscape of untended fields and decapitated hills "to break up comparatively good old road, or commence an unnecessary new one, leading from nowhere to anywhere."

On the evening of June 25, 1846, large crowds gathered in both Houses of Parliament. In the upper house, the visitors jostling for seats in the Strangers' Gallery hoped to see history made by the passage of the Corn Law reform. In the lower house, the crowds hoped to see a less elevated but more thrilling event, a political coup. For weeks there had been rumors about a plot to take down the Peel government, and a name that appeared prominently on almost everyone's list of intriguers was that of Lord George Frederick Cavendish-Scott-Bentinck. "How little we know what we can do until we try," the *Illustrated London News* declared when the handsome Lord George, a famous racetrack habitué, suddenly emerged as leader of the Tory protectionists. Bentinck's ambitious lieutenant, Benjamin Disraeli, whose suits were so sharp they "would cause a country tailor to commit suicide with his own needle," was also among the suspected conspirators, as was William Smith O'Brien, a resolute opponent of the Protection of Life Act, the hated Irish crime bill. Lord John Russell was not directly implicated in the plot, but several prominent Whigs had been seen meeting with Bentinck and Disraeli. Peel had heard rumors of the intrigue and saw no reason to doubt them. Bentinck and Disraeli wanted revenge for the Corn Law reform, Smith O'Brien wanted the Irish crime bill killed, and Lord John wanted to be prime minister. Moreover, the plotters had enough votes to defeat the Protection of Life Act, and a defeat on a piece of legislation as important as the crime bill would bring the government down.

Entering the Commons on the evening of the twenty-fifth, the prime minister looked like a man who had been invited to his own funeral. At eight P.M., the debate on the Irish crime bill was interrupted by messengers from the Lords: the upper house had passed the Corn Law reform bill; the legislation, already approved by the Commons, was now law in Britain. After the hurrahs had died away, debate on the crime bill resumed. The prime minister, expecting to lose on the bill by twenty votes, lost by seventy-three. "A much less emphatic hint would have sufficed," he joked to Graham. The night ended with a valedictory speech by Peel: "I shall leave a name execrated by every monopolist . . . [but] sometimes remembered with . . . good will in the abodes of those who . . . labor."

Then a report of the evening's proceedings was dispatched to Queen Victoria via a special train. One of the most consequential economic debates in modern history had come to an end. The Commons emptied out, and the MPs and spectators, exhausted and heavy with the emotion of the night, vanished into the June darkness. Among them was a diminutive figure in a top hat: Lord John Russell, the next prime minister.

In early July, Ireland was visited by a new miracle. Just enough food and work were being provided to prevent famine. Instead of "death and death and death," there would be deliverance this summer. A great calamity had been averted, and people knew it. "Peel is a true man of Old Ireland," said a Kerry countryman. "Almighty, bless our Queen," said a laborer. In the food lines and at work sites, there was also praise. "All classes of people are full of . . . commendation," reported Colonel MacGregor, the head of the Irish Constabulary. Even the Irish press (albeit sometimes grudgingly) complimented Britain. The "government has done much to alleviate Irish misery," wrote *The Freeman's Journal*. British relief officials felt a deep sense of pride. Routh hailed the "foresight of Her Majesty's Government" in saving Ireland from a "great calamity."

The political economists, who wanted to restructure Ireland, also had reason to feel pleased. Under the weight of mistrust and want, the potato economy was in collapse. Maize was becoming a staple of the Irish diet; free trade had proved itself, though the mercantile men were very angry at the government; and the Irish landed classes—stirred by the demands of conscience, pressured by the British government, and fearful of peasant violence—had made a significant contribution to the relief of the destitute poor, donating a record £98,000. The only major disappointment of the summer had been the public works program. For nearly £700,000 in loans and grants, the British government had gotten another tangled packet of roads that began "anywhere and ended nowhere," and a workforce that often did little work and sometimes none at all.

One day in late June, Routh encountered Edward Lucas, his predecessor as chairman of the Relief Commission, on a Dublin street. "I am bound in honor to acknowledge [your] . . . success," Mr. Lucas declared.

CHAPTER SEVEN

The Great and Glorious Cause of Ireland

Early July brought unsettled skies and enough social diversions to distract those made anxious by the new crop reports. At the Horticultural Exhibition in the Cork Custom House, there was much talk of fuchsias, roses, pelargoniums, and cacti and little of potatoes. At the Limerick County Fair, bright summer skies, gaily colored tents, and milch cows at £13 to £15 a head, lifted spirits. In Doneraile, County Cork, a gladiatorial cock named Pill, victor of a thrilling thirty-minute death match against a challenger from Charleville, kept minds off August and the early harvest. In Dublin, the Kingston regatta offered the anxious the double distraction of a band from the Light Dragoons playing Irish airs, and a prodigious supply of beer and whiskey. At the Cork Temperance Institute, "tea, coffee and confections of various kinds" eased harvest-time worries. With the exception, perhaps, of the tearoom at the Temperance Institute, all the venues offered the further distraction of the latest "Paddy" joke:

> GENTLEMAN: Paddy, what is your belief?
> PADDY: Wisha your honor, I'm of my landlady's belief.
> GENTLEMAN: What is that, Paddy?

PADDY: Wisha and I'll tell you. I owe her five and a half
years' rent and she believes I'll never pay her, and that's
my belief too.

Unlike their social betters, the small farmers and agricultural laborers had no need to seek out distractions. A denied application for a meal
ticket, a rise in food prices, an empty government depot, a breakdown in
the public works pay system: in July 1846, the Irish peasant was rich in
distractions. Despite the abuses in the public works program, not everyone in need of work was employed and hunger was emptying the depots
at an alarming rate. "We have reached the crisis of the struggle," Routh
told Trevelyan on the tenth. "From County Mayo, there is the most earnest demand. . . . I also have strong applications from Loughrea and
Gort [in] county Galway and from Dunmore, all of which I mention to
you that you may understand the pressure that exists through the country." Routh could have cited two hundred other localities. From Killarney
came reports of "frightful destitution"; from Donegal, a warning that "a
few days' disappointment in the procuration of foreign [food] supply
[will] launch thousands . . . into . . . the endless abyss of an awful eternity." In Kilkenny, the July sun shone down on "people without a stitch
of land, without work, without food, [and who] at this moment [are]
staggering thro the streets with hunger." Skibbereen, a market town in
southwest Cork, was already in the early stages of a crisis that would
make its name synonymous with famine and mass death. "At present,"
wrote a resident, "there are 100 poor men, who with their families, *have
no means of living* . . . in three weeks from this date there will be 500 men
and their families without food. . . . I defy anyone living to exaggerate
the misery of the people . . . *it is impossible.*"

Toward the middle of July a visitor appeared in the office of Captain
Pole, the director of a small food depot in the Midlands. Better dressed
than the common Irish of the area and a fluent English speaker, he was a
respectable small farmer, a ten- or twelve-acre man. Anyone familiar
with rural Ireland could have reconstructed his biography from that fact
alone. The man lived in a whitewashed cottage, not a cabin; until the
scarcity, he had kept his fields neatly tended, his habits steady, his rent
current, his family well fed, and had harbored aspirations of becoming a

middle-sized farmer, a twenty- or twenty-five-acre man. When the Dublin press spoke about the "bone and sinew" of Ireland, they were speaking about men like him. The visitor removed a letter from his jacket pocket and handed it to Pole. It was from a local priest and said that the bearer and his family were on the "verge of famine." The description did not strike Pole as an overstatement. Skin hung from the man's body like an oversized coat; still, somewhere inside all that sagging flesh, Pole could see the man the visitor used to be. What perplexed the captain was why someone in a state of starvation would walk the twelve miles to his depot; there was a relief committee near the man's home. Pole asked about this. "By going to the Committee," the man replied, "I proclaim myself a pauper." In a letter to Trevelyan a few days later, Pole said, "I have [seen] many . . . people of this description" recently.

Meanwhile, reports of the blight continued. On July 2, the *Western Star*, a Connaught paper, reported that the potato fields around Ballinasloe, a market town in eastern Galway, had become infected; on the third came the report in *The Freeman's Journal*. On July 12, the *Farmers' Gazette*, a respected agricultural publication, announced that its editors had found signs of the blight in potato samples taken from several parts of the country. And on July 15, the *Cork Constitution*, having conducted a similar study, reported a similar result. The leaves on the sample potatoes that the paper examined had "crisped and withered—the stalks, were brown and brittle and the seed . . . greenish and hard." In Donegal, newspaper reading was confined to the local Big Houses—the mansions of the landowners—but every peasant knew what to do when little brown spots appeared on the leaves of his potato plants. By late July, tens of thousands of tons of infected but still healthy-looking potatoes were being sold to unsuspecting merchants, who resold them to unsuspecting shoppers, who watched them turn an inky black in the boiling pot. By the time dumping became wholesale, the Irish Constabulary had been in the field for weeks, monitoring the new potato crop for signs of infection. On summer evenings, officers could often be seen gathered at a rural crossroads or in front of a barracks, discussing their findings. Even out of uniform, the Constabulary officer was often recognizable. He was usually the tallest man in the crowd—the eight-thousand-man force boasted almost two thousand six-footers—and, thanks to the stock, a leather harness worn during training to improve posture, the Constabulary officer stood parade-ground straight even in a potato field.

Many of the officers were seeing signs of infection, but the pattern was new. In 1845, the blight had advanced helter skelter: one field ruined, its neighbor still pristine. Now it was difficult to find a field without a few spotted leaves or wilted stocks. Unless the country got a spell of good weather before October, when the grand or main crop was taken out of the ground, a second major failure seemed unavoidable.

Except in the west, the late spring and early summer weeks had been relatively temperate. In early July, the low, dull, gray skies of April reappeared, but rain, the blight's great ally last year, remained relatively infrequent. A morning squall would be followed by a perfectly mended afternoon sky, a day of showers by a day of sun and clouds. On July 3, a rainstorm had almost forced cancellation of the Killarney races; but in the main, in eastern Ireland the weather held until the third week of the month. Then, abruptly—or maybe the change only seemed abrupt in Irish folk memory—the sky darkened, clouds billowed upward in mile-high columns, and sheets of rain pelted the earth. Deep pools of water formed in the low meadows, piles of gravel and mud washed through the potato beds, pigs sat in cabin doorways transfixed by the steady rhythm of the downpour, and billions of fungal spores washed through the potato fields. "Since Tuesday last, up to . . . this afternoon, it has rained without one single hour's intermission," *The Times*'s correspondent in Dublin reported in late July. To the north, in the port town of Drogheda, a *Belfast News Letter* correspondent, also caught in the weeklong rainstorm, tried to balance bad news about the weather with good news about the potato crop. The correspondent assured *News Letter* readers that the "rumors of the new potato crop being diseased . . . are without foundation." In the west, the weather, bad all month, remained bad. "Yesterday we were visited by a deluge of rain . . . and this morning we have had more than abundant showers," complained a Galway man. To the north, in Mayo, weeks of dampness produced a fog so thick, people "found it almost impossible to venture out [of] dwellings." In Dublin, July concluded with a monsoonlike downpour. "I regret to say the state of the weather . . . at this most critical juncture of the season has . . . raise[d] the greatest apprehensions about the safety of the new . . . harvest," the *Times* man reported. "Old Deruane," a peasant fisherman who was also watching the sky closely that final week of July, heard a clap of thunder and had a premonition: the fairies were angry. "I knew by the signs that it was they [who] were coming." The weather had also made Routh apprehensive. The "disease is reappearing," he wrote Trevelyan.

On a moist early August evening, when the landscape had the washed-out look of a watercolor, surgeon William Wilde sat atop a western-bound mail couch, the wind in his face, his head full of leaping trout and sparkling streams. Despite the dense humidity, it was a pleasant evening for daydreaming, warm and calm, and it remained so until around midnight, then all at once—or at least so it seemed to Wilde—the temperature plunged and "flashing lights and streamers" illuminated the black sky above the carriage. The next morning, when Wilde awoke at his inn, the countryside had vanished—swallowed up by "a mist that covered the high ground as well as . . . the valleys." Later in the day, cresting a hill near a favorite trout stream, the surgeon noticed a "close, malarious [malarial] smell" in the air; the higher he climbed, the more powerful the odor became. On the crest of the hill, the source of the smell revealed itself. The potato fields on the far side looked as if they had been struck by a "heavy flood." Their stalks were "prostrated" and "their leaves had lost their crispness." Within forty-eight hours, every field around the inn was the color of the African night. "The stalks and leaves were blackened . . . and the stench that arose, particularly in early night, from the whole face of the country, was most sickening.

"The potato was gone."

Wilde spoke with a surgeon's precision.

In a matter of seventy-two to ninety-six hours, the better part of the 1846 crop was obliterated, and not just the early crop. With the loosely packed soil churned up by weeks of rain, *P. infestans* was able to slip underground and get at the still maturing "grand" crop—the crop that fed the peasantry from October to May. So swift and comprehensive was the destruction, that a kind of mass disorientation seized Ireland. A few days after the calamity, a traveler saw a laborer standing in a ruined Cork field, quietly singing to himself.

"Why are you singing?" the traveler asked.

"What else are we to do?" The laborer shrugged.

A few fields away, a middle-aged woman was frantically scooping out a potato bed with a shovel; at her feet lay a small pile of tubers, "scarcely larger than plums," and covered with oozing sores.

"Are you going to eat those?" the traveler asked.

"We must eat something," the woman said, nodding toward her children, who were standing on a small rise near the edge of the field.

In another potato garden, the traveler saw "a fine, comely girl of 18," scraping at the earth with a spade. "Again and again she turned up the soil but not a healthy potato appeared. She repeated the exercise several times with similar results; at length she flung down the spade in despair." Immediately after the blight struck, Mr. C. B. Gibson, a relief official in the Cork market town of Mallow, toured the surrounding countryside. In one cabin he found "two naked children lying on a *heap of stones*, a malnourished woman with no suck in her breast and a tale of a newly dead child who had perished for want of the suck. . . . Oh, if the people of England and English ministry could see this," declared Mr. Gibson.

A few days later, a relief officer in the Midlands wrote that "in a circuit of 200 miles . . . [I] saw not one field free of disease." In the west, the most potato-dependent region of Ireland, a Galway man reported "rapid disease within the last week . . . stalks and leaves . . . turned perfectly black." In Ulster, the blight rendered the local potatoes so revolting to eye and nose that even "swine, when hungry, refuse[d] to partake." The destruction, almost universal, revived fears of "death and death and death." In one Cork town, hundreds of "half famished creatures" marched though the streets, "accompanied by their wives and children, whose squalid and ghastly appearance bore the same traces of hunger." In Tipperary, a county famous for violence, a local clergyman warned that the "poor will soon have no choice but to starve or rob." In Roscommon, placards addressed to the local gentry appeared on public buildings, storefronts, and churches. "Gentlemen," warned the placards, "you know little of the state of the suffering poor. . . . Are we to resort to outrage? We fear that the peace of the country will be much disturbed if relief be not immediately, more extensively afforded. . . . We are not joining anything illegal or contrary to the laws of God, unless pressed to it by HUNGER."

In Limerick, Mr. Pine Coffin fell into despondency. Like many of his

Irish peasants digging for potatoes

colleagues, he believed that Britain had done a great and good thing in Ireland; now the achievement had been ruined. "The prospect is so uniformly and decidedly bad that I can scarcely enter into the subject," he told Trevelyan. It was August 18; the harvest season was less than three weeks old, and 75 percent of the potato crop had already been lost.

How to respond to the new crisis?

Officials were unsure. In late July, Trevelyan had ordered that the two arms of the relief program, public works and the food depots, close on August 15. "*Whatever steps it hereafter may be necessary to take to meet future possible emergencies,*" he declared, "*it is indispensably necessary to wind up our present operations and bring them to a close.*" Routh, who thought the order unwise, objected. "If our Depots are removed & the Country left to grinding mercy of [the mercantile men], it [will] require all the Police and Military to maintain the Peace." Trevelyan brushed aside the objection, and not for the first or last time Routh swallowed his misgivings; he instructed his senior staff to shut the food depots. Colonel Jones, a more ornery personality, was less cooperative. August 15! Impossible! declared the colonel. Hundreds of work sites had to be closed, and that took time. Abruptly abandoned, half-finished roads and harbors would become safety hazards. In Clare, a Board of Works officer named Russell predicted that a closure of the public works program would also produce mass unemployment. "The ordinary farmers of the country . . . I fear will not furnish much employment [to] the poor laborers." And how would the peasantry avoid famine, if it had no means of earning food money? In Galway, Archbishop John MacHale of Tuam foresaw a season of mass death. "You might as well . . . issue an edict of general starvation."

However, Trevelyan wanted an interval of quiet to restructure the relief program. Alarmed by the Scientific Commission's estimate of a 50 percent crop failure, the previous season Peel had mobilized a great many resources for what had turned out to be a 25 percent crop loss. Trevelyan may have wanted to get a more precise fix on the 1846 losses before acting. The interval would also allow him to make the program more efficient and less vulnerable to fraud and abuse and less threatening to the disaffected mercantile men. Over the spring and summer, Peel's initial purchase of £100,000 of corn had grown to £185,000, seriously undercutting the private trade's ability to make what its members considered a fair profit. Every time a merchant tried to raise prices, the government would throw another shipment of cheap corn on the market. The politicians also wanted the program ended. In London, the new chancellor of the Exchequer, Mr. Charles Wood, told the Commons that "if the Irish people were taught to rely on the government for a supply of food, it would become not only a great but a growing evil."

"Hear, hear!" roared the House.

In most places, the August 15 deadline was observed.

Toward the end of August, several hundred men, women, and children descended on Westport, in Mayo. The crowd marched past Robinson's Hotel, slatternly now but once the "best hotel in Ireland, finer even than the Imperial in Cork," past paupers squatting along tree-shaded promenades, past cobblestone streets made hot to the naked foot by the late summer sun, crossed over a stone bridge at the end of town, and entered an enchanted landscape of lake, high wood, and emerald lawn. In the midst of this wonderland was a many-windowed mansion, Westport House, the home of the man the laborers with no work, the mothers with no suck, the children with no shoes, and the farmers with no potatoes had come to see. Lord Sligo was a "big lord," one of the most powerful men in Mayo. As "people thronged the steps" of the house, the main door opened and Sligo appeared. Expressing warm sympathy for the privations of the people, his Lordship promised to "strongly represent" their interests to the authorities in Dublin. "What about rents?" someone shouted. "What about employment?" someone else shouted. Sligo slid over the questions with the practiced glide of a man accustomed to avoiding the inconvenient. Put your faith in "the good intentions of those who [are] fully alive to the state of things."

"Kneel, kneel!" shouted another voice. Instantly "the greater part [of the crowd] dropped down, as if the Host had been raised among them." In a report on the demonstration, Captain Perceval, the relief officer in Westport, warned London not to take too much comfort in the crowd's deference. Centuries of Anglo-Irish rule had bred submission into the Irish peasant, but it was an acquired trait and did not stand up well to crisis. "The mind of the people is much agitated at the grave prospect before them. These, I fear, are the beginning of our sorrows."

＊＊＊

On a rainy Dublin evening, about a month before the demonstration at Westport House, the poetess Jane Elgee—willowy, well-born, with "flashing brown eyes" and a secure future as a literary footnote—leaped from a cab, snapped open her umbrella, and dashed across a wet street. Dodging the watery lights of the oncoming coaches, she disappeared into the large crowd in front of Conciliation Hall, home of the Repeal Association, the voice of nationalist Ireland. The prospect of an evening of thrilling political theater, featuring the warring factions of Young and Old Ireland, had lured the famous, the well-born, the obscure, and the curious out into a torrential downpour. O'Connell, the leader of Old Ireland, was in London, but in his eldest son, John, he had a worthy surrogate. Willam Smith O'Brien, tall, cool, pale, and patrician, and Thomas Meagher, with hair the color of a burning bush and a temperament to match, would speak for Young Ireland. Maybe it was the long wait in the rain, but the atmosphere inside the hall—decorated in Gaelic Chieftain kitsch: candelabras, images of Irish wolfhounds and Irish round towers—was testy. "Old Dan" was corrupt, charged the supporters of Young Ireland. The members of Old Ireland countered by accusing Smith O'Brien

Portrait of Daniel O'Connell by T. Carrick,
courtesy of the National Gallery of Ireland

and his "juvenile supporters" of rabble rousing. There were also people in the audience unhappy with both factions. It was July 29; everyone knew a major crop failure was coming. The Repeal Association, the most powerful political organization in the country, should be preparing to meet the crisis, not tearing itself apart. One member of the audience likened the evening's proceedings to "the factions of Jerusalem struggling for the upper hand when the catapults [of the Romans] were beating down the gates."

For three years, Young and Old Ireland had cohabited uneasily in the Repeal Association. United in patriotism, the two groups were divided by religion, class, education, and culture. The men of Young Ireland—many well-born and Protestant, some English educated—embraced an idealistic, nonsectarian vision of Irish nationhood that owed a great deal to German romanticism. The men of Old Ireland, many still with the smell of the peasant's cabin or the shopkeeper's floor on them, defined Irishness the way their ancestors had: Irish Catholic. Profound cultural and educational differences produced profound political differences. In 1844 and 1845, there had been sharp disagreements over educational reform, federalism, and the use of violence in the struggle against Britain. Now, in the crisis year of 1846, the two sides found themselves at odds over the central issue in the nationalist canon: repeal of the Anglo-Irish Union. Young Ireland regarded repeal, the restoration of Irish nationhood, as holy and inviolate. O'Connell, the father of repeal, regarded his creation as holy but not necessarily inviolate.

In the 1830s, the Liberator had agreed to temporarily shelve repeal in return for an unofficial alliance with the Whigs. In early June 1846, when O'Connell was seen leaving the London home of soon-to-be Prime Minister Russell, Smith O'Brien and his lieutenant Meagher feared another sordid political deal. O'Connell would get more patronage to distribute, and the Whigs would get silence on repeal. "NEVER TRUST A WHIG," blared the Nation, the voice of Young Ireland, on June 13. On June 19, O'Connell counterattacked. In an open letter to the Repeal Association, the Liberator lamented "the efforts [of] some of our juvenile members to create dissension." That will take away some "clap traps from the juvenile orators," he joked to a colleague. It did not. In a blistering counterattack, Meagher likened the Whig alliance to "writ[ing]

Portrait of Thomas Francis Meagher by Edward Hayes and portrait of William Smith O'Brien, courtesy of the National Gallery of Ireland

Fool upon the tombstone" of every Irish patriot. Meanwhile, in London, Russell was becoming anxious. Recently, Michael Doheny, an associate of Meagher's, had told a group of Liverpool Irish, "There are times when the issue must be decided by a man's blood." No British prime minister could tolerate such seditious talk. If there was to be an alliance, O'Connell would have to do something about the "juvenile orators."

On July 15, at a meeting of the Repeal Association, members of Young Ireland were given a choice: sign a resolution, committing the signer to nonviolent resistance against Britain (O'Connell's position), or face expulsion from the association. It seemed like the perfect trap, but those expensive English educations had not been wasted on the members of Young Ireland. One of the "junior orators" asked whether George Washington, a particular hero of the Liberator's, would have signed a peace resolution. After several similar observations, the Old Irelanders overseeing the signing gave up. A final settlement of the physical force issue was tabled until a two-day general meeting of the association on July 28–29. On the twenty-eighth, Smith O'Brien again proved himself a deft witness under public interrogation, refusing to absolutely forswear the use of force, while sounding like an advocate of peaceful resistance. Tonight, the twenty-ninth, it was Meagher's turn to speak; Meagher was no Smith O'Brien. He was twenty-two, a generation younger; he was a romantic; and he had a habit of thinking with his mouth rather than with his brain.

What are your views on armed force? Tom Steele, an O'Connell aide, asked Meagher.

Meagher began temperately enough, with a homage to the Liberator. "I am not ungrateful to the man who struck the fetters from my arms whilst I was yet a child and by whose influence my father, the first Catholic to do so in two hundred years, sat for the last two years in the civic chair of an ancient city" [mayor of Waterford].

Whether because of the O'Connellites' taunts and catcalls, or a fatal addiction to hyperbole, Meagher's temperateness was short-lived. There was a brief transitional sentence—"God . . . gave to me a mind of my own"; then, abruptly, he turned into the Mad Hatter. He praised the sword as "a sacred weapon" and declared that if it "has sometimes taken the shape of the serpent and reddened the shroud of the oppressor with too deep a dye . . . , it has, at other times, and as often, blossomed into celestial flowers, to deck the free man's brow." Exasperated, John O'Connell told Meagher to sit down and shut up. Immediately, Smith O'Brien—Harrow and Cambridge educated, and imbued with an English gentleman's sense of fair play—leaped to his feet and accused John O'Connell and Tom Steele of being cheats. "You are charged with being people who will never give fair play to an adversary." Then he turned around and walked out of the hall, followed by Meagher, who had never actually witnessed any of the bloody scenes he described, and by John Mitchel, a Unitarian minister's son and the author of the pamphlet on sabotaging British troop movements. The rest of Young Ireland followed.

Miss Elgee, the future mother of Oscar Wilde, was thrilled.

O'Connell was thrilled too; nonetheless, his purge of the "juvenile orators" was an enormous gamble. On little more than a Whig promise of government reform and patronage, he had split the most important domestic political organization in Ireland on the eve of a national disaster. If the Russell government responded halfheartedly to the new crop failure, people would say that the Whigs had outplayed him again—would say that and a lot worse. In late July, however, O'Connell rated the risk of betrayal as very small. After all, the new prime minister was Lord John Russell, and Lord John had long been a standard bearer of "the great and glorious cause of Ireland."

⨯⨯⨯

One day when the Russell brothers were not much more than boys, William Russell told his ambitious older brother Johnny that if he hoped to make a mark in the world he could find no better showcase for his talents than Ireland. "The gratitude of the millions [and] the applause of the world would attend the Man who would rescue that Poor Country," William declared. Johnny took the advice. Under the banner "Justice for Ireland," Russell, a strong advocate of Irish modernization, labored steadfastly for the "great and glorious cause." There were Russell plans to reform Irish education and to improve landlord-tenant relations and the treatment of the poor. Unlike Peel, though, Russell lacked a commanding personality. He was high-strung, prone to indecisiveness, and self-conscious about his height; next to his predecessor, who had the smoothness and serenity of a great yacht, Lord John seemed like a noisy, tossing little tugboat.

When Russell assumed office in July 1846, his demeanor and temperament raised questions about his ability to lead a cabinet of strong-willed men who disagreed on Irish policy not only with each other but also with him. The three Irish landowners in the cabinet—Lord Palmerston, the foreign secretary; Lord Clanricarde, the postmaster general; and Lord Lansdowne, lord president of the Privy Council—did not want the government to put financial pressure on their fellow landowners. Make the Irish proprietor bear a greater share of the cost of relief, Lord Lansdowne told Lord John, and the Irish proprietor will join the Irish peasant in the poorhouse.

The Russell cabinet also included three Moralists of forceful character: the woolly-haired, irritable "imperial iron pants," Earl Grey, secretary of war and the colonies; his cousin, the good Gray; the home secretary, Sir George Grey; and the most influential member of the Moralist block, the new chancellor of the Exchequer, Mr. Charles Wood, a tall, reedy Yorkshireman whose large, beaked nose and sly smile gave him the aspect of a bird of prey who enjoyed his work. Mr. Wood had a double first in mathematics and classics from Oxford, a former prime minister for a father-in-law, and an unshakable conviction that the predicate for remaking the Irish economy and Irish society was to remake the Irish character. Mr. Wood was also convinced that the most efficient way to bring about "salutary" change in Ireland was through the application of the Moralist principle of self-help, and on his first visit to Treasury he was happy to discover that he had a like-minded colleague in the department. A few days after the visit, Mr. Trevelyan received a note from a new admirer. "I have had the greatest pleasure in our short intercourse & I hope that whatever my official life may be, that life has given me the opportunity of commencing a friendship [with you]." The note was signed "Charles Wood."

In a series of cartoons, *Punch* assessed Russell's chances of controlling such a formidable cabinet as very low. In one, the magazine dressed the diminutive new prime minister in Peel's oversized jacket and trousers and put a worried-looking Queen Victoria over his shoulder, whispering, "Well, it's not the best fit in the world." In case any readers missed the point, a few months later *Punch* put Lord John in a high chair and made Peel his babysitter.

Russell's field of action in Ireland was further constrained by British public opinion. In the past ten months, the British ratepayer had sent £800,000 across the Irish Sea; £600,000 in public works loans, and £185,000 in Indian corn. And while famine had been avoided, perhaps it had been avoided because the scarcity had never been very deep to begin with. In 1845, the Dutch had lost 75 percent of their potato crop; Belgium, 87 percent; Ireland, only about 25 percent; and the 1845 potato crop had been larger than usual. Now, in the late summer of 1846, as a new series of warnings and alarms floated across the Irish Sea, the shopkeeper in Kensington and the housewife in Paisley remembered the stories of idle public works laborers and Irish mothers who'd borrowed each other's children to qualify for a larger maize allotment, and found themselves agreeing with *The Times*: "Alas, the Irish peasant has tasted of famine and found it good . . . the deity of his faith was the government . . . it was a religion that holds 'Man shall not labor by the sweat of his brow.'"

In early August, when the O'Connell-Russell alliance was tested for the first time, it failed. The prime minister ignored the Liberator's pleas for a more generous program of government assistance. Mr. Wood and, through him, Mr. Trevelyan had the prime minister's ear on relief. Depressed, O'Connell left for his annual sojourn in Derrynane, the family estate in Kerry. It was a sad journey, enlivened only by a stop in the Tipperary town of Nenagh, where the local temperance band serenaded him with "See the Conquering Hero Come" and "thousands of brave stalwart men" chased after the O'Connell coach. Then it was back on the road—and miles more of blackened fields and begging peasants before Kerry. On his return to Dublin in early autumn, O'Neill Daunt, an old political ally, was "greatly struck by [O'Connell's] physical decay." "His intellect was as strong as ever, but his voice [was] extremely weak. How different were his faint and feeble accents from the stirring trumpet tone. I doubt if he could be heard six yards off." During the sojourn in Derrynane, the Liberator, who suffered from heart disease, had felt something "fundamental break" inside him. He returned to Dublin a dying man.

⚮

In early September, *The Economist* announced that the nation was in a season of "terrible emergency and must . . . endeavor to produce instantly here and in climes where vegetation is now beginning . . . an additional supply of food." The paper was referring not just to the new crisis in Ireland, but to the situation throughout Europe.

On August 3, *The Glasgow Herald* warned that Scotland, only brushed by the blight in 1845, would not be so fortunate in 1846. "Accounts regarding the failure of the potato do not by any means abate," declared the *Herald*. A few weeks later, in London, *The Morning Chronicle* told its readers that "the mysterious potato murrain," the source of "so much suffering among the poor last year," had reappeared in England. In early August, the Belgian, Dutch, French, and German press also filled with reports of wilting potato stalks and bereft farmers. In the little towns along the Rhine, in the textile factories of Yorkshire, in the farmhouses of Saxony and Provence, men and women braced for a new season of want. By late August, 67 percent of the districts in the Highlands were reporting a 100 percent potato loss. In Belgium, 43 percent of the potatoes were dead or dying; in Prussia, 47 percent; in Holland, 56 percent; and in Denmark, 50 percent. A change of weather broke the blight's momentum on the continent, but the intense, dry summer heat that caused

Sicilian soldiers to swelter in 95-degree temperatures and melted the Alpine summit of Mont Blanc to "naked rock" also destroyed 50 percent of the Belgian and Danish rye crop and 47 percent of the Dutch, as well as 43 percent of the Prussian wheat crop and 25 percent of the French.

On fears of a Europe-wide scarcity, traders in Mark Lane, the center of the London corn market, immediately bid up the price of a quarter (480 pounds) of wheat by almost 50 percent. In Edinburgh, grain prices rose by a third. In Dublin, a stone of potatoes spiked from 10 pence to 14 or 15 pence, while in Limerick, an enterprising Scottish émigré merchant named Russell singlehandedly ran up the price of Indian meal from £10 to £11½ per ton in a matter of days. Colonel Jones, who, like Routh, had reservations about the mercantile men, feared Irish food prices were only at the beginning of a historic rise. Ireland needed nearly a million and a half tons of corn to replace the lost potatoes, and the colonel did not think "the private dealers [would] be able or willing" to provide that much food; even if they did, without a supply of government maize to throw on the market, it would be difficult to prevent them from charging "famine prices." "I am very much afraid that Government will not find *free trade . . . a succedaneum* for the potato," Jones told Trevelyan. The Colonel was right. In positing his imaginary pin factory, Adam Smith had failed to give adequate weight to human avariciousness and incompetence.

⬦

A seventeenth-century French traveler once likened the House of Commons to an amphitheater, but a more apt comparison would have been to a gentlemen's club. In the metropolis of the greatest empire in the world, men transacted the affairs of state in an austere, oak-paneled room not much larger than the nave of a village church. House legend had it that the two red lines between the government and opposition benches was exactly the distance between "two outstretched arms brandishing swords." In the Victorian era, the price of such intimacy was miserable acoustics, horrible ventilation, and—on days when an important vote or speech attracted a large crowd—terrible overcrowding. August 17, 1846, was such a day. Beneath the Strangers' Gallery—crowded with ladies in bonnets and gentlemen in top hats—a great concourse of boisterous MPs chattered, wheezed, chomped at cigars, and waved at guests until a diminutive figure in a black cutaway rose from the government bench. This was Lord John Russell; as he approached the lectern in front of the bench, the great patrician Russell head looked like an oversized bust on an undersized pedestal. Height, the lack of it, had always been Lord John's special burden. The first entry in his diary reads, "Woburn, August 18, 1803: This is my birthday. I am eleven years old, 4 feet two inches high and 3 stone 12 lbs [54 pounds]." Things did not improve greatly thereafter.

The frequent, invariably unflattering comparisons with Peel were another special burden. Lord John believed he had been right earlier, on historic issues like Catholic Emancipation and reform of the voting franchise. Yet no one asked, "What does Lord John say, what [does] he think?" as they did of Peel. Now, political fortune had made the new prime minister a hostage to his predecessor. His minority Whig government was dependent on the votes of Peel's free-trade Tories for survival.

Russell surveyed the House, then began: "Sir, I am sorry to be obliged to state that . . . the prospect of the potato crop this year is even more distressing than last year." To underscore the depth of the calamity, the prime minister read three letters. Two were from prominent Irish proprietors: Lord Shannon, who reported that "the destruction of the potato [was] proceeding more rapidly than could ever have been expected," and Lord Enniskillen, who predicted that not a sound "potato would be left in the country by Christmas." The third letter was from a Board of Works officer, who estimated that "the potato crops for this year will . . . lose three-quarters of their produce." (This was an echo of Routh's July estimate, and in two weeks' time it would sound wildly optimistic.)

Lord John did not believe the British ratepayer should be made to bear a large share of the cost of relieving Ireland for a second season. Therefore, except for a £50,000 fund set aside for very destitute districts, the new relief plan he presented to the House shifted the financial burden to the Irish gentry. The centerpiece of the scheme was a targeted tax called the Labor Rate, which fell on "persons possessed of property in a distressed district." As it had last season, Treasury would advance loans for public works projects, but the loans would have to be repaid in full and at 3½ percent interest. Peel's generous half-grant public works loans

*Political cartoon explains why no one ever asked,
"What does Lord John think?"*

had been eliminated. In another significant departure from the previous season, gentry participation in the relief effort would no longer be voluntary. If a group of landowners in a district refused to organize a work scheme for the local poor, Dublin Castle now had the authority to compel them to do so. The plan also reduced the government corn program from a national to a regional operation.

Heavy lobbying by the private trade had paid off. "If it was to become the established practice of the Government of this country to . . .

purchase food for the people," Lord John declared, the market "would be disturbed . . . and the government would find themselves charged with that which . . . is impossible, I mean, the duty of feeding the people." The prime minister closed on a glorious oxymoron: "The course I propose to pursue . . . will show the poorest among the Irish people that we are not insensible here to the claims they have on us as the Parliament of the United Kingdom; that the whole credit of the Treasury and means of the country are ready to be used, as it is our duty to use them . . . to avert famine and maintain the people of Ireland."

Peel, a chronic "disturber" of the markets last season, embraced the new plan. Out of office and absolved of all personal and historical responsibility for Ireland, the former prime minister now was more concerned with the morally debasing effect of government assistance than saving Irish lives. A second year of relief would "stamp a character of permanency on a relief," he told a colleague. Mr. Trevelyan was also pleased with the new plan—and well he should have been: it was based on an August 1 memo of his. The memo, which reimagined the problem of Irish assistance, owed something to the practical lesson learned from last year's scarcity, something to political and financial considerations, and a great deal to Mr. Trevelyan's desire to partner with Mr. Wood in advancing a "salutary revolution" in Ireland. The new public works pay structure, which replaced the per diem rate with a piece rate that tied wages to productivity, would promote initiative and self-discipline in a peasantry lacking in both; and the new Labor Rate Act would foster moral responsibility in a gentry notorious for irresponsibility. The plan also heeded Adam Smith's and Edmund Burke's warnings about the dangers of government interference in the marketplace. This season traders would be given a completely free hand in commercially developed eastern Ireland; only in the west, where merchants were scarce, would the government maintain the depot system. But, to encourage the private trade, the depots would be kept closed until after Christmas, and, upon reopening, would be required to sell corn at the prevailing market price, not at cost, the policy of the previous season. London would no longer attempt to control food prices. If a merchant in Kerry or Galway pushed up the price of corn from £10 to £15 a ton, the local depots would have to follow suit. Mr. Trevelyan believed high food prices were a good thing, as "nothing was more calculated to attract supplies [to Ireland] especially from America." Not long after writing the memo, its author had a vision: "I think I see a bright light shining in the distance through the dark cloud which at present hangs over Ireland. . . . The cure has been provided by the direct stroke of an all wise Providence in a manner unexpected and unthought-of as it is likely to be effectual." Together Providence and Mr. Trevelyan would save Ireland from the "moral plague."

Mr. Wood, the chancellor of the Exchequer, harbored fewer illusions about the effect of the new relief plan. In a letter to Lord John, he warned, "We shall need iron nerves to go through with it."

⬡

Within weeks of the Russell speech, the three-fourths loss in the potato crop was revised upward to a five-sixths loss, then again to a six-sevenths loss. In the untouched seventh were Mrs. Rule's, an "excellent" hotel just off the Dublin–Derry road where one evening surprised guests were served a bowl of potatoes that "smiled as [potatoes] were wont to smile in former happier years"; Cave Hill in Ulster, where a slope of untouched potato gardens gazed out over a landscape of universal ruin and the petty money lenders, meal merchants, and gombeen men who bought up "whatever comes to market and offer[ed] it again in small quantities at a great price which the poor man cannot pay and live." In the bottom six-sevenths were the parishioners of Richard Ryan, a Cork priest who wrote to the Relief Commission: "For the last time, the people are starving," and the inhabitants of Connemara, where in the last sad days of summer 1846, men and women sat amid sky-reflecting lakes, quietly waiting for death to take them. "The peasantry look forward . . . not merely [to] distress and want," wrote a visitor, "but to famine and annihilation with an appearance of calm resignation rather to be wondered at than described. [They] are like the old sailor . . . who[,] believing destruction inevitable, sits silently over the magazine, awaiting the blowing up of the ship as she burns."

Not long after the visitor departed, a Coast Guard patrol discovered a settlement of starving men and women living near Twelve Pins, a Connemara mountain range. It's "the total absence of food," the local dispensary doctor told the Coast Guard men. When Sir James Dombrain, the Coast Guard's inspector general, authorized the issue of free packets of meal to the villagers, a Treasury Minute publicly rebuked him for violating the ban on distribution of free food. "Sir J. Dombrain was not vested with any authority to order issues to be made from government authorities," and "it must also be observed that Sir J. Dombrain entirely overlooked the instruction which had been" laid down.

⧓

On August 28, *The Times* printed a list of the latest shipment of Irish exports. In the past seven days, over the docks of London had flowed 1,616 quarters of Irish oats; 1,929 packages of Irish bacon; 542 boxes of eggs; 5,606 packages of butter; 892 packages of lard, 1,240 of pork, and 39 of beef; 170 hampers of hams and 178 of malt; 132 live pigs; and 1,488 packages of fresh salmon.

That may have been more food than Routh had. In early September, his reserve amounted to 2,100 tons of Indian corn and 240 tons of oatmeal. Even if the private trade immediately provisioned eastern Ireland (the free-trade zone), which the trade could not, the 2,340 tons would only feed Gallway, Kerry, Donegal, and the other western counties for a few weeks, maybe less. The western zone, which extended west of a line that ran from the Cork market town of Skibbereen in the south to Donegal in the north, contained some of the poorest, most crowded, and most potato-dependent regions of the country. During an emergency meeting in London, Routh requested 2,000 tons of Indian corn immediately. Trevelyan sanctioned the request, on condition that the food was purchased in the United Kingdom. Private traders would be alienated if they found themselves competing against the British government in foreign markets.

A few days later, a Treasury official stood outside the Bishopgate Street offices of Baring Bros. & Co. The narrow streets of the City, London's financial district, baked under an intense sun: the hot, dry continental weather had arrived in the imperial capital. Barings had purchased more than £100,000 worth of corn for Mr. Peel last November; now Her Majesty's government wanted the firm to purchase 2,000 tons for Mr. Routh. Mr. Thomas Baring declared himself "extremely flattered" and "honored" by the request, but said this time he would have to decline.

Baring was a big firm, and Her Majesty's government was making a small purchase; moreover, the government "exclude[d] from its plans all purchases in Foreign countries." Mr. Baring did not allow his visitor to leave empty-handed, however. Someone from Treasury should contact his colleague Mr. Erichsen. Mr. Erichsen was a corn factor, very "capable" and eager to please. He could be found at 110 Frenchchurch St.

Mr. Erichsen, indeed, proved very "capable," but the 1846 Indian corn crop still sat in the distant fields of the United States, Ukraine, and the Levant—and could not be shipped any earlier than December 1846 or January 1847; what was left of the 1845 crop was being snapped up by the continental countries. Even if Mr. Erichsen were able to reproduce the miracle of the loaves and the fishes, he could not reproduce it in the confines of Britain alone, and Her Majesty's government was still insisting that all purchases for Ireland be made in British markets.

Against all odds, on August 27 Mr. Erichsen did succeed in outbidding an aggressive pack of Dutch, French, Prussian, and Belgian agents for 1,000 quarters of white Indian corn, but that was beginner's luck. The next day he could not find a single quarter for sale in London. The corn factor had not seen such demand since 1816, the last year of deep international scarcity. Little towns along the Rhine were purchasing Ukrainian wheat and Tuscan corn; the French, who usually exported grain, were importing English new wheat, and the pitiful Belgians were buying anything anyone would sell them. Mr. Trevelyan suggested purchasing floating cargoes (those on a ship still at sea). "There are two or three buyers for every seller," an exasperated Mr. Erichsen replied. On September 14, a miracle! Five hundred to 600 quarters up for sale. But Mr. Erichsen had to purchase the corn on his own account. The seller wanted 46 shillings per quarter, 6 shillings above the Treasury's price ceiling. The seventeenth was another day of tribulations. Mr. Trevelyan wanted 5,000 quarters of Indian corn, deliverable to the west of Ireland in November and December. The best Mr. Erichsen could do was 900 to 1,000 quarters, deliverable in December.

Meanwhile, in Ireland, panic was taking hold. The big government depots in Sligo town and Westport were under such intense pressure that the plan to close the depots until after Christmas had to be temporarily postponed. The Sligo facility alone dispensed over 650 tons of provisions in a matter of weeks. Cork city, a center of the Irish corn trade, which should have been well provisioned, was not: 217 men and women applied for relief on a Tuesday; 301 on Wednesday, 579 on Thursday, 742 on Friday, 1,000 on Saturday, and 1,419 on Sunday. Confronted with the threat of frank famine, Trevelyan finally agreed to lift the ban on foreign purchases, but he had waited too long to act and he knew it. He told Routh that "very large orders are believed to have been sent out of the United States, not only from merchants, but by the governments of Belgium and France . . . and only a limited quantity of produce . . . remains in store at the [U.S.] ports."

In total, during August and September, Mr. Erichsen purchased 7,300 tons of Indian corn, 200 tons of maize, and 100 tons of meal—a remarkable feat, considering the international demand. Still, what was 7,600 tons against the nearly 1.5 million tons of food Ireland needed? In theory, the Irish mercantile community would supply much of the remainder, but Irish merchants were exporters by trade, not importers, and most were reluctant to enter a market they neither knew nor understood. After prevaricating through twelve months of scarcity, on August 21, 1846, Mr. Robert Hall of R & H Hall, Cork, screwed up his courage and told his London agent, James Prevost, that should "our friends . . . float a cargo of Galantz [corn] which seems to be liked here . . . I shall be happy to take charge of it and have little doubt about obtaining a good price." However, when his bid was rejected as too low, Mr. Hall evoked the credo of the prudent Cork man: "I do not think it is safe to speculate on too high prices." Over the next several months, this pattern repeated itself. A bid on a shipment of Tuscany or Black Sea corn would be rejected as too low, and, fearful that domestic food prices would plunge before the shipment arrived in Ireland, Mr. Hall would refuse to go higher. Mr. J. N. Murphy, a colleague of Hall's, also lived by the Cork credo, though more uneasily. In strangely confessional letters to his New Orleans agent, Mr. Murphy would reproach himself for his lack of entrepreneurial zeal and speak enviously of the importers who were making fortunes. Mr. Murphy would do everything except import corn. Irish traders, declared Routh, "are a very different class of men from our London, Bristol and Liverpool Merchants. I do not believe that there is a man amongst them who would import direct a single cargo from abroad."

By the final weeks of the summer, historic crop failure, scarce imports, and the continuing export of food had made a major famine all but inevitable. Many officials believed that, with wholesale prices at £14 to £15 a ton, the retail price of maize would become unaffordable for most of the peasantry, and scarcity would tip over into a nationwide famine. On September 30, in Cork city, corn sold for £16 a ton, up almost 50 percent from the September 1 price, £11.

⊃⊄

The almost complete collapse of the potato-based barter economy exacerbated the food crisis. In early September, Routh passed hundreds of acres of oats growing "over ripe" in the late summer sun for want of harvest labor. With potato ground no longer an acceptable unit of payment and most farmers unable to pay laborers a cash wage, the Irish agricultural workforce was fleeing to the market towns of Roscommon, Donegal, Wicklow, and Waterford, to agitate for an immediate reopening of closed public works sites. In Cork city and in Skibbereen, the unemployed marched military style, shovels slung over their shoulders.

Petitions demanding an immediate reopening of the public works flooded into Dublin Castle. In one, a group of County Wicklow laborers said that they had been thrown into destitution when their local relief committee began charging 10 pence a stone for corn the committee had given away for free earlier in the summer. Without work, declared the laborers, they could not purchase food. "If it were not for the goodness of one or two gentlemen and the farmers in the neighborhood, many of us would have perished." In Cork, many of the unemployed were already in a state of starvation. "A stranger would wonder how these wretched beings exist," wrote a local Constabulary man. "Clothes being pawn[ed] for food . . . they sleep in their rags," and they have no bedding, having pawned that for food as well.

In many places, predatory landlords aggravated the employment crisis by evicting small tenant farmers. One morning a landlord's agent and a crew of burly men armed with crowbars and axes arrived at the Mayo farm of Thomas Brien. It did not take more than a half-hour or so for the visitors to strip Brien of everything he owned. His cabin was torn down, his sheep seized for rent, and he and his family turned out on the roads.

A few days later, some friends of Brien killed the agent's dog and shot the landlord's prize mare.

Even at the height of the first scarcity, occupancy rates in the 100,000-bed Irish workhouse system never rose above 50 percent. Now, in September 1846, with work and food scarce, peasant panic overcame peasant aversion, and the unemployed, the potato-less, and the evicted began to mount a sustained assault on the Poor Law system. On the night of September 15, a guard in Cork heard noises on the perimeter of the workhouse. A torch was lit. A group of men were scaling the wall. "What do you want?" the guard shouted. "We want food, we are starving." The guard was astonished: the men were trying to break *into* the workhouse. In many facilities, occupancy rates quickly rose to 60, 70, 80 percent of capacity. In a County Fermanagh workhouse, officials, fearing an occupancy rate of 100 percent or higher, drew up a series of new economic measures. The number of meals served per day would be reduced from three to two; the change would result in a savings of three pence per person per day. The staff was also reduced, from twenty to eleven.

With agitation for employment mounting, in early September the government announced that a number of abandoned public works sites would be reopened on an interim basis. In Dublin Castle, Routh, recently promoted sole overseer of relief in Ireland, was plunged into despair.

"The whole country is expecting miracles," he told Trevelyan.

❦

On the morning of September 10, Elizabeth Smith, the "pretty, lively" wife of Colonel Henry Smith, late of the East India Company, sat down at her writing desk for the first time since July. Abroad for most of the summer, Elizabeth thought that "nothing" she had seen in all her travels was as "satisfactory" as the scene before her now: the "sparkling Liffey," its "agreeable curves" twisting through miles of brilliant green meadow; and off in the distance the Wicklow mountains, silent and glorious in the morning light. Elizabeth's happy mood did not last long. In her absence, Biddy, the parlor maid, had burned "five or six" holes in the drawing room rug and cut up Elizabeth's favorite bedroom rug and carpeted the backstairs with the cuttings. The kitchen girls had also been more than their usual neglectful selves. There was "no butter or eggs . . . nor meat . . . nor poultry" in the pantry for breakfast, and a boy had to be sent around to Blessington, the local market town, to fetch provisions. A few hours later, Biddy, the burns in the rug, and the empty pantry had all been forgotten. One of the Smiths' tenants, old Mrs. Quinn, Red Pat's mother, was dead and James Doyle, another Smith tenant, was likely to die unless James's brother in America sent the long-promised £10. The blight, come and gone in Elizabeth's absence, had left death and want in almost every cabin on the estate. More misery soon followed. On September 22, a heavy rain destroyed the last of the healthy potatoes on the tenant farms; then a whooping cough epidemic broke out at the local school. In Blessington, prices rose to unprecedented levels, and confrontations between town residents and paupers in from the countryside became a daily occurrence. By the final week of September, Elizabeth was in despair. The government relief plans "don't at all meet the emergency," she wrote in her diary. The landed classes, burdened by mortgage debt and falling rental incomes, were incapable of funding relief on the scale that the Russell plan demanded, and, freed from the pricing pressure exerted by the government corn, "the capitalists were buying up all the grain to retail really at an exorbitant price. . . . What laborer's wages can support his family at [such] rates and how can wages rise when there are double the number of workmen than are wanted?"

On September 25, as the price of Indian corn surged past £15 a ton in Cork city, Elizabeth wrote in her diary: "Here comes the famine."

CHAPTER EIGHT

The Mandate of Heaven

On a summer day in 1842, the four-horse *Skibbereen Perseverance* pulled out of Cork city in a southwesterly direction toward the sea. On the roof of the *Perseverance*, a small, gnomelike figure clutched a box marked "Foggerty the Hatter"; his companion, a green-jacketed policeman, sat with a carbine across his legs. Inside the coach, two Cork men were discussing the merits of Irish mares; the third passenger, a heavy set, bespectacled Englishman, had the dour aspect of a provincial banker. This was William Makepeace Thackeray's second trip to Ireland in recent years, and as the silvery streams and emerald meadows of northern Cork slipped by in the *Perseverance*'s window, he pondered the mysteries of the Irish character. "What a chapter a Philosopher might write on them," Mr. Thackeray thought. "They are kind, good, pious . . . [yet] they will shoot a man down without mercy, murder him, put him to terrible tortures, and glory almost in what they do."

One of the Cork men became cross when Mr. Thackeray shared his observations on the Irish character. Look here, the Cork man said with some feeling, do you know what England does to our workmen? "As long as the men are strong and can work, you keep them. When they are in bad health you fling them back upon us." Dismayed by a "peevish and puerile [response] . . . worthy of France itself," Mr. Thackeray returned to the modest pleasures of the Cork landscape. A few minutes later, the *Perseverance* passed a courthouse where a familiar Irish scene was playing itself out. On the steps, an unruly mob was pressing a detachment of beleaguered dragoons back toward the main entrance. "Vitriol-throwers," Mr. Thackeray thought.

The author of *Vanity Fair* was planning a small work on Ireland, *The Irish Sketch Book*. On this trip, Mr. Thackeray planned to explore the wild coast of southwest Cork, one of the great potato-growing regions of the country. On the ride south, Mr. Thackeray kept a notebook at the ready but found few sites worthy of his pen. As morning became afternoon and the Cork air began to smell of sea and salt, the "emerald meadows and silver rivers" in the couch window vanished, replaced by a "sad and bare" landscape of rock, high grass, and uncultivated field.

Poverty in Ireland had an archeological quality. From the local architecture, a visitor could tell when history gave up on a region and left in despair. In Bandon, a market town near the coast, that point had come at the end of the French wars. On the way into Bandon, the *Perseverance* passed two abandoned textile mills and a street where "every single window had three broken panes"; the postwar years had also been unkind to Dunmanway, a town to the west of Bandon. "Crowds of raggedy [paupers] and blackguards" roamed the shabby streets. About a dozen miles from Skibbereen, the town the *Perseverance* took its name from, a brief rush of brilliant vistas flashed by in the coach window—"a bright road winding up a hill . . . the clear cold outline of . . . mountains." Then, just as abruptly, the landscape assumed a dull, slatternly character again. Around two P.M., the *Perseverance* rolled down one of the two good streets of Skibbereen, a "third-rate Irish country town" inhabited by a "stunted, short" race "with Tartar faces." During a twilight inspection of the town, the only point of interest Mr. Thackeray found was the new workhouse; it had a "bastard gothic" front, "insolent" chimneys, and a capacity of eight hundred inmates, though in 1842 the occupancy rate was barely a quarter that.

Skibbereen was the principal market town in a crowded, impoverished, peninsula-shaped district where history had stopped sometime in the late Middle Ages. Outside the local courts and country houses, English was rarely heard, and agriculture was practiced the way it had been practiced from a time well beyond living memory: a man on his knees in a field, face to the black earth, back to the sky, spade in hand. The towns of the region—Skibbereen, Skull, and Baltimore—were like the little towns of the American frontier, fragile outposts of civilization. From a time superseding historical memory, the district had been desperately poor.

In September 1845, the arrival of the blight threw the Skibbereen region into alarm. The population of the peninsula was large—104,000—and, except for a handful of local landowners and merchants, almost entirely dependent on the potato. Yet at the end of July 1846, a month of "pulling want" locally, officials could boast that in ten months of scarcity, not a single starvation fatality had occurred between Roaring Water Bay and Crookhaven. However, the scarcity had also exhausted the small food reserve in the district. By the end of July, people had been living on government meal and waiting for the early crop. When that crop failed, starvation set in immediately.

On August 21, 1846, Mr. Thomas, a transplanted Cornish mining official, warned his superiors in Cork city that even the "small farmers, who in previous years had plenty of provisions, are as badly off as the poorest laborer. Every one . . . will stick to the few small and black potatoes . . . , but this unwholesome food, at moderate calculation, will afford the people a supply only for about three weeks more . . . when it fails, how are they to live?" Mr. Thomas's superior, Major Ludlow Beamish, chairman of the Southern and Western Mining Company, forwarded his report to Mr. Trevelyan, along with a warning of his own. "The western part of this county is, at this moment, in a very alarming state. . . . I fear that unless some steps are promptly taken by the Government . . . serious suffering—if not outright famine—will arise."

In early September, when Mr. Thomas Hughes, temporary clerk, Commissariat, arrived in Skibbereen to take command of the North Street depot, the southern anchor of the new depot zone, a water shortage was exacerbating the famine threat. The hot, dry continental weather had settled over southwest Ireland; local streams were drying up and local grain mills shutting down for want of power. "Three days in succession," a member of the Skibbereen relief committee told Mr. Hughes, "we have [been] sent to get either meal or flour from . . . one of the mills in the neighborhood . . . but the answer was for the want of water to grind, they could send nothing." In the village of Leap, to the east of Skibbereen, drought had also exacerbated the want. "From the shortness of water," the Leap relief committee informed Mr. Hughes, "the mills in this neighborhood are unable to work with their usual power . . . and there exists at the present moment an absolute *scarcity.*"

This was not completely true. There was some cornmeal in the district, but it was selling for as much as £18 a ton. There was also a supply of cornmeal in the North Street depot, but, to preserve the government food supply, the depots would not open until December. "On Wednesday evening last," a local resident wrote, "I [saw] a family of ten, mother, father, and eight children . . . sitting around a dish of mashed potatoes, the color of which almost equaled the ink used to print [news] papers—and the smell from which was sufficient to bring disease."

By September 12, even the blighted potatoes were almost gone.

The twelfth, a Saturday, was market day in Skibbereen town, but on this Saturday there were no boys in blue coats selling buttermilk from stalls, or shoeless old women puffing on clay pipes and singing the praises of bullock hearts. The square was still empty when the late afternoon shadows began stealing down the "insolent" workhouse chimneys. The countrymen and women, with nothing to sell and no hard currency for purchases, had stayed home. When Mr. Hughes walked through the town around five P.M., he did not see one loaf of bread on sale. "*On Saturday evening,*" wrote another man, "*not a single pound of Indian meal or bakers' bread was found in town.*" Early on the morning of the fourteenth, the Skibbereen relief committee held an emergency meeting to discuss "the best means of supplying the people with food." Afterward, a delegation from the committee visited the North Street depot. Famine was imminent, they said. Would Mr. Hughes release a portion of his meal and biscuits?

Hughes was sympathetic but apprehensive. A senior Commissariat officer would be reprimanded for disregarding the December opening date; Mr. Hughes was only a temporary clerk. After several minutes of heated discussion, he agreed to ask Routh for permission to release some of his supplies.

On the fifteenth and sixteenth, under intense public pressure, the

Skibbereen relief committee released the last of its food reserve, a small provision of wheat. On the eighteenth, committee members were followed around town by "great numbers of famishing creatures . . . begging for food." For Hughes, the worst day of a very difficult September was the nineteenth. After a tense six A.M. meeting with the Skibbereen committee, he agreed to release two and a half tons of meal on his own authority. A few hours later, a priest appeared at North Street; the cleric said he feared "returning to his rural district without some food for the people." Again, Hughes released a supply of food on his own authority. His depot was emptying at an alarming rate. Later in the day, when a delegation from Leap requested ten tons of meal, Hughes said no. "Mr. Deputy Commissioner," declared a member of the delegation, "do you refuse to give out food to a starving people? If so, in the event of an outbreak this night, the responsibility be yours."

On the twenty-third, Hughes received permission to release food from North Street, but the permission came with a sharp warning. "I cannot sufficiently explain to you the necessity of economy, for our means of replenishing your depot are very limited." Routh was not exaggerating. Mr. Saunders, a prominent Liverpool merchant, had just warned London that there were "no stocks" available, except for some "inferior Indian corn [from] the crop of 1845."

Meanwhile, outside Mr. Hughes's window, the panic of early September was giving way to fatalism. The streets of Skibbereen were empty now, and the surrounding countryside deserted, except for the occasional sorrowful peasant visiting his ruined potato garden. "This doomed people," wrote a traveler who visited the town at the end of the month. They "realize . . . what [lies] before them, and many seem incapable of mustering the emotional and mental will to [withstand] another season of want. Last year's suffering exhausted them. . . . It [is] not [an] uncommon sight to see the [peasant] and his little family seated on the garden fence, gazing all day in moody silence at the blighted plot that had been their last hope. Nothing can rouse them. You speak, they answer not. You try to cheer them, they shake their heads. I never saw so sudden and awful a transformation."

In ten thousand townlands—in Kerry, in Clare, in Donegal, in Mayo and Roscommon: places as impoverished, overcrowded, and potato-

Engraving of Brigid O'Donnell and her
children, famine beggars

dependent as southwest Cork—other "little families" awaited death in cabins, in fields, and in roadside scalps and ditches. History had made fatalism a habit of mind in Ireland. By mid-September, scarcely a sound potato existed in the latitudes between Tralee in County Kerry and Gweedore in Donegal; and with commercial cornmeal selling for as much as £18 a ton (almost double the June price of £10) and little work available, the government plan to keep the depots in the west shut until December collapsed.

For every peasant in northwest Ireland who still harbored hopes of survival, the big depot in Sligo town became a magnet. In the first week of September, the depot issued 141 tons of meal; in the second week, 217 tons; in the third week, 247 tons. To the north, in Donegal, the small subdepot of Mr. Moore, a Coast Guard officer, had also come under furious assault. "I have one bag [of meal] remaining," Moore told his superior. "We sold 83 [bags] yesterday. I never witnessed anything like [this] and hope I never will again. People coming a distance of 18 miles for a small quantity of meal. . . . Every day is throwing more and more on us. . . . Numbers will die of starvation if you cannot send an immediate [shipment of meal] and keep up a constant supply. I beg of you be quick." Mr. Trevelyan was shocked by the dispersal of such large quantities of food: "If we go on at this rate, we shall soon be bankrupt." A few days later, in an official Minute, the Treasury Lords reiterated the need to preserve "the food in the Government depots in the west of Ireland . . . *as a last resource.*"

Given the shortages in the international markets and the long delivery dates of the era, what happened next should have been anticipated. Dublin, Wicklow, Waterford, and other areas in the eastern free-trade zone developed food shortages and applied for government depots. East and west, divided by government policy, were now united by its failure. In the Midlands town of Enniskillen, the *Erne Packet* reported that "not less than 2,000 souls . . . at this moment [are] in a state of starvation." In Sligo, the local paper, the *Champion,* noted that thirty families "with no other place on God's earth to shelter themselves from the wind" had been turned out of their homes by the agents of Sir Robert Gore Booth. To the south, in Tipperary, Mr. Crawford, a county surveyor, told a group of unemployed laborers he was sorry, but he had no work for them. "It is impossible," declared one disgruntled laborer, as he left the meeting with Crawford. "I have a wife and nine children. . . . Provisions are very dear. How are we to live?" One of his companions pointed to a nearby farm and said, "There is wheat . . . in [those] haggards [enclosures for stacking grain]. Why should a man go hungry in a country when there is plenty of grain?" As the two men walked toward the field, a third— female—voice shouted: "Do nothing mean, boys. . . . Wait with patience a little longer—God is good. I have five children—they are hungry . . . they are in want . . . but do not rob . . . do not disgrace us."

By September 1846, that was not advice many men were inclined to take. The season of the gunman was at hand. In Dungarvan, a Waterford port town, impoverished laborers swarmed through the streets, threatening store owners and taunting top-hatted country gentlemen who had come into town for a public works meeting. Stones were thrown, shop windows broken, carriages surrounded, passersby taunted and pushed into the street; only the arrival of elements from the 27th Regiment prevented serious bloodshed. In Mayo, something like outright anarchy developed. "Deaths innumerable from starvation; plunder, robberies, occurring every day. The bonds of society almost dissolved." In Clare, a local gunman amused himself by terrorizing British officials. "This is a year of famine," he wrote to one potential victim. "Give the people the means of keeping themselves alive; if you do not [you had better bring your coffin with you] . . . I will meet you on this noon day." In the Waterford town of Clashmore, the Earl of Huntingdon, a foolish, vainglorious man, attempted to subdue a starving mob with insults. "You are madmen rush[ing] headlong upon your own destruction!" the earl shouted, riding into the crowd. "We have not tasted a morsel of food for the last 24 hours," one man yelled. We have been "living on cabbage for the past three weeks," shouted another. As the crowd pressed in on his horse, Huntingdon realized he was in grave danger. He flung a handful of coins in the air and fled while people scattered for the sovereigns.

How could the escalating violence be stopped?

To Lord George Bentinck, leader of the protectionist Tories and a man who saw the world in black and white, the answer seemed self-evident. On September 25, at a protectionist fête at the Shire hotel in Essex, the dashingly handsome Lord George looked like the stuff of a shopgirl's dream—wasp-waist guardsman's figure, excellent widow's peak, and waxed mustache twisted into a perfect villain's twirl. As he rose to speak, two hundred spoons clanged against two hundred crystal glasses. The clanging led to clapping, and the clapping to table thumping. The eruption rolled out the half-opened windows across the nighttime lawns of the Shire, to the carriage park, where coachmen huddled in the darkness against an early autumn chill.

Raising a hand for quiet, Lord George observed that the county of Essex had been "the first to raise the banner of protection" ("Hear, hear!").

He denounced the perfidious Sir Robert Peel ("Hear, hear!"), and blamed free trade for spreading the potato blight to Scotland and Egypt. ("Loud cheers!") Finally, Lord George turned to the Irish situation. Citing a *Times* estimate that "4,000,000 people [needed to be] provided for [in Ireland]," he asked the audience, "how were they to [be] provided for? . . . Why, at the rate of a quarter of grain for each inhabitant, they had only to avail themselves of their own super-abundance of grain and keep it at home, and 3,000,000 out of the 4,000,000 would be provided for."

On the twenty-sixth, the day after the Bentinck speech, violence erupted in Youghal, an important export center in northern Cork. "I have never seen anything to equal the state of excitement here," wrote a reporter for the *Cork Examiner.* "It would be impossible to convey any idea of the alarming state of this town." Three days later, "an immense number of people" flooded into Youghal, "determined to sack and pillage." Shop windows were broken, carts tumbled, officials assaulted, soldiers and police taunted; plumes of black smoke rose from sacked warehouses. Fearful of further violence, local merchants donated £2,500 to a municipal relief fund. "Such days of fearful alarm and dreadful excitement were never to be witnessed," said an observer. That same day, the twenty-ninth, Dungarvan erupted in violence for a second time. In the morning, an armed crowd blocked the passage of two lighters (flat-bottomed barges) transporting a shipment of grain to an English vessel in the harbor.

Toward afternoon, the rioters swarmed through the streets, shouting threats to exporters. Buildings were set ablaze, merchants beaten, panicked horses galloped riderless through the streets. When a crowd of rioters ignored an order to disperse, Captain Sibthorp of the 1st Royal Dragoons ordered his troops to open fire. A moment later, half a dozen bodies lay in the cobblestone street, red stains spreading across their shirt fronts. Two of the fallen were dead, the rest wounded.

Punch, always alive to the "incurable madness" of the Irish, took note of the escalating violence in a poem:

> *Och! Paddy, my honey, we've given you the money . . .*
> *In want and starvation, you cried to our nation*
> *To relieve you, we pinch'd our own indigent sons;*

You gained your petition—to buy ammunition
Pikes and cutlasses, bayonets, pistols and guns.

In Downing Street, Prime Minister Russell ordered the twenty-two-gun *Madagascar*, the forty-four-gun *Andromache*, and several cavalry and infantry detachments to Ireland.

On September 28, in the midst of the anti-export riots, Routh warned Trevelyan that the price of cornmeal in Dublin had reached £15 a ton—the famine tipping point. "People [of] all ranks and classes [are] crying out" for the establishment of Commissariat depots and "are astonished when they are told that Indian corn is not in the country [but] has to come 4000 miles [sic]—from America—and cannot arrive in any quantity until 1st December to the 1st January." In London, a plan circulated for bridging the four- to five-month food gap with barley and yams imported from the West Indies. Routh felt a bolder response was needed. Ireland "is full of grain," he told Trevelyan. "[T]hese home supplies . . . must maintain [the people] until the foreign importations arrive."

In a second memo, on September 29, the commissary general pressed the point with uncharacteristic force. "The exports of oats have amounted, since the harvest, to 300,000 quarters. . . . It was this exportation that caused the riot at Youghal. I know there is a great and serious objection [to] any interference with these exports, yet it is a serious evil." On October 2, Trevelyan sent Routh a copy of Burke's *Thoughts and Details on Scarcity* and a note. A "sudden and violent interference with the regular course of trade [would] be regarded by the mercantile community *as the habit of government.*"

Trevelyan had allowed economic ideology to cloud his judgment. Between October 1846 and June 1847, the dead heart of the famine, food imports did exceed exports, and by a five-to-one margin, but the bulk of the imports arrived in the late winter and spring of 1847. In the autumn of 1846, when the Irish grain crop was exported, there was almost no food available anywhere in the world, and the 1846 American corn crop was still several months away. Kept at home, the Irish grain probably would not have prevented famine, but it would have provided the country with a bridge to the American corn, and might well have saved some of the million men, women, and children who were about to die of starvation and disease.

The failure to keep the grain crop in the country was the fourth major miscalculation Trevelyan had made since the Russell government came to power. He also made a grave error in weakening the corn program, the government's price-control mechanism. In modern famines, starvation often arises not from an absolute shortage of food, but from access to food—and among the things that govern who has access and who does not is the cost of food. With no cheap government corn to press down prices, avaricious merchants like Mr. Russell of Limerick were free to foster starvation by pricing food beyond the peasants' reach. Keeping Mr. Erichsen out of the foreign markets until mid-September was also a serious error; by September, there was very little food for sale anywhere in the western world. Trevelyan also put too much faith in inexperienced Irish mercantile men like Mr. Hall and Mr. Murphy. In the winter of 1846–1847, when death was everywhere, a British official would complain bitterly about "the merchants, who last July made promises of all sorts about the stock of meal . . . [and have] done as little as they could have as if the Government had entered on the trade."

In the end, however, a civil servant—even a highly placed, gifted, and strong-willed civil servant—is the creature of his political masters. Kept in check by Peel and by Home Secretary Graham, on balance, Trevelyan was an effective leader during the first year of the scarcity. In the Russell government, the checks were removed because there was no need for them. Trevelyan found the policies of Chancellor of the Exchequer Wood and Lord John deeply congenial. Even in 1863, after famine and emigration had reduced the Irish population by a third, Russell was still insisting that government interference in the corn trade would have "led to a greater number of deaths . . . than the course we thought it our duty to pursue."

⬤

Toward October 1846, a horseman appeared on Castlefarm road, riding hard in the direction of Hospital, a small Limerick town famous for its ruins and its horse fairs. Half a millennium earlier, Castlefarm had been a high forest, teeming with elk and eagles. Now, except for the occasional pair of antlers dug up by the work crews dredging the bogs, no trace of that ancient landscape remained. Passing through this part of Limerick after the French Wars, a British soldier with a mordant eye and a wit to match observed that the region had barely enough tree to hang a man and barely enough soil to bury him in. Soldiers exaggerate, of course, but in this instance not by very much. Every turn in the road and every rise in the land brought into view the same desolate scene: peat-covered rocks, high grass, stony earth, and bog. Except for the parties of men who occasionally appeared in the fields next to the road, the countryside was empty. The interlopers were public works laborers, and they were marching south toward a distant hill line. Having exhausted the road-building potential of the plains, the public works gangs in the neighborhood were now decapitating the hills.

The rider, Mr. Thomas Kearney, a surveyor first class for the Board of Works, was en route to Hospital to attend a presentment session. In normal years, presentment sessions, at which local public works projects were proposed and debated, were a routine and relatively peaceful part of local government, but 1846 was not a normal year. A decade after the famine, one attendee recalled how desperate peasants would crowd into a "session until there was scarcely space to sit or air to breathe," and how members of the gentry, fearful of violence, would approve employment scheme after employment scheme "without knowing or even caring about their purpose and cost or about the most advantageous plan of executing them." If the projects failed to soothe the crowd, often a landowner would rise, ask why it was that so many families in the district were unemployed in a time of such terrible want, then point to the Board of Works representative.

The day before, in Kilfinane, another Limerick town, Mr. Kearney had found a great many fingers pointed in his direction. "Certain gentlemen" had denounced him and the board in the "most violent language; the accusations incited the audience, and their shouts inflamed a "very large mob" outside in the town square; "riot and confusion" ensued, and Mr. Kearney fled Kilfinane, pursued by a crowd of "several thousand people hissing and hooting."

The meeting in Hospital also began on an ominous note. After the session was gaveled to order, several members of the gentry made "injudicious speeches." The "outrageous" tone of the speakers put "the people in a fury," and "police with loaded carbines" had to escort Mr. Kearney from the meeting hall. Outside, in the street, the surveyor "came under the most awful grinding and pelting of stones"; then, for the second time in as many days, he was chased out of town by an angry mob. This time, though, Mr. Kearney's pursuers were so set on doing him bodily harm that they "disencumber[ed] themselves of their coats, shoes, and stockings, to enable them to run faster." On his return to Limerick city, Mr. Kearney told his superiors that, but for a good horse, he would be dead now.

The second crop failure transformed public works employment from the source of easy money into a matter of life and death for millions. Without hard currency, food was unobtainable, and without a position on a public works road gang, hard currency was unobtainable by all but the most fortunate of peasants. The only wage small and middling farmers were offering was the traditional barter of labor for potato ground, which no one wanted, and many large farmers and landowners were not hiring at all. The gentry seemed to be holding back until they had a better sense of where the country was going. "Out of a population of 11,000 of the poorest beings on the earth's surface," wrote a man who visited Skibbereen in late September, "707 only are employed, and the rest? God only knows how the people have tried to hold to life. . . . [T]hey are in the most abject and horrible state of destitution. . . . They are subsisting on sea-weed . . . [and] raw tainted tubers [which] have been crunched and swallowed with more than a beast's avidity by the famishing people!"

On October 1, the Board of Works had fewer than twenty-six thousand men on its rolls, and the Irish press was in a fury about the numbers. "WHY ARE NOT THE PEOPLE EMPLOYED?" cried the *Ballyshannon Herald*. "UNACCOUNTABLE DELAY AND PROCRASTINATION AT THE BOARD OF WORKS," shouted the *Kilkenny Journal*. "PAUPERIZATION OF IRELAND," lamented *The Nation*. "DAMNED POLITICAL ECONOMY," exclaimed *The Kerry Examiner*. "DANGER TO PUBLIC PEACE," declared the *Cork Southern Reporter*.

In February 1847, the board would have ten thousand overseers and five thousand pay clerks, engineers, inspecting officers, and other specialists, but in late September 1846 the agency had fewer than a hundred and twenty-five employees—and a million and half pounds' worth of loan applications for public works schemes to sort through. The result was a new round of chaos and gridlock. "A stranger can form no idea of our . . . work," Colonel Jones told a colleague. "[Our] passages and corridors are blocked up with deputations and expectants for office, and this we cannot prevent, unless our doors [are] kept locked constantly."

In October, the pace of job creation did rise, but with the harvest season ending, and with it the last significant source of private employment, the demand for work rose even more quickly. In the Kerry town of Tralee, hundreds of unemployed laborers, "armed with spades, shovels, and other rude weapons," swarmed through the streets like banditti. Municipal officials were threatened, carts upturned, food shops sacked, passersby assaulted. When a resident rebuked the protestors, he was told to take himself out to Clahane Road. There he would find the body of a man who had starved to death for want of work and whose "family has not a single penny to buy a coffin." Dungarvan, which came out to protest food exports, also came out to protest the lack of work. This time, however, the protest ended with bodies in the streets. There was "terrible excitement," said a reporter for a Tipperary paper. Three days later, two companies of infantry and a reinforced troop of Constabulary patrolled the town. Overnight, the hills above Dungarvan had gone ablaze with "signal fires," and rumors of an invasion by several thousand unemployed men from Tipperary circulated through the town lanes. Through a herculean effort, by the end of October the board had expanded the labor force more than fourfold to 114,000, but as employment grew a new set of grievances arose.

There were not enough construction tools for laborers; £10,000 had to be requisitioned to pay for the purchase of shovels, spades, wheelbarrows and other implements. There was not enough currency to pay wages; £75,000 had to be rushed over from England. There were also bitter complaints about the board's new hiring policy. The previous summer, work tickets, the certificates that entitled a man to a day's labor at a road site, had been handed out with such abandon that Mr. Trevelyan decided to restructure the hiring system. The local relief committees, which had issued the tickets, would continue to compile lists of employment applicants, but, under the new system, a Board of Works inspecting officer would decide who received a work ticket and who did not. Last, and above all else, there were complaints about Mr. Trevelyan's new wage scheme. Board officials claimed that on the new piece-rate system, an average laborer could earn as much as he had the previous summer under the flat-rate system, ten pence to a shilling a day, and a good worker from one shilling, four pence to one shilling, six pence (twelve pence equals a shilling). While not implausible, the board's estimates failed to take into account how much a lack of tools, slothful coworkers, a cold autumn rain, malnourishment, and exhaustion could reduce the productivity of even an energetic young worker. The board estimates also neglected the wage delays associated with the piece-rate system. At the end of each day, a board officer had to calculate the length of a ditch dug or the amount of road cleared by every man on a work crew; then the calculations had to be sent to the Board of Works office in Dublin to be translated into wages, and the wages sent back to the work site. While he waited, a laborer did receive a portion of his wage—but two, three, four weeks might elapse before he received the rest. When told that they were being placed on the piece-rate system, a Cork work crew "put their spades on their shoulders and returned home notwithstanding the poverty and absolute want of their families, the greater number of the men refused pleas to return to work."

Laborers did have the option of remaining on the flat-rate system, which paid a guaranteed wage no matter how much work a man did. But the flat rate was set two pence below the average wage in the district where the work site was located. In many places, the average per diem worked out to about eight pence a day. With a stone of cornmeal already selling for 2 shillings, in many places, eight pence was a famine wage. A laborer needed three working days to earn 2 shillings, and if he was part of a family of seven (not an unusual size in peasant Ireland), a stone of meal would provide each family member with a bit less than half a pound of food a day for four days. "Sir," a Roscommon laborer told a Board of Works officer, "I have a wife and nine children, provisions are very dear—eight pence is no more than will support myself—and what is to become of the other ten?"

Worker anger over low pay, late pay, lack of tools, and stricter hiring standards was exacerbated by the relentless rise in the cost of food. When the price of corn rose from £10 to £15 in three weeks, the *Cork Southern Reporter* warned that "the people are barely able to support life with the weight of food they are enabled to purchase." In many parts of the country, food prices and worker violence rose in tandem. The Board of Works overseer, ganger, pay clerk, or inspecting officer who refused to inflate a pay sheet or to give a man work, or who pushed a road crew too hard, invited a range of retaliations. In the Clare town of Ennis, five men in ladies' hats burst into a board office and assaulted a pay clerk. Another Clare officer, George Andrews, was dragged from his horse and beaten by a mob, who also kicked the horse "several times in the belly." By November, assaults on board men in Clare had become so common martial law was proclaimed in several districts. In Galway, where a board officer was pistol whipped, work sites were closed. "No one but a person on the spot can form any adequate idea of . . . the opposition and difficulty thrown our way," wrote one aggrieved officer. "The insults heaped on [us] as well as the odium cast. . . . Who can stand it?"

As autumn progressed, nervous breakdowns, desertions, suicide attempts, and resignations among board men rose precipitously. "With feelings of deep regret," an officer in Galway informed board headquarters in Dublin, "I am called to acquaint you . . . [with] the melancholy circumstances of Mr. ———, the officer stationed in this town. . . . At the hour of half past eight this morning [he] placed a pistol loaded with powder and a ball to his head and fired it." A few days later, another Galway officer went "quite out of his mind." In Limerick, a frightened Mr. Kearney resigned and an overwhelmed clerk named Owen walked off a public works project "without telling anyone and not even leaving the documents . . . needed to enable the laborers to be paid."

In Dublin, the new Whig viceroy, Lord Bessborough, issued a warning about the attacks:

> The Lord Lieutenant has . . . been informed that a disposition has . . . been manifested by the laborers employed in public works to resist the arrangements . . . which the Board of Works officers have arranged . . . as well as endeavoring by violence to obtain a high rate of wages. . . . The Lord Lieutenant confidently relies on the continued support of the magistrates and other [individuals] of station and influence to maintain tranquility.

Colonel Jones believed that the Irish press—not high food prices and low pay—was responsible for the violence. All those terrible headlines in the *Cork Southern Reporter* and the *Kerry Examiner* had soured the Irish public on the Board of Works. In early October, a novel idea began to percolate in the colonel's head: a publicity campaign. Jones knew that there existed a secret correspondence between the Russell cabinet and the board, which showed agency officials to be frequent defenders of Irish interests. Publication of the correspondence would burnish the board's image in Ireland. Mr. Trevelyan, who had a more sophisticated appreciation of press relations, told the colonel no. The newspapers would feel compelled to respond to the cabinet correspondence, the board would feel compelled to respond to the press, and a fruitless cycle of accusation and counteraccusation would ensue. As a consolation prize, Mr. Trevelyan sent Jones a copy of *Thoughts and Details on Scarcity.*

❧

On August 17, as the noxious odor of rotting vegetation curled up into the Galway sky, *The Times* announced that the cost of assisting Ireland during the new crisis would impose "a poll tax of one shilling on every man, woman and child" in England. Eleven days later, on August 28, Parliament enacted the Labor Rate Act, which transferred to Ireland financial responsibility for the relief. Henceforth, employment projects such as road building would be paid for through a new tax, the labor rate, which fell most heavily on Irish landowners, large tenant farmers, and other well-to-do members of Irish society. Lord Monteagle, a prominent Limerick proprietor and former Whig chancellor of the Exchequer, read the act and sighed. In a time of falling rental and agricultural income, asking Irish property to relieve Irish poverty was like asking the "Hindoustanis to build Manchester." The thing could not be done. Lord Devon of Devon Report fame agreed. Soon the Earl of Lucan, destined to win immortality for his role in the charge of the Light Brigade, took up the cry: The thing could not be done!

From Lord Lucan, the cry spread to the country houses of Tipperary, Roscommon, Cork, Antrim, Monaghan, and Kerry, where Sir A told Sir B, who told Sir C: The thing could not be done! Within weeks, unhappiness in Kerry, Cork, and Tipperary spilled over into unhappiness in the

Cabinet Room at 10 Downing Street, where the Irish landlords in the cabinet, Lord Palmerston, Lord Clanricarde, and Lord Lansdowne, told Lord John: The thing could not be done!

Aroused proprietors, farmers, and municipal officials poured into courthouses and meeting halls across Ireland to second the motion. The thing could not be done!

Declared a gathering of gentry in County Westmeath:

> The expenditure . . . under the present act [the Labor Rate Act] formidably increases the future difficulties of our position, and would eventually ruin the landowner by exhausting his capital.

Resolved a group of landlords in County Mayo:

> We shall keep down the necessity of a *ruinous taxation*. . . . If we do not do this or something like it . . . we shall be swamped in a mass of misery and taxation. . . . We must do or die.

To opponents, the new tax seemed self-defeating as well as financially ruinous. If the British government was serious about modernizing Irish agriculture, why make the Irish landowner and large farmer spend his limited capital funding the construction of more useless roads?

Even *The Nation*, no friend of the Irish landlord, found the prospect of another season of road building depressing. "Cutting down a hill that might as well be filled up again . . . commencing a canal in the wrong place . . . laying down roads that lead no whither . . . [are all a] stupid and perverse waste" and have turned the Irish landscape into "a wonder and a horror of mankind."

There was also a question of whether Her Majesty's highway system could survive another assault by Board of Works road crews. Recently, Lord Farnham had taken a most awful fright when his coach nearly tumbled on one newly built board road, while Lord Sligo and the Dublin Mail barely survived their encounters with another new road.

In September, Lord Monteagle, Lord Devon, Mr. William Monsell, and several other prominent proprietors advanced a proposal that would make the labor rate more acceptable to the gentry. Millions of peasants were in urgent need of employment. Why not allow proprietors to use their tax money to make private improvements on their estates? These would create work for the peasantry and allow landowners to modernize their agricultural operations. "What is asked," said one supporter of the plan, is that "the contribution which each [proprietor] should have to pay [under the labor rate] should, if he pleased, be spent on his own land in a useful manner." The new Irish viceroy, Lord Bessborough, was sympathetic. While presentment sessions argued and board officers searched for the shortest distance between two points, unemployment was pushing whole districts in the south and west into famine. Bessborough took the landlords' idea and redrafted it. He proposed that the government make loans available to landowners who organized private improvement projects on their estates.

Prime Minister Russell was horrified. "If parliament . . . were told the personal interest of Irish landlords were to be served by loans of public money, . . . no Gov. could withstand it." Even worse, "soon the whole landed property of Scotland and England" would be demanding to be "drained, fenced and furnished" with government funds. Chancellor Wood was even more appalled by Bessborough's proposal. "Why," he asked, "cannot Irish gentlemen do as English gentlemen do?" in periods of scarcity—borrow money from a bank to create employment projects for the poor. In a letter to Monteagle, Wood warned that feeling in England was "very strong against . . . the never ending [Irish] requests for money. . . . If the Irish won't, can't save themselves, [then] who will save you?" Only weariness halted the chancellor's assault: "I have written my fingers off."

At a cabinet meeting on September 25, Mr. Wood and the other two Moralists in the cabinet—Sir George Grey, the home secretary, and Earl Grey, the colonial secretary—helped to defeat Bessborough's proposal. Two days later, on September 27, the three leading figures in the Irish government met at Dublin Castle. Bessborough believed the domestic situation had now become so grave that "the very existence of the Country" was at stake. Henry Labouchere, the Irish chief secretary, and Thomas Redington, the Irish undersecretary, agreed. During a long, tense morning of discussion, the men came to agreement on two other points: Russell still did not fully grasp the gravity of the situation in Ireland and had to be told "exactly the state of the country," and the Bessborough proposal or some version of it had to be approved. The public works program was not providing sufficient employment at sufficient speed. Two more months of mass unemployment and there would be mass death, or rebellion, or both. In one of his letters, Lord John had suggested a change that would make the use of government funds for private projects more acceptable to the cabinet: make the loans available only for one or two types of improvement. Accordingly, the new version of the Bessborough proposal that Mr. Redington carried to London a few days later offered loans only for drainage to convert waterlogged land into farmland.

At Treasury, Mr. Redington got a lecture on political economy from Mr. Trevelyan, "wholly inapplicable to Ireland," and in Westminster, a lecture on Scotland as a model of self-reliance and enterprise. Otherwise, the trip went well. In early October, the cabinet adopted the revised proposal. "You shall have all the help we can give you to make the measure work," Mr. Wood promised Bessborough. The chancellor was franker about his feelings in a letter to Lord Monteagle. "Nothing done, nothing attempted, nothing even suggested, except a larger outlay of public money."

In Whitehall and Westminster, and, perhaps even more, in the mind of the British public, the Irish—Catholic and Protestant, gentry and peasantry—were melding into a single impoverished, slothful, whining mass, and all the various branches and divisions of this great glutinous sludge of humanity suffered from the same horrible affliction: the "present habit of dependence on government." The landed classes expected the British government to give them loans to improve their estates, while the Irish poor expected the government to provide food and work. At Treasury, Mr. Trevelyan and Mr. Wood examined the two crop failures, pondered, prayed, considered—and then looked into the mind of God. Inside, they found a message: end the present habit of dependence on government in Ireland.

⚎

The 1840s were the Age of Atonement, a period of intense religiosity. The early Victorians believed that God roamed the life of the world, smiting acts of wrongdoing. Volcanoes, floods, earthquakes, and famines were not random natural disasters; they were Visitations of Providence, indications of divine displeasure, calls for redemptive change. In the case of the Irish crop failures, English public opinion was divided about the cause of the Visitation. Some held that the potato had failed a second time because God was punishing the Irish for being papists; others, because the Irish were a violent, unhygienic, ungrateful, and morally inverted people. Still others held that the Irish had fallen out of God's favor because they were Irish. Mr. John Walter, "chief proprietor" of *The Times*, was a leading proponent of this view. "The blacks have a proverb," he told Parliament: "If a nigger were not a nigger, the Irishman would be a nigger."

Mr. Wood and Mr. Trevelyan were more tempered in their views. They believed the crop failures of 1845 and 1846 constituted a Providential judgment on a specific aspect of Irish life, the potato culture. The potato's ease of cultivation lay at the root of Irish dependency and Irish backwardness. When a man had to tend his garden for only a few weeks to produce a year's supply of food, he became lazy, undisciplined, unenterprising, prone to drink, and inclined to rely on others to take care of him.

Mr. Wood and Mr. Trevelyan also believed the crop failure represented a call for "salutary" change in Ireland, and already they saw signs of such change. During the first year of the blight, Prime Minister Peel had advanced the Irish modernization project by introducing a new and higher food—Indian corn, a grain—and, through the public works program, a wage salary system, the first step in establishing a monetary economy in rural Ireland. The relief plan Mr. Trevelyan drew up in August was intended to further advance "salutary" change by fostering a new culture of initiative, industriousness, and self-reliance.

To employ relief policy as an instrument of social and behavioral change in the midst of a historic famine entailed risk, of course. If the peasantry proved incapable of earning a living wage under the piece-rate system; if the Irish gentry proved financially unwilling or unable to support Irish poverty; if merchants, unchecked by competition from cheap government corn, made food unaffordable, there would be a great tragedy. But unlike the morally blinkered, who saw only hunger, misery, and death in the ruined potato fields of Kilkenny, Kerry, Cork, and Roscommon, Mr. Wood and Mr. Trevelyan saw the restless hand of God at work. The "blight has precipitated things with a wonderful impetus so as to bring them to an early head," declared Mr. Wood. "Supreme Wisdom had educed permanent good out of transient evil," agreed Mr. Trevelyan.

To fend off critics like Lord Monteagle, who believed that the government had a responsibility to keep society together, and Nassau Senior, an influential economist who believed the government should treat the blight as it would a foreign invader, Mr. Wood and Mr. Trevelyan began to cultivate the London press. Religiosity was an uncommon virtue on Fleet Street. Nonetheless, many editors and journalists were troubled by the cost of relief, the attacks on Board of Works officers, and the character of the Irish people. And nowhere was the concern more pronounced than in Printing House Square, home of the London *Times*. In 1846, *The Times* came closest to fulfilling the boast of its rival, *The Daily News*, that "newspapers were the intellectual life of the 19th century." Read by nearly everyone who mattered, the most prestigious paper in the English-speaking world had new, steam-driven presses, a circulation of over fifty thousand on very busy news days, a cadre of professional journalists divided into subspecialties such as parliamentary reporting, and an aggressive young editor in chief, Mr. John Delane, who was eager to make a name for himself.

Over the autumn, a symbiotic relationship developed between Treasury and *The Times*. Officials would leak documents on relief operations to the paper, and the paper would reflect the Moralist perspective in its coverage of the Irish crisis. *The Times* ran dozens of editorials on the perils of Irish dependency—"There are times when something like harshness is the greatest humanity," began one particularly memorable example. Delane also supported the Irish modernization project. "An island, a social state, a race is to be changed. The surface of the land, its divisions, its culture . . . its law, its language and the heart of the people . . . are all to be created anew," the paper declared in another memorable piece. *The Times* also continued to enjoy the services of its irrepressible commissioner, Mr. Thomas Campbell Foster, who this season was in Scotland reporting on the Highlands crop failure. Every week or so, Mr. Foster would write a profile of a Highlands community organizing and funding its own relief. After reading one of his paeans to Scottish pluck, many *Times* readers must have put down the paper wondering, What's the matter with the Irish?

The Economist, which like its chief proprietor, Mr. James Wilson, believed "It is no man's business to provide for another," was already an enthusiastic advocate of Irish self-help. For "the government to supply the people with work is just as injurious as . . . to supply them with food," declared the paper in August. A few weeks later, the editors summoned up the high gods of political economy to attack even the minimalist Russell relief policies. The Whigs, the paper declared, are "forgetting all . . . the mischievous errors that prevailed before [Adam] Smith wrote and Malthus lived." They follow "the creed that it is good for the Government to try to feed and employ the people."

The paper also kept a sharp eye out for relief officials whose behavior suggested a secret sympathy for statism. A year ago, Mr. Hewetson had been an obscure half-pay officer living quietly in Southampton. If he had ever had any economic thoughts, unlikely in itself, he kept them to himself. Then, one morning in September 1846, he awoke to find himself branded an enemy of capitalism. The charge grew out of *The Economist*'s review of the recently published government blue books, a compilation of relief correspondence during the 1845–1846 scarcity. "The first letter" in the blue books, the paper declared, "is from a half-pay officer, Commissary General Hewetson, dated November 5 [1845] to Sir R. Peel recommending the *prompt and secret* purchase of Indian corn. . . . It remains to be added that the suggestive Hewetson was naturally rewarded by being placed on full pay and employed in Ireland to carry his own plan into execution. He is a theoretical political economist, who has formed his opinions of society from government . . . [and who] . . . sets deliberately about regulating market prices."

Punch also needed little encouragement from Treasury. The *Punch* Irishman was either at the Englishman's feet or at his throat and not infrequently in both places at once, while also picking the Englishman's pocket. One much-reprinted cartoon had a menacing character labeled "Young Ireland" selling arms to a peasant under the caption, "Young Ireland in business for himself." Images of dangerous "Paddy" had a powerful effect on British public opinion, especially after the assaults on the Board of Works officers began. In the early autumn of 1846, the Earl of Shaftesbury, an Irish sympathizer, wrote in his diary, "Give orders that no more potatoes should be bought for the house. We must not, by competing in the market, raise the cost on the poor man." By December, several months of sensational headlines about Irish violence had turned the earl's sympathy to anger. "We expend money for their maintenance at a rate of £127,000 a week; and the starving peasantry can save from this effort of money and munificence enough to purchase arms to a greater extent than was ever known before for the assault and overthrow of their benefactors."

An unflattering caricature of the Irish,
from Punch, *1848*

As more and more was heard about attacks on board officers, less and less was heard about the Bessborough proposal, now called the Labouchere Letter in honor of Irish Chief Secretary Henry Labouchere, who had drafted the drainage amendment. In the months after the cabinet approved the amendment, Treasury quietly placed so many restrictions on drainage loans that hardly anyone bothered to apply. Bessborough's attempt to supplement the public works program with an extensive network of private employment failed. Drainage projects produced only 27,000 jobs.

The crowning irony of the autumn, however, was the immense popularity of the government public works loans repayable under the labor rate. After the rate had been denounced from one end of Ireland to the other, the first month the loans were put on offer, applications totaled over £1.5 million. Having pledged to "do or die" to avoid "ruinous taxation," the landowners of Mayo chose to do. They applied for over £400,000 in loans; County Cork, £600,000. British officials were perplexed. Why was the gentry piling up such an enormous debt? Colonel Jones, who knew Ireland better than most Englishmen, believed the paradox was no paradox at all. "People do not expect to have to pay back the money," he told Trevelyan.

CHAPTER NINE

A Sermon for Ireland

In 1846, Killorglin, a Kerry river town to the south of Dingle Bay, had 163 homes and 863 souls, most of whom spoke a Gaelic-flavored dialect called home English. To the extent that Killorglin was famous for anything, it was famous for the Puck festival—the only goat festival in southwest Ireland—and poverty. Including the local bridge, the hotel, and the new Church of Ireland chapel, the valuation of the town was a little over £2,500, a small sum even for a west of Ireland town. Beyond Killorglin, a single track of unshaded road carried local exports—salmon and corn—eastward, to Dublin and Cork, and tourists southward through a landscape of stream, hollow, and bog, to a small mountain range reputedly inhabited by a race of shepherd scholars who spoke Latin as well as a priest.

Near Dingle Bay, the road passed a small lake, a hill, a ridge, and, below the ridge, a potato field. One morning in early autumn, the families on the ridge were surprised to see a top-hatted stranger doing a walkabout among their ruined potatoes. After marching a quarter or halfway down a row of wilted stalks, the stranger would stop, bend over, pull a stunted potato from the earth, and roll it around in his hand like a jeweler examining a precious stone. Anyone with an eye for such things could tell the stranger was an Englishman—who else would wear a top hat in a potato field?—and, from the way he held himself, probably a military man in mufti. After examining the last row of stalks, the stranger scaled the ridgeline. The cabins on top were "class four" dwellings, the type that Irish census takers designated the crudest form of human habitat—a mud-walled, thatch-roofed, single-room cabin; typically such cabins were furnished with a stool, straw bedding, and a pot for cooking and bathing, and heated by a turf fire, burning between four scorched stones.

Inside the first cabin, the stranger introduced himself as Mr. William Hewetson and said he would like to ask some questions. How many potatoes had the family salvaged from the crop failure? How many did they have left? Mr. Hewetson was making a personal assessment of the food supply in southwest Ireland, which was now under his command, and had stopped in Killorglin to check the local food supply. The previous summer, after the Lee Mills had closed and milling operations were transferred to the private trade, Mr. Hewetson had been made director of the big government depot in Limerick, replacing Mr. Pine Coffin, who was ordered to Scotland to oversee Highland relief. Arriving in Limerick a few weeks later, the new director found the government depot empty, except for the meal he had transferred from the Lee facility, and most of western Ireland in or about to fall into famine. From Clare, there were reports of country people selling their clothing for provisions; from Galway city, of crowds gathering outside bake shops to "watch the batches of bread coming out of the ovens, and almost kill[ing] each other for it." Killorglin appeared to be better provisioned than Galway, though not dramatically so. In four to six weeks, the final extremity (starvation and death) gathering in the fields would be ready to make an assault on the ridge line. Several of the families on the ridge said they expected their potatoes to run out by the end of October, and it was now the end of September.

A few days later, the temperature fell, the autumn rains began, and the mood of the country darkened visibly. The initial shock of the crop failure had worn off, and people were beginning to think about what lay ahead. In Limerick, Lord Monteagle predicted "dearth," then "a battlefield." In Ulster, the Belfast Vindicator raised the specter of universal famine. No one would escape the effects of what was coming, the paper warned.

The cry is heard in every corner of the island. It startles and appalls the merchant at his desk, the landlord in his office, the scholar in his study, the lawyer in his stall, the minister in his council room, and the priest at the altar.

"Give us food or we will perish!"

In Dublin, Colonel Jones told a colleague, "There is an undefined notion that something terrible is about to take place. Men's minds are in a very unsettled state."

⨯

In London, there was also deep concern. Toward the end of summer, Routh had warned Trevelyan that he would need 16,000 tons of Indian corn to stock the depots in the west, and half that amount, 8,000 tons, by Christmas. Then, in September, Routh had asked for an additional 25,000 tons. When the *Vindicator* published the "Give us food" editorial, on October 3, there were 3,100 tons of corn in the depots, and almost no unbought food left in the world. The Port of New York had only 50,000 bushels of Indian corn; the Port of New Orleans "not more than three cargoes." The Mediterranean markets were nearly empty as well. Except for 3,000 quarters, the 1846 Egyptian wheat crop had been bought out, and in Malta, an important entrepôt, speculators had cornered the grain market. In mid-October, when Trevelyan boasted of sending 100 tons of meal to the Westport depot in Mayo, Routh lost his temper. "You speak of 100 tons for Westport. There ought to be 1000 tons."

In November, the *Satronizza* out of Venice was scheduled to deliver 800 quarters of corn (roughly 200 tons) to the depot in County Sligo; and the *Pigeon*, a Corfu vessel, 750 quarters to Westport. Provisions were also en route from Marseilles and Genoa, but what was coming was only the smallest fraction of what was needed.

To safeguard the small government food reserve, Treasury announced that the depots in the west—kept open by public pressure—would close until after Christmas. That left only commercial food available, and with no government corn to act as a counter, food was selling at famine prices or close to them in many parts of the country. "We foresaw this. . . . [W]e admonished the government, we again forewarn [them] that no pledge to merchants . . . no maxims of political economy should deter [officials] from satisfying the people's hunger," declared the *Cork Southern Reporter.* By late October, a pound of meal that had sold for a penny in the spring cost between 1½ to 1¾ pence, and a stone of meal that had sold for a shilling cost 2½ shillings (30 pence). In the mercantile houses of Cork, the river of gold grew deeper and broader. "£40,000 to £80,000 [is] spoken of as having been made by merchants" in the city, Mr. Hewetson reported in December.

Believing even a prudent Cork man could not lose money in a market where prices were rising 50 to 60 percent, Mr. Robert Hall of R & H Hall finally placed an order for a hundred tons of maize with an agent in Calcutta. Mr. Russell, the enterprising Scottish émigré, was well ahead of the prudent Cork men. In late October, the mills of G. W. & J. N. Russell, "the great corn factors" of Limerick, were grinding 500 tons of corn per week, and selling the meal, which had cost £15 a ton in September, for £17 a ton into some of the poorest districts in Clare and Kerry. Perhaps owing to the influence of Mr. Trevelyan, who believed high prices a useful tool for rationing food, as well as a lure to Ohio farmers, Routh had become just as ruthless about the cost of food prices. In October, he told a delegation from Achill Island in Mayo: "It is essential to the success of commerce that the mercantile interest should not be interfered with."

Father Malachy Monahan, the priest on Achill, asked why the new regard for the private trade. Last season the government had sold corn at cost.

That was a "bad decision," and had produced "bad habits" in the Irish people, Routh declared. This season the government would observe the "enlightened principles of political economy." Was Father Monahan familiar with the works of his "illustrious countryman," Mr. Burke?

Monahan was incredulous. The people of Achill Island were going to die if food prices did not fall. What had political economy to do with that?

A few days after the interview, the *Clare Journal* denounced Routh as that "pert official" who "puffs on perfumed cigars" and amuses himself "teaching a starving people the novelties of philosophy." The paper also called the government's free-trade policy in food "insane."

In early October, the depots in the west, some still open and distributing supplies, received a second shutdown order. "Cease supplies! You can do it," a Dublin official wrote in a note of encouragement. Mr. Wood, director of the small subdepot on Achill, protested the order. He could not close his doors, not on Achill, not without people dying. Wood received permission to issue provisions in instances where food was "absolutely necessary to the preservation of human life." Mr. Dobree, director of the big depot in Sligo, also resisted the order. On October 12 he told Mr. Trevelyan that there were thousands of people "whose potatoes are quite gone, who have grown no oats, who have no work, and that for this description of person, I must on occasion issue relief." Two weeks later, when another shutdown order arrived, Mr. Dobree again protested. Closing the Sligo depot would leave the local people at the mercy of the private trade, and in this part of the country, Dobree said, the private trade had "hitherto [been] exclusively confined to *exportation*. . . ." Local traders were "quite unprepared . . . to reverse their business with the rapidity which the emergency demands." However, Mr. Lister, director of the depot in Westport, embraced the shutdown order. "We are not prepared to open our depots," and would state this "in the most strong and unequivocal language." Fearing a "fury" if the depot closed, Lord Sligo protested to Dublin. The protest was ignored. Routh was again laboring under the delusion that the cabins of the peasantry were stocked with secret caches of food, which would be consumed if the depots were closed.

The government was more sensitive to the concerns of the private trade. On October 18, relief committees throughout western Ireland received a reminder that committee prices had to be kept high enough to "enable traders selling at the same rates to realize their profits." Mr. Lister was again enthusiastic. "It obviously would be extremely prejudicial to owners of grain, inasmuch as at present extraordinary prices can be realized."

In Skibbereen, where a public works laborer named Denis McKennedy dropped dead on a road crew, a thousand men marched "ten abreast" through the town to protest the closing of the North Street depot. Bugles blared, whistles blew, half-dressed soldiers swarmed out of the local military barracks; a detachment of Constabulary officers took up positions near the town square. One frightened resident described the marching laborers as "very alarming and imposing [in] appearance." Only intervention by a local officials prevented a sacking at North Street and the plunder of local food shops. In Galway, where the depots were also closed, a starving crowd stole a heifer, killed the animal, and left nothing behind on the road but the "hide and part of the fat."

As October progressed, signs of famine began to appear in eastern Ireland. Faces grew narrow, eyes bulged; the dry, musty odor of starvation permeated coach stops and clung to glens and hollows until the rain washed it away. Measured by food imports, the experiment in free trade was working: imports were rising in the east. Measured by food prices and human suffering, the policy was failing. With speculation and hoarding rampant in Cork, the price of wheat, oatmeal, and flour rose 50 percent in a single week. Be patient, government officials counseled the municipal authorities. High prices attract foreign provisions. In the spring, all the corn of the Ukraine, the United States, and Egypt will flow into Ireland, and prices will drop dramatically. What about November? officials in Cork, Dublin, and Waterford asked. Between October 8 and October 10, sixteen districts in eastern Ireland applied for a government food depot. Between October 12 and October 14, depot applications rose to seventeen. The magistrates of Cork city said the price of commercial food was so high, even the employed were starving. Cork's request for a depot was denied. Officials in Youghal, the export center in northern Cork, had a powerful case to make for a depot. During the export riots in September, food shops were sacked, warehouses burnt, merchants intimidated, soldiers dragged from horses and thrashed. Mr. Johns, a local relief official, told Routh that "food fit for immediate use *must* be forwarded . . . instantly . . . *if human life is not to be sacrificed* under the most fearful circumstances, probably both *by famine and sword*." Invoking the pledge Her Majesty's government had made not to interfere in "the Provision Trade in the Eastern Division of Ireland," Routh told Johns no. Youghal would have to make do without a depot.

By late October, the market towns of Ireland were crowded with men and women of "the most wretched and squalid" description. Attacks on food convoys had become routine. Exhaustion, malnutrition, rain, and unseasonable cold were thinning out the public works gangs, and thousands of families had resolved to board themselves in their cabins and die together when the potatoes ran out. Life was becoming elemental. In Mayo, a flock of crows and a local family, the Kellys, fought over possession of a week-old horse carcass.

Toward the end of October, the last of the domestic grain crop—12,000 barrels of oats—sailed out of Cork harbor on a British merchantman.

⚶

One morning a few weeks later, Mr. Trevelyan, now director of Scottish as well as Irish relief, kissed his family good-bye and vanished into a waiting carriage, suitcase in hand. "I am so pressed to provide for several million people in Ireland and Scotland," he told an acquaintance, "I have left my family . . . & am living in Lodgings that I may work early and late."

Of Trevelyan's two commands, Ireland was in more urgent need of attention. The relief plan was clearly failing—but why?

Mr. Nicholas Cummins, a prominent Cork magistrate, had an important insight into that question. In a letter to Trevelyan, Cummins said that most of the imperfections in the plan arose from a central flaw: the plan presupposed conditions that existed only in a nation with a modern economy and a modern infrastructure, and, except for the regions around Belfast and Dublin, Ireland was one of the most backward countries in Europe. Unlike Britain and France, she had no significant class of rural shopkeepers to distribute food in the interior; and the relief committee system was an imperfect substitute, particularly in remote regions of the west and midlands, where local gentry was lacking to organize a committee and the nearest source of commercial food might be twenty or thirty miles away. The Irish economy was also too small to efficiently regulate food prices through market competition, as the British economy did; and the deficiency of domestic mills meant that, in a time of acute food shortages, relief provisions had to be ground in England or sent 1,300 miles away, to the mills at the big British naval base in Malta.

As the famine worsened, Mr. Trevelyan decided to make several changes in the relief plan. A flotilla of depot ships was stationed in Clew

Bay (in Mayo) and in Sligo to act as a kind of rapid response force. When a remote region fell into starvation, the vessels would rush in an emergency supply of provisions. Steps were also taken to increase the food supply. Under a new "buy afloat" policy, British officials were permitted to purchase cargoes on the high seas, and commissariat officers at the large British naval base in Malta were ordered to scour the Mediterranean basin for corn and barley. Plans were also drawn up to import yams from the Caribbean and rye from Germany. Captain Larcom, a public works commissioner, urged Trevelyan not to "overlook the [Irish] crop of *grass*." It has been "enormous this year."

Few of the schemes turned out to have any practical merit.

The waters of Clew Bay and Sligo harbor were too shallow to accommodate depot ships, and the small delivery vessels attached to the ships often found the treacherous inlets and beaches along the west coast unnavigable. "I never saw anything like" it, a relief officer said, after witnessing one failed attempt to deliver provisions. When the supply ship first appeared, people ran "from house to house with the news [and] numbers went off immediately to purchase the meal." Soon a crowd of hundreds had gathered on the shore, waving and shouting, but a turbulent sea forced the ship to retreat, and the people "returned to their children with empty bags" and in tears.

The plan to purchase food in Malta also failed. Local speculators "had recently . . . bought up" most of the grain on the island "at a high price evidently for Ireland." Captain Larcom's plan to use the grass crop came to naught as well, as did the proposal to import yams. On reflection, London concluded that yams, a tropical vegetable, would not stand up to the cool, wet Irish climate. The rye proposal was pursued with considerable vigor, though little success. The Germans, facing scarcity and food riots, wanted to keep their rye at home. They would only release 765 quarters—less than 200 tons—for export to Ireland.

Trevelyan did have some success establishing a milling operation. Still, even with three large Admiralty mills and two private mills in England and several mills in Malta, he was unable to keep up with demand. In November, with the famine daily gathering strength, hundreds of tons of unground corn sat in warehouses in Ireland, England, and Malta, for want of milling power. Mr. Hewetson had an idea. Why not just dis-

A relief ship in the West of Ireland

pense with milling? A colleague of his, Captain Perceval, had created a recipe for unground corn that was wonderful in all ways except one. Corn à la Perceval "[had to] be steeped for 12 hours in cold water and well boiled [for] three and a half hours the next morning." That was 15½ hours, roughly as long as the first day of fighting at Waterloo.

Mr. Trevelyan had a better idea: hand mills. With a hand mill, the Irish peasant could grind his own corn. Mr. Trevelyan wrote to Mr. Byham, at the Board of Ordnance: Did Ordnance have a "plantation mill"? Popular in the American South, plantation mills were reputed to be quite sturdy. Next, Mr. Trevelyan wrote to Mr. Traill, a Scottish official: "Could you send to me at the Treasury a hand mill of the simplest form in use in the Shetland Islands?" A third letter went out to Mr. Melvill, director of India House: "If there happens to be a common Indian hand mill in the museum at the India House or anywhere else in your reach, I shall be much obliged to you to send it to me." A few weeks later, a subordinate of Mr. Byham's at Ordnance sent Trevelyan a coffee grinder, and a subordinate of Mr. Traill's sent a hand mill so primitive, it was "now out of use."

India House sent an Indian mill. Meanwhile, Trevelyan acquired a fourth hand mill, from Lord Monteagle. Of Irish design, this mill had "two horizontal stones working on each other, with a little hollow on the surface of one; a little hole or hopper in the middle."

One day Mr. Trevelyan looked at the Irish mill, the Scottish mill, the Indian mill, and the coffee grinder—and had an inspiration. "By putting all [the mills] into the hands of skillful workmen," he declared, "I hope to produce something that may be of service." What began as a suggestion in a Treasury minute now became an odyssey that led through France, Ipswich, and the workshops of the Royal Engineers, ending in Kilkee, County Clare, where a relief officer named Mann established a manufactory that produced reasonably efficient mills, though at an unaffordable price: 15 shillings. Charitable donations were solicited to buy Kilkee mills for the poor.

Trevelyan also made one other important change in the relief plan. He suspended the Scotland-first policy, which gave the Highlands preference on relief provisions. Except for the fact that the Scots were viewed as the "good" Celts—unlikely to attack relief officers or demand government assistance—there was little to justify the preference. Six hundred thousand people were at risk of starvation in the Highlands, four to five million in Ireland. Moreover, the diverse Scottish economy was better equipped to cope with a famine threat. Having lost most of her industry, Ireland had little employment to offer when the agricultural system collapsed, except public works. A Highlander in need of food money could migrate to the Scottish Lowlands and find work in one of the new textile factories.

Routh was greatly relieved to hear that the Scottish preference had been suspended. "I tremble when I think how many depots we have to fill," he told Trevelyan.

❧

On November 20, 1846, *The Times* reported that eight merchantmen had arrived in the Port of Cork since the previous Saturday:

> The *Narcisse* from Bordeaux (Maize)
> The *Neptune* from Alexandria (Beans)

The *Wanderer* from Marseilles (Maize)
The *Royal William* also from Marseilles (Maize)
The *Science* from Smyrna (Maize)
The *Foxhound* from Malta (Wheat)
The *Iris* from Venice (Maize)
The *John Anderson* from New York (Maize)

Eight merchantmen in four days! Jubilant, *The Times* proclaimed that free trade had saved Ireland. "The constant arrival of . . . grain . . . [is] daily reducing prices; within the last ten days, Indian corn had fallen . . . from £15 to £13 per ton in Cork City. Everything betokens a winter of abundance." Ten days later the "winter of abundance" ended and the price of cornmeal rose to almost £17 per ton in Cork. In early December, the Constabulary barracks in the city was surrounded by a large crowd shouting, "Work! Food!" One protestor, naked from the waist up, had pawned his shirt for food money earlier in the day. Near him another man was crying, "We are dying and starving; we have been dying."

In Skibbereen, half the children admitted to the local workhouse since October 1 were dead or fated to die. In Galway, a public works laborer named Thomas Mollone dropped dead on his way home from a road site. In Waterford, a young pregnant woman named Mary Byrne collapsed and died. Inquiries revealed that Mrs. Byrne's shoemaker husband had recently deserted her. In Kerry, a traveler came across the bodies of a father and three young children, neatly laid out by the side of a road. Death was growing more squalid, as well as more common: "a dying man . . . [in] a naked room," surrounded by "miserable children . . . and a poor [wife] . . . striving to suppress [her] agony." In Ballina, Galway, those were the circumstances in which the poor died, according to Mr. Francis Kincaid, a member of the local relief committee.

Toward December, the Irish landscape began to acquire the wild, feral look of a bloodlands. Bands of armed men, "wolf like" in appearance, roamed the roads, begging, looting, intimidating, and killing. "Every man has a gun, blunderbuss or pistol . . . [and] people do not disguise their firearms. . . . They walk about with them in the noonday," noted the *Tipperary Constitution*. In Mayo, gangs of itinerant peasants drifted through the wet autumn meadows, slaughtering cattle. "Many a man's heifer and bullock has been driven . . . from remote places and slaughtered in the night by . . . miscreants." To the south, in the Cork town of Kinsale, a crowd of four hundred, "not having tasted food all day," pillaged the local bake shops. In King's County (now County Offaly), sheep were slaughtered. From Limerick came reports of masses of "perfectly unmanageable" people arming themselves with "spades and pick axes"; from County Westmeath, of "half clad wretches howling at the door for food"; and from Galway, of parties of "starving and famished wretches" assaulting food convoys. In Clare, where public works violence now bordered on the insurrectionary, laborers at a hill cutting hurled several tons of earth and rock down on a passing food convoy, killing two horses and burying the drivers under piles of wet dirt and rock.

In Waterford, the peasantry turned on the large farmers. In the middle of the night, dozens of the eighty- and hundred-acre men, who had rented out potato ground in the spring, awoke to the loud *boom! boom!* of fists pounding on the door. Two or three masked figures would burst into the house waving pistols, pin the farmer to the floor, and demand a rent refund. Why should a man pay for potato ground that produced only dead potatoes? The rhetoric emanating from certain segments of the Catholic clergy, usually a force for restraint, also was becoming incendiary. "If my poor people be doomed to die of starvation as in all appearance they are," declared Thomas Hardiman, a Galway priest, "it is because [of] our rulers. . . . [They] believe our destitution imaginary [and] our hunger merely hypochondriacal—caused by our native indolence." A hundred more clerics like Hardiman, and the entire British army would be required to maintain public order.

In late autumn, a report issued by the Central Committee of the Irish Quakers, a small but influential community, warned that the Irish economy was collapsing under the weight of the famine. "The small shopkeepers . . . [lose] their trade. The business of the wholesale dealer and merchant [is] diminished. The various branches of manufactures [feel] the want of demand; many of the work people [are] discharged. Few houses [are] repaired or built, and masons, carpenters and other tradesmen connected with building [are] left unemployed. The demand for clothes . . . decrease[s]. Tailors, shoemakers, and other tradesmen of this class accordingly suffer."

In the countryside, the economic collapse was particularly visible. Traditionally, in November, the spring crops were laid down, but during a mid-month tour of the countryside around Skibbereen, Mr. Hughes, director of the North Street depot, passed one deserted field after another. "All is blank," he told Routh. A few weeks later, Colonel Douglas, a British army officer attached to the Board of Works, reported that bank deposits, which usually fell in the autumn as large farmers and landowners withdrew money to fund agricultural operations, had doubled in late November. The implications were obvious. Not only were landowners not creating special employment schemes for the poor; they were abandoning ordinary employment projects, like sowing. Instead of doing what English gentlemen do in periods of scarcity, Irish gentlemen—at least, some Irish gentlemen—were putting their money in the bank. "It is useless to ask what the landlords are doing," said one Irish paper in disgust.

The reluctance of the landed classes to give employment greatly increased the burden on the Board of Works. Except for a brief period in August, the previous summer the board workforce had ranged from 70,000 to 100,000. Toward the end of November, the public works rolls swelled to 284,000—almost a twelvefold increase since September 30; by the end of December, the rolls stood at 441,000, a remarkable though inadequate accomplishment. "Work!—there are tens of thousands of human beings asking vainly for work," declared the *Cork Southern Reporter*. In parts of Galway, two thirds of public works applicants had to be turned away for want of things to build; in parts of Tipperary, the turnaways ran as high as 75 percent. In November, in Mayo, where 400,000 people were destitute, only 13,000 were on the county public works rolls. Daily, the crowds of unemployed, surging through Irish towns and villages, grew larger, and daily the atmosphere in the presentment session became more dangerous. "I have attended meetings [for] the last three days," wrote one proprietor. "At one, I thought we should be impaled by pickaxes. . . . The people fancy that they must have food and work." Leaving a presentment session at a courthouse in northern Cork, Baron Stuart de Decies, a local landowner, was set upon by a howling mob. "For God's sakes man," de Decies shouted to his coachman as he leapt into his carriage, "get away from here." A few days later, de Decies issued a public statement on the attack: "In the first place, it is not true that any tenants of mine . . . were guilty of taking part in the disturbances which occurred upon the occasion in question. . . . In the next place, it is very unlikely that any expressions of a violent character should have been directed against me on account . . . of my subscription being limited to £5, as it is well known that I have contributed in no such niggardly fashion to the relief funds of the district."

"The landlords are frightened," Colonel Jones told Trevelyan.

⚒

Jones was right about the landlords, but wrong about another important issue as he had claimed in an earlier memo to Trevelyan. The "boys," as he called public works laborers, were not being overpaid. By late autumn, high food prices, bad weather—on rain and snow days, workers received half pay—and the new piece-rate system had seriously eroded the value of the public works wage. Between October 1846 and June 1847, the average daily wage for public works was 7¼ pence, barely half the shilling a day that the board had promised the average laborer. Moreover, piece-rate wages were often not paid promptly. On December 1, under the headline "More Deaths from Starvation in Skibbereen," the *Cork Southern Reporter* carried a story about the death of three local laborers who had gone unpaid "*for four consecutive weeks.*" To supplement family income, women and children joined the work gangs. It was "melancholy in the extreme to see the girls and women laboring," wrote an English traveler. "They [are] employed not only in digging with the spade and with the pick, but in carrying loads of earth and turf on their backs . . . and breaking stones like men." Younger children also became a familiar presence at work sites. While mothers, fathers, and older brothers and sisters dug fields and trenches, four- and five-year-olds would gather around a turf fire or, on wet days, under a wagon. "They were haggard with hunger . . . their sprightliness [is] entirely gone," remarked a relief official.

Deepening starvation and the approach of winter made the workhouses as agonizing as the Stations of the Cross. At the North Dublin facility, the occupancy rate rose from from 1,700 to 2,506; in Cork city, it more than doubled, from 2,000 to 4,400. "The miserable creatures, finding the door open, rush [in], the stronger trampling the weak," said one man. In Killaloe, County Clare, the number of those on the waiting list at the local workhouse rose to six thousand. At the Swinford workhouse, in Clare, "multitudes of men, women and children" daily came to the door to "solicit with prayers, just one meal of food." As wages fell in value, public works laborers were often forced to send their wives and children into the system. At the workhouse in Carrick-on-Shannon, a visitor saw "a most painful and heart rending" sight: a party of women, each with six or seven children, begging a workhouse official "that two or three of [the children from each family] might be taken in as their husbands were earning but 8 pence a day," not enough to support the entire family.

The hundred-thousand-bed system, built to rehabilitate the chronic pauper and to provide a temporary refuge for the displaced small farmer, collapsed under the weight of national disaster. "Children appear to be dying in the act of . . . extract[ing] sustenance from the dried-up breasts of parents," wrote a visitor, while "others more mature in years [are] propped up by some relative or acquaintance who [is] fast hastening to a similar state of weakness." After inspecting a workhouse in Enniskillen, County Fermanagh, a medical officer named George Nixon wrote, "The sewers were inadequate and flooded the laundry ward. . . . The interior of the workhouse was not whitewashed. . . . There was no ventilation. There [were] not enough clothes . . . meals were irregular and inadequate. [And] the overflowing cess pool was causing disease. . . . [The place resembled] the Black Hole of Calcutta."

Watching a work gang trench a field above a sea cliff in sleet and wind, Hugh Dorrain, a Donegal man, was visited by thoughts of genocide. "Here is where the government advisors dealt out the successful blow, and it would appear to be premeditated. Getting rid of the people . . . by forcing . . . hungry and half starved men to stand out in the cold and the sleet and rain from morn till night, for the paltry reward of nine pennies per day." Dorrain was half right: British relief policy was never deliberately genocidal, but its effects often were. Passing through southwest Cork in early December, one traveler could barely credit the things he saw: "Fever, dropsy, diarrhea and famine rioting in every filthy hovel and sweeping away families, . . . seventy-five tenants ejected here, and a whole village in the last stage of destitution there . . . dead bodies of children flung into holes hastily scratched in the earth without shroud or coffin—wives traveling ten miles to beg the charity of a coffin for a dead husband, and bearing it back that weary distance—a government official offering one tenth of a sufficient supply of food at famine prices—neither mill nor corn store within twenty miles—every field becoming a grave and the land a wilderness."

Believing the Irish crisis had reached a decisive point, Routh urged Trevelyan to reopen the government food depots immediately rather than wait until after Christmas. "There is no certain way of putting [violence and disorder] down" except by "placing food at given points for sale." "It would be a great object to hold out [until official opening day], . . . but I am anxious to have the means ready if the event rises, to issue at once, and I fear it will arise."

Trevelyan refused the request. England was in a scarcity, too; an early opening of the depots in western Ireland would threaten the English food supply at a time when no source of resupply was available. "My purchases are carried to the utmost point short of transferring the famine from Ireland to England," he told Routh. In "A Sermon for Ireland," *The Times* delivered a little homily on mutual suffering: "The Irishman is destitute [this season, but] so is the Scotchman and the Englishman. . . . It appears to us . . . that there is nothing so peculiar, so exceptional in the condition which the [Irish] look on as the pit of despair. . . . Why is that so terrible in Ireland, which in England does not create perplexity and hardly moves compassion?"

※

On December 7, 1846, in a speech in Dublin, Daniel O'Connell said publicly what he had been saying privately for months: London was not providing enough assistance. The speech was compelling. Like Winston Churchill, O'Connell was a conjurer whose words formed pictures that moved, inspired, and gave courage. By December, though, the denunciation was too little, too late. For most of the autumn, O'Connell had avoided criticizing the Russell government, and he had paid a price for his reticence. In October, protestors disrupted Repeal meetings in Dublin, Limerick, and Cork; in November, an influential prelate, Bishop Blake of Dromore, publicly condemned the Liberator's divisive purge of the Repeal

Association. "O'Connell's position in the country . . . [is] becoming untenable," declared Charles Gibson, a prominent Church of Ireland vicar.

A month after the Gibson warning, London rescinded its pledge to act as a supplier of last resort in the west of Ireland; henceforth, the government would agree to provision the region only "as far as we are able." The alliance with Russell and the Whigs had always been a riverboat gamble; now the gamble had been lost.

With O'Connell gone, the way opened for Young Ireland, but Young Ireland remained immobilized by its high-mindedness. Under the direction of William Smith O'Brien, the group had devoted September and October to promoting "the intellectual and moral discipline that best fits men for freedom"—a praiseworthy pursuit, no doubt, but not very good preparation for the season of mass death that lay ahead.

CHAPTER TEN

Snow

From deep within the Eurasian steppe a fierce autumn wind swept westward across the European archipelago. The Channel seas rose, and the sky over Ireland darkened.

On the morning of November 29, Elizabeth Smith looked out her bedroom window. Snow, lovely and silent, was fluttering softly down through the gray air. A week later, it was still snowing. In Donegal, the mountain roads became impassable. In Galway, waist-high drifts forced riders to dismount and walk their horses. During the final weeks of autumn, it snowed almost continuously. Snow fell down through the cold still world, covering the decapitated hills, the half-dug ditches and upturned earth, the emigrant-crowded Liverpool packets, and the tidelines and turnip fields, where shoeless, jacketless women and children searched for seaweed. It snowed on the five thousand paupers shivering in the doorways of Cork city; on "the half starved" country people in the streets of Thurles, in Tipperary. Snow covered the schoolhouse and military barracks in Skibbereen; the Board of Works pay office in Ennis, Clare; the Commissariat depots in Mayo and Sligo; and the uncoffined dead, who had come to their final end in the shadow of the cold mountains.

It was December now, and mass death was beginning.

One day not long after the snow commenced, Bridie Sheain came home and found her sixteen-year-old daughter dead. Bridie, who had already buried her husband and son, "got some water and washed [the girl] and dressed her up." Then, recalled an old storyteller, "Bridie went out to the garden where there was a little haycock and gathered enough hay to twist a rope. She put her dead daughter on her back, holding her up with the rope.

"Bridie . . . carried her load until she reached the chapel," the story-teller said, "but having reached it the poor woman couldn't make a hole. Eamon [Sheehy, a neighbor] saw her and came to her.

" 'It's a terrible story, Bridie,' he said.

" 'Christ's story was worse,' Bridie replied.

"Gregory Ashe [another neighbor] saw Bridie too and he came over and together they buried [the] daughter. Later, after the girl was laid out in a hole next to her father and brother, Bridie came and stood over the bodies. 'God bless . . . all of you,' " she said. " 'Nobody else will join you now. There is only me left and there will be nobody to look after me to bury me here or anywhere else.' [Then] she . . . made her way back home very slowly."

In September 1845, *The Gardener's Chronicle* had asked, "Where will Ireland be in the event of a universal potato rot?" The question now had an answer. In the event of a universal potato rot, there would be a great mortality in Ireland. In Waterford, a center of the coffin-making industry, on any given day a traveler might see a dozen or more country-women, each balancing an empty coffin on her head, walking toward the mountains off in the distance. Unable to keep up with demand for coffins, many workhouses were forced to bury their dead in reusable wooden boxes with fall-away bottoms. In areas where coffins were unavailable or unaffordable, burials were held at night to hide the shame of putting a family member into an uncoffined grave, or the departed were wrapped in cardboard boxes or old newspapers, secured with a piece of rope. "In this town," wrote one observer, "I have witnessed today men—fathers—carrying their only child; its remains enclosed in a few deal boards, patched together."

Funeral in Skibbereen, from Illustrated London News, *1847*

With no coffins for the dead and no mourners to mourn them, wakes and funerals disappeared. The Irish "have lost all those kindly sympathies . . . for the . . . departed which formerly characterized their natures," lamented the *Cork Southern Reporter*. Social breakdown, previously limited to the public sphere (marches, demonstrations, and the like) now began to penetrate the private sphere. "The wife's eye is stony and her lips without a quiver as she hears the death rattle in the throat of her gasping husband. . . . Every tie of blood and friendship . . . is extinguished," said a Cork man.

In Mayo, where people were selling their clothing to raise food money, December offered the novel spectacle of public nakedness. "Amongst the thousands I have met, I have not seen one who had . . . clothing corresponding to the bitter cold," wrote a Polish visitor. "[T]he emaciated, pale, shivering and worn out farm people [are] wrapt in the most wretched rags, standing or crawling in the snow barefoot." In Dublin, in the parish of St. Mary's, a correspondent for *The Freeman's Journal* found "whole families in a complete state of nakedness." Most of the pawned clothing ended up in England, where it was pulped in paper mills. The manifest of the *Erin* records a shipment of four tons of clothing. In Liverpool, an enterprising importer thought Irish hair would also fetch a good price. The manifest of the Liverpool-bound *Forget-Me-Not* records a shipment of twenty six "bales."

December also offered the novel spectacle of animal die-offs. On a cold winter's night, in the King's County hamlet of Philipstown, the residents were startled by a piercing, screeching sound. Toward dawn, the sound died away and the residents fell back to sleep. The next morning the town awoke to a crow mortality. There were dead birds in the fields, on rooftops, in outhouses and gutters. Upon examination, the crows "were found to have been reduced to skeletons and to have been actually starved to death." The hunger and hard weather were also killing domestic animals. "The mortality among the horses is becoming very alarming," Deputy Commissary General Dobree reported from County Sligo. "The pigs . . . have also ceased to exist and the poultry . . . have likewise disappeared. The dogs are dying fast and preying on one another."

In Dublin a few weeks before Christmas, two young Irishwomen sat in a cheerless, unheated room and calculated the days remaining to them. "We have been talking, Mary and I," one of the young women told an American visitor. "The furthest the good God will give us on this earth cannot be more than fourteen days."

"You are willing to live longer?" the American asked.

"We cannot see how," the young woman replied.

⋇

As the young women conversed with the American, the *Rhadamanthus* and the *Stromboli* were taking on corn in England, and H.M.S. *Shannon* was en route from Malta with a supply of provisions. By December 28, opening day for the depots, Routh would have most of the eight thousand tons he had requested in September, but eight thousand tons looked much smaller in December than it had in September. Last summer, in the midst of a moderate scarcity, the peasantry had consumed eight thousand tons of meal in two months. How long would that much last in a deep famine? Two weeks? Three? Then what? Delivery of the 1846 American corn crop was being delayed by a shipping shortage, and the international markets remained empty. On December 16, an agitated Routh reminded Trevelyan that "the principal point [is] food. . . . If we fail [to provide it], all our other success will count for nothing." He suggested sending British warships to America to transport the 1846 crop. Mr. Wood thought the idea preposterous. The prime minister proposed a less radical solution: waive the duty on foreign grain entering U.K. ports and suspend the Navigation Acts, which required that goods bound for Britain be carried in British ships. The measures were adopted, but had little effect. The famine deepened; the mortality increased.

"The people are starving," wrote a Board of Works officer in Clare. "I have stated this frequently but I consider it my duty to state it again and again." Among officials in Ireland, dissatisfaction with the government relief plan was growing. The plan, effective at imposing bans—on the sale of food below market prices; on outdoor relief—was much less effective at saving lives. Dissatisfaction bred rebellion. In Donegal, Lord George Hill, chairman of the relief committee in Gweedore, announced that his committee would no longer honor the market price rule. The merchants in Gweedore were demanding two pence a pound for meal. If his committee matched that price, food would become unaffordable, even to men on the local public works gangs who labored daily in open fields, in snow and sea wind. Relief committees in Cork and Kerry also ignored the rule, producing furious protests from local mercantile men. The workhouses were even more defiant. As early as September, many of the houses had begun providing proscribed forms of help: free meals to nonresidents, individual admissions—families were required to enter a workhouse together—and outdoor relief. In Cork city, the local workhouse served an outdoor breakfast to 1,440 people each morning; in Kilkenny, 2,000 people gathered daily in the courtyard of another workhouse to be fed.

Alarmed by the rampant infractions, the Poor Law commissioners, who oversaw the Irish workhouses, cajoled and threatened. When bullying failed, the commissioners got a court to declare the workhouse guardians in breach of the 1838 Irish Poor Law. When the guardians ignored the court order, the commissioners issued a public rebuke. "We . . . deem it our duty to point out to the Guardians the inevitable evils of endeavoring to give relief in a manner not sanctioned by the legislature." When the rebuke was ignored, the commissioners sat back and waited for the workhouses to go bankrupt. Between the hard weather, which interfered with the collection of the poor rate, and the overwhelming demand for relief, it did not take long.

By early December, many facilities were forced to curtail not just outdoor relief but basic services. Food and fuel bills went unpaid, local merchants cut off credit, sleeping galleys went unheated; daily meals were cut back from three, to two, to one; sanitation was ignored. In the fortnight before Christmas, the weekly death rate in the workhouse system approached 2,700 people, and unburied bodies piled up in workhouse corridors and courtyards for want of gravediggers and coffins. In the two months between November 5, 1846, and January 7, 1847, the morbidity and mortality rate at the Skibbereen workhouse was over 50 percent. In a facility built for 800 inmates, there were 266 fatalities and 332 cases of famine fever. The loci of the death and disease were the drafty, unheated stables that the guardians had converted into emergency dormitories. The stables were open to wind and cold; melted snow leaked through cracks in the roofs, causing puddling in the stalls, where thinly dressed inmates slept on beds of straw, fumed with horse manure and human excrement and urine. By New Year's Day so many inmates were dying, "there were scarcely as many able bodied paupers [in the workhouse] . . . as can bury the dead [who] are taken out for interment three at a time."

On December 21, Edward Twisleton, the resident Irish Poor Law commissioner, warned the Home Office that many workhouses were nearing financial collapse. Sir George Grey, the home secretary, wondered why. According to the newspapers, Irish bank deposits were still rising. Sir George hoped the workhouses were not going to throw themselves on London. If Irish ratepayers had enough money to put in the bank, they had enough money to fund their workhouses.

In mid-December, official disagreements over relief culminated in a conflict over Circular 38, a proposal that ignored both the spirit and letter of the official relief plan. It surprised Treasury, not at all, that Viceroy Bessborough was behind the circular. In Treasury's view, Bessborough represented a graver threat to "sound principle" than any number of wayward workhouse guardians and relief committees. "I am an Irishman," Bessborough had boasted upon arriving in Dublin Castle the previous summer. And so he was; but he was also an Englishman and a

Whig grandee whose sense of entitlement produced some egregious acts of insensitivity. In November, while public work sites across Clare erupted in violence, Bessborough and his current paramour, Mrs. Maberly, a romance novelist half his age, were at the viceroy's 27,000-acre estate in Kilkenny, and in December Bessborough refused to allow the appearance of mass death to disrupt the holiday season at Dublin Castle. In December 1846, the castle held the usual complement of Christmas balls and fêtes. Toward the end of a gossipy letter about the holiday season, the viceroy added in an offhanded sentence: "39 deaths [in Galway], people having been found dead in hovel & in the field." Still, Bessborough's boast, "I am an Irishman," was not entirely groundless. Believing that, in a famine, even the rules of political economy had to be bent to save lives, in September he had championed changes in the Labor Rate Act; now, in December, he was prepared to support Circular 38, knowing full well the measure violated every "sound principle" Treasury held dear.

Before next year's crops could be laid, the land had to be prepared, and with the peasantry fleeing to the public works program, the land was being ignored. Continued neglect would bring famine in 1847 even if the blight did not reappear. Bessborough believed that Circular 38, created by Richard Griffith, a public works commissioner, would entice public works laborers back to the land. Under the Griffith plan, each fortnight a man would be paid to drain a certain amount of his land. If the man finished the allotted amount of work early—say, in seven or eight days—his pay would continue, even if he spent the remainder of the fortnight cultivating his plot or working for a local farmer. Despite an energetic lobbying by Bessborough, Prime Minister Russell refused to have anything to do with Circular 38. How could he explain such a measure to the British farmer? Mr. Wood seemed more bemused than upset by the Circular. "Paying a man for the ordinary cultivation of his ground!" Who had ever heard of such a thing? It was an even more fantastical idea than sending the Royal Navy to America to transport the Yankee corn crop.

In December, with private employment schemes still scarce, the public works rolls swelled by 185,000, to 441,000. This should have terrified the landed classes. Through the labor rate, they were now funding an organization larger than most armies, but, like Mr. Micawber and Lucius

O'Brien, the lieutenant of Clare, the landowners believed something would turn up before the bill came due.

❈

On a cold late autumn afternoon in Mayo, an inquest was held into the death of James Byrne, a public works laborer who had collapsed a few days earlier on a road gang.

The first witness was Mary Byrne, the deceased's wife.

The judge asked Mrs. Byrne about the circumstances of her husband's death.

She either misunderstood the question or was preoccupied by a more recent incident. Yesterday, she told the judge, she had sold her coat for meal, and, except for the meal, the only food in her cabin was the turnips a local farmer had let her gather from his fields.

The judge gently brought Mrs. Byrne back to the subject. What were the circumstances of her husband's death?

"Jimmy," she said, would often tell her how good everything "would be if he had a bit of food or nourishment."

Did she have an opinion about the cause of his death?

Yes, Mrs. Byrne replied. To the best of her belief, her husband had "died for the want of food."

The next witness was the coroner, James Browne, Esq., M.D. Dr. Browne told the court that the only substance in the "deceased's body was a small quantity of thin feces in the lower portion of the large intestine." There was "no food in the stomach or the alimentary canal." Except for severe malnutrition, Dr. Browne said, Byrne had been a healthy young man.

Every day in December, 400,000 laborers awoke in the predawn darkness, walked three to seven miles to a Board of Works site, and labored in wind, sleet, and snow until nightfall. The most destitute workers—landless agricultural laborers who had thrown themselves on the public works program in September and October—often worked shoeless and coatless; the least destitute—small farmers forced off the land in November and early December by want and evictions—in thin outer garments. Many of the men had not eaten in the past twelve hours, many more not in twenty-four hours, some not in two or three days; and almost no one had consumed a meal larger than a handful of grain or a bowl of soup for a month or more. The healthy young men the Board of Works said could make 1 shilling, 4 pence to 1 shilling, 6 pence a day under the piece-rate system no longer existed. Some, like James Byrne, were dead; others too ill to work. A Churchtown, Cork, man wrote of a laborer: "a poor fellow name Courtney, [who] after a few days working on the public roads, badly fed and worse clothed, caught cold . . . and horrid to relate . . . was obliged in his pitiable state, to depend on . . . cabbage to support existence." The hard December weather, which turned ungloved hands the color of lobster claws and exacerbated the effects of fever, malnutrition, and exhaustion, broke many men. "One wretch drops his head with a convulsive shiver . . . ; he sinks lower, lower—the hammer drops from his hand,—he falls prostrate on the unbroken pile of stones . . . Raise him and bear him home!—his fate is certain." The Irish press lamented the terrible suffering of road crews. It "is horrible, it is cruel," declared one paper; but what choice did a man have? His family had to be fed, and a stone of meal now sold for as much as three shillings. So each morning, hundreds of thousands of laborers would wake in unheated cabins to the sound of the wind; march three or four miles on an empty stomach to a work site; force themselves to work through rain, sleet, malnutrition, fever, and exhaustion—and send their wives to the doctor to find out why they felt like they were dying.

"What ails him?" Dr. Donovan, director of the infirmary in Skibbereen, asked one woman.

"He has pains in his limb."

And your husband? Donovan asked the woman next to her.

"He won't keep anything in his stomach."

The husband of a third woman had "swelled up in his legs and arms and head."

Another wife told Donovan that her husband had gone "on the road every day . . . though he was getting worse . . . but today and yesterday, he can't, sir."

Under the weight of famine, low wages, and desperate working conditions, men grew angry and began to arm themselves. "Fire-Arms Mania," a Tipperary paper reported, noting that since early November 1,191 stands of arms had been purchased in the town of Clonmel alone.* "The sale of fire arms [has] become a first rate trade," observed the *Westmeath Guardian*. In Clare—"the most troubled, relief-hungry county" in Ireland—violence had become so pervasive, one Board of Works officer complained that many of his colleagues would rather resign than give an unpopular order to a work crew. The most turbulent part of the county was west Clare, a primordial region of "peat and moor, barren rocks, [and] black mountains," interrupted by a single sizable town, Ennis, which had twelve thousand residents, many illiterate Irish speakers, and "only two streets [that] rise above the rank of lanes." The coast to the west of Ennis was inhabited by a "vast army" of unemployed squatters. In the autumn of 1846, when Captain Edmond Wynne arrived in west Clare as a Board of Works inspecting officer, a good part of the population had given up all hope of survival and were waiting to die. "Such is the state [of the people's] alarm and despair that thousands never expect to see the harvest," Wynne wrote. A month later, the captain wondered whether he would be among the departed.

Under Treasury guidelines, public works employment was restricted to the absolutely destitute—to men who had no means of earning a wage and no possessions. After examining the records in the courthouse in Ennis, Wynne concluded that upward of ten thousand local public works laborers failed to meet the criteria. Some laborers held ten, fifteen, twenty acres, and had been put on the work rolls by a proprietor eager to insure that he received his rent. Others were the sons of prosperous farmers. Still others, though poor, were not quite poor enough to meet the official criteria for destitution. They owned a cow or two, or had a wife or a child on the work rolls. Wynne branded such laborers the "undeserving," and in November he announced that he would replace them with the "poor and starving who had been neglected because nobody had a direct interest in their welfare." In west Clare in December 1846, that was a brave thing to do—within the last few weeks, one board officer in the district had been assassinated and another attacked, but Wynne's sensitivity to injustice was overshadowed by a blindness to the moral ambiguities of

*A stand is a complete set of arms for one person: musket, cartridge box, bayonet, belt.

famine. Many of his "undeserving" were marginal farmers, men whose only assets were two or three acres of snow-covered ground or a cow that was more rib than cow. Without work, such men would die just as surely as a landless laborer. West Clare knew that, and hated Captain Wynne for his work roll culls. Even more, West Clare hated Wynne for turning his self-righteousness into a sacrament. Instead of quietly culling the work rolls in his office, Wynne would position himself in front of an audience at a public works meeting and read through the work rolls, name by name; when he came to the name of an "undeserving" he would shout, "Gone!" or words to that effect, and scratch a black line through the man's name; then, amid hoots and threats from the audience, he would proceed down the list to the next "undeserving." There would be another brusque "Gone!"—and more angry shouts and threats.

One evening, entering a meeting in Killane, Wynne saw a man "half starved and considerably more than half naked, [with a] bare head, bare legs, and arms." This will "bring color to their cheeks," he declared, as he grabbed the pauper and dragged him into the meeting to illustrate the unfairness of the employment system in the district.

"This officer is better suited to dealing out slugs and bullets on a battle field than work tickets," complained the *Clare Journal*. On December 4, during a meeting in Ennistymon, a small town north of Ennis, there was a bitter confrontation between Wynne and several members of the local gentry. One man, a small landowner, accused the captain of high-handedness, and autocratic behavior. Then the local priest stood up, waved a fist at Wynne, and said that the only thing that kept him from throwing the captain out of the hall "was the Roman collar around my neck." Leaving the meeting, Wynne had a troubling thought. The accusatory land-owners, the angry priest, the outraged shouts of the audience: "the sole purpose" of the meeting had been to "hold . . . us up . . . to the assassin."

The captain was right about the assassination, wrong about the intended victim.

Early the next evening, the fifth, one of Wynne's overseers, a man named Hennessy, was leaving a public works site near the village of Clare Abbey when an assassin leaped from a ditch and shot him pointblank in the thigh with a blunderbuss. There were three soldiers about twenty yards ahead of Hennessy, two behind him, and a pay clerk by his side.

None of them attempted to apprehend the assailant, who fled down the ditch in the direction of Clare Abbey. As Mr. Hennessy lay against a fence in "great agony and torture," the clerk walked over, bent down, and examined his wounds. "Boys, what have we done?" he shouted, then vanished with the soldiers. There was just Mr. Hennessy, the snow, the cold, and the three-quarters of a mile of road between himself and his home in Clare Abbey. By the time Hennessy staggered to his front door, the light was gone and a cold afternoon had become a bitter night. Nonetheless, as news of the shooting spread through the village, gaunt, gray figures as spectral as walking graves appeared on the snow-covered village lanes. Soon a crowd had gathered outside the overseer's home; from his bedroom, Mr. Hennessy could hear people "laughing, joking" and "signifying their complete approval of the outrage."

Two days later, on December 7, Captain Wynne ordered the public works project at Clare Abbey shut down until Hennessy's assailant was apprehended. Two and a half weeks before Christmas, nine hundred laborers and their families were deprived of their only access to food. Conditions in the village grew intolerable. Wynne became racked with guilt. Every starving figure became an accusation. "I ventured through the parish this day," he wrote to a colleague on Christmas Eve, "[and] . . . although a man not easily moved, I confess myself unmanned by the intensity and extent of the suffering I witnessed more especially among the women and little children, crowds of whom were to be seen scattered over the turnip fields like a flock of famished crows, devouring the raw turnips, mothers half naked shivering in the sleet and snow uttering exclamations of despair while their children were screaming in hunger."

In a famous scene from the *Heart of Darkness*, Joseph Conrad's novella about colonial Africa, Kurtz, a brutal ivory trader, who has inflicted great suffering on his black workers, lies on his death bed shouting "the horror! the horror!" The visit to the turnip field seems to have evoked a similar sense of remorse in Wynne. He ordered the Clare Abbey work site reopened and the labor force increased by 150.

※

On December 16, in a strongly worded letter, Henry Labouchere warned Downing Street that the relief plan was failing. "Decisive measures" were required. Lord John found it impossible to disagree. The mass death in the west and southwest was spreading to the peasantry in other parts of Ireland; now, with the "heavy weather" closing public work sites and disrupting food deliveries, and with prices still rising, the middle and lower middle classes, who had escaped serious hardship in the summer of 1846, were falling into destitution and starvation. A new relief scheme would have to be devised; in the meanwhile, Russell authorized a series of interim emergency measures.

The collapse in Ireland also affected British public opinion. Crop failure and scarcity were part of the normal cycle of nineteenth-century life, but what was happening across the Irish Sea was beyond living memory. Medievalists suggested a possible parallel in the Great Famine of 1314/15–1322, which claimed up to 10 percent of rural Europe. For a time, anti-Irish sentiment, a particularly robust strand of nineteenth-century British thought, subsided. *The Times* and *The Economist* stopped lecturing the Irish on sloth, violence, ignorance, superstition, personal hygiene, and dependence on government; there were fewer comparisons with the Eskimos and South Sea Islanders; the adjective "aboriginal" was used less frequently to modify the noun "Irish," as in the construction "aboriginal Irish"; Mr. Trevelyan stopped talking about "a bright light shining in the distance." Ireland was in the midst of a "stark, staring, downright, actual famine," he told Routh. The swell of sympathy produced a surge of charitable giving that far exceeded the £14,000 the Indian Relief Fund had raised in the spring, mostly from Irish soldiers and East India Company officials, and the £42,000 the Irish Relief Association had raised in September after the second crop failure. From the queen and the prime minister to the greengrocer in Bristol and the butcher in Birmingham, everyone became involved. "There were ladies' associations without end to collect small weekly subscriptions and make up clothes to send to Ireland. The opera, the fancy bazaar [also] rendered tribute," Mr. Trevelyan recalled later.

The Society of Friends compiled a particularly distinguished record during the crisis. On November 13, leaders of the three-thousand-member Irish society met in Dublin to form the Central Relief Committee. In an address to the meeting, Jonathan Pim, the co-chairman of the new committee, pledged that the CRC would devote itself to a single purpose:

saving lives. Everything else—"property rights," moral education, the sensitivity of the mercantile men, and the religion of the relief recipients—would be made subservient to that goal. "The people must be kept alive, whoever pays for it," said Pim.

A few weeks later, William Forster, an English Quaker, who had come to Ireland to assist his coreligionists, stood outside a workhouse in Carrick-on-Suir, Tipperary. The admission line was long—about a hundred people—and, except for height, it was hard to tell the adults from the children; the tight press of skin against bone gave eight- and nine-year-old faces the "look of premature old age." They are "dying like rotten sheep," a workhouse administrator said, nodding toward the line. At sixty-seven, Forster was old to be traveling across Ireland in the midst of the worst winter anyone could remember; still, his Quaker conscience and duty compelled. The CRC wanted to establish a network of soup kitchens, and Forster had operated soup kitchens in England. West of Tipperary, the weather grew harder, the sky lower, and the famine deeper. In the Donegal village of Stranorlar, Mr. Foster saw people so weakened by hunger they "were scarcely able to crawl"; in Dunfanaghy, a fishing village on the Donegal coast, more than half the population was "living on a single meal of cabbage." In a town of twisting lanes above an ice-covered sea cliff, he listened to a crowd of panicked country people howl "in despair on learning that not a single pound of meal . . . was available at any price." It did not require much foresight to know what was going to happen next.

Stepping out of the Dublin Mail coach on a brisk early winter morning several weeks later, Forster's, twenty-eight-year-old son, W. E. Forster, found the streets of Westport crowded with "gaunt wanderers sauntering to and fro with [a] hopeless air." In front of the hotel where young Forster and his father were to meet, "a crowd of beggars [cried out] for work." The next day, as a morning wind chased the last of the night clouds into the Atlantic, father and son traveled into the Mayo countryside to see what mass death looked like. In a small village where thirteen people had died in the past week, the lanes were silent except for the low moans coming from the doorless cabins and the crunch of boots on the frozen snow. The village animals had long since been slaughtered for food. Even the "dogs that used to bark . . . are gone," the younger

Forster wrote in his journal. Arriving in the Galway town of Clifden a few days later, the Forsters were told that the previous night an old woman seeking shelter against the winter night had crawled into an out-house and been eaten by a pack of dogs. "In two cases" in Clifden, the young Forster wrote, "my father . . . had applications for money not to keep people alive, but for coffins to bury them; . . . to those who know the almost superstitious reverence of the Irish peasant for funeral rites [this] tells a fearful story." In Cleggan, another Galway village, the young man was "surrounded by a mob of men and women [who looked] more like famished dogs than fellow creatures." Though the light had almost left the sky, the young Quaker resolved to tour the village. In one cabin he found "two emaciated men lying at full length on the damp floor in their ragged clothes"; in another, a dying young man whose "mother had pawned everything, even his shoes, to keep him alive. . . . I never shall forget the resigned uncomplaining tone with which he told me that all the medicine he wanted was food," Forster wrote.

In the south of Ireland, too, famine, death, and bitter cold were pro-ducing unimaginable sights. "I have never seen anything more frightful," said an English visitor to Cork city. "All [the] wealthier streets and places of resort [are] literally in the possession of the most squalid and wretched human beings. . . . These creatures wander restlessly up and down the [streets], now clustered in groups, now singly, besetting the entrance of every shop, surrounding every person . . . with clamorous importunities. Under gateways . . . miserable creatures . . . lay in extreme exhaustion. . . . Six persons died in the streets the night I passed through."

Magistrate Cummins, Trevelyan's correspondent, sent an urgent let-ter to London. "In the whole city and port of Cork there [are] only 4,000 tons of breadstuffs. Unless great amounts reach us from other quarters the prospects are appalling." A few days later, Routh also enclosed a warning with a request for supplies. Mr. Trevelyan became exasperated. What did Routh mean, "I am truly afraid of the result"? Didn't the man ever listen? In a sharp reply, he reminded Routh that "our purchases, as I have more than once informed you, have been raised to the utmost limit, short of raising prices on the London market."

Further south, in Skibbereen, Mr. Bishop, a local Commissariat officer, counted seventeen fatalities in the workhouse and half again that many dead in the back lanes, where packs of rats and dogs lived on human remains. The whole region "is but a theatre for famine, disease and death," declared *The Cork Examiner*. "One, two, three, four victims in one hovel. Old women turned into maniacs. . . . The hourly presence of death in every appalling shape has extinguished every human sympathy." The paper also noted the rise of a savage new type of pauper: "A knock is heard at a hall door. Who is it, some poor wretch seeking a morsel of bread? Open it. What!—a starving mother thrusting her dead child before her and begging, not for . . . bread, though she is gaunt and fleshless with famine and her eyeballs roll fearfully—but for a coffin."

Mr. R. B. Townsend, a Church of Ireland vicar, estimated that the death rate in the Skibbereen region was approaching ten thousand; the Reverend Mr. Fitzpatrick, the local Catholic priest, predicted a third of the population would be in their graves by April; and Dr. Donovan, the workhouse physician, warned that Skibbereen and all of Ireland stood "on the eve of a pestilence that will reach into every class."

By mid-December, when the Board of Guardians at the local workhouse met to discuss the crisis, Skibbereen was a national story in the

Queen Victoria on a visit to Ireland. *From* Illustrated London News, 1849

United Kingdom. As the meeting opened, Mr. James Barry, a member of the board, took note of the attention, solemnly observing that "the eyes of Ireland and England [are] on the movements of the board [this] day." After a round of "Hear! Hear!" the chairman of the board, Mr. Somerville, rose and introduced a proposal to create outdoor soup kitchens. Mr. Barry immediately objected. It was all well and good for a private individual like the Reverend Dr. Traill, a Church of Ireland vicar, to establish a soup kitchen. But soup kitchens were a form of outdoor relief, and as a public institution, the workhouse could not legally administer outdoor relief to the able-bodied poor.

Chairman Somerville thought there might be a way around the law: they could lend food to the poor. Would that be legal? Maybe, said Mr. Downing, another board member. But the food would have to be repaid. Under Section 55 of the Poor Law, "the guardians [were required to] recover the amount [of the loan] from the persons so liable."

Mr. Barry was unpersuaded. Section 55 did not authorize outdoor relief under any circumstances. Recently "the Cork Union Workhouse [had] given outdoor relief in the shape of breakfast . . . and the [Relief] Commissioners [had] restrained them from doing so."

The board voted to table the soup kitchen proposal for further study.

Trevelyan had recently called a Board of Works report on Skibbereen the "most awful" thing he had read; still for reasons of policy he was unwilling to alleviate the town's misery. Under Treasury guidelines, only a local relief committee could distribute government provisions, and, at present, Skibbereen lacked a relief committee. Given the wealth in the community, that was scandalous. The owner of the town, Sir William Wrixon-Becher, had an annual rental income of £10,000 (using the multiplier of 100 and the $4.80 value of the 1846 pound, that is the equivalent of almost $5 million a year today); and Stephen Townsend, a local Protestant clergyman, had an income of £8,000 per annum. Nonetheless, the fact remained that Skibbereen did not have a relief committee, and if an exception were made for Skibbereen, other towns and localities might demand exemptions. A run on the government food supply would result, and the government food supply was thin. On December 18, Trevelyan told Routh that "principles" must "be kept in view."

The eighteenth was a day of bad news for Routh. A new Board of

Works report blamed the mortality in Skibbereen on want of provisions—a clear attack on the Commissariat, Routh's service. "Food is not lacking" in Skibbereen, he told Trevelyan. "The money to buy it is." Technically, both assertions were correct. Many local families were starving because even men with work tickets were unable to find employment on Board of Works road gangs. There was also food in Skibbereen; there were provisions in the North Street depot and in the warehouses of Mr. Swanton, the local miller; at the local inns, a diner could still order many of the items on the menu. The defect in Routh's argument was access. For most of Skibbereen's residents, the local food supply might as well have been on Mars. The North Street depot was closed until after Christmas, and Swanton and the local inns were charging unaffordable prices. More than anything else, though, the situation in Skibbereen—and in hundreds of other starving Irish towns—arose from a failure of local responsibility. Together, the twelve leading proprietors in the Skibbereen region had an annual income of £50,000, almost £25 million in modern money. Two and a half centuries after Spenser first proposed a plantation of Ireland, the plant had not yet fully taken root. Many members of the Anglo-Irish gentry, and most British absentee owners, remained unwilling to assume responsibility for the well-being of the people they ruled.

❧

One morning a few days before Christmas, Mr. Cummins, the Cork magistrate, stood in a cabin in South Reen, a small village below Skibbereen. At his feet lay "six famished and ghastly skeletons, . . . their sole covering . . . a ragged horsecloth [from which] their wretched legs hung [out]." Suddenly, a "low moan" arose from the horsecloth. The skeletons were alive! Cummins lifted the cloth. Underneath, "four children, a woman and what had been a man" were lying together in a ball of sweaty flesh. All six had the fever. Leaving the cabin, Cummins felt someone tugging at his arm. A woman; and she was holding "an infant, just born . . . the sole covering of herself and the babe . . . [was] the remains [of the] filthy sack . . . across her loins." After Cummins departed for Skibbereen, the police opened another cabin in the lane. Inside, they found "two corpses . . . lying upon the mud floor, half devoured by rats." Later in the day, in another lane, "a mother, herself in fever, was seen dragging the corpse of a girl of about twelve" out of a cabin. The mother stopped in the middle of the lane and began to cover the girl's "perfectly naked" body with stones.

Arriving in Skibbereen, Cummins was told that Dr. Donovan, the workhouse physician, had just "found seven wretches lying unable to move, under the same dark cloak. One [man] had been dead many hours but the others were unable to move either themselves or the corpse."

⸗⸗⸗

Nine days after Mr. Cummins's visit to South Reen, it was Christmas Eve. In London, the day began like most days. Along the frigid Thames, cones of thin yellow light danced up and down in the gray river dawn. The light came from lanterns attached to the chests of the toshers, the top-hatted, velveteen-coated, staff-wielding scavengers who prowled the banks of the river for coins, copper, and anything else of value. Beyond the river, in the narrow holiday streets, the pure finders, who collected dog excrement, and the bone pickers, who scavenged the bones of all formerly living things, stamped their feet on the pavement against the Christmas cold. In windows, candles flared; at street corners, young children congregated in front of shops to admire the displays of holly sprigs; strolling carolers sang "God Rest Ye Merry, Gentlemen." In every corner of the imperial capital on this day before Christmas, joy and good cheer reigned—except at Treasury, where a new report had plunged Mr. Trevelyan into despair. Eastern Ireland, the free-trade zone, had fallen into such a perilous state, Routh believed a government intervention might be necessary. Trevelyan regarded such an action as out of the question. The government had promised the mercantile men a free hand in eastern Ireland, and Mr. Wood was "firmly resolved to allow no deviation from the decision." He told Routh, "We rely upon you to avoid even the appearance of a concession on this point."

Across town, in Printing House Square, *The Times*'s new steam presses had finished the day's print run. Within a few hours, the Christmas Eve edition would be in the hands of readers in metropolitan London; by late afternoon, readers in Manchester would have a copy, and within a day or two, so would readers in Glasgow and Aberdeen. Five or six weeks hence, the Christmas Eve edition would be in New York and Cape Town; and sometime in late March or early April, a battered copy of the day's paper would find its way to a hill station in India and make a sweltering, sun-burned subaltern sick with nostalgia for a damp, cold, overcast English Christmas.

As was the custom in the nineteenth century, advertisements blanketed the front page of the December 24 edition. For readers contemplating emigration to Canada, Australia, or the United States, the Cunard Company and the Great Western Steamship Company offered inexpensive fares, and for readers suffering from neuritis, neuralgia, inflamed livers, and gout, the front page offered a potpourri of "miracle" cures. Inside the paper there was a story about Queen Victoria, who was spending the holiday in the country; a new French plan for governing Algeria; and a pretty, sad, confused, Spanish princess. On page six there was also an open letter to the Duke of Wellington from Mr. Cummins about the state of things in Skibbereen:

> My Lord you are an old and justly honored man.
>
> It is yet in your power to add another honor, to fix another star [to your name]. You have access to our young and gracious queen. Lay these things before her. She is a woman. She will not allow decency to be outraged.
>
> Once more my Duke, in the name of the starving thousands, I implore you to break the frigid and flimsy chains of official etiquette and save the land of your birth, the kindred of that Gallant Irish blood you have so often . . . entrusted to support the Honor of the British name and let there be inscribed upon your tomb
>
> Servanta Hibernia

Meanwhile, in Ireland, it was snowing again. Snow "was falling on every part of the dark central plain, on the treeless hills, falling softly on the Bog of Allen and further westward softly falling into the dark mutinous Shannon waves. . . . It was . . . falling faintly through the universe . . . like the descent of their last end, upon all the living and the dead."

CHAPTER ELEVEN

The Queen's Speech

E arly on the afternoon of Tuesday, January 19, 1847, the gates of Buckingham Palace swung open and a pumpkin-shaped carriage emerged. Inside sat Queen Victoria, looking young, slim, and regal in "a magnificent white something or other"; the prince consort, Albert of Saxe-Coburg; and two royal guests, the Duchess of Sutherland and the Marchioness of Douro. An Irish reporter with a weakness for sun metaphors, and the foresight to bring a chair to stand on, peered over the crowd. A few days later, readers of *The Cork Southern Reporter* would learn that the duchess glowed like the "setting sun" while the marchioness shimmered like the "noon day sun." On this gray January afternoon, the royal guests may have been the only things shimmering between Ealing and Barking. The night before, a dense miasma of moisture, sea salt, and industrial pollutants had settled over the imperial capital, turning St. Paul's into a silhouette and the Thames into a rumor. In Hyde Park, walkers out for a morning constitutional complained that the fog had become so dense it was impossible to tell where the park lawns ended and the ponds began. As the carriage passed the reporter's chair, he became disoriented by the daytime darkness and fell backward into the arms of Her Majesty's bankruptcy commissioner, Mr. Charles Phillips. "Hurrumph!" exclaimed

Mr. Phillips, who was the subject of a popular new pub ditty, "Oh, Charlie My Darling."

Near Parliament, the fog lifted slightly, and the face of the queen became visible in the carriage window. "Never had she looked near so well," declared one onlooker, "matronly and dignified" yet retaining "the first blush of early womanhood." The onlooker was particularly pleased by a recent change in the royal mouth, which he had hitherto considered the queen's "principal defect." Through the carriage window, the formerly prominent royal orifice could now be seen sitting in contented harmony between the royal nose and the royal chin, making Victoria "a really beautiful woman." In front of Parliament, every branch of the royal household awaited the royal carriage. There were white-wigged footmen whose brilliant-colored livery gave them a resemblance to "polished copper stew pans"; jowly, mustached Beefeaters in white gloves and ketchup-colored jackets; and battalions of nervous, chattering ladies-in-waiting, every one in a hat large enough to match anything the navy could put into the water.

Above a catacomb of dripping black umbrellas, a buttery cone of yellow light illuminated the midday darkness. The gas lamps in the House of Lords had been lit early against the "darkness occasioned by the fogginess." This afternoon, the upper house, always crowded at the opening of Parliament, was especially so. Lord John, fearing opposition on Irish relief measures, had waived the autumn sitting of Parliament. By one o'clock, the Strangers' Gallery was full and hordes of guests wandered the aisles like the lost tribes of Israel. A group of well-dressed ladies, who had occupied a bench reserved for peers, put up a frightful row when asked to give up their seats. All the firmness and courtesy of the House attendants was required to remove the "fair applicants."

Somewhere out in the fog, a clock chimed two. A trumpet sounded, and the queen entered the upper house. As one, members and guests rose. Simultaneously, a side door opened, and the Duke of Wellington, aged, stooped, and hook-nosed, appeared bearing the Sword of State; he was accompanied by the Marquess of Lansdowne and the Earl of Zetland. The three officers of the household escorted the royal couple to the throne chairs at the front of the chamber. Albert took the smaller chair to the left. Then, following custom, the House of Commons was summoned.

After the MPs arrived, Victoria rose and addressed the gathering. The queen surveyed the domestic and international scene, then turned to the crisis in Ireland.

> My Lords and Gentlemen: It is with the deepest concern that upon your again assembling I have to call your attention to the dearth of provisions which prevails in Ireland and parts of Scotland. In Ireland the loss of the usual food of the people has been the cause of severe sufferings, of disease, and of a greatly increased mortality among the poorer classes. Outrages have become more frequent, chiefly directed against property; and the transit of provisions has been rendered unsafe in some parts of the country. . . . The deficiency of the harvest in France and Germany and other parts of Europe has added to the difficulty of obtaining adequate supplies or provisions.

In a House of Commons speech six days later, Prime Minister Russell publicly acknowledged that the government relief plan had failed. "Destitution and want in Ireland have become so great, it is desirable to attempt some other . . . scheme," he declared.

For eighteen months and through two prime ministers, Downing Street had held fast to the notion that government "cannot feed the people." Now, with every alternative exhausted, tens of thousands dead, and hundreds of thousands likely to die in the coming weeks and months, the British government had concluded that it could feed the people. Under the new Temporary Relief Act, in March the public works labor force, presently approaching 700,000, would be disbanded. "There will be no rude dismissal of the people," Lord John promised the House. The public works program would be closed in stages and, as work sites disappeared, soup kitchens would arise to feed the dismissed laborers, who would return to the land to plant the 1847 crop. The new scheme also included a £50,000 loan fund, which the government hoped proprietors would use to purchase potato and grain seed for tenants, who had consumed their own seed for food.

Lord John, however, only touched briefly on the most important measure in the new government plan. The labor rate act had transferred some of the relief costs to Ireland. In August, when the soup kitchen program closed, the new Poor Law Extension Act would transfer the rest. The act also created a new entitlement: outdoor relief for the aged, the infirm, orphans, destitute widows, and in some cases even the able-bodied poor. A year earlier, upon hearing a similar scheme proposed, Home Secretary Graham had done a few quick mental calculations—two and a quarter million Irish chronically destitute, and perhaps an equal number destitute for a part of each year—and exclaimed, "The locusts will devour the land!"

Lord John did give Irish landowners the debt reduction they had been hoping for. London would forgive half the £9 million in public works debt. But measured against the outdoor relief entitlement, which would keep poor rates high in perpetuity, even £4.5 million did not amount to much. In the weeks after the Russell speech, an end-of-days mood settled over the country houses of Anglo-Ireland. The rolling summer lawns, the manicured gardens, the great still rooms bursting with afternoon light— all of it would go to the rate collector. Two and a half centuries of Anglo-Irish life would end in the quiet shuffle of papers in a morning session of chancery court. Men who bore historic names, men whose ancestors had come over with Cromwell and had stood with William of Orange— William of "glorious and immortal memory"—at the Boyne would end their days in a shabby set of rooms in Dublin or London, the only reminder of their glorious patrimony, portraits of ancestors in black cockel hats and vandyke beards staring down reproachfully from the walls. In County Wicklow, where a state of anarchy and starvation prevailed, Mrs. Smith fell into despair for herself and for her class. "I don't know what will become of us before spring. . . . We have brought our miseries upon ourselves."

✷

On a cold winter morning, five hundred leading Irishmen from all walks of life gathered in the Oval Room of the Rotunda Hospital in Dublin. If the new Poor Law accomplished nothing else, it had united all shades of Irish opinion. Under the banner of the Irish party, Repealers, Unionists, Catholics, and Protestants, men who until recently had been blood enemies, agreed to set aside their differences and together create an Irish relief plan for Ireland. After a gloomy speech by the Earl of Arran, who warned that "Ireland now stood on the precipice," and a rousing speech by Lord Bernard, another prominent landowner, who "rejoiced to [see] such unanimity . . . amongst . . . gentlemen of such various opinions," the meeting got under way. God had ten commandments; by nightfall, the Irish party would have twenty-seven, though all of them boiled down to a single point, one that Isaac Butt, a prominent Dublin barrister, had addressed in an article in the *Dublin University Magazine.* If the Union really did make Britain and Ireland a single nation, Butt wrote, then "what could be more absurd—what could be more wicked than to talk of Ireland being a drain on the *English* treasury. . . . If the Union is not a mockery, there exists no such thing as an English Treasury." To English ears, that sounded as if the Irish plan for Ireland was more money from England.

"Audacious beggars," declared a *Liverpool Mercury* reader in an angry letter to the editor. "You [Irish landowners] ought every one of you . . . to have a begging staff and cap added to your coat of arms."

The era of Irish national unity lasted a little more than a month. By early February, the Irish Party had split into warring factions, and with the domestic elites preoccupied, Lord George Bentinck, hitherto exclusively devoted to high food tariffs and fast race horses, appointed himself spokesman for the Irish peasantry. On February 4 Lord George appeared in the Common wearing one of his signature £2 cravats, and presented the Bentinck plan for ending the Irish crisis: a large British-scale railway project. Rail work would create 110,000 new Irish jobs and feed 550,000 people; moreover, Lord George pointed out, the means to create such a project were already in hand, or almost in hand. London had approved a plan to construct 1,523 miles of railway in Ireland, and only 123 miles of rail had been laid. To finish the other 1,400 miles, all that was required was £16 million. £16 million! On top of half the Irish relief debt just forgiven and the £4½ million still outstanding? Good God, what next? What next was Mr. J. A. Roebuck, the MP from Bath. An unpleasant little fellow once not unjustifiably likened to "a ferret in consumption," Mr. Roebuck held to the *Economist*'s credo: it is no man's business to provide for another. Mr. Roebuck surveyed the house with his ferret eyes for a moment, then asked his fellow English MPs how many of them would be "prepared to suffer [their] poorer constituents to be taxed . . . for the purposes of employ[ing] the capital of this country in speculation" on an Irish railway scheme. The *Hansard* reporter either forgot to note the number of ayes, or thought it too small to be worth recording.

Daniel O'Connell had no plan for Ireland—he had nothing except an appeal to common humanity. On February 8, 1847, in his final appearance before the Commons, O'Connell—his breath shallow, his voice so weak he could barely speak above a raspy whisper—pleaded with Britain not to abandon her Union partner. The Irish "were starving in shoals, in hundreds—aye, in thousands and millions. Parliament was bound then to act, not only liberally but generously. . . . She [Ireland] was in their hands—in their power, if they did not save her, she could not save herself."

O'Connell's listeners, while respectful, were unmoved. Lord John's January speech had been more persuasive, especially the last sentence: "Help yourselves and Heaven will help you."

❧

One evening in December 1846, while awaiting the Dublin train in the Kingston station, Asenath Nicholson, a Vermont Quaker woman, overheard a policeman tell a story about a woman who had killed the family dog to feed her children. "I would not say that I actually murmured . . . '[Here] was why I [was] brought to see a famine,'" Mrs. Nicholson wrote, "but the thought occurred to me." A few weeks later, in the Liberties, among the meanest of Dublin neighborhoods, Mrs. Nicholson opened a private relief station. On winter mornings, long before first light had stolen over the animal carcasses in the lanes of the Liberties, the poor would gather at the corner of Cook Street (also known as "Coffin Street," because it was a center of municipal coffin manufacture) to await the Yankee lady and her basket of bread. Dispensing food in the Liberties was a dangerous enterprise. Starvation had the people half crazed. When Mrs.

Nicholson's basket was empty, the "hungry ones," who arrived too late to receive a piece of bread, would chase her down the lanes demanding something—anything—to eat. One day, workers at a nearby coffin manufactory sent a gift to the kindly "American lady": some coffin shavings for her fire.

By early 1847, the mass press and fast ships had turned the famine into an international event, stirring the conscience of Vermonters, such as Mrs. Nicholson, and New Yorkers, such as Horace Greeley, as well as Berliners, Parisians, and Florentines. In Oklahoma, the Choctaw Indians, no strangers to poverty and injustice, raised $170 for Ireland. In Boston, New York, Washington, and Montreal; in South America, in Scandinavia, in central Europe, charitable drives were organized. British sympathy, first aroused by the early reports of mass death, grew more pronounced, though many British politicians still did not expect it to last. When a Cork clergyman suggested issuing a Queen's Letter on Ireland—a public appeal for charitable donations—Home Secretary Grey said no. The Irish might be less disliked than previously, but the British public would never countenance a charity drive, not while Irish gunmen were donning ladies' hats and shooting British public works officers, and Irish grand juries were indicting Prime Minister Russell and Commissary General Routh for the "willful murder" of famine victims. Mr. Wood agreed with the home secretary.

Mr. Trevelyan, a more acute student of public sentiment, did not. Even the most entombed English conscience could only withstand so many stories of dead Irish children. The London diarist Charles Greville, another shrewd reader of public sentiment, also sensed a new spirit of "pity and generosity" in England. In early December, as the first changes in English feeling were becoming evident, Mr. Trevelyan sensed an opportunity to do well by the Irish, while also doing well by Treasury. In the current atmosphere, a Queen's Letter on Ireland might raise enough charitable contributions to permit Treasury to restrict its financial outlays for relief. It took less than a month for the idea to become a reality.

On January 1, members of the newly formed British Association for the Relief of Extreme Distress in Ireland and Scotland gathered at the St. Swithin's Lane offices of Baron Lionel de Rothschild. New Year's Day was a public holiday, but in the City—London's financial district—avarice slept with one eye open even on public holidays. As the members of the association gathered, candles and gas lamps illuminated windows across the financial quarter. The association's steering committee included two prominent barristers, Thomas Hankey and Abel Smith, a cofounder of the BA, and three prominent Irishmen: Mr. J. J. Cummins, of Cork; Thomas Spring Rice, a son of Lord Monteagle; and Mr. Pim, the Quaker relief official. Sixteen days later, the British government issued the Queen's Letter. Before Michael Jackson and "We Are the World" there was Mr. Trevelyan, the Queen's Letter, and the first celebrity-heavy international charity event. In addition to the English donations—which included £2,000 from Queen Victoria and £1,000 from the Worshipful Company of Grocers—the sultan of Turkey donated £1,000 to Irish relief; Florence, almost £1,000; St. Petersburg, £2,644; Constantinople, £620; and Denmark, over £1,000. All in all, the British Association raised £470,000. Mr. Trevelyan, who believed private charity morally superior to public assistance, and private charity administered by the British Treasury the most superior form of charity, quickly turned the association into a quasi-governmental body. The BA was given access to Commissariat depots and Royal Navy vessels. When it employed commercial ships, the Treasury paid the insurance, freight, and shipping charges.

In January 1847, when the association began operations in Ireland, the food crisis had reached its gravest point. On the sixteenth, the day the government issued the Queen's Letter, Mr. Hewetson told a Limerick priest, "Our resources are at present far too scanty to meet anything like the present wants of the people." The gentlemen of St. Swithin's Lane—most, experienced businessmen—concluded that the quickest, most effective way to bring the British Association's resources to bear would be to act as a supply center for the relief committees; the latter had distribution systems already in place, but often no food to distribute. The situation in Skull, a locality to the west of Skibbereen, was typical. The local committee had seven pounds of meal left. In Carrickbeg, Waterford, the Ladies' Soup Society and the Ladies' Needle Work Society were feeding 2,373 residents; the local committee had no food at all. Under the BA system, after an association agent certified the existence of a food shortage, provisions were released to a committee.

One of the first agents the BA put into the field was Paul Edmund de

Strzelecki, a handsome former Polish army officer. Association officials thought de Strzelecki's Catholicism would be an asset in Ireland, while de Strzelecki thought his knowledge of hunger, acquired when he ran out of food in the Australian outback, would be an advantage. The day he arrived in Westport, the Pole realized that his Australian adventure had taught him nothing about hunger. "No pen can describe the distress by which I am surrounded," he wrote of the scenes outside his hotel window. "It has actually reached such a degree of lamentable extremes, that it becomes above the power of exaggeration and misrepresentation."

De Strzelecki was not being hyperbolic. Ireland now offered sights the human mind was incapable of comprehending. Outside Skibbereen, a young English midshipman came across several "babies . . . lying lifeless on their mothers' bosoms." Before dying, one of the "infants [had] bitten [through its] mother's breast . . . trying to devour nourishment from [her] wretched body." In Mayo, Mrs. Nicholson asked a passing stranger, "Are they dead?" pointing to the stone cottage behind her. She had knocked on the door several times and gotten no reply.

"Worse than dead," the stranger replied. "They are on . . . the bleak sea shore waiting for death . . . lingering out the last few hours of suffering."

In Dublin Castle, Viceroy Bessborough, who had suddenly fallen mortally ill, raged against the mercantile men like a dying Lear. "It is difficult," he told Lord John, "to persuade a starving population that one class should be permitted to make 50 percent, by the sale of provisions, while they [the poor] are dying in want of them." Bessborough's complaint was ignored. London believed high prices were an effective way to ration the food supply.

⚔

Toward the end of January, a visitor stood on Galway dock, gazing out at the bay. It was eight A.M., and the sounds of the rising workday echoed across the buckled wharves: stevedores shouted to each other from work boats; seagulls cawed, laborers grunted as they lowered cranes into place. Out in the harbor, half a dozen food transports lay at anchor under an unmolested morning sky. The air was dry and had a winter crispness to it. The only suggestion of an impending meteorological disturbance was a mild breeze out of the west-southwest. Two of the ships, the *Manchester* and the *Emma of Prescott*, swayed slightly under the light wind. An hour later, their pitching had become pronounced; the wind had picked up, and out on the horizon a black cloud mass was spreading across the blue Galway sky like an ink stain. Occasionally, a thunderclap would startle the livestock in the holding pens above the docks. By ten A.M. it was raining hard, and the wind above the churning white sea was blowing at almost gale force. In the warehouses below the livestock pens, doors slammed open and shut.

Then, "without any apprehension," the sea rose and flung itself over the docks and "swept like a deluge [across] every part of the shore carrying away the embankments and protection walls at Salt-hill and Fair-hill . . . [and] pursuing its course up to Dominic Street . . . and Flood Street." Above the coursing water, roof beams and shingles cantilevered in the wild January air. On one street the floodwaters swept a dead child out of a house and plunged his body into a stream of chairs, pots, pans, and clothing. A man leaped into the water and began swimming toward the body. The swimmer was later identified as the dead child's father. In the harbor, the wind had begun to tear apart the wharves; planks ripped free and flew away in the direction of Salt-Hill or up toward the cattle pens. The "splendid" *Manchester* snapped her stern moorings and "was thrown on her beam ends." The *Emma of Prescott*, caught by a sudden gust, hurtled over the harbor swells toward the rocks at Renmore Point. A moment later, there was a sharp crack—and the mast of the *Redwing* disappeared into a rain squall. On the other side of the harbor, the wind had the *Lee*, out of Marseilles, pinned against the mutinous sea.

"No boat [can] venture out in such weather," wrote a relief official about the ferocious January gales that had left the west coast of Ireland "ironbound." Vessels that did try to make food deliveries ended up like the *Redwing* and *Emma of Prescott*, with holds full of waterlogged provisions— or like H.M.S. *Dragon,* a food transport, ripped apart by sea and wind. Occasionally, though, the sky would clear, and the sea and wind calm. On such a day, H.M.S. *Scourge* arrived in Skull harbor with a cargo of meal. Even by the standards of a country that abounded in back places, Skull—perched at the tip of a peninsula at the most southwesterly point of Cork—was remote. It was also deeply impoverished. According to Samuel Lewis's *Topographical Dictionary of Ireland*, Skull comprised 84,000 statute acres, most "rocky and very uneven, rising in some places into mountains," and only one village of note, Ballydehop, a settlement of seventy-nine homes. Many of the ruined redoubts and castles on the landscape dated from the medieval period, when the district had been a plaything of the O'Mahoneys and O'Donnells.

Except for the population, which now stood at eighteen thousand (nearly three thousand above Mr. Lewis's 1837 figure), and the new road up to Skibbereen, Skull remained much as the *Topographical Dictionary* had described it. Outside of farming, which Mr. Lewis called "very backward," and fishing, a peasant avocation now frequently disrupted by the winter gales, the only significant source of employment in the area was the slate quarries of the West Cork Mining Company. Most of the slate was sent to London, a place the Irish-speaking population of Skull knew only as a name, if they knew it at all. London knew Skull, though; all England did. In January 1847, the region may have been, next to Skibbereen, the most renowned bloodlands in Ireland. Even in good weather Skull's remoteness had made it difficult to provision, and the weather had not been good for months. Reporters returning from Skull brought back stories of suffering and degradation so wrenching that they strained credulity.

Now that his ship was in Skull, Commander Caffin, the captain of the *Scourge*, decided to see how closely reality matched up to the lurid press accounts. While the *Scourge* unloaded, the captain toured the district with the Reverend Dr. Traill, the local vicar. In Ballydehob, Caffin followed Traill past the Constabulary barracks; then the two men turned in to a lane. In the first cabin, they found an emaciated girl of about eight or ten, propped against a cracked wall; a few feet away, her mother was sprawled "naked upon some straw." The mother was "writh[ing] like an animal in pain." Caffin gave mother and daughter a week to live. Outside another cabin in the lane, Dr. Traill stopped and stuck his head into "a hole which answered for a door." "'Well, Phillis, how is your mother today?'

"'Oh sir, mother is dead.'"

The visitors moved on. In the next cabin, "the doorway was stooped with dung," and Caffin had to bend to enter. Inside, an old woman sat next to a bed with a body on it. Four days earlier, the dead man had asked if he could stop and rest; the woman said yes; the man lay down on the bed, closed his eyes, and died. The cabin, six feet square across, was permeated with the sickly sweet smell of death. Dr. Traill tried to ask a question, but the woman had gone quite out of her mind. "She had been a wicked sinner," she said, and "longed to depart, to be at peace"; she said she planned to "block up the door that she might not be disturbed in her final hours." Another cabin presented "the most wretched picture of starvation possible to conceive": a man so debilitated by hunger, he was unable to speak. Upon opening his mouth, nothing came out except a rush of foul breath; his wife, "little better," was crying out for food and the "mercy of God." God and his mercy were nowhere to be found in Skull on this day. In other cabins, in other lanes, Caffin encountered "bodies half eaten by rats"; dead dogs; cadaverous children in clothing fouled by urine, excrement, and blood. In one lane Caffin saw a woman carrying the corpse of a dead child in a burlap sack. "These are things which are everyday occurrences" here, he wrote in a report on his visit.

Not long after the *Scourge*'s visit to Skull, the window of good weather shut and the snow began again. Horses struggled in three-foot drifts, provision carts got stuck in ditches or tumbled over on icy roads; the lack of food became unbearable. Potato gardens were dug up for a third and fourth time; people ate the diseased carcasses of cattle, dying now in their thousands from an epidemic of pleuropneumonia; old men and

A deserted famine village

women got down on their hands and knees and foraged through the snow for grass. People ate anything—animal or vegetable—no matter how long dead or how foul smelling. After exhausting all local sources of food, the country people would walk ten, fifteen miles through the snow to the nearest town. "Daily, hourly," wrote a young Commissariat officer named Hunt, "multitudes of starving men, women and children . . . swarm into town in search of food." In Cahersiveen, a "crowd of 1,000" attacked a local food depot, "breaking the windows with a pick axe"; in Mayo, a group of fishermen executed a daring nighttime raid on the provisions schooner.

In Irish port towns, long lines of scantily dressed men and women— their worldly possessions compressed between two pieces of cardboard— gathered on wharves in the cold and snow to wait for a British packet to rescue them. "Even in the depth of a winter of unusual severity . . . vast numbers are emigrating," the *Dublin Evening Post* reported on February 16. "[In] Limerick some hundreds of small farmers . . . and mechanics are to embark for the United States this week." Even the peasantry, which had no tradition of emigration, was leaving. Anyone able to "beg or borrow a few shillings [was taking] deck passage on the steamers or sailing vessels to Liverpool, Bristol, Newport, Glasgow, or some other seaport in England or Scotland." The swelling emigrant tide alarmed Lord Brougham, a former lord chancellor of England. On February 4, in an impassioned speech, Brougham accused the Irish poor of defying the will of God. "Providence, who sent the potato disease, meant that many should die," he declared—not that they should emigrate to Brixton, Buxton, Vauxhall, or Merseyside. In one recent forty-eight-hour period, Brougham noted, three thousand Irish paupers had arrived in Liverpool: 240 from Cork, 701 from Sligo, 692 from Drogheda, 272 from Newry, and 911 from Dublin.

Lord John was also alarmed by the swelling emigrant stream. What was the "use in sending men from starving in Skibbereen to starve in Montreal?" Besides, the Irish would turn Canada into a Catholic country, and set a bad example for the impressionable Canadians. "Before we fill our colonies with them," the prime minister told a colleague, better to improve the Irish first.

Lord John was also concerned about the public works program. In

January, when he announced that the program would be closed, there were 570,000 laborers on the rolls, and the monthly cost of operations was £736,125. In February, employment rose to 708,000 and monthly operating costs to £944,144. (That works out to almost $500 million a month in modern money.) On February 22, the Board of Works ordered its inspecting officers to begin reducing the workforce. That was easier said than done. Despite the new corps of Inspecting Officers, the local relief committees still retained a great deal of control over hiring, and for reasons ranging from humanity to fear, the committees were reluctant to cut the work rolls. From Clare, Colonel Douglas, the army officer on temporary relief duty, reported that the committees in his districts not only refused to honor the reduction order but were even adding laborers in "packs [of] fifties." In County Leitrim, a relief committee told a board officer named Bull that if he dared to pare its rolls, the committee would send "the starving and dead bodies" of the dismissed men to his home "in carts."

By March 7, the public works labor force stood at 734,000, and the daily cost of operations at £40,000 (almost $20 million). Treasury blamed the numbers on the culture of dependency in Ireland; the real reason was more elementary. With cornmeal selling for up to 3½ shillings a stone and little private employment, road work offered peasants the only chance of being alive come spring. "The want of food and support is strikingly visible [and] causes [the poor] to be almost entirely dependent on the Public Works," wrote Captain Layard, a board officer in County Leitrim. In the margin of a report by another board officer, Routh scribbled, "When the country tailors and shoemakers are obliged to go to road work . . . there must be great local distress."

People unable to find employment threw themselves on the workhouses. The system now held 116,000 inmates, 16,000 above capacity. In the Cork city facility, inmates slept five and six to a bed, and the chamber pots in the wards overflowed with "the discharge of the inmates . . . diffusing a stench most disgusting," wrote Dr. Stephens, a Board of Health official. Other aspects of the sanitary system were "so disgusting," Stephens said, that he "refused to enter upon [them]." In Fermoy, southwest of Cork city, the local workhouse, built to house 800 inmates, held 1,800; fever raged in the wards; and, for want of funds for a fever shed, the healthy and the infected shared the sleeping galleries and dining halls. In Skibbereen, a workhouse built for 800 held 930 inmates. "Deaths . . . average 25 a day [and] the majority of bodies are buried without coffins," reported a workhouse official. In many facilities, semi-nakedness was rampant. Before admission, inmates often sold their jackets, shirts, and shoes for food, and, unable to collect the poor rate, the workhouses could not supply new clothing. "The poor creatures . . . are huddled together in the tattered rags," a Commissariat officer wrote after a visit to the workhouse in Ballinrobe, Mayo. The indefatigable Mr. Erichsen was asked to find a wardrobe for the inmates. A few weeks later Mr. Trevelyan sat in his office, examining samples of "winter clothing" originally made for "female Negroes" in the West Indies. He examined the price list Mr. Erichsen had sent along. The imperial Treasury could purchase petticoats for 3 shillings 3 pence, shifts for 1 shilling 3 pence, and stockings for a shilling. What if anything Trevelyan ordered is not recorded.

In Tralee, County Kerry, where a workhouse built for a thousand held twelve hundred inmates, the administrators called in the police to break up the squatter camp that rejected applicants had set up in the courtyard. When the police arrived, the squatter women held up their infants and begged not to be sent back onto the winter roads. An hour later, the yard was empty except for piles of human waste, chewed-over bones, and burn marks on the cobblestones from the camp fires. Inside the Tralee facility, bodies were stored in corners, in carts, under stair wells, in washrooms and sleeping galleries. In normal times, the staff swept the workhouse for bodies every twenty-four hours, but so many inmates were dying now, the carts were unable to keep up. In the workhouse at Enniskillen, where famine fever raged, an official recorded a conversation between a medical officer, a clerk, and a sub-sheriff:

> SUB-SHERIFF: A pauper in fever would be better thrown behind a ditch than in a poor house.
> MEDICAL OFFICER: Ye sentenced in one day two hundred persons to death [a reference to the number of new admissions].
> CLERK: We did not, they sentenced themselves to death.

MEDICAL OFFICER: There are 24 people dying of fever in the house and the rain is dripping down on them at this moment.

CLERK: Mr. Otway [a Poor Law official] said that there were seventeen poor houses in Ireland worse than ours.

After inspecting the South Dublin workhouse, Mr. Barden, a municipal relief official, declared the facility a "haunt of desperate suffering" and a "disgrace to a civilized country," then went home and shot himself.

The architects of the workhouse system had failed to anticipate a situation in which admissions would rise 20 percent and 30 percent above capacity and blizzards, gales, and a general collapse in ratepayers' incomes would make it impossible to collect rates. When the Tralee workhouse fell £1,700 into debt, local merchants threatened to cut off supplies. In other districts, workhouse guardians had to personally guarantee payment before the local mercantile men would deliver food or fuel. Under the 1838 Poor Law, a financially pressed workhouse could strike a new rate—that is, collect a new round of taxes. In the chaotic conditions of late winter 1847, though, this was easier said than done. The Tralee workhouse, which was bleeding funds, raised its rates twice in a matter of months, and before the second rate was "half collected," a third had to be struck. Under pressure from ratepayers, a County Dublin workhouse stopped providing coffins. Others facilities employed reusable coffins. In Dingle, a Royal Navy man named Brown reported that "an open coffin or bier [is] made use of; the corpses are carried to the burial ground and shot . . . into a large hole." In Clare, a local workhouse tried to economize by purchasing unground corn; in retaliation, angry inmates spiked nails into the Trevelyan hand mills provided to grind the corn. In October 1846, 4 out of every 1,000 inmates in the system died each week. In January 1847, the mortality rate rose to 13 per 1,000, and by mid-April it would rise to 25 per 1,000. In March, Parliament was told that if current trends held, the total number of workhouse deaths in 1847 would be 77,630.

On January 16, under the headline "Widespread Mass Extermination," *The Nation* announced the beginning of a new phase in the Irish crisis. To reduce costs before the Poor Law Extension Act was enacted, landowners were organizing mass evictions. The most frequent target were small farmers. Unlike the twenty- or thirty-acre tenant, who often paid up to half the poor rate on his holding, the small farmer—who held land valued at £4 or less—had his entire rate paid by the proprietor. Ejecting four or five hundred small tenants could produce a significant drop in an owner's rate. On February 1, the *Manchester Guardian* reported that in the past few weeks, in Mayo, where 75 percent of the holdings were valued at £4 or less, local landowners filed between five thousand and six thousand eviction notices and civil bills, demands for immediate payment of rent that were tantamount to eviction notices. In time, many of the evicted families became like the other ruins on the Irish landscape. Passing through Mayo in the winter of 1847, the Quaker Richard Bennett reported that one saw "only the remnants of families" now.

Among the proprietors the *Guardian* singled out for special notice was Lord Lucan, who in less than a decade would achieve immortality of a sort in the Tennyson poem that thrilled every public school boy in England, "The Charge of the Light Brigade":

> *Half a league, half a league*
> *Half a league onward . . .*
> *Into the valley of Death*
> *Rode the six hundred.*

Lord Lucan was the man who ordered the six hundred into the valley of death.

As a young man, Lucan had been prettier than a professional soldier ought to be, but in 1847 he was forty-seven, as old as the century: balding, thickening around the middle, and out of uniform. He had taken temporary retirement from the army to oversee the family estates in Mayo. Literal minded, violent, and possessed of a unwarranted belief in his own intelligence, George Bingham—Lucan's given name—was by every account a difficult fellow. He had been difficult when he commanded the 17th Lancers, and he was difficult in County Mayo, where he earned a reputation as a bully and a despot. Lord Lucan was also cost-conscious. In September 1846, in his role as chairman of the Castlebar Board of Guardians in Mayo, he had ordered that the workhouse, which was only about a quarter full, shut to keep the poor rate down. Not long afterward, George Poulett Scrope, an English MP, told the Commons that the "closing of the workhouse" had been a great boon to the rate-payers of Castlebar, as the local peasantry were now either starving to death or fleeing to Britain and throwing themselves on ratepayers in Liverpool and other British cities. When passage of the amended new Poor Law became a certainty, Lucan summoned the crowbar brigades, compiled lists of tenants, and found ways to work around the traditional three-month grace period for payment of rent. Two thousand people were driven from the Bingham properties in Ballinrobe, Mayo. Lucan also moved against a family property in Castlebar.

Early on a winter's morning, the town streets echoed with the bark-ing of dogs. Curtains parted in the sturdy stone houses of the Protestant merchants. There was a group of rough-looking men on the local high street. The men had their hats pulled down against the cold and carried crowbars, pickaxes, and sledgehammers. The barking dogs were running in and out between their legs. The men walked past the military bar-racks, past a row of pubs, past the building that had housed the Republic of Connaught (its lifespan briefer even than the 1798 uprising that spawned it), and past Lord Lucan's personal cricket field. Then the men disap-peared toward the far end of town, where the neat stone houses and cobblestone streets ended in unpaved roads, mud cabins, and fields of high grass. About half an hour later, the heavy thud of collapsing walls began to echo back up toward the center of Castlebar; shortly after, crowds of wailing peasants streamed up the high street and disappeared onto the winter roads.

Captain Arthur Kennedy, who was stationed in the west of Ireland during the famine, told a friend, "There were days when I came back from some scene . . . so maddened by sights of hunger and misery I had seen in the day's work that I felt disposed to take a gun from behind my door and shoot the first landlord I met." Proponents of a measure called the Encumbered Estates Act believed that there was a simple, less violent solution to the problem of the Irish gentry: follow the Scottish example and restructure the class.

During the first half of the nineteenth century, industrialists from the lowlands had bought out impoverished Highland aristocrats and the change had proved quite beneficial. Between the newcomers—serious-minded, solvent men—and the Scottish Free Church, the potato-less Highlands was currently funding its own relief. Advocates of the Encumbered Estates Act, which would make it easier to strip an indebted Irish owner of his property, argued that restructuring would advance the modernization project in Ireland and with rental incomes down and British public opinion hostile, the gentry was vulnerable now. And, indeed, except for the London insurance companies, the gentry was. The companies held a lot of Irish mortgage debt and did not want hundreds of estates flooding onto the market at once, depressing property values. However, Mr. Wood, a proponent of the act, did not regard industry opposition as an insurmountable obstacle. The Encumbered Estate Act was put on the government's late winter legislative agenda.

CHAPTER TWELVE

Pestilence

One day in 1849 John Callanan, a Cork physician, received a letter from *The Dublin Quarterly Journal of Medical Science*. The *Quarterly* was compiling a scientific record of the recent pestilence. As part of the effort, the editors were asking subscribers to complete an enclosed questionnaire. The first question—"When did the fever begin in your district?"—required little thought. In Dr. Callanan's part of Cork, the epidemic had begun in January 1847. But something about the answer—"From the commencement of 1847"—bothered Callanan; perhaps he thought a date too trivial to describe the biomedical disaster that had engulfed Ireland two Februarys earlier. In the blank space below the question he added a further observation. In the winter of 1847, "fate opened her book in good earnest and the full tide of death flowed on everywhere around us."

From historical experience, Irish medical men knew the blight was likely to produce a major pestilence. The fever epidemic of 1740–1741 had been preceded by two years of historic cold; grain and potato fields turned as "red as foxes"; famine developed, and pestilence followed. In a nation of a little less than 2.5 million, between 250,000 and 400,000 people died.

"Scarce a house in the whole island escaped tears and mourning," wrote a contemporary. In 1816, the year after the French Wars ended, another historically severe winter put the crops at risk. This time, though, there was a second environmental insult: the harvest season of 1817 was also very wet. That September, potatoes came out of the ground as small as eggs and as hard as Sheffield iron, and what grain remained was barely edible. Another season of "tears and mourning" followed. Two amateur epidemiologists, Dr. John Cheyne, a transplanted Scot, and Francis Barker, a professor of chemistry at the University of Dublin, estimated that between 1816 and 1819, fever infected a million and a half people, of whom 65,000 died: a high morbidity and mortality rate in a nation of six million.

Even between epidemics, Ireland was never entirely free of fever; inadequate sanitation combined with primitive habits of personal hygiene to create a permanent reservoir of disease. In the first half of the nineteenth century, the small Irish health system was devoted largely to fever care. The country had 101 county fever hospitals, most small and underfunded, and 664 dispensaries. In 1843, the workhouses were also mandated to offer fever care. After the famine, George Nicholls, the chief architect of the Irish Poor Law system, claimed that by 1845, the workhouses had made "considerable progress" in equipping themselves to meet this new responsibility. The most charitable thing that can be said about Nicholls's assertion is that he was, by nature, a glass-half-full man. In the autumn of 1845, only 50 out of the 128 workhouses (two had yet to be completed) had fever facilities or were in the process of constructing them. On the eve of the famine, in large swaths of rural Ireland, the only fever treatments available were hot whiskey, the "fairy doctor," and a dozen Hail Marys.

Typically, a gap of several months existed between the appearance of famine and the appearance of fever. In March 1846, when Parliament enacted the Temporary Fever Act, which created a central Board of Health, it seemed time to act; six months had passed since the first crop failure. Then the unexpected happened: nothing. In April, May, June, and July 1846, there were fever outbreaks in Cork, Galway, Carrick-on-Shannon, and several other localities, but none rose to the level of an epidemic. The "summer of 1846 [has] passed over without producing much cause for alarm," reported the Board of Health. On August 31, 1846, the Temporary Fever Act was allowed to expire. The decision was odd. By the end of August, everyone knew a second, terrible crop failure was coming. After a relatively uneventful September and October, in November 1846, "Fate opened her book." Officials in Mitchelstown, Cork; in Dublin; and in Clonmel, Tipperary; reported a sharp rise in the incidence of fever. As fears of a nationwide pestilence grew, medical science stepped in to calm public anxiety. After reviewing twelve years of admissions to the Dublin fever hospitals, a group of leading Irish medical men announced that the fever threat was exaggerated. In 1840, the admission rate had been higher than it was at present, and no epidemic had developed. Furthermore, for the past several months female admission rates had been higher than male rates, and prior to a pestilence male patients typically predominated in the fever wards. Reassured by medical science, in late January 1847, Mr. Labouchere told Parliament that Dublin Castle would rely on the "ordinary law" to deal with the rising incidence of famine fever.

⋙⋘

On a February morning in 1847, an American visitor stood in a courtyard in Skibbereen; a few feet away, a hundred or so paupers were queuing up in front of a soup shop in the rain. The American was youngish rather than young and had a classic nineteenth-century Yankee face: long, narrow, and high-cheekboned. Elihu Burritt, thirty-seven, was an example of the American progressive, circa 1847. A Connecticut shoemaker's son, a fervent abolitionist, and a temperance advocate, Burritt had never met a good cause he could resist, or a war he could support. On this unpleasant Irish morning, the founder of the League of Universal Brotherhood and editor of the *Citizen of the World* and *The Peace Advocate* was in Skibbereen to investigate a rumor about a fever epidemic. The Yankee visitor, who also wrote regularly for the New York and New England papers, scanned the soup queue; there were no obvious fever cases in the line. Near the front, a woman was wailing—but from exhaustion and despair. The mortality in Skibbereen had created such a shortage of burial space, people were digging up each other's dead and burying their own departed in the empty graves. The woman had spent the night guarding her husband's grave. Further back in the queue was a shoeless pauper with feet as red as an August tomato and swollen to twice normal size. Behind the pauper, a tall, dark-haired laborer with "jaws so distended he could scarcely articulate" held a young child in his arms. The laborer's older children were sitting on the ground, trying to shelter "their naked limbs " from the rain. The line suddenly lurched forward, and Burritt found himself swept into the soup shop. "The dispensary bar [where the matrons served soup] was choked with young and old of both sexes . . . some . . . upon all fours like famished beasts." The children in the shop looked as if "they had just been thawed out of ice." Someone at the back of queue shouted, "For the honor of God, give us food!"

Later in the day, Burritt tracked the epidemic rumor to a water-house—a storage shed—in a cemetery near the soup shop. The house was reputed to be "an unholy sepulchre" where "living men, women, and children festering with fever . . . went to die." Reality proved even more compelling. Inside the waterhouse, about a dozen men and women lay on the ground amid pools of vomit, waste, and blood. Some of the waterhouse inhabitants had swollen heads, oozing sores, and bleeding hemorrhages; others, distorted limbs, parched lips, and jaundiced skin. Burritt was not sure anyone was still alive until one corpse murmured: "Water! Water! Help! Help!"

By midwinter, epidemic fever was widespread. Counties Meath and Wicklow were stricken in January 1847; Dublin and Cork city in February; and County Carlow in March. To one Carlow physician, a Dr. Roache of Bagenalstown, the pestilence seemed to fall out of the sky. "Previous to [the] outbreak, the health of the district was [as] good . . . as at any time in the last eight years." In April, epidemic fever appeared in Kilkenny and King's County, and in May, in Waterford, Galway, Limerick, and parts of Ulster, including Belfast. By late spring, fever seemed to be everywhere, but what kind of fever? Initially, Irish physicians were unsure. In Ireland, the most common form of famine fever was typhus, a disease with a distinctive clinical profile: red blotches on the arms, back, and chest; a fever so intense, some patients jumped out a window or into the water in search of relief; memory loss; violent twitching of the limbs; excruciating muscle pain; and progressive mental impairment, including confusion and a drunken gait. Dr. Cavet, a Waterford physician who contracted typhus while autopsying a victim, described the mental symptoms as "furious." Perhaps the most distinctive feature of typhus is the course of recovery: if a patient survives the crisis period of the disease, recovery is usually uninterrupted.

However, during the 1847 epidemic, many patients with symptoms that resembled typhus were relapsing three, four, five times. History, memory, and science solved the mystery. The epidemic was being driven by two different illnesses: typhus and relapsing fever, a disease uncommon in normal times, hence many Irish physicians were unfamiliar with it. According to Dr. Lynch of Galway, who treated many cases during the epidemic, seven to fourteen days after the initial attack, "ninety nine out of a hundred victims relapse, and if the relapse is accompanied by uncontrollable vomiting, great thirst, very rapid pulse . . . delirium . . . involuntary evacuations, [and] intense heat of the skin," the patient was likely to die.

Initially, there was also confusion over another important point. Dominick John Corrigan, the five-time president of the Irish Royal College of Physicians, believed malnutrition was the root cause of epidemic fever. This was the traditional explanation of pestilence, and it had the support of both medical logic—hunger weakens the body, which increases vulnerability to disease—and personal observation. Could anyone remember the last famine in Ireland that killed more rich people than poor? No, and for good reason, said Dr. Corrigan. The wealthy do not starve in periods of want. The commissioners of health sided with the lion of Irish medicine. In a postmortem report on the epidemic, they emphasized the close relationship between food prices and the incidence of fever. "In 1845, when prices were still at normal levels, there was no epidemic. In 1846, the scarcity was first felt and fever began to show itself, and as prices . . . continued to rise in the winter of 1846 and the spring of 1847, the effects of want of food were seen in an alarming increase in fever." None of Corrigan's medical colleagues questioned the role of hunger in the genesis of epidemic fever; but, as the pestilence deepened, many physicians found the hunger theory insufficient to explain how a fever outbreak grows into a full-scale epidemic. One Kilkenny physician with an acute clinical eye—a Dr. Lalor—postulated that the genesis of the transformation might lie in factors that become more common in periods of social upheaval, like "overcrowding, the assembling of people in masses and vagrancy." Time, the germ theory, and a better understanding of the common louse would prove skeptics like Lalor correct.

✳

A wonder of evolutionary adaptability, the lowly louse is exquisitely sensitive to all its prey's vulnerabilities. It has evolved strong legs and claws with which to cling to human skin; powerful mouthparts to pierce the epidermis and suck out human blood, its principal food source; a thick, glutinous saliva to attach its eggs to the host's hair; and a size—0.5 millimeter to 8 millimeters—small enough to avoid easy detection. Like humans, lice are also highly vulnerable to *Rickettsia*, the genus to which the several typhus pathogens belong. The *Rickettsiae* multiply in the cells of the louse's intestinal wall; the cells burst, and the *Rickettsiae* spill out into the intestine and are evacuated in the feces. Some years ago, the biologist Hans Zinsser turned the death of an infected louse into a Shakespearean tragedy. "In eight days he sickens, in ten days he is in extremis, on the eleventh or twelfth day his tiny body turns red with blood extravasated from his bowel and he gives up his little ghost." Zinsser's description omits one important detail. As death nears, the louse often transfers to a new host and bites it; the host scratches the irritation; the scratching produces breaks in the skin, and the *Rickettsiae* slip through the opening and enter the bloodstream.

Bites, however, are only one of several possible routes of transmission. Infected louse feces are so dense with pathogens that even a minor skin abrasion can create a portal of infection. Poor personal hygiene also plays a role in disease transmission. On unwashed bodies, the infected louse feces turns to powder on the skin; when the host rubs his eyes or nose, the dust enters the body. The dust may also fall or be blown off the skin, and those in immediate proximity to the host become infected. In the human body, *Rickettsiae* gravitate to the skin cells, producing grotesque blotches, and to the brain, producing delirium. Autopsying a typhus victim, Dr. Pemberton, a Mayo physician, noted that "the brain vessels . . . [become] filled with dark fluid blood, the sinuses also, and a quantity of fluid blood [is] extravasated at the base of the brain." The word "typhus" derives from *typhos*, Greek for "mist." In Gaelic, the disease has a more evocative name: *frabhras dubh*—"black fever"—and it was deeply feared, for good reason: untreated typhus has a mortality rate of between 10 percent and 60 percent.

The common louse also transmits relapsing fever, though through a different pathogen. A spirochete is forty times longer than *Rickettsia*, more threadlike than tubelike in shape, and it inhabits the body and limbs of the louse, not the intestines. Spirochetes are also transmitted to a human host through a different mechanism. When a louse is injured or killed in a traumatic event, such as a slap, spirochetes pour out of its crushed body and onto the skin of the host; the blood of the host is infected by way of a cut or abrasion. In some cases, the period between infection and the onset of symptoms is so brief, the victim claims to have sensed the moment of infection. "Nothing was more common than for persons to perceive a bad smell going along the road and immediately sicken," recalled a Galway physician named French.

There were several major outbreaks of relapsing fever in the eighteenth century, but the disease's nineteenth-century appearances were confined to the occasional medical report. In 1842, the Coolock and Santry dispensary in County Dublin treated nineteen cases; in 1843, seven cases. Despite their initial confusion, Irish physicians developed a good grasp of the disease. Some of the descriptions in the 160-year-old *Dublin Quarterly Journal* survey can stand comparison to the modern profile of relapsing fever. In the survey, many physicians said that, on average, the initial bout of fever lasted five days; the interval between relapses, seven to fourteen days; often three or four relapses preceded a full recovery. According to the profile of the disease compiled by the U.S. Centers for Disease Control, the first bout of fever lasts an average of three days, though some patients recover as quickly as the second day. The interval between relapses is seven days, and the average number of relapses is three.

Of the two types of famine fever, relapsing fever was the more aggressive. On entering a district, it would often muscle out typhus and establish itself as the dominant form of infectious disease. It also showed a tropism for the poor. "Each class was liable to a particular form [of fever]," observed Thomas Kehoe, the medical officer in Skull. "The poor had famine [relapsing] fever, the persons better off . . . typhus." There was also a second important class difference. In the homes of the middle and upper middle class, relatively high sanitary standards often prevented the fever from spreading beyond the patient; in the cabins of the peasantry, three or four family members frequently fell ill within days of each other.

⌘

One winter morning in 1847, Mr. Joseph Driscoll stood in the front of a half-ruined stone house in Skull. Not much had changed since Captain Caffin's visit; thirty-five people a day were dying in the district, and "children, in particular . . . were disappearing with awful rapidity." "Frightful and fearful" is how Dr. Traill, the local vicar, described the mortality; it was also putting a heavy financial strain on the local Poor Law system, which had to provide fever care—hence Mr. Driscoll's visit to Skull. Driscoll was a tax collector and he was at the cottage to collect a long-overdue poor rate from a ratepayer named Regan. Tax collecting was a difficult occupation in Ireland, and it was scoundrels like Regan who made it difficult. Mr. Driscoll knocked on the door. No answer. Mr. Driscoll was not surprised. Regan was a blackguard if there ever was one. While he shivered in the wind, Regan was probably sitting inside by a fire, smiling to himself. Driscoll pounded on the door again. Still no answer. More than most professions, tax collecting taught a man the virtue of patience; still, it was very cold. Driscoll lost his temper and "punched in the door." To "his astonishment," inside there were "*three dead men*": Regan and two others. Driscoll did not recognize Regan's companions, but he had seen enough of the pestilence to know what killed them.

In Galway, there was another macabre incident. Three strangers were infected by the same fever victim, a local gentleman who had died of the disease. The village barber fell ill while shaving the gentleman's corpse, went home, and died. The physician who administered an enema to the same gentleman on the eve of his death also fell ill and "sank on the fourteenth day after passing through a most malignant form of typhus." The gentleman's coachman was the last of the three victims to be stricken; he fell ill "while acting as a pallbearer at the gentleman's funeral."

In normal times, the sedentary character and provincialism of Irish life acted as a firewall against epidemic disease, but the chaos of mass death, mass flight, and general social breakdown had burst the firewall. Despite the hard weather, by February 1847 the roads were crowded with lice-bearing orphans, paupers, peddlers, laborers, evicted farmers, and emigrants. Many of the travelers had no idea where they were going, except that it was away from where they had been. On winter evenings, a group of strangers would appear at a cabin door and beg for shelter; the cabin owner—mindful of the peasant code: "never . . . refuse admission to the poorest"—would take in the strangers; one of the visitors would slap his neck or hand; and, within days to weeks, the cabin owner, his family, and almost everyone they knew would be ill or dead.

Ditches, glens, coach stops, abandoned cabins, the peddlers who sold lice-infested clothing on the roads, the unburied dead: there were disease vectors everywhere now. In a winter of seminakedness, few people could pass up a well-clothed corpse. Within a week or two, the man who had taken a jacket or shirt from a body was often dead himself, or in an infirmary, burning with fever and ranting like a lunatic. The swelling emigrant tide made port towns especially potent disease centers. In Dublin and Cork city, peasants who had not had a proper washing in months slept five and six to a bed in emigrant lodging houses that had not had a proper cleaning since the French Wars.

Fever outbreaks on the small Liverpool packets—Liverpool was a popular emigrant destination—were especially lethal; by the time the packet was in the Mersey, 15 percent of the passenger complement might be dead and another 15 percent vomiting with fever. Pestilence in a confined space like a gaol also produced a high mortality. Toward the end of winter 1847, Dr. Dillion, the prison physician at the Castlebar gaol, urgently requested a supply of hospital beds. The inmate population was now at more than double the building's capacity; many inmates were in "a state of nudity, filth and starvation," and half of the cases in the prison hospital were people suffering from a low-grade, relapsing fever. Dillion's request for extra beds was denied, the number of inmates sharing a bed grew, and a few weeks later "a state of actual pestilence" developed. Before the fever burned itself out, "we had fully one fifth of the inmates in bad maculated typhus," Dillion recalled later. "Our Roman Catholic chaplain, deputy governor, deputy matron, and a turnkey fell victim. Every hospital servant was attacked; and, from our wretched, overcrowded state, the mortality was fearful—fully 40 percent." At the public works sites where laborers worked and ate together, and at the soup kitchens, where a hundred people could be in a queue, the appearance of a single case of fever could produce a mortality.

The pestilence also took a heavy toll among caregivers. In one Connemara district, two of three physicians died; in the region between Clifden and Galway city, four doctors; in County Cavan, seven. Of the 473 government medical officers seconded to fever duty, one in thirteen died. The mortality among Catholic priests was high, and among Church of Ireland vicars, significant; the dead included Dr. Traill, who had opened one of the first soup kitchens in Ireland. The mortality among caregivers, which often deprived the ill of treatment, was among the ways the pestilence fed itself. "I have . . . seen whole families lying in the fever at the same time, with perhaps a child of eight or nine [as] the anxious nurse tender of its father, mother, and from four to six brothers and sisters," said one physician.

Early in the fever epidemic, dysentery—another disorder associated with famine—made an appearance. In periods of social disruption, unclean fingers, contaminated food, and flies become common. Once in the body, the dysentery bacilli lodge in the intestinal tract and multiply; the intestine becomes inflamed, ulcerated, and occasionally gangrenous, producing painful bowel colic and violent, bloody diarrhea. Bloody stool is such a common symptom of dysentery that in Gaelic the disease is called *ruit fola*: bloody flux. Despite its often florid, violent course, dysentery can produce a strangely peaceful death. "There was no complaint of pain, no want of rest, or of appetite," wrote a Galway physician of one victim. "The pulse was natural, the tongue clean, and the patient expressed himself comfortable and well, but he could not leave the bed; he took his nourishment greedily, yet he became obviously weaker . . . the face became paler, the limbs . . . more and more attenuated . . . the voice weaker. . . . Patients seemed to die by inches. . . . They gave themselves up, they said day after day that they knew they were dying but were resigned to their fate and grateful for the attention shown them." In combination, fever and dysentery almost always proved fatal. "Epidemic dysentery is a serious disease in itself," said a Dr. Kennedy of Dublin, "but joined to fever, it becomes a truly formidable affliction. . . . I saw cases of dysentery, which had continued for several days, suddenly put on signs of fever and so carry the patient off."

During the winter of 1846–1847, scurvy, a disease uncommon in prefamine Ireland, also increased dramatically. Whatever the potato's deficiencies as a promoter of moral virtue and self-reliance, it is a good source of vitamin C. Indian corn is not, and without vitamin C the body is unable to synthesize collagen. In the early stages, scurvy produces appetite loss, diarrhea, rapid breathing, irritability, and discomfort in the legs; in advanced stages, bleeding from the gums and eyes, tooth loss, skin blotches, and protruding eyes.

No one can say for sure, but pestilence may have killed ten famine victims for every one who died of starvation; still, the signature image of the famine remained a starving peasant and by the winter of 1847, newspaper artists had become adept at drawing the lines of a gaunt Irish face, though even the best of the press artists, men like James Mahony of the *Illustrated London News*, exercised a degree of self-censorship. Mahony's iconic sketches of the famine, like most contemporary newspaper sketches, depict starvation at midpoint in the cycle. The body has begun to cannibalize itself—bones protrude, the face is hollowed out, muscle and skin hang from the frame—but the most hideous changes have not yet occurred. In the later stages of starvation, the eyelids inflame; the angular lines around the mouth deepen into cavities; the swollen thyroid gland becomes tumor-sized; fields of white fungus cover the tongue, blistering mouth sores develop, the skin acquires the texture of parchment; teeth decay and fall out, gums ooze pus, and a long silky growth of hair covers the face. When the victim lies on his back, the articulations of the spine protrude through the skin of the stomach. Hunger edema— grotesque swelling—is also common. Elihu Burritt was already familiar with edema when he visited Skibbereen. Passing public work sites in Ireland, he had seen men "with limbs swollen to almost twice their natural size" digging ditches and pushing wheelbarrows. In a cabin in Skibbereen, Burritt encountered edema in its most florid form: a boy of about twelve, with a "cold watery face" and "a body swollen to nearly three times its natural size." Nothing could be more hideous, Burritt thought; then, from a darkened corner of the cabin, a toddler appeared with "a body . . . swollen to the size of a full grown person."

The day after the visit, Burritt wrote, "Yesterday has haunted me . . . like Banquo's ghost."

On a raw January day in 1847, H.M.S. *Hibernia* emerged out of a cloudless Atlantic horizon, cleared the shoals off Winthrop Peninsula, passed Deer Island, and entered the inner harbor of Boston, where she was welcomed by the three hills of Shawmut Peninsula: Beacon Hill, where proper Boston lived; the North End, where proper Boston used to live; and Fort Hill, where its Irish domestics lived. Somewhere off to the west, just beyond icy Charlestown Point, lay Somerville, now an "Anglo-Saxon wasteland," soon to be a teeming Irish colony. The arrival of the *Hibernia,* one of the fastest ships of the day, had been eagerly awaited. The famine had become a major story in the city, and the British newspapers in the *Hibernia*'s mail pouch would bring the Irish laborers and domestics in Dorchester, East Boston, and Fort Hill up-to-date with events in the "old country," as of January 5. For the next few days, extracts from the papers, reprinted in the *Boston Herald* and the *Boston Daily Advertiser,* were read aloud in kitchens and parlors across the city. Some of the listeners must have secretly thanked God that they had gotten out in time; many more, though, thought of the snow and gales and unburied dead and wept. On February 7, at the ten o'clock mass at the Cathedral of the Holy Cross on Franklin Street, Archbishop John Fitzpatrick, leader of the Boston diocese, addressed recent events in Ireland. The archbishop took for the text of his sermon the mail pouch of the *Hibernia.*

> A voice comes to us from across the ocean . . . it is the voice
> of Ireland. . . . The loud cry of her anguish has gone through
> the world. She calls upon all, she calls upon you especially,
> dearly beloved brethren, to look upon her sufferings with
> eyes of compassion, to enter her wretched cabins, to go over

her desolate fields, to climb her hillsides and descend into
her valleys, to view on all sides her poor children who have
fainted away searching vainly for food, consumed by fever's
fire, frantic, mad with the pangs of hunger, and expiring . . .
in the most excruciating of pains.

Years later, one observer recalled the "ghastly stillness" in the nave
when Fitzpatrick finished speaking. "These people had known hard times
in Ireland . . . but here, in vivid terms [was] . . . a situation more serious
than any they had imagined or experienced. In stunned quiet, they med-
itated. Most of them could remember Ireland, see the fields, envision the
rotting crops, the wretched shacks of the cottiers and the not much better homes of the tenant farmers; many had fathers and mothers, brothers
and sisters, some wives and children who were caught in the horror,
helpless to break the shackles of starvation, doomed."

By early 1847, news from Ireland was arriving almost daily in American port towns, galvanizing public opinion. A rally in Washington, D.C.,
was attended by George M. Dallas, the vice president of the United States;
the mayors of New York, Boston, and Philadelphia; and a dozen or more
senators, members of the House of Representatives, and justices of the
U.S. Supreme Court. The featured speaker, Massachusetts senator Daniel
Webster, described the events in Ireland as "unprecedented in Christen-
dom in this age." Wasn't it astonishing? Webster declared. "Improvements
in communication [have made] the cries of suffering Ireland almost as
fresh and strong as if they had come from our own country." The next
speaker, Congressman Robert Dale Owen of Indiana, also spoke of the
impact of modern communications on human understanding. "Railroads
and telegraphs are bringing nations that were far apart . . . together. And
as it is in the physical, so it should be in the moral world. Advancing
civilizations should attach men's hearts to one another."

However, even with the aid of the railroad, the telegraph, and the fast
mail ship, America remained three to eight weeks behind events in Ireland. Elihu Burritt's February 26 letter in the *Albany Evening Journal*
contained no mention of the latest development. Feeding off one another, fever, dysentery, scurvy, and starvation had melded together and

thrust Ireland into a biomedical catastrophe. In Ulster, "typhus fever of the most malignant character . . . attack[ed] all classes, ages and sexes . . . and dysentery and diarrhea [had become] very frequent, severe, and, in many cases . . . fatal." In Ballinrobe, County Mayo, "scarcely a cabin escaped the desolating influence" of dysentery, scurvy, and fever. On the Aran Islands, the local magistrate warned a visitor that the "entire island was now in a state of flagrant pestilence." In Cork city "*one third* of the daily population . . . consist[ed] of . . . fever, dysentery and famine [victims] stalking along to general doom."

In *The Decameron*, an account of the Black Death in medieval Florence, Giovanni Boccaccio described how fear of contagion could corrupt any human heart. "Almost without exception, people took a single and very inhumane precaution [against infection] namely to avoid and run away from the sick. . . . [A] great number of people departed without anyone at all to witness their going." While the famine Irish stood up to contagion panic better than the medieval Florentines, Paul de Strzelecki, the British Association agent, witnessed many instances of inhumanity. It was "painful . . . to observe . . . the recklessness of mothers to their children [and] of adult children to their aged parents." Some of the reports of Mr. Bishop, the Commissariat officer in Skibbereen, could have been lifted directly from Boccaccio: "The instant fever appears in a cabin, the neglect is fearful, the nearest friends, neighbors and even relatives . . . cannot by any persuasion be induced to afford the sufferer any assistance." In Cork, municipal officials stationed guards at the approaches to the city to protect residents from the country people who were flooding into the city in search of food and bringing disease with them. Shortly after Cork took action, the Dublin police asked permission to station groups of "well disciplined" men at the principal entrances to the city.

By the end of February, the workhouse system was also engulfed in pestilence. In Lugan, the small local workhouse had ninety-five fever fatalities in a single week. In the Belfast workhouse, fifty to sixty inmates were dying weekly from a combination of fever, smallpox, and measles; during one particularly horrendous week, sixteen infants also died. In the Cork workhouse, where 757 inmates were infected, the guardians invoked a law that required fever hospitals to accept diseased inmates. Patient dumping, charged officials at the municipal fever hospital, and refused to accept any more workhouse transfers. The guardians at a Kilkenny workhouse were cannier: they managed to convince a local gaol to accept their infected. Pestilence erupted in the gaol; the superintendent, his wife, their servant girl, and dozens of prisoners fell desperately ill.

As fever killed doctors, orderlies, and administrators, the appalling sanitary conditions in the workhouses worsened, facilitating the spread of disease. One workhouse official wrote that the pestilential smells that greeted him each morning were "so morbidly fetid and laden with noxious miasma . . . that on the door being opened, I was uniformly seized with the most violent retching." Overcrowding also fed the pestilence. In Fermoy, the 900-bed workhouse held 1,533 inmates; the 800-bed Kilmallock workhouse, 1,500 inmates. "The unwillingness of many workhouse and hospital officials to harden their hearts and refuse further admissions had disastrous consequences," wrote a public health official.

In the winter of 1847, nothing could have prevented a collapse of the workhouse system but a lack of foresight among the workhouse guardians made the catastrophe worse than it had to be. Despite a December 1845 circular reminding the guardians of the responsibility to provide fever care, and despite a March 1846 law that created a national Board of Health with the power to compel workhouses to offer such care, a significant number of guardians did nothing. Erecting a fever shed or renting a house to treat infected inmates often necessitated an increase in the poor rate, which made guardians very unpopular with local ratepayers. In February 1847, the Central Board of Health, disbanded the previous August, was reconstituted; a new Temporary Fever Act was passed, and the cost of fever care transferred from the workhouses to the relief committees, which were less susceptible to ratepayer pressure. These measures did improve the situation. Three hundred seventy-three new fever facilities were eventually built; still, much more was left undone. In June 1847, fever sufferers in Kanturk, in County Cork, were still sleeping in the streets; in Ballina, Mayo, fever cases were housed in leantos: planks propped diagonally against the walls of the local workhouse.

Under a report on the situation in Cork and Mayo, Trevelyan scribbled a single word:

"Why?"

✴

In early March 1847, an old man stood by a window in a Sussex lodging house, staring at the sea. A few hundred meters beyond the tideline, a small flotilla of fishing boats bobbed up and down in the black Channel swells. To the west, the skyline was dominated by church steeples; beneath the spires, neat lines of white-trimmed brick houses circled down to the sea; the narrow cobblestone streets were crowded with fishermen and purposeful Victorian tourists, guidebooks in hand. Above a castle ruin on a nearby hill, the March sun shone down on the peaceful Channel village of Hastings. For the first time in months, Daniel O'Connell, in grievous health since the previous October, thought he might live. A few days later, a party of visiting English Catholics spoiled the illusion. The well-wishers, deferential to a fault, acted as if they were talking to a dead man. After the visitors departed, O'Connell added two new codicils to his will. Since returning to England in late January, the Liberator had become notably more infirm. On February 8, a few hours before his final appearance in the Commons, he was unsure he had the stamina to make a speech. "They deceive you . . . who tell you I am recovering," he wrote to a colleague. The pestilence was also depressing his spirit. "To the all prevalent famine is now superadded dysentery and typhus in their worst shapes. Nothing can be more appalling."

Two years after rolling out of a Dublin gaol in a gilded carriage with a flutist on the roof and half the city in the streets, O'Connell had been reduced to Yesterday's Man by physical infirmity and political marginalization. The previous September, when he recast himself as a man "above party" and called upon Protestant and Catholic members of the gentry to join together to meet the famine threat, O'Connell seemed to have found a new political role. In January, when leading figures of Catholic and Protestant Ireland gathered in the Oval Room of the Rotunda Hospital to form the Irish party, the Liberator could, with some justification, claim that the attendees were acting on his vision. But except for distrusting the British government more than each other, the members of the Irish Party had little in common. Lacking any predicate for political success, the party quickly dissolved. Now, O'Connell's own political organization, the Repeal Association, was on the edge of collapse. In the autumn of 1846, when the association called on members to exercise "PATIENCE, PEACE, AVOIDANCE OF CRIME AND RESIGNATION TO HIS HOLY WILL," rank-and-file members in Dublin, Limerick, and Cork rebelled. On October 26, the Dublin rebels drew up a "remonstration," a formal protest; the Dubliners objected to the Whig alliance and to O'Connell's refusal to entertain the idea of armed struggle.

In December, when the Dublin rebels met again, O'Connell found it harder to ignore their protests. Mass death was appearing, and even some Catholic clerics, traditionally O'Connell loyalists, were questioning his leadership. Then, in January, Young Ireland broke with the Repeal Association and created its own organization: the Irish Confederation. By early February, the Repeal Association was on the verge of bankruptcy and O'Connell reduced to seeking sinecures for old colleagues. On a last visit to Downing Street, he had persuaded Lord John to appoint P. V. Fitzpatrick, a longtime aide, as assistant registrar of deeds in Dublin. The Liberator's last major public appearance was the Commons speech on February 8, 1847. Half a century of public life had ended in begging; without British assistance, one fourth of Ireland's population would perish.

❧

I won't go!

O'Connell grew truculent as his scheduled departure for Rome and meeting with the pope drew near. If he was "not strong enough to return to Ireland in such weather as this," how could he possibly travel to Rome? His doctors were adamant. The warm Italian climate would have a restorative effect. In Hastings, where he was accompanied by his confessor, the Reverend Dr. Miley, and several members of his personal household, O'Connell spent most of his time in prayer. "It is most edifying to witness his demeanor in this respect," said Dr. Miley. He prays "not alone by day but also by night." O'Connell's other principal diversion was tinkering with his will. There was a £630 bequest to the Repeal Association, and another large bequest to his oldest son, Maurice. Before leaving for Hastings, the Liberator had ordered the faithful Fitzpatrick to sell his remaining assets. "My illness is very expensive, and the times are indeed bad."

Three weeks later, on March 22, O'Connell stood on a wharf in Folkestone harbor, thirty miles east of Hastings. The harbor still bore signs of a recent dredging by the South-Eastern Railway Company. The company was planning a new London-to-Dover link and expected the railroad to greatly increase tourist traffic in Folkestone. Off in the distance, the French coastline was just visible. It was somewhere in this general area that the blight had jumped from the continent to England in the summer of 1845. A cross-Channel steamer approached; an hour later, O'Connell was gone.

CHAPTER THIRTEEN

Atonement

T oward the beginning of March, Mr. Trevelyan received a letter from one of his most trusted Irish sources, Mr. Nicholas Cummins, the Cork magistrate and author of the Christmas Eve appeal to the Duke of Wellington. The 1846 American corn crop was now arriving in bulk, wrote Cummins, but the crisis was still deepening.

> The distress and misery spread daily wider, and affect in some way or other all classes in the community if I may except the corn merchants. The mortality in the western districts . . . continues unabated. This week's reports make it even larger than at any previous time and those portions of the country which have hitherto been comparatively well off, are now inundated by hordes of wretched objects flying from still more wretched homes, who bring with them infection and disease. . . . It is now, indeed, too manifest, that no supplies of food can prevent the loss of a fearful amount of life.

On March 9, two weeks after the Cummins letter, Mr. Smith O'Brien, the leader of Young Ireland and the MP for Limerick, told the House of Commons that he understood that "as many as 240,000 starvation deaths" had already occurred. He asked the Irish chief secretary, Mr. Henry Labouchere, if the government had any figures on the mortality. No, replied Mr. Labouchere. The government did not, but "regarding Mr. Smith O'Brien's 240,000 figure," he, Mr. Labouchere, "did not believe anything of the kind was the case." A few weeks later, Lord George Bentinck asked Labouchere whether the government had had an opportunity to compile figures on the mortality in Ireland. No, Labouchere replied, not yet. Bentinck was incredulous. There had been "tens of thousands, hundreds of thousands of deaths, [yet Parliament] could not learn from the government how many." Labouchere may have known more than he was saying, but compiling an accurate death count was challenging in a country where people were burying their dead in cabin walls (for retrieval later, when the family came into coffin money) and under metal sidings, and where the fields and ditches were littered with unattached body parts that might belong to one person or five. Moreover, in late February, when Mr. Cummins wrote Trevelyan, the principal priority of the British government was not ascertaining the scope of the mortality, it was bringing the wholesale mortality to an end.

The average daily wage of public works laborers had fallen to 7½ pence, so even the inexpensive Yankee corn often remained unaffordable. "Most of the laborers are in debt to the hucksters [the gombeen men] as deep as those hucksters will let them go," wrote Mrs. Smith, the landlord's wife. The public works program, created to protect the Irish peasant from the moral depredations of free food, had failed, a victim of snow, gales, exhaustion, malnutrition, and the ideological fixations of its creators.

Under the new Russell relief scheme, by this spring, a nationwide network of two thousand soup kitchens would be established, and the public works program, having failed to check the famine, would be closed and the laborers returned to the land to plant the 1847 crops. Funded by government loans and operated by reconstituted relief committees, the soup kitchens would provide free soup to dismissed laborers, their families, and virtually everyone else in Ireland except the able-bodied employed.

The appointment of General John Burgoyne to head the soup operation was a measure of the importance London attached to the program's

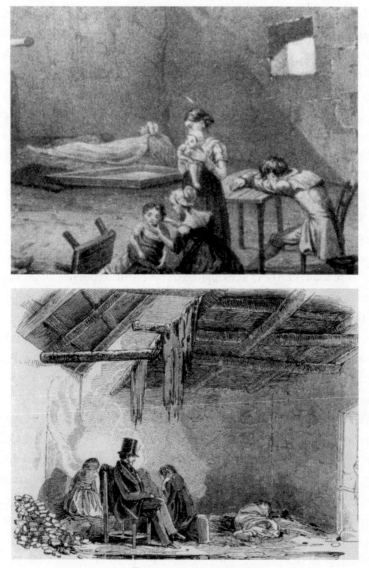

Famine-era cottages

success. Burgoyne had been the general of fortifications, Great Britain, and director of the Irish Board of Works; before that, he had served in the French Wars and fought in the Battle of New Orleans. Sixtyish, still cavalryman-slim and handsome in the dashing Anglo-Saxon man-of-affairs manner, the general bore a slight resemblance to C. Aubrey

Smith, the English actor who presided over the British empire in Hollywood movies of the 1930s. Not every general looks like a commander of men; Burgoyne, among the most admired and competent officers in the British army, did. In February, he sailed for Dublin with a letter of congratulations from an excited Mr. Labouchere—"Your name will inspire . . . confidence and respect"—in his pocket and a new title: chairman of the Relief Commission.

On arriving at Dublin Castle, the general was greeted by his fellow relief commissioners: Mr. Edward Twisleton, the resident Poor Law commissioner; Colonel Jones, of the Board of Works; Thomas Redington, the Irish undersecretary; and the sulky former chairman of the Relief Commission. No, Routh said when Trevelyan asked him to serve under Burgoyne on the reconstituted commission: "I do not see how I can find the time." A few days after that exchange, Trevelyan wrote Routh an uncharacteristically sensitive letter. He assured his disappointed subordinate that Burgoyne planned to consult him on everything. Routh remained inconsolable. He felt he had been demoted, and he was right; he had—and not just because Burgoyne was a famous general. Routh had become notorious in the Irish press for lecturing starving peasants on the virtues of the free market and was derided in Dublin Castle for being Trevelyan's poodle. Nearly every colleague, including Richard Griffith, a commissioner at the Board of Works, complained that Routh "consult[ed] nobody [on relief decisions] but Trevelyan, who, of course, knows nothing about Ireland." Trevelyan also knew little about patience. When Routh failed to reply to his sympathetic letter, he sent the former chairman of the Relief Commission a sharp note: "You will obey any orders with respect to [serving under General Burgoyne]."

Viceroy Bessborough, though now quite ill, was also on hand to greet the general. Like Griffith, Bessborough felt Trevelyan knew nothing about Ireland, and in Burgoyne he believed Dublin Castle finally had a man with the stature and force of character to stand up to Trevelyan. This remained to be seen. As the general was settling in, a note arrived from London: "We shall be obliged to you to follow the same practice which the Board of Works and Sir R. Routh adopted with great advantage to us all. . . . Send me, *as you receive them*, copies of the reports of your Inspecting Officers and other documents . . . to keep the government informed of all that is going on in different parts of the country." The note was signed C. E. Trevelyan.

><•><

Despite orders to have two thousand soup kitchens in operation by June and the first group of kitchens up and running within six weeks—that is, by mid-March—Burgoyne resolved to put a sound infrastructure in place before serving a single bowl of soup. Unlike Peel and Graham, who last April had been willing to tolerate a certain amount of fraud and abuse in the half-grant loan program in order to keep relief flowing, Burgoyne's first priority was to create an orderly, fraud-proof program, even if the cost of caution was a needless loss of life. The scandal-ridden public works program was an object lesson in the dangers of haste and carelessness. In February, as hunger deepened and pestilence spread, the College Green headquarters of the soup program produced fourteen tons of documents: ten thousand record books, eighty thousand sheets of paper, and three million food cards that would wrest order out of chaos. Deep into the bitter February nights, the general's subordinates scrutinized every detail of the soup kitchen plan. Instructions were issued on who qualified for relief, how to color-code index cards, who should stand where in the soup line, and what to do when a relief recipient failed to respond when his name was called (send him to the back of the line to wait his turn again). Officials gave special attention to the kind of soup the kitchens should serve.

College Green had three specifications: the soup had to be nutritious, flavorful, and cheap. The hundreds of charity kitchens in Ireland were contacted. Alas, none served a soup that met all three specifications. Some soups, while flavorful and nutritious, were too expensive to employ in a mass feeding program; others, though inexpensive, were as vile-tasting as the ox-head (without tongue) and turnip soup on offer at a Queen's County kitchen. Then, on February 10, the soup problem appeared to solve itself. In the letters column of *The Times*, a Frenchman named Alexis Soyer announced a plan to create a "soup for the poor" that acted as "generously on the digestive organs as a change of air does on the convalescent," yet cost a pittance to make. The letter caused an immediate sensation; in his own sphere, the thirty-eight-year-old Soyer was as eminent as General Burgoyne. He was chief chef at the Reform Club, patronized by Prime Minister Russell and half the cabinet. He was the author of a bestselling cookbook, *The Gastronomic Regenerator*; he was an inventor of the gas oven and—his greatest achievement—the creator of a new "scientific" approach to food preparation. Soyer's interest in soup kitchens was a byproduct of his other consuming passion, social climbing. Some of the fashionable ladies who visited his new "scientific" kitchen at the Reform Club complained about the poor quality of soup in the London charity kitchens where they did volunteer work. Soyer investigated. *Sacrebleu!* The English could not even make a proper soup. When the government announced plans to establish a soup kitchen program in Ireland, the Frenchman saw an opportunity to do well for himself by doing good for others.

In a second letter to *The Times*, on the eighteenth, Soyer apologized "for the delay" in publishing his new soup recipe. His "experiments . . . with various kinds of farinaceous ingredients" had been unexpectedly time-consuming. There was good news, though. Soup No. 1, as the Frenchman called his creation, had been tasted and praised by "numerous noblemen, members of Parliament and several ladies" of distinction. His letter also included the recipe for Soup No. 1.

A *Times* reader who wrote under the nom de plume No Cook examined the list of ingredients:

A quarter of a joint of leg of beef	1 penny
Two ounces of dripping fat	½ penny
Two onions and other vegetables	1 penny
Half a pound of flour	1½ pence per lb.
Half a pound of pearl barley	3 pence per lb.
Three ounces of salt, with half an ounce of brown sugar	¼ penny
Fuel	1 penny
Two gallons of water	0
Cost	6 pence

No Cook complained that M. Soyer should call his creation "poor soup" instead of "soup for the poor." Medicus, another *Times* reader, described Soup No. 1 as a "reckless," "preposterous," and "debilitating" experiment. Medicus also warned that, alone, even good soup was insufficient to sustain the human body. M. Soyer and "the best judges of the noble art of gastronomy at the Reform Club" would discover this if they "restrict[ed] themselves to a bellyful of soup . . . for two or three weeks [while] laboring hard every day." The British government looked at Soyer's cost projections and decided to ignore the criticisms. Whatever its deficiencies, Soup No. 1 only cost ¾ penny per quart—about half the cost of the average soup kitchen soup, which ranged from 1¼ to 1½ pence. Soyer was invited to Dublin to set up a model soup kitchen.

On a gusty spring day six weeks later, a "large and brilliant assemblage" of Dublin notables—including Viceroy Bessborough, who looked alarmingly unwell; his daughters, Ladies Emily and Kathleen, both with long Ponsonby faces; the "lovely" Mrs. Williams; the Misses Brady, who rarely missed a social event; and the lord chancellor, Mr. Connellan—stood on one side of a wooden building in the courtyard of the Royal Barracks, watching soldiers and Constabulary officers herd a large crowd of paupers into a line on the other side. The building in between the two groups, forty feet long and thirty feet wide, was a repository of Soyer's ideas about scientific gastronomy. The entrance, which zigzagged to enhance crowd control, led to a kitchen with two large rectangles. The inner rectangle held a bread oven, cutting tables for meat and vegetables, and a three-hundred-gallon cast-iron soup boiler that resembled a spaceship in a Jules Verne novel. The outer rectangle, the dining area, was lined with rows of narrow tables. The tables measured eighteen inches across and had a perforated surface. Inside each perforation was a quart-sized enamel soup basin with a metal spoon attached by a chain. To maintain order and maximize efficiency, Soyer limited seatings to one hundred people. Upon entering the serving area, diners were required to stand at attention in front of their chairs until the check clerk had counted a hundred people. Then, a bell rang, and the diners sat down to say grace; a second bell signaled eating time; a third bell, the end of the meal. Upon leaving the kitchen, each diner received a quarter of a pound of bread or a biscuit.

The "scientific" Soyer soup kitchen

On opening day, the "honored" guests exposed themselves to every facet of soup kitchen experience. Entering through the zigzag passageway, each guest passed the gruff check clerk, who pressed his metal counter, which made a little clicking sound, and stood in front of a chair in the dining area until the dining bell sounded. Soyer had created several soups for the poor, and as they were served, a reporter for the *Morning Chronicle* watched "the guests discussing the merits of each." When the end-of-meal bell sounded, and the "brilliant assemblage" was replaced by a group of authentic paupers, the "sudden and bold" change of scene startled the *Chronicle* man. "A moment before, a great number of lively faces smiled their approval [at] everything." Now, the kitchen was filled with faces "upon which it would be hard to say whether time or hunger had made the most havoc." Another reporter, an Irishman, was watching Viceroy Bessborough's daughters, Ladies Emily and Kathleen, Mrs. Williams, and the Misses Brady. The ladies had stayed behind and were standing in the inner rectangle, examining the new diners as intently as they might an interesting new addition to the Dublin zoo. "Was it humane, was it kind, was it decent, to make such a public display of wretchedness?" the reporter wondered. "Could not this afternoon, the feeding of the poor have been arranged without outraging every feeling of rectitude, every principle of humanity?"

Routh, who considered M. Soyer an "artist," told Trevelyan that the Frenchman's scientific approach to gastronomy ought to be incorporated into the Irish modernization program. If the Soyer method "could be extended throughout the cities and large towns, it would not only afford effectual aid in the current dearth, but go far to change the habits of the people by giving them a new taste of a higher order."

⚬

The Times, though pleased by M. Soyer's success, was absolutely tickled by another recent piece of Irish news. According to a newly released set of figures, between January 1, 1846, and January 1, 1847, bank deposits in eastern Ireland had increased by £26,000, from £965,000 to £991,000; in Ulster, by £47,000, from £621,338 to £668,787; and in the south, where the depth of the famine would seem to argue for a decline in savings, the rise was steeper still: £62,000, from £1,045,584 to £1,107,280. Even in the impoverished west, where the deep crop losses had produced widespread mass death, savings were up, from £131,156 to £140,781. *The Times* could barely contain itself: "Let all Europe, which watches our domestic affairs with so benevolent a curiosity, take note, Ireland, starving Ireland, oppressed Ireland, at this very acme of her woes, is putting by more money than ever." This was demagogic nonsense, and the paper's editors had to know it. Irish bank deposits were up for all the wrong reasons. The middle and upper middle classes were putting money aside to emigrate, and, even with the spring planting upon the country, large farmers and landowners were still delaying agricultural operations. From Mayo came reports of little agricultural activity even at "this, the eleventh hour"; from Cork, there were accounts of men turning their backs on the "ungrateful soil"; and from Tipperary, warnings that there was "*very little* preparation for sowing oats or anything else." In late February, with the public works rolls at a new high—708,000—and the lack of planting, threatening a third year of famine even without the blight, Board of Works officers were instructed to overcome all resistance and start reducing the labor force. At a meeting in a Mayo courtroom, a young board officer named Primrose found that easier said than done. As Mr. Primrose struck workers' names from the rolls, a priest in the audience leapt to his feet and shouted: no "alleviation of . . . distress could take place while such blackguards were sent amongst us taking pleasure in hastening . . . death by withholding the relief intended for them." The words brought the rest of the courtroom to its feet; there was shouting, cursing, waving of fists. "Willful murderer!" cried one man. "Clear the courtroom!" shouted an alarmed magistrate. The order got everyone out into the hall, but there a great commotion erupted. The courtroom doors flung open, and before Mr. Primrose knew what was happening half a dozen men were chasing him down an aisle. In a report on the "outrage," the chastened young officer expressed grave reservations about "carrying into effect . . . the measure"—the work reduction—"soon to be commenced."

At Downing Street, Lord John, who planned to call a general election later in the year, alternated between fears of a third year of famine and dread at having to explain to Devon, Dorset, and Derbyshire why he was spending £944,000 a month in Ireland to build impassable roads, decapitate hills, and fill in holes. The time for bold action had arrived. On March 10, the Board of Works announced that on the twentieth, ten days hence, there would be an across-the-board 20 percent reduction in the public works rolls; further reductions would follow at two- to three-week intervals. On the next day, the eleventh, laborers learned who would be cut first: men who held ten acres or more; this in some districts amounted to 25 percent or 30 percent of the workforce. On the thirteenth, there was another board announcement: laborers with physical infirmities would be struck from the rolls immediately. On the fifteenth, the government authorized relief committees in compliance with the Soup Kitchen Act (as the Temporary Relief Act was also known) to begin serving soup. Not much soup was served on the fifteenth. Eager to implement the work reduction, the government had ignored its pledge not to close construction sites until soup kitchens were available to feed dismissed laborers and their families. The first hundred kitchens would not be in operation until March 26, and they would only be able to feed a fraction of the 146,000 laborers scheduled for redundancy. On March 19, Sir Lucius O'Brien, the Lieutenant of Clare, predicted disaster if the government proceeded with the cuts.

The next day, Saturday the twentieth, the 146,000 laborers were dismissed. The redundancy put roughly 600,000 to 700,000 people—if the laborers' families are included—at imminent risk of starvation. If London did not know this, and if General Burgoyne, who bore much of the responsibility for the kitchen shortage, did not know it, the men at the work sites knew it. "Be it recorded," wrote one man, that the laborers "walked off the works . . . without offering any resistance . . . except rending the air . . . most *terrifically*, with cries and shrieks and almost death groans." Another man overheard a group of laborers telling each another, "Let us go now, and dig our children's graves."

Men at a County Cavan work site drew lots to determine who would be dismissed. The losers "raised a cry which still rings in my ears," said a man who witnessed the drawing. In Cork, another man watched a group of laborers disappear into the lanes. He wondered what principle of political economy had been served by "send[ing] men to till the land [who] have neither seed nor subsistence." In Westport, an altercation occurred on the morning of the twentieth. The board officer charged with enforcing the workforce reduction instructed the local relief committee to pare the rolls; "the committee refused, . . . the officer grabbed the rolls and . . . marked off with red ink every 5th person." In Galway, the damp March streets filled with dismissed laborers marching under the banner "Bread or Employment." In Limerick, a dozen laborers burst into a church and smashed a soup boiler; in the town of Kilfenora, a soup boiler was thrown into a lake. To destroy soup boilers made no sense, of course, but life in Ireland no longer made sense. A few days after the reduction, an MP read a letter from a public works officer in the House of Commons. The savage press coverage of the shutdown had damaged the board's reputation; the letter was intended to repair it by highlighting an overlooked act of kindness. To wit: the Board of Works had paid the dismissed laborers on the twentieth, a Saturday, though they were not entitled to be paid until the following Tuesday or Wednesday.

Meanwhile, the Irish Constabulary was out in the unsown fields counting bodies. In April, a Constabulary report would put the mortality at 400,000.

⬥

In November 1846, when Armagh organized a day of solemn prayer and humiliation, British officials began to think of doing something similar on a national scale. In November and December 1846, public sympathy for Ireland was still strong. Even *The Non-Conformist,* the voice of British dissenters—Baptists, Methodists, Presbyterians—was urging readers to "Give, give, liberally." A national observance for Ireland could raise more charitable contributions, especially if the day was built around the theme of atonement. The public viewed the crop failures as a Visitation of Providence, and expressions of divine displeasure required acts of atonement. The only vexing question was what to atone for. In the case of Ireland, there was a multitude of possibilities: the potato culture, sloth, violence, large families, "the drink," and dependence on government. In the case of England, however, no obvious answer suggested itself. Finally, it was decided that England should atone for its pride and wealth and for allowing the Irish to slip beyond the bonds of human civilization. Before March was many days old, Downing Street announced that the United Kingdom would observe a national day of fast and humiliation on the twenty-fourth, four days after public works shut down in Ireland.

In Kent, March 24 began with farmers and laborers crowded into pews, heads bowed and purses open. In Dublin, too, the churches filled early. "Never within the memory of man," declared the *Dublin Evening News,* "was there such a universal attendance of Divine Worship in this city. . . . The earnestness of supplication, the deep humility of heart and the ardor of devotion were truly affecting." In Frensham, Surrey, the faithful listened in hushed silence as Leslie Badham, the vicar, described where things stood in his native Ireland. "The living envy the dead . . . [and] the dead are either allowed to putrefy . . . or [are] flung into the earth coffinless and unwept. . . . Oh! [the] depths of misery . . . even the ties of affection are burst asunder."

The next day, the British press described the observance as an outstanding success. Like many journalistic statements, this was a half truth.

While a goodly number of Englishmen and women fasted to atone for their pridefulness, resolute fasters appear to have been few. Early in the day, Lord Morpeth, the commissioner of woods and forests, had a lapse and consumed "a small crust of bread, some salt and fish." Remorseful, Morpeth attended five church services on the twenty-fourth. Press claims that the day was unmarred by "appearances of pleasuring" were also an exaggeration. Though the sky was partly cloudy and the March wind still had some winter in it, a fair portion of London's "rising generation"—scriveners, clerks, shopgirls, and mechanics—skipped church and took themselves off to Greenwich to admire the Naval College, to picnic on the pleasant rises near the Royal Observatory, and to watch the play of sun and shadow on the early spring lawns. Here and there, one heard some talk of Ireland, though not enough to spoil the holiday mood. "Greenwich had quite an Easter Sunday look," declared a visitor who encountered many examples of "pleasuring." "Blackheath, with its donkeys, was all alive; the tea shops . . . crowded and, of course, the public houses were not empty . . . the entire neighborhood formed a picture in which groups engaged in eating, drinking, smoking and dressed in their Sunday clothes, formed prominent objects." There was also little talk of Irish suffering on the wharf beneath London Bridge, where hundreds of day trippers stood in line, picnic baskets under arm, waiting to board the Gravesend and Richmond steamer. "Miso-Humbug," whose letter appeared in the March 24 edition of *The Morning Chronicle*, wished to know "by what authority . . . Her Majesty's Ministers . . . presumed to direct the vengeance of Omnipotence?" Two other letter writers—"Not A Fast Man" and "Facts Opposed To Fiction"—also warned that Providence could not be ordered about like a junior minister. An exasperated John Stuart Mill complained that blaming the potato blight on Providence was as nonsensical as blaming it on "a thunderstorm."

In central London, however, the twenty-fourth did have a somber, Good Friday feel. The crowds were dressed in solemn colors, black, dark brown, and blue—though in Mayfair and Belgravia the ladies in black tended to look more stylish than repentant. In the business districts of the imperial capital, shops and offices were shuttered, and the streets, while crowded, lacked the usual kinetic energy of a London weekday.

Not once were the pigeons atop the Duke of Wellington statue or Nelson's Column startled into flight by a sharp noise. Even in Southwark, where it was sometimes possible to see a "perfectly naked woman dancing to the fiddler's tune," only the occasional rumble of a passing coach and the bark of a dog disturbed the stillness. Having had several weeks to prepare for the day, London's clerics mounted the pulpit in full war paint. At St. Paul's Cathedral—the great gold dome looking faintly papist under a dull March sky—the canon, Mr. Bennett, warned the repentant: "If there be in the land famine, if there be pestilence, blasting, mildew, locusts, or there be caterpillars, if their enemy besiege them," then the only hope of "turning away divine wrath was . . . national repentance." At St. Philip's in Kensington, the Reverend Mr. Repton was also in a militant mood: "Nation shall rise against nation, Kingdom against Kingdom." However, like Mr. Bennett, Mr. Repton failed to explain what any of that had to do with the uncoffined dead inhabiting the unsown fields of Ireland.

At St. Mary le Strand, the Reverend J. F. Denham declared the day "a day for a man to afflict his soul, to spread sack cloth and ashes under him." At the German Jews' Synagogue in the Duke's Place, Aldgate, Dr. Nathan Adler, the chief rabbi, offered some of the most sensible advice of the day: "Do good and observe charity." A *Times* correspondent, who sounded mildly astonished to find himself inside a synagogue, reported that the congregation "bore the same appearance as at one of their holidays, the ladies' gallery also being very full." In St. Margaret's, Westminster, where the House of Commons observed the day, the Venerable Dr. Delany also avoided apocalyptic imagery. "For their hearts were not right with Him," Dr. Delany told an audience that included Prime Minister Russell; former prime minister Peel; Sir George Grey, the current home secretary; Sir James Graham, the former home secretary; Lord George Bentinck; Mr. Roebuck; and Mr. Benjamin Disraeli, whose act of atonement was to dress as inconspicuously as his colleague.

Meanwhile, in Ireland, the mortality continued unchecked. "In some parts," wrote Henry Brennan, a Sligo priest, in *The Freeman's Journal*, "the fields are bleached with bones of the dead . . . previously picked [apart] by the dogs. About a month [ago], two died in a waste house near my residence. . . . Two days ago . . . two little girls who are recovering from fever [agreed] to drag out the bodies. Now both [corpses] . . . lie in a drain, to the rear of my house with a slight covering over them. One body [is] covered with worms and has had one of its thighs devoured by dogs." In Skibbereen, a man "encountered the head of a person" in one part of a graveyard; in another part, the person's "arms, and elsewhere the legs and last of all the bowels—the dogs ha[d] devoured most of the flesh." One morning, a young woman cradling a baby appeared in a shop and asked for food. Later that day, the shopkeeper, who had given the woman some milk, passed her corpse on the road. "The baby was still alive in her arms."

Nassau Senior, a leading Victorian political economist, observed that after the first crop failure in Ireland, the English had made three promises to themselves: "[We] resolved that Ireland should not starve. We resolved that for one year at least we would feed them. But then we came to a third resolution. We resolved that we would not feed them for *more* than a year." The Poor Law Extension Act was how the British government intended to keep the third promise. Under the terms of the legislation, in August, when the soup kitchen program ended, the new Poor Law, which was expected to win parliamentary approval in May or June, would transfer the entire cost of Irish relief to the Irish ratepayer.

The former home secretary, Graham, predicted that when the transfer was effected, "the consequence will be a complete revolution in property, the ruin of the landed proprietors, and the downfall of the Protestant Ascendancy." This was not hyperbole. Even by Lord John's calculation, the new law could raise Irish property taxes from £400,000 to £1,800,000. The Irish ratepayer, who had felt that asking him to bear the burden of the Labor Rate Act was like asking the "Hindoustanis to build Manchester," now felt that he was being asked to build London, Paris, and Rome as well.

In February, a deputation of sixty-four Irish peers and forty-three MPs visited Downing Street to warn Lord John that the extended Poor Law "would produce social disorder" in Ireland. In March, when Catholic members of the Irish party announced that they would support the new Poor Law, Anglo-Irish members created their own organization, the

Irish Council, to agitate against the law. The Russell cabinet was also deeply divided over the measure. Lord Lansdowne, who was both lord president of the council and a large Irish landowner, warned Lord John that the high rates in the bill would crush Irish property. Lord Palmerston, the foreign minister, called the measure "that black dose," and Lady Palmerston said that if the bill became law, her husband would have to start sending money to his Irish estates.

The new Poor Law did entail risks. If rates rose too high, a class war could erupt between the Irish proprietors and large farmers, who paid most of the rate, and the poor small farmers and laborers, who consumed most of the relief. Nonetheless, Lord John believed the law's benefits outweighed its risks. The great invasion of Irish paupers that had given two generations of British politicians sleepless nights was now here. Since the late autumn of 1846, London, Liverpool, and every other sizable port in Britain daily had been inundated by hundreds, sometimes thousands, of the Irish poor, and in Norfolk, Suffolk, and everywhere else, people were in a fury about it. These days, it was hard to pick up a newspaper without encountering a headline such as "What is to be the End of it?" or "The Irish Ulcer." Lord John believed the outdoor relief entitlement in the new Poor Law would encourage Irish paupers to stay home, and that would benefit not only British ratepayers, who were paying for pauper relief, but his general election prospects.

In a little book called *The Irish Crisis*, Mr. Trevelyan described some of the other benefits of the new Poor Law, including how it would foster a commonwealth of mutual interests in bitterly divided Ireland. The law would draw into the commonweal the landlord, by making it less expensive for him to give the poor man work than to pay for his relief, and the peasant, by expanding his social safety net in the form of the outdoor relief entitlement. Here, as evidence, Mr. Trevelyan quoted a Dingle priest. One Sunday during Mass, the cleric (according to Trevelyan) told his flock, "Heretofore, landlords have had agents who collect their rent. . . . Now, for the first time, the poor man has an agent to collect *his* rent. That agent is the poor-rate collector." In his book, Mr. Trevelyan also cited two other benefits of the law. It would "insur[e] that landowners and [large] farmers either enable the people to support themselves by honest industry or dispose of their property to those who can and will perform this indispensable duty." And, last, and perhaps most centrally, the law would help excise from the Irish national character "dependency on government." "The attraction of 'public money' . . . eats like a canker into the moral health and physical prosperity of the people," declared Mr. Trevelyan. "All classes make a 'poor mouth.' . . . They conceal their advantages, exaggerate their difficulties and relax their exertions. . . . There is only one way in which the relief of the destitute ever has been, or ever will be, conducted consistently with the general welfare, and that is by *making it a local charge.*"

In the final weeks of a March so unseasonably cool that one contemporary complained of "a backward spring," the climactic debates over the new Poor Law devolved into a family quarrel between the Anglo-Irish MPs, who felt their class under existential threat, and the English MPs, whose commitment to Irish self-help was fortified by the hysterical scale of Irish immigration. Catholic and nationalist MPs, who had decided to support the bill because of its peasant protections, were largely bystanders to the quarrel. Like many family quarrels, the one over the new Poor Law was often bitter and ugly. Much of what was said during the final debates was highly personal, mean, heated—and often off-subject, as one side or the other aired long-ago slights, resentments, and hurts. One evening, things got so out of hand, an exasperated Mr. Labouchere interrupted to remind the Commons that nothing would ever get done "if on every Irish Bill . . . we are to resume a debate on the Union, on the distinction of Celt and Saxon, taxation, and other subjects."

The admonition was ignored. In one exchange, Mr. Walter, the chief proprietor of *The Times* and a Tory MP, said the Irish had no more talent for self-rule than "the blacks"; in another, Mr. Roebuck called the Irish proprietors "slave holders." Every English MP who participated in the debate seemed to have a favorite example of the Irish landowner's reckless improvidence and cravenness. Stunned by the vicious tone of the attacks, Mr. Frederick Shaw, MP for Trinity College, Dublin, protested that English gentlemen "seemed not to think it beneath them to rake up anecdotes . . . of [Irish proprietors] who had kept more horses or dogs than the Gentleman approved of, and not given as much as they should have . . . to the poor." What if "Irish Gentlemen pried into all the residences of . . . Belgravia Square or the county seats of the English aristocracy, and when they found money or extravagance that might have been given to the starving poor of Ireland, held [English Gentlemen] up to . . . obloquy." Mr. Bateson, another Irish MP, warned that if the new Poor Law was enacted "the whole of Ireland [would become] a monster workhouse with the Prime Minister of England [as] the head relieving officer."

Rejected by Catholic Ireland and mocked by English colleagues, on many nights the Anglo-Irish MPs must have left the Commons wondering where they belonged—or, indeed, if they belonged anywhere at all.

On March 29, the deadlock over the bill was broken by Mr. William Gregory, a Tory MP for Dublin. Mr. Gregory's future accomplishments would include service as parliamentary spokesman for the Confederate States of America; champion of Sunday museum-going; and the colonial governor of Ceylon; but March 29, 1847, was the night Mr. Gregory's name entered Irish history as a curse. His amendment to the Poor Law Extension Act, which passed by a 117–7 majority, denied relief to small farmers unless they agreed to surrender all but a quarter acre of their land. With its addition, the new Poor Law became as much an instrument of social engineering as a tax bill. In the high poor rates, the British government had a means of restructuring the landed classes, and in the quarter-acre clause, a means of crushing the small-farmer class. Within six years, the number of small farms in Ireland—those amounting to between one and five acres—would fall by 52 percent.

The new Poor Law seemed as perfect a legislative expression of self-help as any Moralist could hope for, but in an article in the *North British Review*, the leading Moralist of the age, the Scottish cleric Thomas Chalmers, pointed out a distinction that the bill's Moralist supporters had overlooked. Visitations of Providence come in two forms: ordinary and special. In an ordinary Visitation, God worked through natural law: He created manageable natural disasters, regional crop failures, floods, and so forth, to test victims; and, through the testing, to bring the weak, the dependent, and the doubtful to self-reliance. Special Visitations were a different matter. In a special Visitation, God transformed Himself into the angry, wrathful God of the Old Testament. He suspended the workings of natural law and intervened directly in the life of the world, creating catastrophes of such enormous magnitude that individual initiative was overwhelmed. Because "extraordinary Visitations" produced "extraordinary suffering,"

Chalmers said they had to be "met by means alike extraordinary," not by self-reliance and private charity alone, but by government assistance. The Irish famine was an example of a special Visitation.

Mr. Trevelyan, Mr. Wood, and the other Moralists in the Russell government were unmoved. The two crop failures were proof enough that Providence had rendered a judgment on the Irish potato culture and had commanded the British government to "commence a salutary revolution in the habits of a nation long singularly unfortunate." Besides, there was that third promise: "Not for more than a year."

On the evening of April 10, 1847, ten feet above the graves of the long dead Norse kings of Dublin, a stout, balding gentleman who looked like a Lille butter merchant was presented with an "elegant snuff box" in appreciation of his services to the Irish people. The presenter, T. M. Gresham, Esq., a noted barrister, thanked M. Soyer for his efforts to improve the "condition of the country" and told the audience gathered at Freeman's Hall that, while it was true that M. Soyer's "efforts were not approved by all Irishmen, they were fully appreciated by those who were the best judges of what was likely to improve the condition of the country."

After thanking Mr. Gresham for the gift, M. Soyer gave a farewell address in which he made frequent but "modest" allusions to his own "profound knowledge of the culinary arts." When M. Soyer finished, an official reminded the audience that this coming Saturday they could visit the Soyer model kitchen to watch the poor eat. The admission fee, five shillings per person, would be donated to the lord mayor's charity. A few days later, the future inventor of the Soyer "magic kitchen," which cooked food on the table, and the future author of *Soyer's Charitable Cookery*, which sold for a sixpence, returned to London.

On April 24, two weeks after the Frenchman's farewell, the public works labor force, reduced by 20 percent on March 20, was reduced by a further 10 percent. The second cut brought the total number of dismissed laborers to 209,000. Not enough, London complained. Half a million men or more were still on the rolls. Orders were issued to quicken the pace of redundancies; otherwise, the British ratepayer would end up funding two expensive relief operations—public works and the soup scheme—simultaneously. In response, Colonel Jones issued Circular No. 84: Board of Works engineers were to shut down all public works projects in their districts on May 1, unless otherwise instructed. Even Mr. Trevelyan, who had been pressuring Jones to hasten the pace of redundancies, found Circular 84 too audacious. Two million people could be affected by the order; how would they be fed? In early May, only half of the two thousand planned soup kitchens were in operation, and in most of the thousand kitchenless districts, distress was increasing. A Galway relief officer blamed the rising mortality rate in his locality directly on the failure to establish kitchens; in County Roscommon, a relief official in one district was feeding the local people out of his own pocket.

During the early weeks of spring, the pressure on the workhouses, the repository of all national sorrows, increased relentlessly. In one overcrowded Cork workhouse, a Board of Health physician counted 102 inmates in a dormitory of 24 beds, and 120 fever patients in a sick ward of 45 beds. In a Galway workhouse, with more bodies than gravediggers, another visiting Board of Health physician found the dead buried next to the fever shed, which was near the workhouse well. At the time of the physician's visit, fever had already killed the master and his wife, and two doctors at the facility were dying.

One day, during a debate in the Commons, Mr. Smith O'Brien reminded Mr. Labouchere of a promise Lord John had made in January: no public works sites would be closed in a district until the district also had a soup kitchen. The chief secretary feigned amnesia. Had the government really said that? "If the government [had], they would have acted very improperly." Again, Mr. Labouchere knew more than he was saying. Worried about the slow pace of kitchen creation and the ever deepening mortality, government officials tabled Circular 84 and slowed the pace of redundancies to 106,000 in May, giving Burgoyne time to establish more kitchens. In the first week of June, when the work rolls were cut by a further 318,000, there were 1,989 soup kitchens in operation, and the kitchens were feeding 2,729,824 people—a remarkable achievement. The general's delays may have been costly in terms of human suffering, but, like many British officials in Ireland, he was competent.

The second part of Lord John's emergency relief plan—transferring the labor force back to the land to plant the 1847 crops—was less successful.

Dismissed laborers often had nothing to plant, having eaten their seed potatoes and grain over the winter. The government did establish a £50,000 loan program in hopes that proprietors would borrow money to buy seed for tenants, but many proprietors thought that supplying seed to a tenant was self-defeating; the tenant would only "consume the crop and not pay . . . the rent." Meanwhile, some of the dismissed laborers who had seed were refusing to plant for fear "the landlord [would] pounce on the crop as soon as it is cut." Planting was also down among large and middle-sized famers, many of whom planned to emigrate, and among proprietors, many of whom continued to put their money in the bank.

With hunger certain to return when the soup kitchens closed in August, almost half a million people arrived at the same conclusion in April 1847:

"I shall arise and go now."

CHAPTER FOURTEEN

"I Shall Arise and Go Now"

A t the beginning of May, spring remained in a "backward" state. "The air . . . is cold, and the atmosphere heavy and gloomy as it could be in the month of November," *The Times*'s man in Ireland reported. A few days later, the Dublin papers warned that the 1847 crops had the look of decay about them. "The wheat look[s] very badly and oats slowly coming up. . . . [And] there is by no means, such a breadth of potatoes sown . . . as I anticipated."

The news was enough to give the wavering, the undecided, and the fearful resolve; it was time to go. In 1846, emigration, though large—116,000 people left Ireland—had had an orderly character. By the spring of 1847, people were not leaving Ireland; they were fleeing, the way a crowd flees a burning building: heedlessly, recklessly, with no thought other than to get out. In 1847, 215,000 men and women sailed to North America, and another 150,000 to Britain. And the emigrant ships carried not just the middle classes and upper peasantry, groups with a long tradition of emigration. Hidden Ireland—the ancient Gaelic-speaking peasant nation that had gone into exile in the back places of the south and west after the Cromwellian conquests—was also fleeing. Men who had never ventured five miles beyond the place of their birth now spoke of Albany, Boston, Philadelphia, and Cincinnati as ancient Israelites spoke of the Promised

Land. Overnight, bonds of memory forged like geological layers over innumerable generations were shattered. Men who knew the genealogy of every resident in the townland—who knew the son of the son of the son; who knew the local hills and dales as intimately as they knew the faces of their own children—became barefoot pilgrims on the road to the nearest port, with nothing to sustain them but the hate in their hearts.

> The Englishman's hand is strong and harsh—
> the might of his laws and the slaughter of his victories—
> his promise is a lie, his blade bloody—
> and it's high time for me to flee across the sea.

In a letter to *The Nation*, Michael Doheny, a Young Ireland official, recounted several instances "where a mother and father went away by night and left [their] little children, scarcely more than infants, to a person to take to the poorhouse the next morning." In England, where depopulation was widely viewed as a necessary precondition for the modernization of Ireland, the outflow was cheered. *The Times*, always reliably nasty on such occasions, predicted a second plantation of Ireland by "thrifty Scot and scientific English farmers, men with means, men with modern ideas." In a few years more, "a Celtic Irishman will be as rare in Connemara as is the Red Indian on the shore of Manhattan." Miss Jane Elgee, poetess and future mother of Oscar Wilde, was glad to see the back of the Gaelic-speaking peasantry and their language. "No new light of thought has flashed [through the Irish language] for a thousand years," she wrote.

The landlords, eager to consolidate their land and lower their poor rate, were also happy to see the Gaelic speakers go. Stewart & Kincaid, estate agents to the foreign secretary, Lord Palmerston, advised Palmerston to offer his most destitute Irish tenants free passage to upper Canada. Leasing ships for the voyage would be expensive, Joseph Kincaid, a principal at Stewart & Kincaid, told Palmerston, but your "estate will be of more value . . . with the population reduced. These people are a dead weight on you." Major Mahon, a large Roscommon landowner, received similar advice. Mahon's agent calculated that it would cost the major £11,534 per annum to keep his tenants in the local workhouse, twice the cost of transporting the tenants to Canada (£5,768). Major Mahon instructed the agent to contact a shipping company. Upon learning that only ten tenants in Ardtarmon, one of his County Sligo properties, had paid any rent since 1840, Sir Robert Gore Booth ordered the shipping men called in. Proprietors too impoverished to fund transatlantic travel gave their deadweight packet fare to Liverpool; inmates in overcrowded workhouses were also provided with fare money.

One day in May, three strangers offered thirteen-year-old James Gormally, an inmate in a Galway workhouse, seven shillings to go to England. In Dublin and Cork, strangers stood in front of the docked Liverpool packets, handing out free tickets. "Beyond all doubt," complained a Liverpool magistrate, "the towns on the seacoast of Ireland and many of the landed proprietors . . . [are] furnishing the wretched Irish with the means of coming [here]." Another English official who interviewed several newcomers said he "was told over and over again that some strange gentleman on the quay in Dublin gave them their tickets." Peasants with no landlord or workhouse to subsidize an escape turned to friends and neighbors. "Trifling objects" were auctioned off to raise fare money; subscriptions were raised in pubs and shebeens, and family members, especially those who lived abroad, were solicited for ticket money. "I cannot hold on long," a Kerry woman told her children in Boston. "I know I need not state that I am now dependent on ye." "For the honor of our Lord Jesus Christ and his Blessed Mother," wrote another parent, "hurry and take us out of this." In the bleakness of the Canadian spring, a farmer named Rush sat at his kitchen table, reading a letter from his daughter, Mary, in County Sligo: "Pity our hard case . . . don't let us die of the hunger."

In many parts of Ireland, townlands melted away almost overnight. Some Galway villages lost a third of their population to emigration during the spring of 1847. In the County Roscommon diocese of Elphin, the Catholic population shrank by 10 percent to 17 percent in a few months. "There are very few boys left on our side of the county," a Wicklow woman wrote. In the Cork village of Edward Ronaye, "every house on . . . the street ha[s] been long since torn down, most of the people having died and a few managing in some way to go to America." Only one in three Irishmen born in Ireland around 1831 would die in Ireland of old age.

The desire to go was so powerful, people left without luggage, without money, without forethought, without shoes. They left in unsafe ships; they left from little-used, ill-equipped ports like Westport in Mayo and Kinsale in Cork. They left on ships that had fought through the French Wars and they left without sea stock, the extra provisions essential for the typical eight weeks' crossing in an emigrant vessel. Later, the grand-children and great-grandchildren of the emigrants would grow misty-eyed when Bing Crosby sang, "I'll take you home again, Kathleen, Across the ocean wild and wide." But the people standing on the wharves wait-ing for the Liverpool packets wondered why, in God's name, would any-one want to stay? No, said an ailing new mother when offered refuge on shore the night before her ship was to sail. "[I] would rather start with hope . . . of arriving in America soon than to remain [in Ireland]." On the wharves that desperate spring, the talk was all of the death of "Old Ireland." "Anywhere than here"; "Poor Ireland's done"; "This country is doomed," the people on the crowded decks told one another. Mornings when the packets were late and there was time to think of all that had been lost—the dead wives, husbands, children, and parents; the land—sorrow would overcome the crowds like a strong wind.

> For every hope is blighted
> That bloomed when first we plighted
> Our troth, and were united
> A gradh geal mo chroidhe!

In Cork city, a major emigrant port, Father Theobald Mathew, the temperance priest, watched, horrified, as the streets filled with "shadows and specters." "No Tongue can describe, no Understanding can Con-ceive the Misery and Wretchedness that flowed into Cork." In May, when news reached the city that Daniel O'Connell had died in a hotel room in Genoa, the quantum of sorrows on the quays of Cork became commen-surate with those in the hills of Jerusalem.

The more superstitious emigrants surely took it as an ill omen that the journey west began with a voyage to the east. In the 1830s and 1840s, the first sea that two out of every three Irish emigrants crossed was the Irish Sea, an expanse of gray-blue light embroidered with hundreds of frothy white ship wakes, most leading to and from the mouth of the

Mersey, entrance to the great bazaar of the Victorian world economy: Liverpool. The "bully of the litter" of eighteenth-century English port cities, Liverpool was as clever as she was amoral. Through the American wars and the French Wars, through slave revolts and slave suppressions, through the Rights of Man and the Declaration of Independence, Liverpool had grown steadily wealthier on the high-end vices of the white man: African slaves, sugar, and tobacco. In 1807, when Britain abolished slavery, Liverpool—nimbler than other English seaports—identified emigration as the next growth area in human trafficking. By the 1820s, the city offered regular passenger service to North America. By the 1830s, Belfast, Londonderry, and Dublin—the traditional Irish immigration ports—had become spokes in a wheel that led to Liverpool, whose port offered the emigrant a cheaper fare and more regular passenger service to North America than any Irish port.

In theory, the packets that carried the Irish to Liverpool sailed under the providence of the Passenger Acts, a series of laws that mandated regular ship inspections and an adequate complement of lifeboats; in practice, a passenger who stepped aboard a Liverpool packet stepped beyond the laws of God and man. Though packet advertisements promised travel times of as little as eleven hours, even the new, screw-driven steamers rarely made the crossing in under twenty hours, and the sailing ships in the packet fleets could take up to four days.

"Nine out of ten [Liverpool passengers] had not the remotest idea of what they faced," said John Besnard, the Port of Cork weight master. Deck tickets, the only kind of ticket an Irish peasant could afford, cost 5 shillings, and that 5 shillings did not buy food, water, shelter from wind and rain, or a place to perform the offices of nature. Stewart Redmond, an English journalist who made the Liverpool crossing, recalled waking to the pungent odor of human waste and the sight of men and women covered in "one another's . . . dirt and filth." On many packets, crew members sold bottled water for 6 pence, and an hour or two in the warm engine room for 12 pence. As May became June, passengers looked forward to a more temperate passage, but even in summer the maritime air retained a November sharpness, and in all seasons the surly Irish Sea remained mutinous and unpredictable.

Mr. Redmond spent his night passage to Liverpool sailing through whistling black canyons of water thirty feet high and dodging hurtling bodies and tumbling cargo crates. With the crash of a large wave, Redmond's packet would pitch violently; suddenly, there would be the rapid *snap, snap, snap* of breaking rope, the ominous thud of large objects becoming displaced; then everything—people, belongings, sea barrels, and human effluvia—would slide across the deck and pile up in a great heap on the opposite side of the ship. In the morning, when the sea had calmed, Redmond went out on the bridge. In between pools of water and shattered cargo containers, he saw "50 or 60 . . . people, including 4 to 5 children," sitting "perfectly stiff and cold" amid the debris, waiting for the sun to reach their corner of the deck. The storm produced one fatality, a young girl, and one near fatality, "a fine looking boy" who was revived after being laid before a fire and rubbed down with hot water.

The passengers on another Liverpool packet, *Londonderry*, were less fortunate. On a sunless morning of high winds and rogue seas, a furious storm caught the packet off the west coast of Ireland. The 170 deck passengers were ordered into a twelve-foot-by-eighteen-foot crawl space below deck; the crew threw a tarpaulin over the entrance; the tarpaulin blocked the flow of air; and people began to suffocate. The next morning the crew found the bodies of "seventy-two . . . men women and children . . . piled . . . indiscriminately over each other, four deep." The dead presented "the ghastly appearance of persons who had died in agonies of suffocation; very many [were] covered with blood, which had gushed from the mouth or nose or had flown from the wounds inflicted by the trampling of nail-studded brogues." The captain of the *Londonderry*, a Mr. Johnson, rode out several tides before he could bring himself to sail the packet into its next port of call.

⌘

Herman Melville, a young American sailor who arrived in Liverpool on a morning tide in the third year of the famine, full of Yankee swagger, pronounced himself disappointed with the city; Liverpool seemed "deficient in the marvelous." Maybe to Melville, a New Yorker accustomed to clamorous South Street, where the forest of ship masts was so thick, gazing across the water at Brooklyn Heights was like peeping through a keyhole. But for an Irish peasant whose conception of urban space was a two-lane village with a blacksmith's shop the wonders that lay below the Bell Buoy at the mouth of the Mersey were beyond all imagining: "lofty ranges" of warehouses, a vast "Parliament of masts," and "long China walls of masonry." Those China walls—the Liverpool docks—produced a wealth so prodigious, even Kublai Khan would be envious. To Liverpool, the Mersey docks were what Waterloo Bridge and Nelson's Column were to London: symbols of municipal glory. Who but a Liverpudlian would think to name docks Trafalgar, Waterloo, Victoria, Albert, King's, Queen's? Each dock was built like a great man-of-war: its masts, the spindly dock cranes that scraped the Liverpool sky; the top decks, a latticework of gates, huts, cranes, and sheds; and its crew, skinny, tattooed navvies, heavy with a mastery of rude Anglo-Saxon verbs and short on front teeth.

Behind the port lay another Liverpool marvel, the churning polyglot streets of Merseyside, where all the children of the Victorian world economy paraded: ponytailed Chinamen; Sikhs in gloriously colored turbans; Lowland Scottish merchants in black frocks and top hats, any one a suitable model for Mr. Dickens's Scrooge; former West Indian slaves with begging bowls; sleek, cigarillo-chomping Yankee cotton merchants in Panama hats, as avaricious looking as the canny Yankees were reputed to be; feral-faced dock runners searching the crowds for easy marks; Negro cooks off the American ships, walking arm and arm with white women; French sailors with Côte d'Azur tans and red-pompommed mariners' caps; every manner, color, and shape of prostitute—Liverpool had 714 known houses of ill repute—and, amid this gaudy, hurly-burly celebration of empire, greed, and bad intentions, the strangest sight of all: parties of neatly dressed, orderly German immigrants, an hour off the train from Hull, where they had been deposited by German packets from Bremen and Hamburg.

The purposeful Rhinelanders, Prussians, and Bavarians, who were also fleeing crop failure and industrial dislocation, provided a striking contrast to the Irish streaming off the Dublin and Cork packets at Clarence Dock. "Drenched from sea and rain . . . suffering from cold [and] . . . seasickness, scarcely able to walk," the Irish came off the packets like sea creatures crawling ashore to die.

Two hundred and ninety-six thousand, two hundred thirty-one Irish emigrants arrived in Liverpool between January 13 and December 13, 1847, and almost half—116,000—stayed, usually because they were too impoverished to travel further. The accusations of "pauper dumping" made by Liverpool officials were not exaggerated. The mysterious strangers who prowled the Irish docks generally provided the would-be emigrant with just enough money to cover the fare to Liverpool. Still, the city had no one but itself to blame for its position as chief burial ground and relief station for the "deadweight" of Ireland. The "men with the gallows in their eyes" and the "puny mothers holding up their puny babies" at Dock Wall, a beggars' site near the harbor, were the price Liverpool paid for ruthlessly manipulating Irish agricultural prices. "Of all the seaports in the world," declared Melville, "Liverpool perhaps most abounds in all the variety of land sharks, land rats, and other vermin which make the helpless . . . their prey."

Liverpool, beyond shame and insult, was also beyond hyperbole. Almost everything said about her was true. Chief among the "land sharks" who preyed upon the hapless emigrant were dock runners, like the gang, the Forty Thieves, who would gather each morning at Clarence Dock to wait for the Irish packets. As the crew drove the passengers down the boarding planks with sticks, the runners would pick their marks. An enterprising runner could turn an emigrant with a little capital—a forty- or fifty-acre farmer with £50 or £60 in his money belt—into a source of multiple commissions. Steering the emigrant to a ship broker who booked transatlantic crossings could earn the runner a 7½ percent commission; visits to the lodge keeper and the chandler (the merchants who sold sea stock) produced further commissions. Though possessing little capital, the small landholder—innocent, illiterate, Irish speaking—sometimes made an even better mark. Gullible, lost, and frightened, the emigrant would buy a canceled ticket from a runner, believing it valid; a half-fare child's ticket, believing it was an adult ticket; a ticket to Baltimore, believing it was a ticket to New York; and, when the runner offered him two dollars U.S. for his £10 gold coin, he would count himself blessed to have met the only honest man in Liverpool. On one occasion, a party of 150 Cork men from the backplaces of the county, disembarking at Clarence Dock, were greeted by a runner employed by a ship broker named Keenan. The runner asked the Cork men whether they planned to travel to North America. Yes, replied one man; he and his mates had purchased tickets in Ireland from the agent of a Mr. Shaw, and they were on the way to Mr. Shaw's office now, to settle the outstanding balance on the tickets. The runner kindly offered to escort them. Ten minutes later, the Cork men, all with a shaky grasp of English, were settling their balances in the office of the runner's employer, Mr. Keenan.

It was also not uncommon for a passenger to arrive at the assigned dock on the assigned day of departure, only to find a note posted to a pole stating that the sailing date had been changed. Two pence to four pence, the daily rate at the average Liverpool lodging house, was not high, but a small farmer with £10 in capital could be beggared by a three- or four-week sailing delay. Forty percent of the Irish who came to Liverpool as emigrants ended up indigent.

Under the provisions of the English Poor Law, Liverpool ratepayers had to feed the paupers. In the third week of December 1845, the city relieved 888 "casual Irish poor"; by the third week of December 1846, the figure was 13,471; by the week ending January 23, 1847, 130,795; and by the week ending January 30, 143,872. Liverpudlians who visited the Fenwick Street relief shed could be forgiven for thinking that the Irish public works program, with all its fraud and abuse, had been reborn in their city. Family size determined the amount of soup and other food dispensed to an applicant, so Irish paupers borrowed one another's children. Finally, a sharp-eyed Ulsterman named Austin caught on to the ruse.

Every time a list of new arrivals from Ireland was posted, the Liverpool press grew faint with anxiety: "240 from Cork"; "701 from Sligo"; "692 from Drogheda"—who would pay for them all? Not Liverpool, insisted old Lord Brougham, who gave a speech on the city's agonies in the Lords that would have made Becky Sharp weep. Brougham put out all the colors: Liverpool as the thin red line of empire; Liverpool under pestilential threat; Liverpool under financial strain. Brougham said the city was entitled to assistance from the central government. London said Liverpool would have to assist itself. Frantic, the city fathers invoked the Removal Act, a complex, time-consuming deportation procedure. It did little to alleviate the situation. The pauper population continued to swell, and the Liverpool poor rate went where no poor rate had gone before.

Between 1845 and 1847, municipal expenditures on Irish paupers rose from £2,916 per year to £25,926: an 889 percent increase.

Even before the famine, Liverpool had had the highest municipal death rate in Britain: 36 per 1,000, compared with the national average of 22 per 1,000. The rate owed much to the Irish who had come over in the 1820s and 1830s to work on the docks. In an 1841 report, Dr. William Henry Duncan, the "Medical Officer of Health" in Liverpool, described the Irish emigrants as the "least clean in their habits, the most apathetic about everything that befalls them . . . and the most resistant to being removed to hospital." "As long as the native inhabitants are exposed to . . . numerous hordes of uneducated Irish," Dr. Duncan warned, "it will be in vain to expect that any sanitary code can cause fever to disappear from Liverpool." After the Duncan report was issued, the municipal authorities closed the fetid abandoned cellars where many of the dock workers lived. Now, six years later, the cellars had been reopened by the famine emigrants. By midsummer, Liverpool had an underground city of 27,000, with its own burial society—a halfpenny a week guaranteed against a pauper's grave—and its own Via Dolorosa: Vauxhall, the ward immediately to the east of the port.

For the thousands of Tipperary, Wexford, and Antrim peasants who had fled Ireland crying, "Anywhere than here," anywhere turned out to be a crowded, pestilential cellar five feet under a Vauxhall field. Visiting one reopened cellar, a city coroner counted "seventeen human beings [crowded] together without so much as even a bit of straw to lie down on" in a space "so small, a person could not stand upright." None of the inhabitants would live out the week: the coroner was sure of it. In one cellar on Bent Street, another municipal official found four fever victims sharing a bed; in another, "twenty-four young men and their sisters . . . sleeping in a filthy state." When authorities attempted to remove the body of a typhus victim from a Thomas Street cellar, his mates, who had planned to bury him the coming Sunday, protested vehemently. On March 13, Dr. Duncan warned about "the objectionable practice of retaining the bodies of the dead," but by then typhus had already mobilized itself for a full-scale assault on the city. On Lace Street, 181 people died within a few months, not including residents who died in municipal hospitals and fever sheds.

By April, it had become possible to imagine funeral pyres on the Mersey and columns of fetid smoke rising from the fields of Vauxhall. The infection rate in the ward now approached 1 in 17. The local cemetery on Brownlow Hill briefly became as crowded as Clarence Docks. "The dead are taken by relatives . . . at all hours of the day and sometimes at night, in coffins, sometimes nailed, sometimes not, and if the gates happen to be closed, [corpses] are put over the walls." One day in the spring of 1847, a Liverpool police officer had to be posted over a body to prevent rats from tearing it apart.

By late spring, the prevailing winds carried the Irish biomedical miasma eastward across the Irish Sea. In Liverpool, a metropolis of 250,000, there were now 60,000 cases of fever, 40,000 cases of dysentery, and 60,000 cases of diarrhea. By the end of the year, more than 7,000 people were dead. Home Secretary Grey ordered a quarantine station established on the Mersey; the Removal Act was also simplified to expedite the deportation of Irish paupers. Otherwise, Liverpool was left to save itself. Municipal pleas for a ban on Irish emigration were ignored; requests for government funds were ignored. The register general, called upon to issue a report on Liverpool's *annus horribilis*, instead rendered a biblical judgment on the city. "Liverpool, created in haste by commerce—by men too intent on immediate gains—reared without any tender regard for flesh and blood and flourishing while the working population was rotting . . . has . . . for a year been the hospital and cemetery of Ireland." *The Times,* always happy to engage in a little schadenfreude, announced that Liverpool was "the most unhealthy town in this island" and a "mass of disease."

Liverpool remained unrepentant. "That the scum of Ireland come to Liverpool and die in thousands is true," admitted the *Liverpool Mail*, "but whose fault is that?"

❦

For almost every Irish emigrant who disembarked at Clarence Dock, Liverpool represented a first encounter with modernity, and it would be the most profound experience many of the newcomers ever had. Irish peasant culture, though medieval in character, was good at a few things; one was affording a deeply impoverished people with a sense of dignity and worth. Every Irish townland had its wise man, its storyteller, its keeners; every district its schoolmaster, its traveling poets, and its songsters. Under the sheltering umbrella of peasant culture, even the most humble could be esteemed. Of course the peasant knew he was very poor, but that was the result of being outmatched by life, and where was the shame in that? Many a man—many a fine man—had been outmatched by life. Besides, the peasant's language, Irish, was such a glory, the saints in heaven spoke it.

In Liverpool, modernity pitilessly deconstructed all the comforting myths of peasant culture; the emigrant suddenly found himself an object of horror and contempt. On his approach, pedestrians turned and walked the other way; storekeepers bolted the door or picked up a broom; street urchins mocked his shoeless feet, filthy clothing, and Gaelic-accented English. In Liverpool, the emigrant was forced to see himself—judge himself—by the standards and values of the modern world. The historian Robert Scally has called this change in perspective the "Liverpool Mirror," and it was as cruel as any pestilential Vauxhall cellar. Standing in front of his reflection, the peasant saw the poet, honored for his perfect image of the moon, and the "scholar," revered for his "priest's knowledge of Latin," dissolve into *Punch*'s "aboriginal Irishman: illiterate, savage," a speaker of a language "through which no light of thought had flashed for a thousand years." Thomas Carlyle, the leading public intellectual of the era, warned his countrymen not to be deceived by the emigrant's poverty and wretchedness. "In his rags and laughing savagery . . . [he] is the sorest evil this country has to strive with." Of course, along Dock Wall, and in Vauxhall, Carlyle might as well have been the man on the moon; but every time the Irish pauper looked into the eyes of a policeman or Poor Law official, or saw a mother tuck her child into her skirt on his approach, he saw his new self staring back at him.

Many of the Liverpool emigrants did eventually acclimate to the modern world, but some were broken utterly and completely by it. One day in early August 1849, a relief official climbed down the stairs of a Vauxhall cellar. Liverpool was in the midst of a cholera epidemic, and the official had come to inquire into the health of the cellar's occupants, a family of Irish emigrants, the Culkins, who had come over in 1847. When the officer arrived, a small body was lying on the table: two days earlier, one of the Culkin children, an eight-year-old girl, had died of cholera. A second body was lying on the straw mat: the girl's mother had died the previous night. The dead woman's husband, Patrick, was lying beside her, his arm draped around her corpse. The bodies would have to be buried quickly, the relief official said. There was a cholera epidemic in the city. Culkin was an educated man—he had been a schoolteacher in Ireland—but in Liverpool he had lost his way. Two years of indignity and humiliation would end with his wife and daughter lowered into a pauper's grave. The next day, when the official returned, Culkin's two remaining children were dead. The schoolteacher had slit their throats, then tried to take his own life, but he had failed even at that. When the official arrived, Culkin was lying on the bed, gurgling and choking in a pool of blood.

⬥

For the emigrant wealthy enough to stay in a roominghouse instead of a Vauxhall cellar, smart enough to avoid the runners, and lucky enough to have his ship leave on schedule, the Liverpool passage was often a three- to ten-day kaleidoscope of sights and sounds: the parliament of masts; the mêlée of bodies at the Clarence Dock; the villainous odor in the lodging house; a visit to the harbor to check the latest fares, which could fluctuate by the hour (in general, though, the Canadian passage cost around £3 and the American around £5); and, finally, a visit to the medical station for a physical examination, which usually consisted of a single request: "Stick out your tongue."

On the eve of departure there might be a boisterous "American wake"; then, early the next morning, his worldly possessions packed in a cardboard suitcase secured with string, the emigrant would be off to the docks. Boarding was usually close to departure time, because cargo was loaded before passengers. As the top deck filled with newcomers, passengers with fiddles and pipes would take out their instruments, and the ship would pull out of its berth to the sound of dozens of dancing feet thundering across the top deck. Rowboats with late-arriving passengers often followed departing ships like minnows. The idea was to throw the late arriver and his belongings onto the deck, but sometimes the rowboat crews missed, and the emigrant and his luggage would tumble into the Mersey to the strains of "Pat Toomey's Wake."

Three or four hours later, the twinkling lights of the Lancashire shore would be memory and the ship dark, except for the cabin lanterns and the rising of the moon over the coal-dark sea. Robert Whyte, who left Dublin for North America "in all the freshness of early summer," said the sight of the open sea was "calculated to inspire the drooping soul with hope; auguring future happiness." Such optimism rarely lasted long. The Irish peasantry, having spent the winter of 1847 dying in public works ditches, under carts, on public streets, and in snow fields, would spend the summer dying across three thousand miles of ocean. In 1847, the death rate on vessels on the Liverpool-to-Canada route was over 15 percent; on the Cork-to-Canada route, over 18 percent.

The armada that carried more than 214,000 Irish famine victims across the Atlantic in 1847—116,000 from Liverpool, the rest from Irish ports—was a by-product of the Canadian timber trade. In the early 1800s, shipowners eager to monetize the otherwise empty westward leg of the crossing began constructing temporary passenger decks in their empty cargo holds. Boards would be thrown across the beams in the hold and two rows of passenger berths installed. By the late 1840s, emigration often contributed as much as timber to the balance sheet, but the new revenue only occasionally found its way into passenger comforts. On a 400-ton vessel, 250 to 300 passengers might find themselves squeezed into two temporary decks, each 96 feet long, 26 feet across, and 6 feet high. The uncaulked deck floor—uncaulked because the decks were torn up to provide storage space for timber on the return voyage—became a collection point for filth and a snare for clothing, and the windowless hold a receptacle for cooking and body odors. Within a ten-foot space on an unventilated deck, one passenger might be cooking food, another performing the offices of nature. "We had not been at sea one week, when to hold your head down the fore-hatch was like holding it down a suddenly opened cesspool," the young mariner Melville recalled.

Despite the 1842 Passenger Act, the latest upgrade of the 44-year-old acts, the 1836 assessment of a parliamentary committee of inquiry remained true in 1847: ships "of the United States [were] superior to those of a similar class among ships of Great Britain." Under American law, each passenger had to be provided with fourteen square feet of space; under British law, ten feet. Under German law, the weekly passenger ration was two pounds of beef, one pound of bacon, five pounds of dried bread, and three and a half pounds of dried vegetables. On most British ships, the weekly food allotment was seven pounds of breadstuffs. The 1842 regulations did mandate medical exams for passengers, but John Griscom, an American physician who visited the Liverpool docks, dismissed the exams as risible. "The inspection[s] I saw [were] conducted through the window of a little office, and consisted in nothing but [a medical officer] looking at the tongues of the passengers, as they presented themselves in rapid succession. . . . There was no certainty even that the person presenting the ticket was the passenger named on it and that its real owner was not at the moment laboring under small pox or typhus fever, in some other place and was represented at the examining office by a conniving friend." Dudley Mann, the American emigration officer in Bremen, described the British system as "exceedingly imperfect." By the spring of 1847, the flood tide of emigration had seriously strained the resources of a British emigrant fleet that was prone to deficiencies in normal times.

At the end of the 1846 Canadian emigration season, the *Sarah and Elizabeth* had limped into the St. Lawrence River with nearly half her 260 Irish passengers lying dead under canvas covers on the upper deck. Dr. George Douglas, the medical superintendent at Grosse Isle, the immigration station in the St. Lawrence, warned Montreal that the mortality on the *Sarah and Elizabeth* had not been a fluke. Filth, overcrowding, and inadequate food had increased the death rate among Irish immigrants during the 1846 season.

Immigration to the United States and Canada traditionally stopped in the winter, but when ice-free American ports continued to receive immigrants into January and February, British officials knew the coming spring and summer would be a season of historic emigration. Despite parliamentary pressure to stiffen the 1842 passenger regulations, the colonial secretary, Earl Grey, hesitated.

What kept the colonial secretary awake nights was not six-foot-high decks, terrible ventilation, rancid air, and inadequate rations; it was the commercial buzz and hum of Buffalo, New York. "On the American side [of the border] all is bustle and activity, on the [Canadian] side . . . with the exception of a few favored spots . . . all seems waste and desolation. The ancient city of Montreal, which is naturally the commercial capital of the Canadas, will not bear the least comparison in any respect with

Buffalo, which is a creation of yesterday." Earl Grey, regarded as an imperial visionary, would look at the map of upper Canada, run his hand across the vast empty spaces, and sigh. So much land, so much timber, so much wildlife, so few people. There were a million inhabitants north of the border, 23 million below, and every year Canada lost a large complement of her Irish to the United States; the emigrants sailed to Montreal or Quebec City to take advantage of the cheaper Canadian fares, then walked south to Maine and Vermont.

Higher fares would make Canada even less attractive to emigrants. And adopting German or American standards would force shipowners to raise fares. Earl Grey would agree to a few tweaks in the 1842 regulations, but only a few. On March 15, he told Parliament that the 1847 emigrant season would be a historic success. Grey had to know that this was mendacious nonsense.

Days after leaving pestilential ports like Liverpool and Dublin, many emigrant ships suffered horrible disease outbreaks. In February, ship fever—typhus—had driven several vessels on the Liverpool–Canada run into Cork. In March and April, crews returning from the winter crossing had come back with harrowing tales of midocean "plagues." The crew of the *Erin Queen*, which lost seventy-eight passengers on the crossing, refused to remove the dead from the hold unless they were paid. On another vessel, no amount of money could persuade the crew to enter the hold. The captain had to carry the diseased bodies up on deck himself. A few weeks out of Ireland, the cry "Ship fever!" went up on the vessel carrying the Dublin emigrant Robert Whyte. The captain ordered the passengers locked in the unventilated hold. A rebellion ensued, and the crew had to force the passengers into the hold at gunpoint. Waiting among the dying for death to come, Whyte distracted himself by keeping a diary:

> **Friday**
> This morning there was a further accession to the names upon the sick roll. It was awful how suddenly some were stricken. A little child who was playing with [her] companions suddenly fell down and for some time was sunk in a death like torpor . . . when she awoke, she commenced to scream violently.

Sunday

The moaning and raving of the patients kept me awake nearly all night. . . . It made my heart bleed to hear the cries for, "Water, for God's sake, some water." Oh! It was horrifying.

Wednesday

Passing the main hatch, I got a glimpse of one of the most awful sights I ever beheld. A poor female patient . . . lying in one of the upper berths—dying. Her head and face . . . swollen to a most unnatural size. . . . She had been nearly three weeks ill and suffered exceedingly. . . . Her husband stood by her holding a "blessed candle."

As the weeks passed, passengers and crew fell into the same state of stuporous resignation that the characters in Albert Camus's *The Plague* succumbed to as they watched the pestilential city around them die. "None of us was capable of exalted emotion [any longer]. . . . People would say it's high time it stopped. . . . But when making such remarks we felt none of the passionate yearning or fierce resentment of the early phase. . . . The furious revolt of the first few weeks had given way to a vast despondency." Toward the end of the epidemic, Whyte allowed himself an evening on deck. It was a lovely night; the moon on the trades, and with the Canadian Maritimes just over the horizon now, the smell of land was in the air again. Whyte looked out over the rail. The "phosphorescent appearance" of the nighttime ocean was "very beautiful," he thought. "We seemed to be gliding through a sea of liquid fire." The next morning—another shimmering summer morning—the remnant of the passengers assembled on deck.

"The appearance of the poor creatures was miserable in the extreme. We now had fifty sick passengers, being nearly one half of the whole number. . . . The brother of two men who died on the sixth . . . followed today. He was seized with dismay from the time of their death, which no doubt hurried on [his] malady to its fatal termination. The old sails being all used up, his remains were placed in two meal sacks, and a weight . . . fastened at [the] foot. . . . He left two little orphans, one of whom, a boy seven years of age, I noticed in the evening wearing his deceased father's coat. Poor little fellow!"

The mortality on Whyte's ship, though severe, was not extraordinary. After inspecting the *Larch* and the *Virginius*, which carried tenants from Lord Palmerston's County Sligo properties, a Canadian official wrote, "The Black Hole of Calcutta was a mercy compared to the hold of these vessels." The official, who had just inspected a vessel carrying German emigrants, was struck by the contrast. "As if in reproof of those on whom the blame of all this wretchedness must fall," he wrote, "Germans from Hamburgh and Bremen are daily arriving; all healthful, robust and cheerful." Shipwrecks also claimed many lives. When the *Carricks* out of Sligo went down off Cap des Rosiers, 187 people drowned; 60 died on the *Miracle* when she sank off the Magdalen Islands; and there were 207 fatalities on the *Exmouth*, which "foundered at sea." Steven de Vere, an Anglo-Irish gentleman who made the crossing in steerage in order to "bear witness," blamed the carnage on the Colonial Office and Parliament. The 1842 Passenger Act was egregiously inadequate to the crisis, de Vere told a parliamentary inquiry. "In the ship that brought me out, the supply of water . . . served out to passengers was so scanty that they were frequently obliged to throw overboard their salt provisions and rice . . . because they had not water enough both for the necessary cooking nor to satisfy their thirst afterwards. . . . No cleanliness was enforced, the beds never aired, the master [captain] during the whole voyage never entered the steerage and would listen to no complaints."

In 1849, Herman Melville was a crew member on a "good" emigrant ship, the *Highlander*; and he found the rigors of the journey such that he howled from one side of the Atlantic to the other: "Stowed away like bales of cotton, and packed like slaves in a slave ship, confined in a place that during storm time must be closed against light and air, [unable to do any] cooking nor warm so much as a cup of water"—and Melville was a healthy young man. For a forty- or fifty-year-old—or a five- or six-year-old—emigrant weakened by months of malnutrition, death at sea may have been inevitable, even on a "good" ship.

Word of the great mortality at sea quickly filtered back to Ireland; still, the cry "Anywhere than here!" continued. Through the spring and summer, hundreds of thousands of emigrants, country men and women who knew the ocean only as a rumor, continued to rush to ports that had no business calling themselves ports and boarded ships that had no business on any ocean. Almost 98,000 of the emigrants were en route to Canada.

✳

In British North America, spring had begun with arctic temperatures, ice floes as steep as "hills" in Montreal harbor, and deep apprehension in the picturesque hamlets nestled between the sunless high forests of the St. Lawrence Valley. In the 1840s, the Canadian immigration season began in May, when the St. Lawrence was free of ice, and ended in autumn, when the river began to freeze over again. Toward the end of the 1846 immigration season, the character of the immigrant stream changed. The sturdy, industrious merchants and farmers—the traditional Irish immigrants—disappeared, replaced by hordes of "low Irish": indigent peasants who had come off the ships half "naked, malodorous and filthy." In Montreal, the ancient capital of British North America, concern spread through government offices. How could a nation be made from such people? In Grosse Isle, the Canadian immigration station, Dr. Douglas warned Montreal that 1846 was just the beginnning. "Next [year], the number of sick will exceed that of any previous year." By February 1847, Quebec was in a fright. In the towns and villages of the province, there was a general sense that something terrible was coming the province's way, though its shape and nature remained hidden in the crowded port towns of Britain and Ireland. Joseph Signay, the archbishop of Quebec, issued a pastoral letter on Irish immigration that breathed fear and despair. The citizens of Quebec City expressed concern about the imminent "Irish invasion" in a letter to the colonial secretary; the provincial press attacked the Canadian Legislative Assembly for temporizing on the immigration threat. In the hamlets along the St. Lawrence, people were seized by the fear of pestilence. In 1832, an Irish ship had ignited a cholera outbreak that swept down the St. Lawrence Valley all the way to Detroit, killing seven thousand.

On April 16, 1847, *Le Canadien*, a Quebec City paper, warned readers that "emigration from the British Isles, and from Ireland, in particular, toward this continent is readying on a vast scale." On the twenty-third, with the new immigration season now barely a week away, *Le Canadien* issued a second warning: "In a few short weeks Ireland and Scotland will jettison onto our shores their hungry and their dying." As the gray spring skies and unseasonable temperatures lingered into the final week of April, news from Canada's neighbor to the south stirred further disquiet. The American press was fond of depicting the United States as the friend of the famine Irish. "The soldier, the merchant, the mechanic—the very children of America—all vie with each other in their endeavors to feed the starving and stop the work of famine and fever," boasted *The New York Herald*. The boast was true enough, though it did not follow that Americans wanted the Irish in America. The fourteen-feet-per-passenger space regulation enacted by Congress in February not only made American passenger ships safer, it made American fares too expensive for the average emigrant. New York State, which imposed an immigrant head tax of $1.50, and Boston, which now required shipowners to post a $1,000 bond for each passenger, created their own deterrents. "Give me your huddled masses yearning to be free" was the song of another American generation. On April 28, *Le Canadien* denounced the American measures as a further example of Yankee perfidy. "God forbid that we should wish to close the doors of Canada to the unfortunate immigrants of Ireland. Not only the federal congress but also individual state legislatures of the United States have adopted strict and isolationist precautionary measures, which tend to shift the tide of emigration . . . away from the American Union; emigration which up to this point had been so profitable for the States . . . is now thrown upon the shores of Canada."

On May 1, the traditional opening of the immigration season, the St. Lawrence was empty. The persistent frigid temperature had kept the region so cold that residents of Nicolet, a small town near Quebec City, observed May Day by planting a maypole in the frozen river. In Montreal, the harbor remained speckled with floes of brilliant blue ice. On May 12, as the river waited for the spring sun to release it, the editors of *Le Canadien* permitted themselves a final outburst: "With utmost energy [we protest] the idea that certain politicians in Ireland and England have to swamp Canada with the indigent population of Ireland. . . . The conditions in Ireland are the result of poor administration of the miserable country; are we to be the ones to bear the distress?"

Two days later, Dr. Douglas, a sturdy young Scotsman with a bristling black warrior mustache, stood on a hill at Grosse Isle, surveying the river. There was a mast on the horizon: the *Syria*, out of Liverpool, the first immigrant ship of the 1847 season, had arrived. Every foreign vessel entering the St. Lawrence was required to stop at Grosse Isle for inspection. Passengers designated "disease free" were confined to the whitewashed quarantine sheds on the island for two weeks, long enough for a hidden infection to surface; fever patients were kept in the station hospital until deemed a healthy risk. The need to keep disease-bearing vessels away from the major population centers of Quebec City and Montreal had led to the selection of Grosse Isle as an inspection site. The island was located in one of the most isolated sections of the river, in a landscape of primordial beauty. To the north lay the Gulf of St. Lawrence, whose immense corridors of light, water, and high forest suggested what geological time might look like. To the south lay the Plains of Abraham and the "sparkling spires" and gun batteries of the ancient fortress, Quebec City. Grosse Isle itself offered a series of charming views, a coast of lovely inlets and bays and an interior of deep forest. Except for Dr. Douglas, who had a large farm at the far end of the island, and a few of his subordinates, the island was empty from September to May.

The *Syria* was closer now, approaching the island through a backdrop of wide river and high timber. On the opposite side of the river, neat little slate rooftops warmed themselves in the May sun. From his vantage point on the hill, Douglas could see orderlies running from the empty quarantine sheds. In a moment they would be at the wharf, unmooring the craft, which would carry Medical Superintendent Douglas out to the *Syria* for a passenger inspection. Despite the apprehensive tone of the Quebec press, Douglas was less worried about the 1847 immigration season than he had been last autumn. In April, at a public meeting in Quebec City, Douglas had told his fellow Scot Dr. Joseph Morin that "nothing extraordinary" was being done at Grosse Isle by way of preparations except "placing the establishment in perfect order and in his opinion, it had been so placed." Fifty new iron hospital beds had been purchased, raising the number of beds to 250, and three new staff members hired. For his foresight, Douglas had received a commendation from the Emigration Commissioners in London. The medical superintendent also told Dr. Morin that certain "parties" (presumably the press, the public, and Bishop Signay) were, in his opinion, unnecessarily alarmed.

Coming from Douglas, such reassurances were not as comforting as they sounded. Unlike Dr. Duncan of Liverpool, a highly skilled physician of international reputation, the Scotsman was a journeyman doctor whose training consisted primarily of an apprenticeship under his brother, a physician in upstate New York. Douglas's knowledge of public health was largely limited to his experience at Grosse Isle.

From a distance, the *Syria* showed no signs of distress, but when Dr. Douglas entered her hold he counted nine dead and fifty-two fever and dysentery cases. The next day, May 15, Owen Wood died, having spent twenty-four days on this earth, twenty-three of them in the hold of the *Syria*. This was the first on-island fatality of the season. On the fifteenth and on each morning thereafter for three days, the river remained empty except for cargo ships—unprepossessing colonial tubs of weathered timber—and the occasional billowing white sail of a pleasure craft. The interval allowed Douglas time to deal with a crisis in the quarantine sheds. Many of the healthy *Syria* passengers were falling ill; the fifty-two fever cases of the fourteenth had became seventy, then ninety, and finally 125 cases. On the nineteenth, the horizon filled with masts again. There were two ships out of Dublin: the *Perseverance*, which had nine dead and twenty cases of fever and dysentery, and the *Wadsworth*, which had fifty dead and eighty ill. The next day, the *Jane Black*, out of Limerick, arrived; she had thirteen dead and twenty fever and dysentery cases; many of her sick would die within days. "[I] never contemplated the possibility of every vessel arriving with fever as they are now," declared Douglas.

It was just the beginning. Intelligence reports indicated that since April 10, at least ten thousand emigrants had left British ports for Canada. On May 21, four new ships arrived at Grosse Isle. They carried 112 dead and "twice that number" of fever and dysentery cases. Douglas sent an urgent request to Quebec City for medical supplies, physicians, and nurses. Two days later, May 23, the number of sick on the island climbed to 695, more than double the capacity of the hospital. Douglas ordered the quarantine sheds cleared of healthy passengers and converted into aid stations.

By May 30, there were twelve hundred patients on the island and thirty-five immigrant ships in the St. Lawrence, with 12,175 passengers, "many falling ill and dying." On May 31, the number of waiting ships rose to forty and stretched downriver for two miles.

The immigrant season was not quite three weeks old.

During the first week of June, the number of sick rose to eighteen hundred. Four large hospital tents, each with a sixty-four-bed capacity, and 266 "bell" tents, each with a twelve-bed capacity, were rushed up from Quebec City, but the Commissariat officer who sent the tents forgot to include wooden planks for the floors. To the agonies of typhus and dysentery were added the agonies of sleeping on cold, damp ground. Another bureaucratic oversight produced quarantine sheds with no bathrooms. Piles of human waste collected in the low brush around the sheds. Toward the beginning of June, Douglas lost his only medical assistant, Dr. Benson, a Dublin physician who had come over on the *Wadsworth* and agreed to stay on Grosse Isle and help care for the ill. For a few days after Benson's death, the medical superintendent and his assistant, Collingwood, a former orderly in the guards, were the only medical men on an island of almost two thousand sick men, women, and children. On June 1, two volunteer physicians arrived from Quebec City. Other medical volunteers followed, but Grosse Isle was now perhaps the most concentrated area of pestilence in the Americas. Most physicians fell ill within eighteen to twenty-one days of arrival. At one point, twelve members of the fourteen-member medical staff were incapacitated. Urgent efforts to recruit female nurses from Quebec City failed. Ever mindful of cost, the Canadian government offered only three shillings per diem. That was less than a nurse could make in Quebec City, minus vomit, excrement, naked bodies, disease, and threat of contagion.

As more ships arrived, the similarities with the cellars of Vauxhall grew. In the hospital sheds, the sick slept two and three to a bed; they slept with the dead, and they slept in each other's excrement. The waste of immobilized patients in the upper berths dripped down to those below them. In the fever sheds the cry "Water! Water!" was incessant. Jean Baptiste Ferland, a Quebec priest, described the suffering in the sheds: "The sick [lie] in their own excrement for days [and] . . . go without drinking water for 10 or 12 hours." When Father Ferland asked why the calls for water were ignored, he was told that the orderlies could not "carry water from the river to quench the thirst of so many persons." The number of daily deaths on the island rose to forty; a shortage of gravediggers developed; "coffins were piled one on the other" in shallow graves. On rainy days, human effluvia seeped up to the surface and formed little pools of waste in the spring grass. "If infection does not arise it will be a fortunate thing," said one visitor. Under the press of time, inspections grew perfunctory, making it easier for fever cases to escape detection. Upon arriving on "our vessel," recalled one passenger, the doctor "hastily enquired for the captain, and before he could be answered . . . he was enquir[ing] if we had sickness aboard?—its nature?—how many deaths? How many patients at present? These questions being answered . . . he snatched up his hat" and disappeared into the hold. "Arriving there, 'ha' said he, 'there is fever here!' He stopped beside the first berth . . . felt [the man's] pulse—examined his tongue—then turned around and ran up the ladder. . . . In an instant, he was in his boat."

As conditions continued to deteriorate, questions arose about Douglas's leadership. Father O'Reilly, a Quebec City priest, recognized that Douglas faced an unprecedented crisis but felt the medical superintendant's inability to delegate authority had contributed to the chaos. Inspecting ships and manning the hospitals on the island was full-time work for five men, yet Douglas insisted on performing both duties himself. Testifying before a government inquiry later in the summer, Captain Boxer, a Royal Navy officer stationed in Quebec, blamed Douglas and Alexander Buchanan, the chief immigration officer in Upper and Lower Canada, for allowing concerns about cost to make them "too cautious" in preparing Grosse Isle for the immigrant influx.

Early in the season, Douglas had decided to keep the healthy, the sick, and the dead together until disembarkation, in the belief that it would help prevent chaos on the island. This decision was also criticized. If "this year's melancholy experience" had taught the medical profession anything, declared a visiting Quebec City medical commission, "it was that keeping . . . the sick and healthy congregated together breathing the same atmosphere, sleeping in the same berths . . . causes contagion." The criticism was justified. The *Agnes*, out of Liverpool, arrived in the St.

Lawrence with 427 passengers; on disembarkation, only 150 were still alive. The Canadian government was also culpable. In the spring, when Douglas asked for £3,000 to prepare the island for the coming season, Montreal balked and approved only a £300 grant. The most serious mistake the government made was failing to provide a flotilla of small naval craft. The removal of healthy passengers from arriving ships would have reduced the mortality on waiting vessels.

On June 9, Archbishop Signay appealed to "the Catholic Bishops and Archbishops of Ireland" to halt the emigration. "Already, more than a thousand human beings have been consigned to their eternal rest... precursors of thousands of others who will join them there if the stream of emigration from Ireland continues to flow with abundance." The ninth also found Dr. Douglas deeply apprehensive. The two-week quarantine period had been shortened to reduce overcrowding on Grosse Isle. "Of the 4,000 or 5,000 emigrants who have left this island since Sunday," he told Alexander Buchanan, the immigration agent, "at least 2,000 will fall sick somewhere before three weeks are over. . . . Give the authorities of Quebec and Montreal fair warning from me. . . . Public safety requires it." As "healthy" emigrants began pouring into the major population centers of the province, *Le Minerve*, a Quebec paper, advanced a "modest proposal": send the Irish to the West Indies to replace the freed slaves.

Toward the end of June, it began to rain heavily; the ground in the unfloored hospital tents turned to mud; a shortage of fresh bedding developed; nothing would dry in the wet weather. In the hospital tents, fevers spiked and mortality rose. In July, the rain was replaced by "calm, sultry" weather. Sheets and other bedding reappeared on the clotheslines, but the dense, windless July air trapped the smells of disease and human waste, and the sheets came off the line fouled with odors. Out on the St. Lawrence, temperatures rose in the holds of the ships awaiting inspection, and a quarter to a third of the passengers died. By the time Robert Whyte's ship arrived off Grosse Isle in early August, death and disease were being processed on an industrial scale. Among the stands of high timber and sandy coves, hundreds of "helpless creatures" stumbled over the rocks on their way to the hospitals; on shore, piles of canvas-wrapped bodies lay waiting to be loaded into burial boats. Occasionally, a mourner would accompany a body to the cemetery on the other side of the island, more often the boats were empty "save for the rowers."

Whyte's visit to Grosse Isle produced one other notable memory: a German ship leaving the crowded harbor one afternoon, her entire passenger complement—five hundred hardy, well-scrubbed, young and middle-aged men and women standing on the top deck, "singing a charming hymn . . . spreading the music of their five hundred voices upon the calm still air." In his report on the 1847 emigration season, Dr. Douglas noted that among the 7,500 German emigrants who passed through Grosse Isle during the past season, the incidence of disease had been no greater than it would be "in the same class [of people] living in their native villages." The Irish would leave behind 5,294 dead, a Celtic cross of granite, and a bitter cry of rage in Gaelic:

> Thousands of the children of Gael were lost on this island
> While fleeing from the foreign tyrannical laws and an
> artificial famine in the years 1847–8. God bless them.
> God save Ireland!

About thirty miles upriver from Grosse Isle, the St. Lawrence narrows, the land rises, and Quebec City appears. The Algonquin Indians called this part of the river Kebec, Land Where the Water Narrows. The French adopted the name for a settlement they founded there. Quebec City's position astride the river made it an important commercial center, but it also put the city in the path of anything coming downriver, including an invading American army in 1787 and, in the summer of 1847, the immigrant Irish from Grosse Isle. In June, Dr. Douglas gave the city fair warning: a pestilence was on the way. By July, the number of municipal deaths was close to forty a day, most from typhus, and the city's Marine and Emigrant Hospital and the hastily constructed sheds next door were so overcrowded, the municipal Board of Health petitioned Montreal for access to an empty cavalry barracks on the Plains of Abraham above the city.

In the harbor area, the doorways along the narrow cobblestoned street became frescoes of human suffering: people starving, people shivering uncontrollably, people soiling themselves, people with oozing fever sores, people in delirium, people weeping, people vomiting, people calling out for death to take them. The arrival of the *Yorkshire* on July 31, with forty-five sick and fifty dead, made an already dreadful situation worse. In the United States, headlines like "Fearful Mortality on the St. Lawrence" and "Annals of Misery" made New Yorkers grateful for the city's $1.50-a-head immigrant tax and Bostonians grateful for the $1,000 per-passenger bond. For a period in midsummer, Quebec seemed to teeter on the edge of social chaos. A mob of angry citizens tore down the fever sheds near the Emigrant Hospital; the Board of Health, overwhelmed and over-worked, threatened to resign. In the parish of St. Patrick's, sixty people died of typhus in a single week. Disease continued to make "fearful prog-ress among the citizens," the *Quebec Herald* reported at the end of July. In the end, Quebec was saved by its size and mediocrity.

Montreal, 180 miles upriver, was a more inviting destination. It was larger (almost fifty thousand inhabitants), more commercially vibrant, and almost as easy as Quebec to reach from Grosse Isle. Virtually every day, immigrants were delivered to the ancient capital of Canada in lots of up to two thousand by the *Queen*, the *Alliance*, and other large river steamers. On many vessels, the disembarking passengers were "clearly marked" with fever, and on some ships the living and dead huddled to-gether as tightly as "pigs upon the deck of a Cork and Bristol packet." The press of a thousand or more bodies in a confined space produced corro-sive odors. Entering the passenger chamber of one vessel, an immigra-tion agent staggered backward as if "struck." Montreal had also received "fair warning" from Dr. Douglas. In early June, the local Board of Health ordered the streets cleaned and the cheap lodging houses near the harbor closed (they were a chronic public health hazard), but a lack of funding rendered the board's directives meaningless. The streets remained un-clean, the lodging houses open. Typhus appeared as soon as the first wave of immigrants arrived in the capital, and almost immediately a mortality swept through the city.

"Every hour furnishes a new instance of sickness," declared the *Mon-treal Herald* in early July. "With whatever point the stream of misery comes in contact, it leaves the mark of its passage. . . . The clergy and the medical profession—the self-devoted ladies from the convents and the benevolent portions of general society have each furnished victims."

John Mills, the mayor of Montreal, wrote a letter of complaint to Queen Victoria. The influx of "whole cargoes of human beings in a state of destitution and every stage of disease . . . [has] proved a grievous burden to the resident[s]." The queen thanked Mr. Mills for his letter. The mayor wrote to Canada's governor general, Lord Elgin, to request "pecuniary assistance to meet the additional calls upon the city caused by the influx of immigrants." The governor general thanked Mr. Mills for his letter.

In the final week of July, 267 immigrants died in Montreal, most in the marshy recesses of Pont St. Charles, the site of six recently erected fever sheds. The camp's placement enraged the citizens of Montreal. Pont St. Charles was only a mile upriver from the city's water supply. What if effluvia from the camp got into the pipes that carried water into the city? The outcry puzzled the mayor. The river already served as a municipal garbage dump. "Every day," Mills told the press, "the people of Montreal quietly drink the filth produced by fifty thousand of its inhabitants, and they do not conceive that the necessary ablutions of at most a couple of thousand . . . emigrants would much increase the evil."

A summer heat wave added to Pont St. Charles miseries. "Oh, imagine their suffering in the low marshes where not a breath of air can reach them," wrote a visitor. On some nights, as many as fifty people died in the camp. Typhus was responsible for most of the deaths; suicide for others. "On Saturday afternoon," reported the Montreal Gazette, "two brothers, emigrants, threw themselves . . . into the river. They were rescued by the exertions of the police . . . and on being taken to the station said they wished to end their misery." Local reporters described the camp as "hell on earth." They wrote of "wretchedness and misery in the most revolting forms," of "sick males and females, indiscriminately huddled together," of "noxious air" and "piteous creatures," of people lying on rows of fetid straw beds "as if they were already in their coffins." The local press imagined it was reporting an unprecedented mortality, but everything the Montreal papers had to say about the events at Pont St. Charles had already been said a thousand times before in hundreds of newspapers across two continents. By the summer of 1847, newspaper readers in North America and Europe could be forgiven for thinking the only thing the Irish knew how to do anymore was die.

From Montreal—where the typhus mortality may have reached six thousand, including Mr. Mills, eight priests, and seventeen nuns—the fever traveled downriver with the immigrants to Kingston, at the mouth of Lake Ontario. A local paper, the *British Whig*, greeted the newcomers with an editorial denouncing the "barbarous policy . . . of pouring . . . 80,000 to 100,000 of the famished and diseased population of downtrodden Ireland into this province in a single season." From Hamilton, the immigrants carried the epidemic across Lake Ontario to Toronto, where the harbor became "crowded with a throng of dying and diseased objects; the living and dead lay together in horrible embrace." Farmers, fearful of infection, refused to hire Irish immigrants; towns, fearful of epidemics, would not tolerate their presence; passersby "fled" at their sight. One newspaper described the Irish immigrant—half naked, malodorous, diseased—as "a terrible intimation of mortality"—a provincial turn on Spenser's somberly elegant phrase for the misery-haunted Irish "anatomies of death."

On August 13, an agitated Lord Elgin wrote the Colonial Office. In April, London had given Canada a £10,000 grant to help defray the expense of the coming immigrant season. The money was gone, and the Canadian government, having contributed £50,000 to immigrant relief, was running out of funds. Typhus, said Elgin, was still spreading; Grosse Isle continued to receive ships; the roads were filled with unemployed immigrants; and winter was coming. "I much fear that very serious embarrassment . . . will be occasioned unless I am enabled to meet expenditures . . . from imperial funds," Lord Elgin told the Colonial Office.

The colonial secretary, Earl Grey, was vague about further funding but reminded the governor general of the "benefits, direct and indirect . . . which the province has derived from the . . . emigrants . . . in this and former years."

⋙⋘

Next to the famine and the Crimean War, the Irish passage to Canada produced the greatest British mortality of the Victorian era. By the time the St. Lawrence froze over in early October, twenty thousand people were dead, Canadian society was traumatized, and relations with Britain were badly strained. London was accused of indifference and callousness, and port officials in Liverpool and Cork—the embarkation points for the worst of the emigrant ships—were accused of indifference and incompetence. In the hierarchy of Canadian grievances, however, no group occupied a higher rung than the landlords of Ireland, and no group of proprietors a higher position on the top rung than the Big Lords, who had used assisted emigration to clear their estates of "deadweight."

Of the nearly 100,000 Irish who immigrated to Canada in 1847, only about five thousand to six thousand had their passage paid for, but the prominence of the proprietors who sponsored assisted emigration, and the high mortality and morbidity among the emigrants, gave the program a high public profile. Stewart & Kincaid, the firm that organized a program of assisted emigration for Lord Palmerston, the foreign secretary, was among the most highly regarded estate agents in Ireland, but the first ship the firm sent to Canada, the *Carricks*, went down in the St. Lawrence in a May storm, drowning 87 of her 187 passengers.

In mid-June, the *Eliza Liddell*, another Palmerston-sponsored vessel, arrived in Canada with seven dead, six nearly dead, and a hundred passengers in various stages of typhus and dysentery. The foreign secretary's connection to the *Carricks* had gone largely unnoticed, but the fate of the *Eliza Liddell* attracted so much attention that for a time it was feared that "the name of one of Her Majesty's Principal Secretary [might become] mixed up [in] the affair." Moses Perley, the immigrant agent in St. John's in New Brunswick, the principal immigrant station in the Canadian Maritimes, was assigned to investigate the *Eliza Liddell* case. Mr. Perley was a competent, conscientious officer with a record of defending immigrant passengers, but the *Eliza Liddell* was a Palmerston ship, and Mr. Perley had been in government service long enough to know what that meant. "There has been nothing irregular with respect to the passengers [of] the *Eliza Liddell*, nor any wrong done them," he wrote in his report.

Mayor Mills was harder to intimidate. In a letter to Queen Victoria, the mayor made a not-so-veiled reference to the foreign secretary. "Your petitioner [has] learned with equal surprise and pain that some Irish landlords, among whom is said to be one of your Majesty's Ministers, have resorted to the expedient of transporting the refuse of their estates to Canada." The next two Palmerston vessels, the *Numa* and the *Marchioness Breadalbane*, arrived in Canada with forty-four dead; then, in

November, the *Aeolus*, a vessel jointly chartered by Palmerston and his County Sligo neighbor Mr. Robert Gore Booth, slipped through a corridor of treeless hills in the Bay of Fundy and limped into St. John's in New Brunswick with eight dead, twenty-two dying, and scarcely a single able-bodied man or woman among the remaining 377 passengers. "[Ninety nine] out of 100 must be supported by the charity of the community," concluded Dr. W. S. Harding, the medical officer at St. John's. The only passengers able to muster on deck for examination upon arrival were the young, and, although it was a cold November day, they mustered stark naked, except for "blankets and other articles of bedding tied around the waist with rope yarn." One passenger, a ten-year-old boy, was completely naked. A sailor threw a bread bag around his shoulders. The hold of the *Aeolus* contained the "deadweight" of the Palmerston and Gore Booth estates: the "superannuated," the chronically ill, and those with "broken down constitutions." When news of the *Aeolus*'s losses reached Dublin, Mr. Stewart said to Mr. Kincaid, "I don't know what to think. . . . I fear we did not inform ourselves well enough of the circumstances of the place they [the passengers of the *Aeolus*] were sent & the suitable season."

In December, Adam Ferrie, chairman of a Canadian Emigration Committee, addressed an open letter to Colonial Secretary Grey. Ferrie did not stop at accusing prominent Irish landowners of "emigrant dumping . . . without regard to humanity or even to common decency"; he named names. In addition to Palmerston, he singled out Major Denis Mahon, late of the 1st Lancers, who had recently come into possession of Hartland, a large property in County Roscommon. Earlier in the century, Hartland had been one of the glories of rural Ireland: a handsome Italianate-style Big House, surrounded by several thousand acres of deer parks, leaf-shaded oak, and beech walks, and so many gardens a full-time staff of fifteen was required to maintain them. But under the previous owner, a sweet-tempered clergyman who was declared mad by the courts, Hartland had gone badly to seed. By the time Mahon took possession of the estate in 1845, hundreds of small, unprofitable plots cluttered the land, and the tenantry was £13,000 in arrears on the rent. In the spring of 1847, Mahon took the advice of his cousin, the estate agent, John Ross Mahon, and organized a program of assisted emigration.

Of the first Mahon vessel to arrive in Grosse Isle—the *Virginius*—Dr.

Douglas wrote that she left Liverpool "with 476 passengers, of whom 158 died on the crossing including the master, [first] mate and nine of the crew. . . . Three days after the arrival of this ill fated ship, there remained of the ship's company only the second mate [and] one seaman, a boy able to do duty." Douglas described the *Virginius's* passengers as "without exception the most wretched, sickly, miserable beings I have ever witnessed." Two days later the *Naomi*, another Mahon ship, arrived at Grosse Isle city; she had 110 dead. The *Erin Queen*, a third Mahon vessel, lost 78 passengers during the crossing.

On an autumn evening a few weeks after the emigration season ended, Major Mahon was riding home from a meeting in Roscommon with a friend, Dr. Terence Shanley. There was not much light left in the sky; Mahon looked at his watch. "Ten minutes before six," he told Shanley. "We should be home half past six." As he finished speaking, two brilliant yellow flashes illuminated the gathering darkness. The major lurched forward, exclaimed, "Oh God!" and died.

For years to come, it would be said that on the night of Mahon's murder, celebratory bonfires were lit on the hills above the Mahon estate.

CHAPTER FIFTEEN

"Yankee Doodle Dandy"

I n New York as in Quebec, the spring of 1847 was unseasonably cold. On March 13, the Hudson remained frozen over from Poughkeepsie to Albany; on March 17, St. Patrick's Day, not a single cargo ship sailed south past the state capital. March "closed [on] a cold wintry day," and April began with an afternoon snow squall that sent the picnickers on Brooklyn Heights scurrying to their carriages. Across the river in Manhattan, cartmen slipped and slid in the spring snow, paupers in the shantytowns above Fiftieth Street lit bonfires, and snowball fights erupted outside the tenements in the First and Second Wards. At the Narrows, the entrance to the Port of New York, the "magic and enchanted" hills of Staten Island disappeared beneath a swirling veil of white wind. Outside the island quarantine station, dog prints formed in the freshly fallen snow; inside, patients shivered under cheap government blankets and cursed the municipal bureaucrat who had deemed a single small wood-burning stove sufficient to heat an entire ward. Some of the curses were in German; most were in Irish or a heavily brogued English.

It was unusual for the quarantine station to be full this time of year, but the crop failures in Ireland and on the continent had kept ice-free ports like New York at or near capacity all winter. In early February, George Bancroft, the American ambassador in London, warned Washington to prepare for a summer of historic immigration. "All Germany is alive on the subject and from the preparation [being] made here [Britain] there is reason to believe that at least three hundred thousand persons will, in the course of the year, remove from Europe to the United States." The ambassador did not have to say that most of the America-bound emigrants would pass through New York City—that was understood: New York was the premier port of antebellum America. On March 12, under the headline "Foreign Immigrants: What Are We to Do with Them?" *The New York Herald* informed its readers that "there is every reason to believe that the importation of foreigners . . . during 1847 will be larger than at any former period of our history." The pro-immigration *Herald* reassured its readers that the newcomers would be "men of health, energy and some capital." No one on Staten Island was buying that line. The island's newly formed Committee of Safety wanted the quarantine station in Thompsonville relocated to a different part of the harbor. Another citizen rebellion was brewing on Hubert Street, in lower Manhattan. Fearful that a proposal to limit immigrant disembarcations to a single wharf at the end of the street would "endanger the health and good morals" of the neighborhood and "seriously affect real estate" values, residents were threatening an injunction if the authorities persisted with the scheme.

Pestilential quarantine stations and overrun neighborhoods were the price the Empire State paid for empire. The Erie Canal, opened in 1825, had placed New York at the center of an international trade route that, on its landward side, ran across the Adirondacks and into the resource-rich Great Lakes region and, on its ocean side, across the Atlantic and down the Mersey to Liverpool. By the early 1830s, longtime rivals Boston, Philadelphia, and Baltimore had faded into provincial entrepôts, while everything in New York continued to go up: population, real estate values, vice, pollution, wharves; exports, imports, and immigrants—especially Irish immigrants.

The Irish were not new to the city. According to one perhaps over-optimistic assessment in 1816, 25,000 of New York's nearly 100,000 residents were either Irish born or of Irish descent. Most were Protestant in religion and lower middle class to upper middle class in background. The city's historic Irish community did include a small Catholic minority, but for reasons of history and acceptance, Catholic professionals and artisans had Americanized their Catholicism. The sensible, unfussy lines of St. Peter's, the first Catholic church in the city, owed more to the architecture of New England than to that of Rome. To Episcopalian and Presbyterian passersby, St. Peter's seemed to whisper, "We're just like you."

The Irish immigrants who began arriving in the early 1830s were demonstrably not just like other New Yorkers. During an 1842 visit to the city, Mr. Charles Dickens was surprised to find Jonathan's Swift's "savage old Irish" living almost next door to City Hall. "Do [pigs] ever wonder why their masters walk upright and why they talk instead of grunt?" wondered Mr. Dickens, after a tour of Five Points, a notoriously violent, squalid, and heavily Irish slum in lower Manhattan. Mr. George Templeton Strong, a prominent Manhattan attorney, labeled the newcomers "scum." Not to be outdone, the *Christian Examiner*, a leading nativist publication, declared the immigrant Irish "repulsive to our habits and our taste." After Irish women were seen handing shillelaghs to their men during a riot in lower Manhattan, the Irish joined the "Red Indians" in the pantheon of things New Yorkers most wanted to avoid. In this hostile environment, two institutions reached out and offered refuge to the immigrants of the 1830s—the Catholic church, in the form of Archbishop John Hughes, a cleric of first-rate mind and third-rate temperament, and the Democratic party, in the form of Tammany Hall, which provided jobs in return for political favors. To natives of a country where the boast "I shook the hand that shook the hand" often brought good things, coming to Tammany was like coming home. Between the early 1830s and 1847, many things changed in New York. The northern border of the city expanded from Houston Street below Greenwich Village almost to Thirty-fourth Street; gas lighting became more common; and a professional police force was established—but the allegiance of the "low Irish" to the Catholic church and the Democratic party remained steadfast. When the famine immigrants arrived in 1847, they found their American identities waiting for them on the wharves of South Street and Hubert Street. They would be Paddies, Catholics, and Democrats, and, as Daniel Patrick Moynihan once observed, this triple identity seemed to embrace all the mysteries of the Holy Trinity itself. "The three . . . one and yet the one, three."

***

In 1847, the first glimpse of New York that the famine Irish got was seaweed. On the *India*, a converted merchantman out of Liverpool, every passenger erupted in "a joy better imagined than described [when] a great quantity" of green vegetation floated past the hull. Seaweed signaled America was near. Three days later, a lookout in the crow's nest shouted, "Land! Land!" In steerage, passengers who still had the strength fell to their knees on the damp planks and "thanked God for his mercy." In April, after a leaked British government report warned that the famine death toll could reach two million, just getting out of Ireland alive seemed like deliverance. "Two million!" a Dublin paper declared. "Do they know what [that] means?" Surviving the cellars and lodging houses of Liverpool had been a second deliverance; surviving the crossing, a third. By the time the *India* arrived at the Narrows, 149 of her 300 passengers and crew had typhus, and 26 of the 149 had died. No Statue of Liberty existed yet to raise her torch in tribute to the vessel's survivors, but Staten Island, riding off the bow, offered a not unworthy substitute. Across a hundred yards of sea boiling with the detritus of the immigrant season—bottles, barrels, boxes, kegs—moss-covered lawns sloped upward toward stately hillside Dutch manors shaded by weeping willows and surrounded by country roads, where an hour might pass before a carriage appeared. For the "future Americans" aboard the *India*, it was a first glimpse of the American dream. The next day a medical officer from the quarantine station paid a visit. The *India* was a British ship, so the officer could not have been surprised by the rows of canvas-shrouded corpses on the deck. The mortality rate in the British emigrant fleet was 30 per 1,000, compared to 9½ per 1,000 on American vessels and 8½ per 1,000 on German. An hour later the passengers and crew were ferried across the Narrows to the quarantine station, where the sick would receive medical care and the healthy quarantined for thirty days.

Despite New York's relatively lengthy internment—on Grosse Isle, healthy passengers were confined for only two weeks—ship fever broke out in Manhattan almost as soon as the 1847 season began. On May 17, the police chief warned that a "terrible epidemic" already "prevail[s] "in this city." In one of its proclamations, the ever vigilant Staten Island Committee of Safety drew lurid pictures of "low Irish" immigrants spreading disease among the unsuspecting passengers on Manhattan-bound paddle steamers. A State Senate committee that investigated the typhus outbreak proposed a more complex etiology. The principal factor in the spread of pestilence, declared the committee, was visitors. If thirty days was long enough for a latent case of typhus to appear in a quarantined immigrant, it was also long enough to invite visits from the immigrant's acquaintances in Manhattan and Brooklyn. On the quarantine station's two weekly visiting days, uncles, aunts, cousins, and friends from the old country could "be seen by the hundreds and by the thousands coming and going in the ferry boats, to and from the city to the island, and the extraordinary spectacle is presented of an unlimited and unrestrained intercourse with an establishment whose great end and aim is to prevent that very intercourse." Crew members, who escaped quarantine early, and the wealthy, who frequently escaped quarantine entirely, also helped spread disease. By December, typhus had jumped into the general population, and 1,396 New Yorkers were dead—a considerable mortality, though New Yorkers had only to look north to see how much worse it could have been. Between June 18 and July 24, there were nearly three thousand typhus deaths in Montreal, and in 1847 Montreal, with its fifty thousand people, was only one seventh the size of New York.

❦

Five miles north of the quarantine station, a skyline of church steeples and warehouses appeared, the river traffic quickened, the corridor of light above the water broadened into a glorious sky, and the swoop of the seagulls became more daring—these were New York birds. Though the Manhattan street grid now stopped only a few blocks south of what would be Thirty-fourth Street, the center of municipal life remained below Houston Street, in the teeming precincts of the ancient colonial city, where dog, pig, rat, and man engaged daily in a struggle for existence in a warren of unnumbered, unpaved, ill-lit, malodorous streets. Lower Manhattan was also home to a three-mile thicket of slips, warehouses, and masts. From Corlears Hook on the east side of the island to Hubert Street on the west side, the air smelled of old rope, tar, fish, and rotting wood. From first light until the last harbor saloon closed, "the number of boats shooting hither and thither . . . or going up and coming down the two rivers on voyages of business and pleasure is amazing," said one New Yorker. On South Street, where the nautical thicket reached its densest point, grain and Indian corn from Ohio and Wisconsin joined lumber and granite from Maine and Massachusetts, on weathered wharves stained with tobacco spit and echoing with a babel of French, German, Spanish, Italian, Swedish, Dutch, and Irish voices. South Street was also a favorite meeting place for the city's dock-runners. In the morning, the runners would gather on the water side of the street to gamble, gossip, and chew tobacco amid a deafening cacophony. The noise drifted across the river and into the parlors and bedrooms of Brooklyn Heights, to the great annoyance of the inhabitants—even then an excessively high-minded lot who considered themselves a race apart from vulgar New Yorkers.

South Street was the compass of the New York runner's life. Directly to the west, on Fulton Street, lay his past as a cartman or a menial laborer; due north, on Greenwich Street and Washington Street—the center of the boardinghouse trade—lay his future as the proprietor of an immigrant lodging house. Thomas Gunn, a nineteenth-century New Yorker who studied the "physiology of the New York boarding house," described the houses as little Prussias, Hollands, Englands, and Irelands. Houses catering to English immigrants served kippers and eggs at breakfast, offered pale ale, and not infrequently were owned by an English patriot who loudly proclaimed the sorrows of exile, but for one reason or another, never returned home to the land of Hope and Glory. The German lodging house was identifiable by the advertisements in the parlor window. Printed in a heavy Teutonic typeface, the ads hailed the establishment's beer parlor and listed midwestern cities with large German populations. The air inside the house had the heavy, cabbagey smell of German cuisine. According to Mr. Gunn, the German boardinghouse proprietor was an amiable fellow, able to abide anything except a guest who played a loud musical instrument. The Irish lodging house was a portrait in patriotic blarney. The proprietor was usually "a thick, squat, muscular" fellow who hid his duplicity under a "mask of blather," favored cravats of emerald green, and often greeted guests under portraits of the sainted Irish: Daniel O'Connell, Wolfe Tone—and Robert Emmet, a political exile who fled to New York after the 1798 uprising. "[I'm from] the ould sod, and love ever sod of it, God bless it!" the proprietor would proclaim to every greenhorn who walked through the door.

The dock-runner's present was the ships coming up from the quarantine station at Staten Island. In the 1850s, *Harper's Weekly* would lament New York's reputational decline. "What was . . . a decent and orderly town," said *Harper's*, "has been converted into a semi-barbarous metropolis." The runners—"without coats, without cravats . . . shirt necks flying open, a large roll of tobacco in each cheek"—bore most of the blame for New York's descent into reputational hell. "As a vessel approache[s] the wharfs," wrote a contemporary, "a rope [is] thrown and tied, whereupon a gang of 300 or 400 ruffians calling themselves runners jump aboard and in the style of plunderers, or pirates seize all the baggage and endeavor to persuade the passengers to such and such lodging house." Like his counterpart in Liverpool, the New York runner was often employed by a lodging house, but polyglot New York allowed for specialization. English runners wrangled English immigrants; German runners, German immigrants, Irish runners, Irish immigrants. It was frequently remarked that the Irish runner's brogue thickened perceptibly when addressing a greenhorn. He was also a man who refused to take no for an answer. One young Irish immigrant had his suitcase snatched by a runner from a lodging house on Greenwich Street, and his toolbox by a runner for one on Washington Street, a block to the west. The tools being more valuable than the clothes, the "future American" followed the runner with the tools.

Testifying before a State Senate committee on immigration, Tobias Boudinot, a New York City police captain, said that some runners hired "bullies" as enforcers. If the runner's pitch for a lodging house proved unpersuasive, the "bullies" would pick up the "new arrival" and bodily carry him to the establishment. Another common ruse was to tell the immigrant, Come to my lodging house; the weekly rate is only $1. On checking out, a week later, the immigrant would discover the real weekly rate was $3 or $4, and the landlord would demand his luggage if he was unable to pay the bill. George "one-eyed" Daley, a "reformed runner" who testified at the State Senate inquiry, described another common ruse of the profession: "tooling." Upon arriving in New York harbor, immigrant ships were required to transfer passengers to packets for the trip to the Manhattan wharves. A "tooling" runner would slip aboard a ship and offer the leader of an immigrant group a bribe to persuade the rest of the group to use the packet the runner represented. "One-eyed" told the committee of a former colleague who offered an immigrant leader his gold watch as a bribe; then, when the packet arrived in Manhattan, summoned the police and accused the immigrant of stealing the watch.

In the years since the Erie Canal made New York the premier American port, two other predatory classes had arisen to feed off the immigrant trade. Commonly, the owner of a forwarding house, which sold rail and steamship tickets, would overcharge westbound immigrants for railway tickets and shipping costs. A Mr. Weaver told a New York State Senate inquiry that he weighed 170 pounds in real life and 274 pounds on a forwarding house scale.

The rise of the bondsman, another class of immigrant predator, was one of the unintended consequences of the 1824 Passenger Act that required ship captains to post a bond of up to $300 for every passenger likely to become a ward of New York City within two years of his arrival. For a fee that ranged from 10 cents to $1 per head, the bondsman relieved a ship's captain of this financial responsibility. In theory, this exposed the bondsman to great risk as any city funds spent on the immigrant during the life of the bond came out of his pocket. In practice, the bondsman had a friend at City Hall: Mr. John Ahern, clerk to the mayor who was supposed to keep a record of all passengers under bond, but did not.

Ailing or indigent immigrants who did fall under the care of a bondsman were likely to find themselves warehoused in unheated, malodorous harbor tenements or in the bondsman's private poorhouse. Through savage cost cutting, the firm of W. J. & J. T. Tapscott of South Street was able to care for its immigrant wards at an even lower daily rate than the municipal alms house. Passenger brokers, the Tapscotts annually brought in seven thousand to eight thousand immigrants, most from Ireland. The indigents who needed care were housed in the Tapscotts' Williamsburg (Brooklyn) poorhouse where they were fed "black meal" and "refuse grease." On February 3, 1847, a day after the New York

Board of Assistant Aldermen and a committee of prominent Williamsburg residents condemned the poorhouse, the Tapscotts invited the
critics to visit their facility. This was a mistake. Mr. Lavendel, an Irish immigrant, told the Williamsburg committee that, in addition to "refuse
grease collected from ships during their trip across the Atlantic," the
diet at Tapscott's consisted of the remains of diseased pigs and lambs.
Margaret Bertram, another Irish immigrant, said that during her brief
internment at Tapscott's two infants had died. A few weeks after the
visit, the Williamsburg committee issued a second report on the Tapscott Private Poor House and Hospital. "To our utter astonishment,
even horror, we found it, if possible, worse than represented, exhibiting
a state of wretchedness not to be borne or countenanced by any civilized community."

On May 5, 1847, the New York State Legislature overrode the objec-
tions of city officials (all spiritual sons of Mr. Ahern) and instituted a series of immigrant reforms. "An Act concerning Passengers in Vessels
coming to the City of New York" created a Board of Commissioners "to
protect the new comer . . . from being robbed, to facilitate his passage
through the city, to aid him with good advice and in cases of the most
urgent necessity, to furnish him with a small amount of money." The
commission's close ties to the forwarding houses and bondsmen insured
that this brief would not be discharged faithfully. The *New York Irish-
American*, a particularly vociferous critic, accused the commission of
"reckless and culpable conduct," of "extravagant expenditure of moneys,"
and gross incompetence. "Hundreds of our people, just cast on shore
from the emigrant ships, parade daily the streets of New York, *howling
beggars*. They sleep in droves in the station houses . . . [and] in the morning, they wander the city *begging*." Finally, in 1855, a central landing
point for immigrant ships was established at Castle Garden (now Castle
Clinton) in lower Manhattan; agents were stationed in Albany to protect
westbound immigrants from forwarding-house frauds, and municipal
almshouses replaced private poorhouses like Tapscott's.

The U.S. government was quicker to impose reforms on the immigration system. On April 24, 1847, two weeks before the New York State
Legislature created the Board of Commissioners, the *Liverpool Mail* accused Washington of erecting barriers to immigration. "The United States

seems to have adopted a more effectual method of restricting, if not putting a stop, to the shoals of emigrants . . . which have been for years and are still weekly landed on their shores." The *Mail*'s complaint, which echoed an editorial in *Le Canadien* a few days earlier, was animated by the federal law (already discussed) that required all immigrant vessels entering American ports to provide each steerage passenger with fourteen feet of space. Since many foreign vessels were built to a ten-foot standard, Europeans viewed the legislation less as an act of emigrant empathy than as an attempt to protect American jobs, the purity of Yankee blood, and Yankee-style Protestantism. On June 6, *The New York Herald* reported that the vast emigrant armada in German, Dutch, French, and British ports was disbanding. "Captains and ship owners refuse to carry passengers . . . and the ports of Rotterdam, Havre, Liverpool and London, are crowded with emigrants disappointed in the object of their arrival."

The number of those who immigrated through the Port of New York between 1847 and 1851—1.8 million—makes the charge of American isolationism hard to sustain. Nonetheless, the tough new immigration laws were designed to deter—and, in 1847, to a degree, they did. During "Black '47," a year of deep famine in Ireland and of hunger and political turmoil in Germany, only 53,189 Germans and 52,946 Irish arrived in New York;* that same year, 98,000 Irish landed in Canada. In 1848, 189,176 immigrants arrived in New York, 98,000 of whom were Irish.

❈

July 1847 was one of those awful New York Julys, the kind that make the city feel like Calcutta in monsoon season. Just dressing in the morning produced a clammy sweat; every afternoon the sable-colored Manhattan sky rumbled with indigestion, and a terrific downpour puddled roofs and floors in the Sixth Ward and washed garbage—and the occasional baby pig—into the Hudson in the Ninth. The rain was particularly heavy on July 22; "Thunder-showers between 4 and 5 o'clock P.M. and [again] in the night," the municipal meteorologist reported. The previous evening,

---

*According to Professor Kerby Miller, 117,000 Irish arrived in U.S. ports in 1847.

people could already feel the humidity building. At the Old Brewery, the big tenement in Five Points, residents dragged their mattresses into the street to escape the heat. Along Water Street in the harbor, windows popped open and prostitutes stuck their heads out and let the fresh sea air wash over them. In the narrow alleys of the Sixteenth Ward, where packs of scavengers boiled animal remains in cauldrons, the "dense" odor of dog, rat, cat—and rain—corrupted the air. Even in Brooklyn, still mostly open country in 1847, the air was close. The evening of the twenty-first was not a time to be indoors, but the heat and filth and noise of the summer night had filled Biddy Nulty with longing for the cool, quiet places of her native Galway. "Do dear Mary," Biddy wrote to her friend Mary Doyle, "get some of our young ladies to write to me. . . . I shall be so unhappy until I hear from Moyode [Biddy's home in Galway]. I hope Mr. and Mrs. Persse and old Mrs. Persse are quite well and the Ladies and young Gentleman. Are they at home this summer? Please give my fond love to all the family . . . and a kiss [to] my sweet dear boy for me. . . . Tell him that I love him better than any child in the world."

As the months passed and the loneliness of the immigrants deepened, the flow of letters to Ireland became voluminous, as did the personal notices in the Irish-American press. In fifty words or less, thousands of anguished, penniless young men and women attempted to bridge the vastness of America. The immigrants who placed the notices were searching for kin who had come out before them, and in many instances the only information they had about the missing relative or friend was that they lived "somewhere north of Boston" or west of Baltimore or out in "Colorado territory."

> PATRICK FITZPATRICK, co. Cavan . . . town of Drumfife, near Croskeys, who arrived in New York in 1839. When last heard from was in the state of Ohio. Any information respecting him will be thankfully received by his brother.
>
> *
>
> PATRICK MCGOORTY, and his sister Bridget, formerly of Lianagrough, county Leitrim, who landed in Quebec in June last. They intended to proceed direct to Iowa Territory. Any

information respecting them will be thankfully received by their father, Hugh McGoorty.

*

MARGARET COLLINS of co. Cork parish of Barryrone. She arrived in Troy [New York] last July and has not been heard from since. Any information respecting her will be thankfully received by her sister Johanna Collins.

*

WILLIAM BURNS and his wife MARY GRADY, who sailed from Limerick on the 1st or 2nd of April last for New York. Their daughter . . . who left Ireland in the middle of April last and landed in Baltimore, is anxious to hear from them.

Visiting the harbor one day, Friedrich Kapp, a German-American member of the Board of Commissioners, overhead a Prussian farmer and a port official arguing over the amount of capital the farmer had declared; the official found it difficult to believe this prosperous Teutonic gentleman possessed only $25. After Kapp took the farmer aside and assured him that his capital would not be taxed, the newcomer opened his money belt and produced $2,700; his two sons, who were standing beside him, opened their belts and produced a like amount. The immigrant stream from Ireland also included a number of prosperous farmers. The "pith and marrow" of the country, the *Irish-American* called them, and claimed that some had come to America with as much as $5,000 in their money belts. But the "pith and marrow" was a pitifully small minority. The average famine immigrant washed up on American shores owning nothing more than the clothes on his back and his dreams. "The scattered debris of the Irish nation," Archbishop Hughes of New York called the newcomers. Alone, confused, unskilled, the immigrant often had no patrimony but the name and address of a relative or friend somewhere in America—that, and a capacity for hard physical labor. The Irish lived in the poorest neighborhoods, suffered hunger and disease, and worked in the most menial and worst-paid occupations. By 1850, three fourths of domestics in New York were Irish countrywomen like Biddy Nulty, but, "being the daughters of laborers or needy tradesmen or persecuted rack rented cottiers," many of the young women possessed as little domestic skill as the maid who had cut up Elizabeth Smith's favorite bedroom rug and carpeted the stairs with it. These girls, wrote a not unsympathetic observer, "are ignorant of the common duties of servants in respectable positions. They can neither wash nor iron clothes. They don't understand the cleaning of glass or a silver plate. They cannot make a fire expeditiously or dust carpets or polish the furniture. Many . . . never saw a leg of mutton boiled or roasted. Several of them cannot even prepare their own dinner pork or bacon." By the late 1840s, Biddy jokes had become popular in upper middle class and upper class New York. Biddy did not know how to answer the door, having never had a door in her cabin. Biddy stirred the fireplace with a gravy ladle, having never seen a fire poker. Biddy thought the punch bowl was a wash basin. One New Yorker said that if his wife ever killed herself, a single sentence in her suicide note would explain everything: "I kept Irish domestics."

The jokes were mean; the Help Wanted advertisements, cruel.

> WANTED—An English or American woman, that under-
> stands cooking, and to assist in the work generally . . . IRISH
> PEOPLE need not apply.
>
> *
>
> WOMAN WANTED to do general housework . . . any coun-
> try or color except Irish.

In 1852, the *Irish-American* boasted that "one half (at least) of the mechanics of New York—machinists, turners, ship-wrights, carpenters, cabinet makers, Smiths of all kinds, practical engineers— . . . were Irish." Like James Tyrone's boast in *Long Day's Journey into Night* that Shakespeare and the Duke of Wellington were Irish Catholics, the paper's claim was one part blarney and two parts ethnic insecurity. The editors were eager to dispel the notion that all Irishmen were ditch diggers, and, indeed, not all were, but—like their wives, sisters, and mothers—the men, many illiterate and some without English, had nothing to sell but their physical labor. As well as ditch diggers, the famine immigrants became cartmen, longshoremen, quarrymen, blastmen, and rock men. The Irishman who came to America thinking himself well versed in the demands of physical labor was quickly disabused of that notion. Despite repeated British attempts to change the work ethic of the Irish peasant, that ethic had remained defined by ancient Celtic rhythms. Market days, fair days, wakes, funerals, and the county races were all regarded as legitimate occasions for a holiday. In America, the immigrant quickly discovered that every day except Sunday was a workday, and that the Yankee workday was longer and the Yankee boss harder than anything the immigrant had encountered in Ireland. "I commenced working in the digging [of] Cellars," a Donegal man named James Dever recalled, "and may heaven save me from ever again being compelled to labor so severely, up before the Stars and working till darkness, nothing but driven like horses . . . a slave for the Americans, as the generality of the Irish . . . here are." Another immigrant said of his American bosses that they "only give you twenty one minutes to eat/ . . . scream, threaten and shout/ While forcing you back to work." In 1846, five hundred Irish longshoremen on the Brooklyn docks struck for a ten-hour workday and an 87 cent daily wage; a few years later, a group of immigrants laying railroad track in a brutal upstate New York winter walked off the job, striking for a ten-hour day and $1.25 daily wage.

Unlike the Germans, the English, and the "pith and marrow" Irish, the peasant Irish were too poor to go anywhere beyond the neighborhoods of lower Manhattan. The heavily Irish First, Second, Third, and Sixth Wards were within walking distance of the harbor. During the famine era, the Sixth became so famous, a visitor from the Midwest, Abraham Lincoln, requested a tour of the ward; so corrupt, in one election the ward returned more votes than it had residents; and so Irish, a resident named Paolo Antonio Vaccarelli changed his name to Paul Kelly to advance his criminal career. The Old Brewery, the most famous tenement in Five Points, was once a charming hotel and drinking establishment; by 1847 the hotel housed a thousand of the poorest people in the city, many of them Irish. To the east of Five Points, along Second Avenue, a mile-long garbage dump ran from First Street to Twentieth. On nights when the wind blew in the wrong direction, the stench from "large quantities of manure and garbage of almost every description" would settle over the narrow lanes of the Sixth. All the other public health hazards that gave mid-nineteenth-century New York a child mortality rate of almost 50 percent—uncollected carcasses, animal and human waste, and garbage—were common features of life in the ward. In his darker moods, Archbishop Hughes feared that the famine immigration had succeeded only in moving Irish squalor from one side of the Atlantic to the other. "It is but truth to say, that . . . the [Irish] cellars and garrets of New York" are as awful as "the . . . hovels from which many of the [Irish were] exterminated."

Between 1847 and 1851, 848,000 Irish immigrants arrived in New York: about four times the population of midcentury Dublin and more than twice that of 1845 New York. While a significant number of the newcomers eventually moved elsewhere, those who stayed were too numerous to be housed in a few steamy wards in the old colonial city at the bottom of Manhattan. By 1847, 56,753 of Brooklyn's 205,250 residents were Irish; in time, building projects like the Croton Aqueduct and the Harlem Railroad would attract Irish laborers and their families to the Bronx. Meanwhile, in Manhattan, the search for cheap living space drove immigrants into the sparsely populated northern regions of the island. In the 1850s, a visitor approaching Sixtieth Street in what is now Central Park would see plumes of smoke rising above the tree line and a moment later enter a squatter camp built along the lines of an Irish townland.

Even if the Irish had been Germans or Swedes, the sheer scale of the famine immigration would have disrupted New York life enormously, but the famine immigrants were not Germans or Swedes. "The Irish," noted Thomas Babington Macaulay, were "distinguished by qualities that tend to make men interesting rather than prosperous. They [are] an ardent, impetuous race, easily moved to tears or laughter, to fury or to love." Most midcentury New Yorkers would have agreed with Macaulay, except for the part about the Irish being "interesting." During the famine era, words like "hairy," "simian," "odorous," "ugly," "diseased," "hungry," "incurable," "leprous," "disorderly," and "quarrelsome" made up the vocabulary of public and private discourse on the famine immigrant. Some of this could be put down to historical prejudice. Henry II's "wild Irish" and Swift's "savage Irish" still resonated in the minds of Anglo-Saxon New Yorkers. However, racial prejudice alone did not turn the police wagon into the Paddy wagon. Removed from the constraints of family and townland culture, the immigrants often behaved in ways that made even Irish leaders despair. "The social training of our people has been sadly neglected," wrote Thomas D'Arcy McGee, publisher of the American edition of *The Nation*. "They were not taught punctuality, soberness, cleanliness, or other minor morals." In the 1850s, the Irish accounted for 55 percent of the arrests in New York, 63 percent of the admissions to the municipal almshouse, 85 percent of foreign-born admissions to the public hospitals, and 35 percent (706 out of 2,000) of the city's prostitutes. As the association between the famine immigrants and social pathology grew, members of the old New York Protestant Irish community began to step away from their Irishness. They now called themselves "Ulster Irish" or "Scotch Irish."

Nativist organizations like the American Republican party, the Native American party, the American party, and the Order of the Star Spangled Banner (the Know Nothings)—anxious about immigration, about Catholics, and about universal male suffrage—saw in the Irish the sum of all their fears. The Irish immigrant posed a threat, in the first place because he was a tool of the priests, the priests were a tool of the papacy, and the papacy occupied the same place in the minds of nativists as *The Protocols of the Elders of Zion* later came to occupy in the minds of anti-Semites. Whether "wise or stupid, good or bad, their priests control their votes," declared Robert Breckinridge, the superintendent of public education in Kentucky. Samuel F. B. Morse—writer, publisher, and inventor of the telegraph—believed the peculiar character of the Irish mind made the immigrants "senseless machines," vulnerable to priestly manipulation. The *Southern Literary Messenger* asserted that Paddy, exposed to "the most debasing influences of mankind," was incapable of the intellectual exchanges that are the basis of free government. His natural sphere, declared the *Messenger,* was "servile employments." It was a special misfortune of the famine Irish to arrive in America just as the "scientific" study of race was becoming popular. The racial "scientists" who studied the immigrants came back shaking their heads in dismay. The Irish had the wrong head shape, the wrong facial contours, the wrong pattern of skull bumps. Being white and European, the Irish had to be classified as Caucasian, but this potential embarrassment was circumvented by dividing Caucasians into an ever expanding array of subgroups. In *Types of Mankind*, the pioneering ethnographers Josiah Nott and George Gliddon succeeded in devising seven such categories. To no one's surprise, except perhaps their own, the Irish were in one of the bottommost categories.

In 1849, when an Irish mob rioted in Astor Place; in 1857, when an Irish gang, the Dead Rabbits, rioted in lower Manhattan; in 1863, when draft riots swept through the Irish neighborhoods of the city; and in 1870 and 1871, when the Orange riots broke out, many New Yorkers saw racial disorder at work. The qualities of the Celtic race, wrote *The Presbyterian Quarterly Review*, were "vehement, impulsive reckless[ness]." The Irish were "an animal rather than an intellectual people . . . a sort of exaggerated or overgrown children." By 1870, the Irish accounted for 21.4 percent of the population of New York, and, with few exceptions, the other 78.6 percent viewed the immigrants as, at best, a dead limb that had to be dragged about at great inconvenience, annoyance, and expense.

Before the famine Irish could be turned into Irish-Americans, someone would have to socialize them.

✳

On a wet Ulster morning before the nineteenth century was many years old, a peasant family draped in mourning black and carrying a small wooden coffin arrived at the gates of a cemetery in County Tyrone. At the gates, the little procession halted and waited while the priest accompanying the mourners scooped up a handful of moist black earth and made the sign of the cross over it. It was the Catholic custom to sprinkle blessed earth on a coffin before it was lowered into the grave, but in the Ireland of this period, Catholic clerics were banned from burial grounds. As the gates opened, the priest handed the blessed earth to one of the mourners. No one incident shapes a life, but as far as one can, the burial of Mary Hughes shaped the life of her older brother, John. As an adult, John Joseph Hughes, archbishop of New York, would say that in his native country, the only moments of freedom he enjoyed were the five days between his birth and his baptism as a Catholic.

Hughes had a moving story, but the hard Ulster childhood produced a hard man. Dagger John—the archbishop placed a dagger after his
name rather than the customary priestly cross—was contentious, narrow-
minded, and quick-tempered, and his sympathies rarely extended beyond
his own people. On the great question of antebellum America—slavery—
Hughes was persistently evasive and opaque, and his evasiveness was all
the more notable because, by the time of the famine, his commanding
personality had made him the most celebrated Catholic prelate in the
United States. A man of the world, he measured success the way worldly
men do—by the amount of money raised, the number of buildings built,
organizations formed, meetings attended, opponents bested. If the archbishop ever had any deep spiritual thoughts, he kept them to himself. Intelligent, forceful, autocratic, and handsome, Hughes was respected by
every man, loved by few. "More a Roman Gladiator than a devout follower
of the meek founder of Christianity," *The New York Herald* said of him.

This was the flawed but gifted Moses who would gather up famine
immigrants in the teeming filthy wards of lower Manhattan and lead
them out of the wilderness. "My lot," Hughes said later, "was cast in the
great Metropolis of the whole country.... I had to stand up amongst [my
people] as their bishop and chief to warn them of the dangers that surrounded them; to contend for their right as a religious community; to
convince their judgment ... in regard to public and mixed questions; to
encourage the timid; and sometimes to restrain the impetuous." When
Hughes arrived in New York in 1838, he put an end to the old Catholic
community's policy of accommodation. There would be no more Catholic churches that looked like Protestant churches, no more going along to
get along, no more Americanization of Roman Catholicism. In the United
States, all religions stood equal before the law. The archbishop used that
constitutional guarantee to expand the church's sphere of influence. When
nativist administrators refused to allow Jesuits to minister at municipal
hospitals and prisons, Hughes harassed city officials; when rioters burned
down Catholic churches in Philadelphia, Hughes told New York officials
that if one of his churches was burned, the city would become a second
"Moscow"—a reference to that city's sacking during the Napoleonic
Wars. Hughes also drove Protestant Bibles out of the classrooms of the
Free School Society, the forerunner of the New York City public school

system. During his tenure, New York became the first of the original thirteen states to prohibit the teaching of religion in public school classrooms. After the Philadelphia riots, Hughes threatened to raise an army of three thousand faithful to guard Catholic churches in the city.

Under Hughes, the Catholic church in New York became a distinctively Irish institution. From the wilderness of potato lands, oppressive landlords, coffin ships, and Sixth Ward slums, the archbishop gathered up the "scattered debris of the Irish nation" and built a homeland for them, where they were free to enjoy "the consolation of [their] religion" and to forget that they were "among strangers in a strange land." Hughes began by "churching" the newcomers.

In nineteenth-century Ireland, the relationship between "Irish" and "Catholic" was not quite what it appeared to outsiders. While the peasantry looked up to the local priest as a community leader, and while the organized church played an important symbolic role in the life of the people, only a minority of Irish men and women actually attended mass regularly, or knew the names of the sacraments or the holy days in the church calendar. After two centuries of British oppression, the Irish church had become more a symbol of national resistance than a religious institution. Hughes would build his new Irish Catholic homeland upon the rock of parish, church, and school. In the decades after the famine, a hundred new churches and fourteen parishes were created, and dozens of temporal institutions established to look after the worldly needs of the famine immigrants, including: two new Catholic colleges, St. John's (now Fordham) and Manhattan; New York's first Catholic hospital, St. Vincent's; a new paper, the *Irish-American*; a Catholic temperance society; a savings society; the beginnings of a municipal cathedral, St. Patrick's; and dozens of parochial schools.

Inside Hughes's enclave, the immigrants learned the dangers of "godless" public education, mixed marriages (Catholic-Protestant unions), nativism, and "red republicanism," but they also learned how to be Americans. At Sunday mass, the faithful were encouraged to develop industry, punctuality, sobriety, thrift, and self-control—the Anglo-Saxon virtues the British nation builders wanted to foster in Ireland. The Sunday homilies also helped the immigrants to see how and where they fit into the American story. Like the Pilgrims—the first European

Americans—the Irish came to the United States in search of religious liberty. Proud, tough, and street-smart Irish New York was also inward-looking, parochial, frequently intolerant, sometimes violent, and very politically astute.

⚶

William Marcy Tweed was a Scotch-Irish Protestant who had little in common with John Joseph Hughes except a flawed character, a knowledge of the way the world worked, and an important role in the Americanization of the famine Irish. A friend to all "future Americans," Mr. Tweed led Tammany Hall, the most powerful and arguably the most corrupt political machine in mid-nineteenth-century America. George Washington Plunkitt, the philosopher king of Tammany, once likened the Tweed machine to a great ocean, and its reformist opponents to waves. "If you know the ropes," said Plunkitt, there was no wave a little patronage could not smooth out. Tweed, Plunkitt, and other Tammany men knew the ropes. In Manhattan alone, the machine controlled almost eight thousand jobs, and at one point thirty thousand jobs citywide.

Formed in the late eighteenth century, Tammany took its name from an Indian chief and its morals from Caligula; it was run by men like Tweed, Plunkitt, and Honest John Kelly—men who favored bowlers and loud cravats; talked out of the side of the mouth; called one another "Brains," "Boss," and "Slippery Dick"; and believed legitimate distinctions could be made between "honest graft" and "dishonest graft." The corpulent Tweed, never a man to deny himself, took both kinds. Estimates of the Boss's personal fortune range from $30 million to $200 million—in nineteenth-century dollars. For the famine immigrant, the virtues of Tammany Hall in particular and the Democratic party in general began with what they were not. They were not the Republican party of Abraham Lincoln; in the eyes of the Irish, the Republicans were only the latest manifestation of a deep strain of anti-immigrant feeling in American life. As early as 1777, John Jay, an author of *The Federalist Papers*, had attempted to insert into the New York State constitution a clause that, to Irish Catholic colonists, sounded like an American version of the Penal Laws. Jay would have deprived Catholic New Yorkers of their civil rights and banned them from holding land unless they swore a special oath of allegiance that included a denunciation of "popery."

Deep differences in sensibility ensured that a certain amount of ill feeling would arise between the New York Republicans—a mixture of well-to-do abolitionists, temperance advocates, and other Yankee progressives—and the famine Irish, who were preoccupied with urgent matters of daily survival and prone to take a relaxed view of human weaknesses. When a reform-minded New York legislature imposed restraints on the sale of liquor, the *Irish-American* denounced the measure as impractical and impossible to enforce. When the Irish tore up Astor Place to protest the appearance of an English actor, William Macready, in the role of Macbeth, the reformers were beside themselves. For heaven's sake, Macbeth was a Scottish king, not an Irish one! At the root of the mutual antipathy lay profoundly different conceptions of government. Reformers saw government as an instrument of progress and enlightenment, a tool to construct Jonathan Edwards's "shining city on a hill"; having suffered through the Penal Laws and seen their grain exported in the midst of famine, the Irish saw government as brutal and oppressive. When President Grover Cleveland rebuked New York congressman Timothy Campbell for submitting an "unconstitutional" proposal, Campbell, a County Cavan man by birth, replied, "Ah, Mr. President. What is the constitution between friends?" The Reformers and the Irish also divided over the race question.

Despite Daniel O'Connell's fervent embrace of abolition, many famine emigrants saw slavery as an American issue and the Civil War as another man's fight. Having escaped a miserable death at home at the hands of the British government, many immigrants wondered why the American government expected them to die a miserable death at Fredericksburg or Cold Harbor. At a meeting in Cincinnati in 1861, the American Catholic church implicitly endorsed this view.

> It is not for us to inquire into the causes which have led to the present unhappy condition of affairs. This inquiry belongs more appropriately to those who are directly concerned in managing the affairs of the Republic. The spirit of the Catholic Church is eminently conservative and while

her ministers rightly feel a deep and abiding interest in all
that concerns the welfare of this country, they do not think
[it] their province to enter into the political arena.

In many parts of the north, the Irish stance on the war aroused further questions about their suitability for citizenship, and in New York the
questions were informed by terrible memories of the 1863 draft riots. Men
like George Templeton Strong; Horace Greeley, the editor of the *Tribune*;
and Thomas Nast, a German-born cartoonist for *Harper's Weekly*, never
forgot the way Irish mobs had torn away the city's thin veneer of civilization, or their brutal attacks on African American New Yorkers. For the
rest of the century, progressive New Yorkers would view the immigrant
Irish as a corrupting influence on government: clannish, violent, brutal to
enemies, subservient to friends, the Irish seemed attached to no political
principle beyond selling their votes to the highest bidder. In an 1876 cartoon, "The Ignorant Vote," Nast placed a simian-looking Paddy on the
scales of justice, facing that other participant in the ignorant vote, the
black man. In an 1871 cartoon, "The Usual Irish Way of Doing Things,"
the cartoonist placed Paddy on top of a barrel of gunpowder with a
bottle of whiskey in one hand and a shillelagh in the other. The Reverend Samuel D. Burchard boiled Paddy's faults down to three words:
"Rum, Romanism and Rebellion." Enlightened New Yorkers longed
for "the decent orderly town" that New York had been before the Irish
arrived.

The Tammany Hall model of politics was closer to the Irish model.
"Study human nature and make government warm and personal," Mr.
Plunkitt advised young Tammany officials. To anyone accustomed to
the way Daniel O'Connell did politics, the advice sounded familiar.
Tammany also had other attractions for the famine immigrant. Tweed
and his associates were as unhappy about the Civil War as he was, and,
outside the Catholic church, Tammany was the only institution in New
York that seemed to understand and care about the immigrants' needs.
In return for his vote and the votes of his family and friends, the Tweed
machine provided food and rent in emergencies, a meal at Christmas
and Thanksgiving, and a government job. It also acted as an advocate
and intermediary in encounters with the state. A Tammany man would

get the immigrant out of jail if he was arrested; if he or a family member needed to be naturalized in a hurry, a Tammany man would see to that, too. In 1868, the New York courts naturalized sixteen hundred people in a day, at the machine's request. "Think what the people of New York are," Mr. Plunkitt once observed. "One half, more than one half, are foreign born. They do not speak our language. They do not know our laws. They are the raw material from which we have built up the state. There is no denying the service that Tammany has rendered the Republic."

In regard to the Irish, Tammany's contribution to the Republic was to teach a politically gifted people how to practice American politics. In the 1840s, the famine Irish came to Tammany as supplicants, their highest ambition a job. By the mid-1850s, many of the more astute immigrants had become saloonkeepers, policemen, and firemen, three professions closely intertwined with politics in late-nineteenth-century New York. Under the tutelage of Tweed and his associates, an aspiring politician tired of the saloon or firehouse could learn the importance of "walking around" money, of knowing how to make a wedding toast in German, and other essential tradecraft of the nineteenth-century New York City street politician. By the 1870s, having become as adept at American-style politics as their mentors, the Irish, in the person of Honest John Kelly, seized control of Tammany. A former sheriff and congressman who was given his sobriquet by a badly misinformed colleague, Mr. Kelly instituted the Irish Ascendancy at Tammany with a Tammany-style coup. To ensure a favorable result in the election that followed Boss Tweed's arrest, Kelly had guards posted at the auditorium where the vote was held. Once in office, he went after the mayor of New York, William Havemeyer. One day, Havemeyer woke up to the alarming news that Honest John had ordered several of his election inspectors arrested. The mayor responded by accusing Kelly of stealing $84,482 from the city; charges and countercharges flew back and forth. The governor of New York, a man named Dix, expressed concern about the political effects of such a public quarrel. Havemeyer spared everyone further embarrassment by having the decency to die. In a postmortem on the dispute, *The Irish World* declared Honest John the victor on the grounds that the deceased mayor had once defamed the Irish by calling attention to the fact that two-sevenths of the convicts in New York State were from Ireland.

Under the Irish aegis, Tammany continued to trade immigrant social services for votes, to make Jesuitical distinctions between honest and dishonest graft, and to put forward politicians whose only discernable qualification for office was their connection to Tammany. In nineteenth-century New York, the Irish commanded more than a fifth of the vote, and very few Irish voters held Providence responsible for the famine. "Until my father died . . . he never said England without adding 'Goddamn her,'" recalled Elizabeth Gurley Flynn, who, like tens of thousands of other first-generation Irish-Americans, received her Anglophobia like "mother's milk" from her parents.

In the Irish saloons of lower Manhattan and Brooklyn, a hundred heads would nod whenever a plaintive voice began to sing the "The Song of the Black Potatoes":

No work of God are these deeds accursed.

However, beyond "England, Goddamn her," the drinkers were incapable of explaining how it happened that they should be standing in a Brooklyn saloon instead of a Tyrone or Antrim field.

In the decade after the famine, that began to change; politically minded Irish journalists and priests assembled a detailed critique of British famine relief policy. The most influential member of the group was a former Young Irelander, John Mitchel, whose talents as a polemicist had impressed men as diverse as Lord Stanley, the colonial secretary under Peel, and Jefferson Davis, president of the Confederate States of America. In *The Last Conquest of Ireland (Perhaps)*, Mitchel, a son of the Ascendancy and an apologist for the Confederacy, took a widely observed fact—the failure of the British relief program—and turned it into a genocidal plot to depopulate Ireland. "These Relief Acts . . . have always appeared to me machinery for . . . destruction." Even the 20,000 tons of corn London imported were a subterfuge, designed to lead "all the world to believe that they [the British government] would provide large quantities [of food] whereas, in fact, the quantities imported . . . [were] inadequate to supply the loss of grain *exported*." Mitchel also made the chaos of the public works program and General Burgoyne's obsessive attention to detail part of the plot. "The unassisted human facilit[y] never could comprehend those ten thousand books and fourteen tons of paper. [And the] insolent commissioners and inspectors and clerks . . . ordering [the bewildered] to study the documents, added further to the obfuscation."

Some of Mitchel's accusations were simply wrong. By the time the famine ended, Ireland had imported far more food than she had exported. Other accusations were distortions of fact: no national relief effort organized in a backward country in the midst of a great national disaster could avoid bureaucratic chaos and dislocation. And some charges were grotesque fabrications. Whatever Mr. Trevelyan's sins—and he had much to answer for in Ireland—he did not draw Irish children into "his government laboratory where he had prepared for them his typhus poison." But to Irish readers the central accusation in *Last Conquest* sounded true: "The Almighty, indeed, sent the potato blight but England sent the famine"—and why would it not sound true to a people who had built roads in the bitter January cold, who had watched British ships sail away with their grain in the midst of famine, and who had put their children into early graves?

For "politically minded Irishmen," writes the historian Kerby Miller, "the government's niggardly relief measures, its failure to stem food exports, and its passage of the fateful Gregory clause [requiring that a man surrender all but a quarter acre of his land to qualify for relief] not only confirmed preexisting suspicions [about the English] but also seemed to form a pattern, not of mere indifference or incompetence but of 'systematic extermination and recolonization.'" What was the English plan to restructure the Irish economy and Irish society if not a plot to drive the peasantry from the land in order to create large English commercial farms? A compelling case for the genocide argument could be made from the pages of *The Times* alone, with its talk of a second plantation of Ireland by Scottish and English farmers.

To a brutalized people, the charge of genocide also had the emotionally satisfying element of scale and weight. Bureaucratic delays and incompetence, shipping shortages, legislative measures and tax policy, cowardice on the part of some officials and stupidity on the part of others—such explanations sounded too small, too trivial, too lacking in supreme malevolence to explain the disappearance of a third of the Irish nation. What famine immigrant wanted to believe that Mr. Trevelyan's sin was taking Adam Smith and Edmund Burke too literally, when he could believe the assistant secretary was poisoning Irish children in his typhus laboratory? "No wonder that a dedicated nationalist like Mitchel became filled with a 'sacred wrath' against England," says Professor Miller, "and that ordinary Irishmen and Irish Americans—who first learned about such callous statements through nationalist channels—soon became equally convinced that their sufferings were intentional." *Last Conquest* also had another attraction for Irish readers. The book ignored the prosperous Catholic farmers who evicted tenants, the Catholic merchants who charged "famine prices" for Indian corn, and the Catholic-dominated relief committees that dispensed food and work on the basis of patronage rather than need.

Men and women who arrived in New York and Boston as immigrants now began to think of themselves as exiles. In the late 1850s, the British spy Thomas Doyle warned London that among the famine immigrants and their children there resided a deep desire "to wreak vengeance on the persecutors of their race and creed." In the 1850s, three-fifths of Irish America believed a revolution in Ireland was not "practicable in the present state of the world," but the Civil War changed Irish attitudes. The war gave many immigrants at least a modicum of economic security, and several hundred thousand young Irishmen military experience—the Union Army alone had trained 150,000 Irish recruits. *Last Conquest*, published in 1861, provided Irish America with an intellectual framework for its rage. The large Irish vote also had made American politicians sympathetic to Irish grievances. Reporting on the visit of the Fenian leader John O'Neil to the White House, Thomas Miller Beech, another British spy, alleged that Andrew Johnson had told O'Neil, "I want you to understand that my sympathies are entirely with you and anything which lies in my power, I am willing to do to assist you." On April 21, 1866, the *Irish-American* reported that an attack on Canada, the nearest British-held territory, was imminent. Five weeks later, General O'Neil led a six-hundred-man Fenian army across the Canadian border near Buffalo. The invasion was not a success. After repulsing a Canadian attack at

Ridgeway, a few miles north of the border, the Fenians, running short of food, retreated back into New York State; O'Neil was arrested by a local sheriff. The second Fenian attack on Canada, in 1870, may have had the strangest ending in the history of human warfare. The penniless invaders had to wire Boss Tweed for fare money back to New York.

The Irish lack "John Browns," sneered George Templeton Strong. The sneer was premature. In time, the Irish John Browns would appear, and one of them, Brooklyn-born Éamon de Valera, would become president of the Irish Free State. However, as people of the Trinity, the Irish were capable of more than one identity. Along with the gunmen and patriots who went back to Ireland, Irish New York also produced a brash new middle class of strivers, sharpies, fast talkers, and wise guys. In the 1930s, when Hollywood went looking for a model for the modern urban American, it was to Irish New York that the moviemakers turned. And, as played by James Cagney, with a smile so sharp you could cut a finger on it and so much energy he seemed to bounce on the balls of his feet, the Irish New Yorker appeared to be the very embodiment of the George M. Cohan song:

> *I'm a Yankee Doodle Dandy . . .*
> *Born on the Fourth of July.*

the beginning of August—having acquired enough prayers to fill Heaven three times over, been the recipient of at least four surrogate funerals, and hailed by everyone from the pope to "the colored people" of New York, the Hero was coming home, though he was still taking his good time about it. The day before—August 1—when the *Duchess of Kent* sailed into Dublin harbor with O'Connell's mortal remains, instead of proceeding directly up the Liffey she had loitered next to the harbor light for over an hour, allowing tension to build in the "prodigious" crowd waiting at the Custom House quay. Another long hour passed while O'Connell's coffin was transferred from the *Duchess*. The waiting mourners might be forgiven for suspecting that the Hero of Christianity was determined to savor every moment of his Last Hurrah.

Finally, at four thirty, the Dublin city marshal; the Liberator's personal chaplain, the Reverend Dr. Miley; his eldest son and political heir, John O'Connell; other family relations; and sundry clerics and dignitaries took their places around the hearse, and the cortège proceeded northward in "spherical silence" to St. Mary's, where O'Connell's body was to lie in state until August 5. The old man who had left for Rome in March, "broken in health and spirit," was not the man in the mind's eye of the crowds standing in the hot August streets. To the rising middle classes, in their English suits; to the peasants, in their patched and repatched jackets; to the shoeless children and their shoeless mothers; to the coffin makers and the tax collectors, the gravediggers and chimney sweeps; to the off-duty Constabulary men, and to the felons and the gunmen: to all of them O'Connell remained forever Kerry handsome and as bold as the wind. He was the man who had restored dignity and pride to an oppressed people, who had led the struggle for Catholic Emancipation, had become the first Irish Catholic to sit in Parliament, the first Irish leader to almost break the Union; and, what the crowd loved most, he had done it all while publicly thumbing his nose at the English. The mourners were not unmindful of the departed's faults: an appetite for jobbery and double-dealing, and a love of pomp and pageantry that bordered on the oriental. And the two grave mistakes of the final years: the failure to see that England would resist repeal of the Union (which was a threat to the empire) more aggressively than it had Catholic Emancipation (which was not), and the fateful Russell alliance, which divided nationalist Ireland and tied O'Connell to the disastrous Whig relief plan. Still, if any people understood that life can sometimes outmatch a man, the Irish did. As *The Freeman's Journal* noted on August 4, all that mattered now was that O'Connell was home. "At last the wish of the Irish people is gratified."

On August 5, Dublin awoke to a peal of church bells echoing from every point in the city. By eight, the boulevards and thoroughfares were full. "Many hours before the appointed time," wrote a visitor, "every street leading to the Metropolitan Church [St. Mary's] presented a stream of well-dressed persons, women, men, and children thronging towards those points from which the sad ceremony could be seen to the greatest advantage. The cities and towns [of] Ireland sent forth their municipal representatives. The prelates and clergy of the church . . . attended from the most extreme points of the land, all that is trusted and honored in Ireland attended to do honor to the memory of her greatest citizen."

※

O'Connell's death was not the only shocking piece of news Ireland received in the spring of 1847. In mid-May, the citizens of Cork city were put into a terrible fright by a report that the blight had reappeared in a field outside the city. The origins of the intelligence were obscure, but what began as a single observation in a single potato field quickly "swelled to portentous size." "The annihilation of the whole 1847 potato crop" is at hand, the people of Cork told one another. Then, one day toward the end of May, an editor at the *Cork Southern Reporter* realized no one had actually examined potatoes from the suspect field. Tests were duly conducted, and a few days later the *Reporter* announced to a grateful city that the sample potatoes from the field "were not spotted and they were not black. . . . We trust this . . . will be sufficient to calm the natural disquietude." It was not. Anxious eyes and anxious minds continued to see signs of the potato disease everywhere. Normal plant blemishes—a spot of discolored leaf, a shriveled tip—were exaggerated into "alarming symptoms," and alarming symptoms exaggerated into apocalyptic rumors and predictions.

There had been so much bad news for so long, people viewed good news as suspect; nonetheless, good news there was in August, and it began with the weather and the crops. Mourners traveling north from

The funeral procession of Daniel O'Connell on August 5, 1847.

Cork and east from Tipperary to attend O'Connell's funeral marveled at a sight that had begun to seem like the stuff of myth: potato fields "in the full bloom of health." After a few brief appearances early in the summer, the blight, unable to tolerate the hot and dry weather, had vanished.

The "glorious summer" weather had ended both "fever among the people and disease in the potatoes," announced Lord Clarendon, the new Irish viceroy. Although Clarendon was overstating the case, still the good weather had reduced the incidence of pestilence, and General Burgoyne's soup kitchens had reduced the incidence of starvation. Having experienced eighteen months of mostly failure in Ireland, the British government had finally discovered a lifesaving relief formula: stop using food as a tool of moral reeducation, and feed the people. At the height of the soup operations, two thousand Burgoyne kitchens were relieving 3,020,712 people daily: a remarkable achievement. The great question before the country on the day of O'Connell's funeral was what would happen when the soup kitchens closed on August 15, ten days hence. The 1847 potato crop, though healthy, was less than a quarter the normal size—the spring warnings about a lack of planting had not been exaggerated. The potatoes would be gone in a few months and, although cheap foreign food was pouring into the country, with the public works program closed the peasantry lacked means to buy it.

In theory, the new Poor Law would replace the 700,000 plus lost public works jobs, but the new law rested on a pair of untested assumptions. After two years of falling rental and agricultural revenues, did the landed classes still possess enough capital to put the peasantry to work? And, assuming the answer was yes, would the Poor Law work the way Mr. Trevelyan claimed in *The Irish Crisis*? Would landowners find it more economically advantageous to hire laborers than to put them on the relief rolls, especially when landowners—and large farmers, for that matter—could just as easily lower their poor rate by evicting tenants?

In August, it was still too early to answer either question, but George Poulett Scrope, an influential English MP, was not optimistic. "The majority [of landlords] look for salvation . . . *in the eviction of their numerous tenantry, the clearing of their estates . . . by emigration and ejectment.*" Assistant Poor Law Commissioner Caesar Otway was also pessimistic. Earlier in the summer, during a visit to Westport, one of the most impoverished regions of Mayo, Otway had found the guardians and the local gentry colluding to keep the poor rate low. Even Mr. *Punch* had noticed the gentry's unhappiness with the new Poor Law and, thoughtfully, had suggested some new arguments they could use against the measure:

> "Because the Irish people are constitutionally given to starvation and an interference with national habits cannot be desirable."

> "Because it will ruin the independence of the poor in Ireland by giving them something to depend on."

> "Because the tendency of the bill is to increase the distress of landlords while attempting to relieve the distress of the whole people."

> "Because the bill . . . was framed in a hurry; and . . . nothing done in a hurry is done well."

In August, when the *Duchess of Kent* docked at the Custom House quay, the only thing that could be said with certainty about the new Poor Law was that it would be very expensive. In September 1846, £21,510 was collected under the old Poor Law; in September 1847, £73,338 was collected under the new law; in October, the comparable figures were £26,805 for 1846 and £121,255 for 1847; in November, £36,639 for 1846 and £151,684 for 1847; and in December, £46,440 for 1846 and £168,860 for 1847.

James Hack Tuke, a York Quaker and a banker, found the arguments for and against the new Poor Law so confusing toward the end of summer he decided to visit Ireland. Several weeks later, Tuke returned to York deeply depressed. In the north and east of the country, he had found the necessary wealth to make the new law work, but not the necessary will. Few proprietors and large farmers were planning to expand their labor force. In the west, where the roads were full of paupers crying, "Won't your honor give us work!" Tuke found the will, "wealth and machinery" lacking, and mass evictions growing.

Visiting Keel, a Mayo fishing village, Mr. Tuke passed dozens of freshly unroofed cabins and dozens of men and women sitting in piles of earth, surrounded by the detritus of their lives. Some of the evictees wept, some tried to comfort their children. As Tuke and his companion, Sir Richard O'Donnell, a prominent local proprietor, were talking, one evictee, an old man, walked over and placed his wife at their feet. The woman was still alive, but only just. The old man asked whether the two gentlemen could please help him.

In early September, Frederick Cavendish, editor of *The Connaught Telegraph*, warned his readers to prepare for a bitter winter struggle between a landed class prepared to resort to mass evictions to protect their financial position, and a peasantry determined not to endure another winter of starvation and mass death. If the common people of the country have "no means of earning their food," said Cavendish, they would seize it by main force.

At Downing Street, the warnings of impending calamity were ignored. The total value of the 1847 Irish crops—potatoes, wheat, oats, and so on—was expected to amount to £40 million. Lord John Russell was certain that forty million pounds sterling was enough to give employment to great numbers of poor peasants. If the Irish landed classes insisted on doing nothing, then the peasantry should be allowed to consume their rent crops (oats and wheat) or sell them to raise food money. "Proprietors . . . have raised up, encouraged and grown rich upon a potato fed population," declared Lord John. "Now that the question is between rent and substance—I think rent must give way."

✴

London's determination to press forward with the new Poor Law owed much to recession fears. In the age of the gold standard, imports had to be paid for in bullion, and over the winter so much foreign food had been purchased for Ireland that by the spring of 1847 a balance-of-payments crisis had developed. Almost immediately, the balance-of-payments crisis was turned into a credit crisis by an 1844 law requiring the Bank of England to withdraw currency from circulation as the amount of bullion declined. Corn dealers, caught between the credit crunch and a sharp drop in food prices, had a particularly unquiet spring. Merchants who had purchased maize at £16 and £17 a ton in January—thinking corn would sell for £25 in April—watched the price fall to £14, then £12 and £10 a ton. Then, in early summer, the railway bubble burst, and the precipitous fall in the price of railway shares—combined with a downturn in the textile industry, the credit crunch, and a wave of bankruptcies—produced what one clever headline writer called a "famine in money." In Dublin, a visitor found a "to let" sign on "every second house."

Lord John was also committed to the new Poor Law because the new outdoor relief entitlement might finally convince Irish paupers to stay home. After nearly a year of "the Irish invasion," Britons were waking up to paupers defecating in their gardens, sleeping in their doorways, and rummaging through their garbage. In London, where a thousand immigrants arrived weekly, the parks and national monuments had become great pauper dormitories. In Manchester, where five thousand Irish immigrants were being relieved weekly, the local poor rate rose and then rose again; in Liverpool, there were corpses in the streets, pestilence in the cellars, and a population afraid to leave their homes. In Swansea and Cardiff, in Falmouth, and in dozens of other small British cities and towns, normal life had been disrupted by the sudden influx of large numbers of Irish-speaking peasants unfamiliar with the habits of modern life. By late summer, in England and in Scotland, where 26,000 immigrants flooded into Glasgow between July 15 and August 17, there was great anger. In pubs and church halls, the immigrants were accused of undercutting working men's wages and of threatening the Protestant character of the country. Paddy was even blamed for the recession. During a meeting at St. Marylebone, a London church, one parishioner, a Mr. Joseph, moved "that the collection of tomorrow . . . not be for the Irish poor but for their own poor who were so much in want of it."

Just before the British general election in July, the *Preston Guardian,* an influential English provincial paper, declared that "the time has arrived to leave the Irish landlord and tenant to their own devices, and allow England and Scotland to apply their resources to the benefit of their own people." Just how many Britons agreed with the *Guardian* was evident in the election results. The Russell government eked out a small parliamentary majority, but the big electoral winners were Mr. Roebuck's Radicals, the "party of no" on Irish relief. In Durham, Devon, and Dorset, in West Sussex and East Sussex, large numbers of people now embraced the Moralist doctrine of Mr. Wood and Mr. Trevelyan: Ireland must learn to help herself, even if the human cost of the lesson was regrettably high.

"There are many individuals of even superior minds who now seem to me to have steeled their hearts entirely to the suffering of the people of Ireland," Mr. Twisleton, the Irish Poor Law commissioner, told a parliamentary inquiry. "They justify it to themselves by thinking that it would be going contrary to the provisions of nature to give any assistance to the destitute in [that] country. It is said that the law of nature is that those persons should die . . . and that you should leave them alone; there is thus a sort of philosophical color given to the theory or idea that a person who permits the destitute Irish to die from want of food is acting in conformity with the system of nature."

✖

Early on the morning of September 1, 1847, a coach stopped in front of the fever hospital in Rochdale, a British Midlands town proud of its

An engraving of an eviction and "tumbling," from Illustrated London News, *1848*

past—which included a mention in the Domesday Book (circa 1086)—and prouder still of its present. In 1847, Rochdale, like Liverpool, was the bully of its particular litter, the cluster of gritty little mill towns that had sprung up around Manchester, one of the hubs of the industrial revolution. Rochdale had two sources of wealth—the local textile mills and an industrial canal—and an ambition to improve its place in the world; hence the town fathers' current infatuation with Victorian Gothic Revival architecture. The style was powerful, imaginative, consequential—everything Rochdale was not but wished to be, now that she had come into a little money.

In the summer of 1847, Rochdale had an aggressive antipauper policy. Every Irish pauper deported brought the local poor rate down, and every ailing pauper deported reduced municipal medical costs and the risk of epidemic fever. It was for this reason that the coach of Mr. Edward Lord was parked in front of the Rochdale fever hospital on the morning of September 1. Mr. Lord had been instructed to transport a recently recovered fever patient, twelve-year-old Michael Duignan, to the train station. From Rochdale, Michael would be transported to Manchester, thence to Liverpool, and finally back to Dublin.

When Mr. Lord arrived, Michael was standing in the hospital portico leaning on a stick. Until he began descending the stairs, Lord did not realize the boy was lame. It was an odd sort of walk Michael had, the coachman recalled at the inquest into Michael's death. "He would put the stick in front of him . . . then slur his feet [forward], as if he had not the power to lift them up." The other thing Mr. Lord remembered about that September morning was the heavy rain. By the time Michael reached the coach, his new linen shirt and black coat—gifts from the hospital staff— were dripping wet. Lord lifted Michael into the coach, put his walking stick on the seat beside him, and closed the door.

Michael was not the first member of his family to be treated at the fever hospital. Since the Duignans' arrival in Rochdale in March, Michael's older brother, Patrick; his baby sister; his mother; and his father had been hospitalized for fever. All but his brother were dead now.

In April, Michael's mother, father, and sister were buried in pauper graves near the textile mills. Pluck, bravery, and his older brother had kept Michael alive. James Redfern, a Rochdale butcher who testified at the inquest, said that he often saw Michael outside his shop, begging. The boy's lameness made him easy to recognize, Redfern recalled, although one could never be sure whether he was completely lame. Redfern was certain of one thing, though; lameness ran in the Duignan family. Patrick, the older brother, had difficulty walking as well.

Thomas Collingwood, the attending physician at the Rochdale fever hospital, also testified at the inquest. He said that on the morning of the deportation, Michael had been free of fever for five days. "I saw him twice every day, . . . [and] he was in a fit state . . . to be discharged with perfect safety." Mr. Lord corroborated this. During the journey to the railway station, the coachman said, Michael "laughed and played . . . and seemed overjoyed with riding." Thirteen-year-old Patrick Duignan, who met Michael at the station, had a different memory of his brother. He thought Michael looked unwell, very thin and pale. Despite his own lameness, Patrick lifted Michael from the coach and carried him into the station. It was still raining when the train left Rochdale, but near Manchester the clouds broke and a bright Midlands sun appeared. Patrick looked over at Michael; he was swaying back and forth in the seat like a pendulum. Patrick reached over and put his arms around Michael to prevent him from falling into the aisle. One of the officers accompanying the deportees walked over to Patrick and whispered in his ear, "Your brother will not live very long."

At Manchester, Patrick put Michael on his back again and carried him across the crowded station to the Liverpool train. The rest of the day was a series of fits and starts. There was a half-hour layover in Preston and another long delay in front of the City of Dublin Steam Packet Company offices in Liverpool. Normally, the purchase of packet tickets took only a few minutes, but the City of Dublin clerk and the officer accompanying the Rochdale deportees got into an argument. There were eleven deportees in the Rochdale party. The officer wanted a bulk discount rate; the City of Dublin clerk demanded full fare for each deportee. It was almost two P.M. by the time the officer returned to the cart; Michael had been sitting in the open under a bright late summer sun for over half an hour. At Clarence Dock, the cart stopped in front of the *Duchess of Kent*, the ship that had brought Daniel O'Connell home.

Robert English, a *Duchess* passenger, was standing on deck when the Rochdale deportees arrived. At the inquest, English said that even in a party of "very bad, weakly and exhausted" men, Michael had stood out. The "boy . . . looked especially stricken: lame, much emaciated and sickly." In September, a 5-shilling packet ticket still bought what it had bought in April—open deck passage across a nighttime Irish Sea. To protect Michael, two Poor Law officials put him between the paddle box and the engine. This was the warmest area of the deck, and under other circumstances the warmth of the engine might have kept him alive until the *Duchess* reached Ireland, but O'Connell had been a trophy assignment for the *Duchess*. In real life, she was a grimy little workhorse of a packet. On this trip out, she was carrying more than five hundred deck passengers, most of them Irish deportees; after months of sleeping in English doorways, they did not have much humanity left in them. When a night wind rose off the sea, and the contest for warm space began, Michael was pushed out onto the main deck, where he was exposed to sea, wind, and cold. Around eight P.M., Mr. English was in his cabin, reading, when someone shouted, "Doctor! Doctor!" A few minutes later, English heard the shuffle of feet. He rose and walked over to the door; two crew members were carrying Michael down from the deck. The *Duchess*'s physician was summoned. He bent over Michael and immediately announced, "All is over with him."

Britons could still be moved by individual stories of Irish suffering like Michael's; in late September, *The Manchester Guardian* devoted an entire page to his inquest. Nonetheless, after months of rising poor rates, crime rates, and fever rates, the housewife in Kensington and the railway worker in Birmingham had learned to separate their feelings about individual cases of suffering from their feelings about Ireland in general and what needed to be done to cure the "*Irish ulcer.*" People read in *The Times*— "there is a nation to be remade, a race to [be] changed"—reminded themselves of that ancient human consolation—"at the dark core of human suffering [lay] the will of God...unfailingly transforming evil into good"—and then looked across the Irish Sea and imagined that they saw good arising from the evil of famine, pestilence, and mass death. The potato culture, the principal source of Irish economic and moral backwardness, was in collapse, and starvation, disease, and emigration were rapidly lowering the Irish population to a size that British political economists believed commensurate with the country's resources.

In the autumn of 1847, many Britons also overcame their personal scruples and learned to come to terms with mass evictions. Of course, turning whole townlands onto the roads was a savage, uncivilized practice. Still, the land had to be cleared, and the new Poor Law, which had inspired the wave of mass evictions, was destroying the small-farmer class. Mr. Trevelyan also saw another "bright light shining" over Ireland. "Dependence on government" was disappearing. "Reason is now able to make herself heard.... Many a warning and encouraging voice [can be] heard from Ireland herself declaring.... We are able to help ourselves, we will no longer be dependent on the precarious assistance received from other lands."

Meanwhile, in the Ireland inhabited by the Irish, mass starvation was reappearing.

⁘

In northwest Mayo, resurgent hunger drove hundreds of climbers onto the ancient cliff faces in search of seagull eggs. Cliff foraging was a dangerous business. The Mayo cliffs were high, jagged, and slippery; the gulls, fiercely protective of their eggs; the sea wind, fierce; and if a man fell, there was nothing between him and the sea but two or three hundred feet of air and a few sharp rocks that would either break his back or impale him. Inland, the resurgent hunger drove flocks of half-naked families into the October fields in search of harvest gleanings. "Like cattle, these poor creatures seem . . . driven from one herb and root to another, using nettles, turnip tops [and] chickenweed, in their turn," wrote a Dublin visitor. In the Mayo market town of Belmullet, the authorities had to station a troop of 151 soldiers to protect the local food depot. From morning to night, the soldiers marched around the depot, singing "Rory O'Grady" and "The Girl I Left Behind Me." Visitors to Belmullet were struck by the contrast between the singers—sturdy, "warlike" men—and "the haggard, meager, squalid" crowds who daily gathered around the depot.

Even a few of the Anglo-Irish gentry were starving now. This had seemed improbable to Mrs. Nicholson, the Yankee Quaker lady, until she was invited to tea by a young Anglo-Irish woman during a visit to Mayo. The young woman, who had lost as many relations to the pestilence as Michael Duignan, lived in a former tenant's cabin with a chair, a bed, and a few tokens from her former life. When Mrs. Nicholson arrived, the table was decorated "with the fashionable ornaments which adorn the drawing rooms of the rich." Hanging carelessly around the hostess's shoulders was another "ornament" of her former life, "a light scarf." "Genteel and pretty of feature," Mrs. Nicholson thought, until she looked into the young woman's eyes. The other guest, a local gentleman named Mr. Bourne, also noticed that their young hostess had "the famine stare."

On the coach ride back to Belmullet, Mr. Bourne became quite agitated. "What can be done with that helpless, proud, interesting girl?" he cried. "She must die in all her pride if some relief is not speedily found. She cannot work, she would not go to the workhouse, and there upon that desolate mountain, she will probably pine away."

As autumn deepened and the dead reclaimed the roads and fields, people began to feel that the famine would never end; life would always be like this. There would always be women begging with dead children; there would always be coffin shortages, pestilence, overcrowded workhouses, and unbounded want. The Reverend Alexander Hoops, a Tipperary vicar, could bear it no longer; he put a bullet through his head. In late September, the Reverend E. L. Moore, a Mayo vicar, published a desperate appeal to the English people in *The Manchester Guardian*. "With all our exertions, deaths are increasing ten fold. . . . [F]ever in all its forms is surrounding us, our wretched funds are expended. . . . I entreat, I implore in the name of Him. . . . Be merciful."

Moore's letter appeared just as the economic crisis was coming to a head. As industrial activity slowed, credit became even tighter and railway share holders even more inconsolable. As the British banking system shook and shivered and the revenues of Her Majesty's government dropped by £1 million in two brief months, Mr. Wood decided that "this must be the end of it." He told the new Irish viceroy, Lord Clarendon: "In the present state of the money market, and depression in all our manufacturing towns," further assistance to Ireland was "out of the question. . . . [She] must keep herself somehow or other. . . . Where the people refuse to work or sow, they must starve."

✂

"Les beaux jours sont passés," Clarendon sighed. We now have "repudiating rate payers . . . landlords and farmers declare they can't employ laborers, doctors promise pestilence again . . . not one fourth of the usual amount [of potatoes] were planted . . . I look forward to a troublous winter, the difficulties of which will not be smoothed by England." The most "troublous" item on the viceroy's list would prove to be the "repudiating rate payers." The architects of the new Poor Law had been half right. Proprietors and large farmers were indeed displaying great eagerness to avoid the rates, but they were resorting to every stratagem, except creating employment, to do so. During the autumn, the Gregory Clause, born on a March evening to end the deadlock over the new Poor Law bill, was reborn as a way for a proprietor to lower his poor rate, though it was not a foolproof way. In a country where the land meant everything, to make relief contingent on its surrender was tantamount to asking a man to slay his firstborn for a meal. Thousands of small farmers like Michael Bradley, of Mayo, refused. A few weeks later, Bradley died a pauper's death on a road outside Westport. According to a relief official in Mayo, hundreds of Bradley's neighbors were "now actually starving but . . . unwilling to abandon their little farms."

An 1843 law that made the landlord financially liable for the poor rate of every tenant who held land valued at £4 or less also made mass eviction a popular rate-containment strategy. Around the time of Michael Bradley's death, Mr. Tuke, the Quaker banker, witnessed a second eviction in Mayo, this one in the town of Mullaroghe, which until two weeks earlier had been home to a substantial community of small farmers. The morning Mr. Tuke arrived, nothing remained of Mullagrobe except "a heap of ruins." "I tried to count the roofless houses and after proceeding as far as seventy, I gave up in despair." An old woman told Tuke that ten days earlier the son of the proprietor, a Mr. Walshe, had arrived in Mullagrobe with two drivers and evicted the residents. "That night [the evicted] made a bit of . . . shelter of wood and straw [but] the drivers threw it down" and drove the people from Mullagrobe like cattle. "It would have pitied the sun to look upon them," the old woman said. "It was a night of high wind and storm and their wailing chordee could be heard a great distance."

Many "repudiating rate payers" resorted to the simplest form of tax evasion: they just stopped paying. By October 31, the uncollected poor rate stood at £854,049, and in many districts the ratepayers were waging war on rate collectors. During one collection attempt, Patrick Martin, a Galway collector, was attacked "by a large number of persons . . . [carrying] sticks and stones." During a visit to another disgruntled ratepayer, Martin was hit over the head with a large rock. Shaken and nursing a head wound, he told his superiors that it was his "firm conviction and belief that no person can, with safety to his life, even attempt the collection of said rates, much less collect [them], unless [he has] the protection of a sufficient military or police force." A few weeks later, an Ulster magistrate named Johnston was shot while riding home. The shooting caused puzzlement, until it was recalled that in a recent dispute between a local rate collector and a party of aggrieved ratepayers, Mr. Johnston had found for the rate collector. In Carrick-on-Suir, the "troublous" Captain Edmond Wynne, recently transferred from West Clare, told his anxious rate collectors that it was their duty to collect the rates "at any risk."

Ultimate responsibility for rate collection rested with Edward Twisleton, who had recently been promoted from resident Poor Law commissioner, answerable to Whitehall, to director of an independent Irish Poor Law Commission. Mr. Twisleton had spent the winter of 1845–1846 fending off attempts by Mr. Trevelyan—and his stalking horse, Routh—to co-opt Poor Law workhouses into the Peel relief program. As chairman of the new commission, Mr. Twisleton now faced an even more daunting task: collect enough taxes from Irish property to feed Irish poverty.

Shortly after taking command of the commission, Mr. Twisleton took a bold step: to end collusion between the workhouse guardians, who set the local rates, and the gentry, who paid them, he shut down several workhouses and replaced the guardians with professional government administrators. In theory, the change should improve rate collection because the appointed administrators were answerable only to the government, whereas workhouse guardians, who were popularly elected, were answerable to local ratepayers. In practice, however, the change had little effect. As autumn progressed, and the weight of want grew, even the Gregory clause and the mass evictions proved unable to keep rates down. In parts of Clare and Mayo, the poor rate rose to 10 shillings in a 20-shilling pound and, in one Clare district, to 12 shillings, 6 pence—a rise of over 50 percent. After two years of scarcity, famine, and falling rents, the Irish landed classes had, in most cases, simply become too poor to pay such rates. In Ballinrobe, Mayo, the government administrators managing the local workhouse told their collectors that £14,126 was urgently needed to keep the workhouse open. Four weeks later, not a single shilling had been collected. By October, a number of high-ranking British officials in Ireland had concluded that Irish property could not pay for Irish poverty—not unaided. *"Ireland cannot be left to her own resources,"* Viceroy Clarendon warned Downing Street. General Burgoyne also lobbied for more British assistance. "We must in common charity afford [Ireland] considerable charity."

London hesitated. Resumption of direct aid would undermine the government's effort to eradicate "dependency on government" in Ireland, and be deeply unpopular in Britain, where anti-Irish feeling was running high again. When London announced plans to issue a second Queen's Letter on Ireland, *The Times* received sixty-two letters of protest from English clergymen in a single delivery. When the letter was issued in October, only £20,000 was raised—less than a fifth of the £116,000 raised by the January letter.

⋙⋘

One morning in between the Twisleton appointment and the second Queen's Letter, a handsome young Englishman strode through the lobby of the Salt Hill Hotel outside Dublin, exciting the interest of the ancient colonels sipping the first whiskey of the day. Mr. Trevelyan was in Ireland to determine what could be done to retrieve the situation, short of committing Britain to another season of direct aid. During the visit—his first visit to Ireland since the famine began—Mr. Trevelyan interviewed, inspected, pondered, and cogitated—then made two changes. Twenty-two Poor Law unions (a union was the geographic area served by a given workhouse) in the west and south, the most impoverished regions of the country, would be designated "distressed" and made eligible for government assistance. However, to receive aid, a union would first have to make a good-faith effort to collect the poor rate. In addition, Mr. Trevelyan ordered the workhouses cleared of the very old, the very young, the infirm, and the widowed, who were put on outdoor relief. The order was aimed at the able-bodied destitute, who became eligible for outdoor relief only when the local workhouse was full. If the price of public assistance was entering a workhouse, Mr. Trevelyan believed healthy young men and women would think twice before throwing themselves on local ratepayers. He also ordered the Commissariat back to Ireland to organize the food supply, and invited the Quakers and the British Association—both groups had won high praise for their work in Ireland—to participate in the new relief program. The Quakers, who disliked the new Poor Law, refused; the British Association, which still had nearly £200,000, accepted.

The letter Trevelyan wrote to *The Times* upon his return to England contained none of the "salutary" changes he had heralded earlier in the autumn. "The unhappy people in the western districts of Ireland," he wrote "will again perish by the thousands this year if they are not relieved." This was incomplete. Tens of thousands of peasants in the other regions of the country were also at risk. Still, unlike Trevelyan's other statements on Ireland, this one at least had the virtue of being something like the truth.

❧

According to Samuel Lewis's 1837 *Topographical Dictionary of Ireland*, the Roscommon market town of Elphin is best approached from the south, whence the traveler would encounter a particularly agreeable view of the rise the town sits upon. The 1837 edition of the *Dictionary* also contained several other interesting facts about Elphin. The town had 260 homes, a wide main street, a public fountain, and a large Constabulary barracks. For a little town, Elphin had a big imagination. It claimed Oliver Goldsmith, the novelist, playwright, and poet (*The Vicar of Wakefield*; *She Stoops to Conquer*), as a native son, and St. Patrick as a visitor. In the flatlands below Elphin, neither claim was widely accepted.

The *Dictionary* also included the names of the local clerics, circa 1837. One was the Reverend John Lloyd, who was both the vicar at Kilmore church and a local landowner. Had Mr. Lewis visited Elphin in 1847, he would have had an exciting story to tell about the vicar. One afternoon toward November, Lloyd was traveling home with his son Percy when two gunmen emerged onto the road from a nearby field. One of the men grabbed the reins of Lloyd's carriage; the other removed a pistol from his pocket, walked over to the carriage, shot Lloyd, reloaded the pistol, and shot him a second time. Percy Lloyd began to cry. The assassin removed the boy from the seat, climbed up into the carriage, reloaded, and shot Lloyd a third time. Then he lifted Percy back into the carriage, handed him the reins, and told him to drive home.

Lord John Russell had been right to fear class warfare. The mass evictions of the autumn brought out the gunmen. In October, Lloyd and Mr. Roe, a prominent Tipperary landlord, were assassinated; in November, Richard Baley, another Tipperary proprietor, and Major Mahon of Roscommon; in December, Mr. Hill, a Limerick landlord, and Mr. Peter Nash, a landlord's bailiff. "The vast and increasing bodies of armed men who nocturnally prowl about the country . . . are frightful to behold," declared a provincial paper.

The mass evictions also produced a new tenants' rights movement. In October, James McKnight, a Protestant and Ulsterman and editor of the *Londonderry Standard*, urged that the "Ulster right,"* which protected tenant farmers in the north against peremptory eviction and exploitation, be extended to Catholic regions of the country. The tenants' rights movement also had the support of Jonathan Pim, the codirector

---

*Under the "Ulster right" a tenant also received compensation for any improvements he made to his plot.

of the Quaker Central Relief Committee; William Hancock, a professor of economics at Trinity College; and, most centrally, the Catholic bishops of the country, who incorporated a version of McKnight's proposal into a memorial on tenants' rights that the hierarchy presented to Viceroy Clarendon. Control of the land—the principal source of Anglo-Irish power since the plantation period—was now coming under serious challenge. In a letter to *The Times*, one weary Irish proprietor wrote, "I am denounced by [the] parish priest . . . as an exterminator and held up in the county paper as an advocate of the clearance [eviction] system. . . . I am in the constant receipt of letters commencing with rude sketches of coffins and informing me that 'my grave has been dug.' . . . I never stir without being armed to the teeth and carefully avoid all banks and patches of wood which may secrete an assassin."

On November 10, a worried Clarendon told Downing Street that if "the present anarchical tendencies increase," extraordinary police powers would be needed to "maintain order in Ireland." A week later, in a second warning, Clarendon declared that no British government could leave "300,000 arms in the possession of some of the most ferocious people on earth, at the commencement of a winter when there will be great poverty and little employment." The prime minister was wearing his "great and glorious cause of Ireland" hat the day Clarendon's letter arrived. He refused the viceroy's second request for expanded police powers and told Clarendon that there was nothing "anarchical" or arbitrary about the current wave of violence. The gunmen were out because the landlords were evicting tenants wholesale to avoid the poor rate. "The landlords in England would not like to be shot like hares and partridges," Russell declared, but "neither does any landlord in England turn out 50 people at once and burn their houses over their heads."

Russell's conviction that the gentry must take responsibility for the peasantry had produced one very ill-conceived piece of legislation, the Poor Law Extension Act. Now it produced a good piece of proposed legislation, the Landlord-Tenant Bill. If enacted, the measure would extend to even the smallest tenant the right to fixity of tenure—a protection against peremptory eviction—and provide compensation for any improvements the tenant made to his holding. As the historian Peter Grey has noted, Russell's Landlord-Tenant Bill amounted to "a conceptual

leap for a British minister." Never before had a member of the British political elite acknowledged the "principle of dual ownership in the soil and
the limitation of private property."

The appalled Russell cabinet was also quick to recognize the bill's
revolutionary character. At the very least, the measure could impede the
modernization of Irish agriculture by making it more difficult to evict
small farmers; at worst, the bill could lead to "a war against property."
The legislation never even reached Parliament.

Clarendon did get his new crime bill, though. The act, which mandated communities to bear the cost of any extra policing they required,
severely limited the right to own firearms and made the failure to assist
in a murder investigation a crime, passed both houses of Parliament with
large majorities.

✠

Late in the afternoon of December 31, 1847, John Costello stood in the
rain, watching a wrecking crew demolish his home. Costello knew most
of the men in the crew. Arthur Blake, the crew leader, was the son of
James Blake, the agent for Costello's landlord; Patrick McNulty was Blake's
lieutenant; and the other two men, Edmund Walsh and Fogerty, were
drivers.

Inverin, the spur of Galway coast where Costello lived, had been described as good "for nothing but a sheep walk" but Costello liked the
wildness of the place: a big ocean sky overhead, Galway Bay to the south,
Inishmore to the west, and under his feet the fine stones he had used to
build the house presently disappearing under the hammer blows of Blake
and McNulty. The eviction had come as a surprise to Costello. He had
not spoken to his landlord in nine or nine and a half years—so long ago,
he could not even remember the date, though he did remember what the
landlord had said to him that last time: "I would rather feed goats than ye."

Then out of the blue, this morning, the driver Walsh had appeared at
Costello's door and told him to pack up his wife and children and get
out. A few minutes later, Blake and McNulty arrived; they must have
stopped on the road. Both men had the smell of drink on them. "For God's
sake, leave the house [standing] until morning," Costello begged. Blake
ignored the plea and ordered McNulty to get the three Costello children

out of the house. They were standing beside their mother now. Two of them—Ann, four, and Coleman, ten—would be dead in two weeks, but Costello had no way of knowing that as he watched the wrecking crew pack up. Blake had timed the visit well. A winter night was gathering out on Galway Bay. After the crew left, the family took shelter in a hollow near an abandoned potato field. Just as the children fell asleep, Costello felt something wet on his face. He looked up. It was snowing again.

In London, the holiday weather was better. Under partly cloudy skies, New Year's Eve revelers drank, kissed, sang, and wished each other a happy 1848. Few gave much thought to Ireland. In the public mind, the healthy 1847 potato crop had become an unofficial demarcation point. The famine was over and it had had an expectedly happy ending: the Irish people were learning how to help themselves.

Afterword

I n *The Last Conquest of Ireland*, John Mitchel accused Mr. Trevelyan of creating a special "typhus poison." Mitchel should have confined himself to the truth. It was incriminating enough.

Mass eviction; widespread unemployment; the reappearance of pervasive hunger, disease, and death—the trends that plunged Ireland back into chaos in the autumn of 1847 persisted into the early 1850s, and, just as in 1847, in 1848, 1849, and 1850, the principal engines of Irish misery were the Extended Poor Law of 1847, which made eviction an efficient way for a landowner to lower his poor rate, and the Gregory clause, which so facilitated the eviction process that one contemporary, Canon John O'Rourke, called it the "perfect engine for the slaughter and expatriation of [the] people." Unlike Mitchel, O'Rourke was not exaggerating. Between 1847 and 1851, the eviction rate rose by nearly 1,000 percent, overwhelming the Irish Poor Law system.

During the early months of 1848, the workhouse population, which had stood at 75,000 during the soup kitchen summer of 1847, rose to 120,000, then to 150,000. By June, a million people were being relieved, 850,000 outdoors and the remainder in the workhouse; and that figure did not include the destitute men and women who had contrived to get themselves arrested because Irish jails served a better class of food than

Irish workhouses. By early summer 1847, a penal system built to house five thousand had an inmate population of thirteen thousand. During the spring, the ever growing demand for relief also produced historic increases in the poor rate. In June, it was 76.5 percent above the comparable figure for June 1847. In some districts, taxes were claiming half of every pound, and many ratepayers feared that if things went on like this much longer, they would join their tenants in the workhouse.

In July, lamentations about the Poor Law and the Gregory clause were briefly interrupted by the specter of rebellion. During the spring and early summer of 1848, a wave of democratic revolutions swept across western Europe. Popular uprisings erupted in the Italian and German states, in Austria, in France, and finally, on July 30, in the Widow Mc-Cormack's cabbage garden in Ballingarry, Tipperary. Inspired by events on the continent, and believing the agrarian crisis had put the peasantry in a revolutionary mood, William Smith O'Brien and Thomas Meagher spent most of June and July in the Irish countryside, trying to raise an army; but three years of famine had taken the fight out of the people. Smith O'Brien fought the battle of Mrs. McCormack's cabbage garden with 118 men—thirty-eight armed with rifles and pikes, the rest with stones. His army was quickly overwhelmed by a contingent of police.

In August 1848, the blight reappeared in parts of Ulster and in the west of Ireland, igniting a new wave of evictions. Lord Lucan, who had already evicted 246 men, women, and children from his Mayo holdings, now evicted another 913. A *Castlebar Telegraph* reporter who witnessed the ejectments wrote: "We, afterwards, at the dead hour of the night, saw hundreds of those victims of landlordism and Gregoryism, sinking on our flagways . . . emitting green froth from their mouths as if masticating soft grass." In the Clare district of Kilrush, mass evictions helped reduce the population from 82,000 to 60,000. Even "the good landlords are going to bad and the bad are going to the worst extremities of cruelty, and tyranny," declared the *Limerick and Clare Examiner*.

The new wave of evictions further strained the relief system and italicized the fundamental flaw in the 1847 Poor Law. Except for a few relatively prosperous regions in Ulster and around Dublin, Irish property was too impoverished to bear the burden of Irish poverty. In parts of the west, the underfunded Poor Law system broke down after the 1848 crop failure, and evicted peasants died for want of assistance. By early 1849, every shade of Irish opinion had turned against the 1847 Poor Law. The *Northern Whig* was vehement, denouncing it as "a cruel and useless experiment"; the *Dublin Evening Mail* called for its abolition. Even Mr. Twisleton had lost faith in the Poor Law system. "The extent of the distress . . . does not seem to be understood in England," he told Home Secretary Grey. In 1849, when Queen Victoria visited Ireland, a group of Limerick priests presented her with a memorial highlighting a chief evil of the Poor Law system—its propensity to encourage mass evictions:

> Madam, in no other region of the habitable Globe would it
> be admitted to two or three satraps [meaning the landlords'
> crowbar brigade] . . . to unroof and demolish at their plea-
> sure, the homes of fifteen thousand human beings, and to
> turn out that multitude . . . to die by the slow wasting of
> famine and disease.

The British government, which officially terminated its relief operations in the late summer of 1847, did provide Ireland with £156,000 in emergency aid in 1848 and a further £114,000 in 1849, but the sums were a pittance compared to the need. Had he been able, Lord John probably would have provided more assistance, but the Irish landlords in his cabinet—Lords Palmerston, Clanricarde, and Lansdowne—and the members of the Moralist bloc—Mr. Wood, Sir George Grey, and his cousin, the colonial secretary, Earl Grey—were now of one mind. Regrettable as the continued suffering in Ireland was, small farmers were disappearing at a remarkable rate, while the high poor rates, and a new Encumbered Estates Act, which eased restrictions on the sale of Irish property, were hastening the removal of improvident, incompetent proprietors. By 1849, members of both blocs could see Mr. Trevelyan's "bright light shining in the distance." The era of large-scale commercial farming was about to commence. To members of the Moralist bloc, its arrival was proof that the blight had, indeed, been a Visitation of Providence; to members of the landlord bloc, its arrival was a welcome opportunity to dispense with all "deadweight" tenants and to transform their Irish properties into lucrative commercial enterprises.

In the immediate postfamine years, the hopes of both groups were sustained.

During the 1850s, Irish farms grew steadily larger and Irish agricultural profits steadily bigger. In 1861, *The Times* hailed the country's remarkably quick recovery from the famine: "Compared with a few years back, the agriculture of Ireland is greatly advanced." Once again, *The Times* had gotten it exactly wrong. In the mid-1860s, peasant agitation for land reform revived. The agitation led to the Land War in the 1870s and 1880s, and the Land War produced a series of reforms that reversed the land seizures of the plantation era. On the eve of World War I, 11.1 million of Ireland's 20 million acres were again owned by Irish proprietors, and, as before the famine, many of the proprietors were small farmers.

A million people dead and over two million fled abroad. Ireland's population reduced by a third or more—it was a high price to pay for a "salutary" revolution that lasted barely a decade.

England, the vital heart of Britain, has a proud and glorious history. In the nineteenth century, she led the world into the modern era. In the twentieth century, at one of the darkest moments in human history, the summer of 1940, she stood up to evil when other nations shrank from the challenge. But the relief policies that England employed during the famine—parsimonious, short-sighted, grotesquely twisted by religion and ideology—produced tens of thousands, perhaps hundreds of thousands, of needless deaths. The intent of those policies may not have been genocidal, but the effects were.

No wonder, in the decades after the famine, so many Irish immigrants were incapable of saying "England" without adding "Goddamn her."

Notes

꩜

Introduction

1   **incident outside Skibbereen:** Lord Dufferin and Hon. G. G. Boyle, *Narrative of a Journey from Oxford to Skibbereen During the Year of the Irish Famine,* Mar. 1, 1847, p. 1.

1   **"sights that . . . poison life til life is done":** Lord Dufferin, "Black Death in Bergen," *Letters from High Latitudes* (1910), p. 38.

1   **mothers begging:** on May 7, 1847, *The Freeman's Journal* reported that the Dublin police arrested a Miss Eliza Holmes, a pauper mother, for begging with a dead infant in her arms on Sackville Street (present-day O'Connell Street), the principal high street of the Irish capital; people scaling cliffs for seagull eggs: Asenath Nicholson, *Annals of the Famine in Ireland* (1851), p. 97; breakdown in family ties: *Cork Southern Reporter,* Jan. 5, 1847, *Cork Examiner,* Jan. 6. 1847, *Nation,* June 13, 1847; P. de Strzelecki in *Report of the British Association for the Relief of Extreme Distress in Ireland and Scotland* (1849), p. 93. Emigrant flight: Kerby Miller, *Emigrants and Exiles: Ireland and the Irish Exodus to North America* (1988), p. 292.

2   **Terry Eagleton's assessment of the famine:** quoted in *Mapping the Great Irish Famine,* Liam Kennedy, Paul S. Ell, E. M. Crawford, and L. A. Clarkson, eds. (1999), p. 15.

2   **famine death and emigration figures:** James S. Donnelly, "Excess Mortality and Emigration," in *New History of Ireland, 1801–1870,* vol. 5 (1989), pp. 350–56; death tolls in Chinese and Soviet famines, Amartya Sen, "The Economics of Life and Death," *Scientific American,* May 1993, p. 44.

2   **Petrarch quote:** *The Black Death,* Rosemary Horrox, ed. (1994), pp. 248–49.

2   **role of bad luck in famine:** Christine Kinealy, *This Great Calamity: The Irish Famine 1845–52* (1994), p. 345; Cormac O'Grada, *This Great Irish Famine* (1989), p. 76.

3   **death toll in Haiti:** The Haitian government claims that 316,000 died in the 2010 earthquake, but the findings of an unpublished U.S. government study suggest the

upward limit on the mortality may have been 85,000. The study was reported on by the BBC on May 31, 2011. Japanese death toll: the website Earthquake Report, earthquake-report.com, noted that as of August 15, 2011, the Japanese death rate was a little over 21,000.

3   **Flow of exports and imports during the famine:** Austin Bourke, "The Irish Grain Trade 1839–1848," *Irish Historical Studies,* Sept. 1976, pp. 160–65.

3   **British use relief policy as an instrument of nation building:** Peter Gray, *Famine, Land and Politics,* British Government and Irish Society 1843–50 (1999), pp. 331–32; Kinealy, *This Great Calamity,* pp. 343–47, 353–54.

4   **genocidal intent of British:** John Mitchel, *The Last Conquest of Ireland (Perhaps)* (1876), pp. 102, 112, 120.

One: The Savage Shore: Three Englishmen in Ireland

5   *Times* **commissioner's route:** Thomas Campbell Foster, *Letters on the Condition of the People of Ireland* (1846), pp. 81–84.

5   **"Monday last":** *Dublin Evening Post,* Aug. 23, 1845.

7   **"fields heavy with potatoes":** T. C. Foster, *Condition of Ireland,* p. 107.

8   **"Well, pardon my ignorance":** J. G. Kohl, *Ireland* (1843), p. 47.

8   **"The earth disowns it":** Thomas Carlyle, *Chartism* (1858), p. 26.

8   **population:** Report of Census Commissioners, Ireland (1841), p. viii; Cormac O'Grada, *Ireland: A New Economic History, 1790–1939* (1994), p. 6; L. M. Cullen, *Economic History of Ireland Since 1600* (1987), pp. 95, 118.

8   **economic growth and the French Wars:** Cullen, *Economic History,* pp. 97, 100, 101; "English visitors surprised": Miller, *Emigrants and Exiles,* p. 31.

9   **post-Waterloo economic decline:** Cullen, *Economic History,* pp. 103–10; Joel Mokyr, *Why Ireland Starved* (1983), p. 12.

9   **fall in Drogheda weavers' pay:** Third Report of Her Majesty's Commission for inquiring into the condition of the poorer classes (henceforth referred to as Report of Poor Law Commissioners) (1836) [43], Appendix C, p. 4; "I begged him," ibid., Appendix C, p. 89.

9   **destruction of textile, shipbuilding, and glass-making industries:** Cullen, *Economic History,* p. 105; Mokyr, *Why Ireland Starved,* p. 14.

9   **decline in Irish manufacturing:** Report of the Commissioners Appointed to take the Census of Ireland for the year 1841 (henceforth referred to as Report of Census Commissioners) (1843) [504], p. 440.

9   **postwar rise in rents, prefamine stabilization in rents:** Cullen, *Economic History,* pp. 112–13.

9   **"People are forced from want":** Report of Poor Law Commissioners, Ireland (1836), [43], Appendix D, p. 75, Appendix F, p. 43.

10   **45 percent of farms were under five acres:** Report of Census Commissioners (1841), [504], pp. 454–55.

10   **"broken down dancing masters":** J. Kohl, *Ireland,* pp. 47–49.

10   **potato dependency:** Austin Bourke, "The Potato Crop in Ireland at the Time of the Famine," *Journal of the Statistical and Social Enquiry Society of Ireland,* vol. 20, (1959–60), pp. 10–12; nutritional content of potato; Mokyr: *Why Ireland Starved,* p. 8; data on Irish physicality, including height and strength, ibid., p. 9.

11   **growing frequency of crop failures:** Report of Census Commissioner, Ireland (1851), part 5, pp. 383–42.

11   **M'Kye memorial:** *Facts from Gweedore* (1854), p. 6.

12   **64 percent of farms in Donegal, Mayo, Kerry under five acres:** Larry Zucker-man, *The Potato* (1998), p. 137.

12   **Dublin cattle show:** Henry Inglis, *A Journey Throughout Ireland During the Spring, Summer, and Autumn of 1834* (1836), p. 4.

12   **Londonderry pawning:** Report of Poor Law Commissioners (1836) [43], Appendix C, p. 79.

12   **murder of Mr. Bell-Booth:** T. C. Foster, *Condition of Ireland*, pp. 5–8.

13   **landlord, gallows:** Report of Poor Law Commissioners (1836) [43], Appendix D, p. 75.

13   **80 percent Catholic population:** Miller, *Emigrants and Exiles*, p. 41; Helen Litton, *The Irish Famine* (1994), p. 10.

13   **Mr. Bell-Booth's sister-in-law:** T. C. Foster, *Condition of Ireland*, p. 8.

13   **reluctance to cooperate with judicial system:** Alexis de Tocqueville, *Journey in Ireland*, Emmet Larkin, ed. (1990), pp. 101–3; see also pp. 43, 21–22.

13   **Devon Commission testimony:** Digest of Evidence taken before H. M. Commis-sioners of Inquiry into the State of Law and Practice in Respect of the Occupation of the Land in Ireland (1845) (hereafter, Devon Commission), Part 2, p. 270.

14   **"unequivocal symptoms of improvement":** Devon Commission, introduction, p. 12; interference with legislature, p. 15; support of Irish landlord, p. 20.

14   **"a uniformly 'unreadable'":** *Times* editorial, quoted in T. C. Foster, *Condition of Ireland*, p. 8; "Whatever the success of present inquiry": T. C. Foster, *Condition of Ireland*, p. 9.

14–15 **Mr. T. C. Foster's biography:** *Oxford Dictionary of National Biography*, oxforddnb.com.

15   **meeting at Bryskett's home:** Nicholas Canny, *Making Ireland British* (2003), pp. 2–3.

15   **Spenser biography:** *Oxford Dictionary of National Biography*, oxforddnb.com.

15–16 **state of savage primitiveness:** Canny, *Making Ireland British*, p. 28.

16   **description of early modern Ireland:** R. F. Foster, *Modern Ireland 1600–1972* (1987), pp. 8–16.

16   **"Old English":** Andrew Hadfield, *Edmund Spenser's Irish Experience* (1997), pp. 29, 64, 199.

17   **Cromwell's Irish campaign:** "The Cromwellian Conquests," Andrew Corish, *New History of Ireland*, vol. 3 (1976).

17   **growth of British population in Ireland, 1600–1750:** R. F. Foster, *Modern Ire-land*, pp. 155–59. Penal Laws, p. 154; "Here I sit in Holyhead": p. 175.

18   **Arthur Young's Arrival in Ireland and description of Dublin:** A. Young, *A Tour in Ireland* (1780), pp. 1–6; Irish per capita income doubles: L. M. Cullen, in *New History of Ireland*, vol. 4 (1983), p. 186.

18   **Anglo-Irish state:** R. F. Foster, *Modern Ireland*, pp. 173–74, 178–79.

19   **eight thousand to ten thousand landowning families:** Miller, *Emigrants and Exiles*, p. 42.

19   **landholding structure:** R. D. C. Black, *Economic Thought and the Irish Question* (1960), pp. 7, 8; Young, *A Tour in Ireland*, pp. 30–32, 35–36, 40–60.

19   **rate of absenteeism:** O'Grada, *New Economic History*, p. 124.

19   **Lord Baltimore's entourage:** Michael McConville, *From Ascendancy to Oblivion* (1986), p. 162.

19   **"Our great farming Landlords":** John Pitt Kennedy, *Employ, Instruct, Don't Hang Them* (1835), p. 81.

20 **"you would hang all the landlords":** Young, *A Tour in Ireland*, p. 62; sexual slavery, ibid., pp. 40–41; characteristics of middlemen, ibid., pp. 17–19.

21 **"Oh Sir," confiscated Irish estates:** Kevin Whelan, "An Underground Gentry," in *18th Century Ireland*, vol. 10 (1995), p. 151.

21 **physical condition of peasantry:** Young, *A Tour in Ireland*, pp. 32–33.

22 **French Revolution's effect on Ireland:** Paul Bew, *Ireland: The Politics of Enmity, 1789–2006* (2007), pp. 20–35; French invasion fleet, ibid., p. 40; British army takes field, ibid., pp. 42–45; Anglo-Irish Union: *Belfast News Letter,* January 2, 1801.

23 **Lord George Hill:** E. Estyn Evans, *The Personality of Ireland: Habitat, Heritage and History* (1973), pp. 85–104. For an Irish view of Lord Hill, that "special blessing on two feet sent by Providence for the neglected Celts," pay special attention to p. 101.

23 **"Facts from Gweedore":** T. C. Foster, *Condition of Ireland*, pp. 100–101.

23 **ascendancy of commercial farming:** Gray, *Famine, Land and Politics*, pp. 8–12; Black, *Economic Thought*, pp. 15–24.

23 **Malthus first proponent of commercial farming:** Gray, *Famine, Land and Politics*, p. 8.

23 **15,000 to 25,000 troops:** Miller, *Emigrants and Exiles*, p. 46.

23 **"I'll make a stir in the world yet":** Oliver Macdonagh, *The Hereditary Bondsman: Daniel O'Connell, 1775–1829* (1988), p. 6.

24 **Catholics denied emancipation:** Bew, *Ireland*, p. 121.

24 **denial of leases:** Devon Commission, part 2, p. 224; Mokyr, *Why Ireland Starved* (1983), pp. 83–84.

24 **plots smaller:** O'Grada, *New Economic History*, p. 114.

24 **"Worse than we are":** Report of Poor Law Commissioners (1836), Appendix D, p. 75.

24 **repeal year:** Oliver Macdonagh, *The Emancipist, Daniel O'Connell 1830–1847* (1989), pp. 239–40.

25 **consensus on big farm Ireland:** Robert Torrens, *Plan of an Association in Aid of the Irish Poor Law* (1838), pp. 5–9; Black, *Economic Thought*, p. 19; Gray, *Famine, Land and Politics*, p. 8.

25 **Irish work ethic:** George Nicholls, *A History of the Irish Poor Law* (1856), p. 163; Gustave de Beaumont, *Ireland, Social, Political, Religious* (1839–42), vol. 2, pp. 19–20; Mokyr, *Why Ireland Starved*, pp. 218–19.

26 **labor resistance in Gweedore:** T. C. Foster, *Condition of Ireland*, pp. 116–17.

26 **land consolidation and disruption:** G. C. Lewis, *On Local Disturbances in Ireland* (1836), pp. 76–82; Torrens, *Plan of an Association*, pp. 5–9.

26 **David Moore interview:** *Dublin Evening Post*, Sept. 9, 1845.

Two: The News from Ireland

27 **European weather:** E. C. Large, *Advance of the Fungi* (1940), p. 14.

28 **degeneracy of potato:** Bourke, *Visitation of God* (1996), p. 129; appearance in Flanders, Bourke, p. 130.

28 **symptoms of potato blight:** *Gardener's Chronicle and Horticultural Gazette* (hereafter *Gardener's Chronicle*), Oct. 4, 1845; odor indicates death of potato: Zuckerman, *The Potato*, p. 188.

28 **crossbreeding of American and Flemish strain of potato:** John Reader, *Potato: A History of the Propitious Esculent* (2008), pp. 195–98. Spread of blight: ibid., p. 195.

28 **blight's spread in America:** Bourke, *Visitation of God*, pp. 129–30.

29   **report of Mr. Parker:** Sir Robert Peel, *Memoirs* (1969), entry for Aug. 11, 1845, part 3, p. 109.

29   **public announcement of blight:** *Gardener's Chronicle*, Aug. 16, 1845.

29   **"visited by a great calamity":** Ibid., Aug. 23, 1845.

29   **international coverage of blight:** Bourke, *Visitation of God*, pp. 140–41.

30   **potato's role in Europe's development:** William McNeil, "How the Potato Changed World History," *Social Research*, Winter 1998, www.newschool.edu/cps/socialresearch/vol. 66, pp. 3–8, online edition.

30   *Leidsche Courant:* Bergman, *The Potato Blight in the Netherlands*, p. 401.

30   **"The whole of the [potato] crops":** *The Economist*, Sept. 6, 1845.

30   **"In Poland, there is":** *The Morning Chronicle*, Sept. 3, 1845.

30–31 **Morren identifies disease as fungus:** Bourke, *Visitation of God*, p. 131; attacks on fungal theory: ibid., pp. 144–35; "hairbrained" and "full of evil passions," ibid., p. 135; copper solution: Reader, *Potato*, pp. 206–8; Lindley on influence of weather: ibid., p. 198; defense of fungal theory by Berkeley: ibid., pp. 203–4; fungal theory loses ground: Bourke, *Visitation of God,* p. 137; how *P. infestans* destroys the potato: Reader, *Potato*, p. 203; Moggridge's copper theory, Reader, *Potato*, pp. 206–7.

34   **mood of Ireland:** T. P. O'Neil, "The Scientific Investigation of the Failure of the Potato Crop," *Irish Historical Studies*, no. 18 (1946), p. 122.

34   **Reports on weather:** *Athlone Sentinel*, July 16, 1845; *Belfast Penny Journal*, July 19, 1845.

34   **"a fearful malady":** *Gardener's Chronicle*, August 23, 1845.

34   **"So little is there to write about":** Elizabeth Smith, *The Irish Journals of Elizabeth Smith* (1980), p. 75.

35   **arrest of suspect in Bell-Booth murder:** *The Times*, Aug. 28, 1845; dispute over Irish beauty: T. C. Foster, *Condition of Ireland*, p. xv.

35   **"If [the potato] fail[s]:"** Peel, *Memoirs*, part 3, Graham to Peel, Oct. 13, 1845, p. 114.

35   **description of Sir James Graham:** T. J. Ward, *Sir James Graham* (1969), pp. 28, 29; Sir James Graham, *Oxford Dictionary of National Biography*, oxforddnb.com.

36   **progress of blight:** Famine Relief Commission Papers (RLFC)/ National Archives, Ireland. Confidential distress reports of Constabulary subinspectors/ RLFC2 /Z13210, Sept. 24, 1845; Confidential reports from counties Antrim, Armagh, Carlow, Kilkenny, Limerick, et al., RLFC2/Z13468, Sept. 9, 1845; reports from counties Meath, Sligo, Donegal, Down, Tipperary, et al., RLFC2/Z13758, Sept. 22, 1845; reports from Counties Tyrone, Wexford, Waterford, Londonderry, Queen's, et al. RLFC2/Z14134, Oct. 19, 1845, Report of Robert Murray: Cecil Woodham-Smith, *The Great Hunger*, p. 41.

37   **Constabulary informs government of crop surplus:** Correspondence explanatory of the measure adopted by Her Majesty's for the relief of distress arising from the failure of the potato crop, H.C. [735], p. 85. (Hereafter, Corr. exp.)

37   **oat crop:** *Northern Whig*, Oct. 1, 1845.

37   **"I am willing to hope":** Peel, *Memoirs*, part 3, Graham to Peel, Oct. 13, 1845, p. 114.

37   **return of rain exacerbates blight:** Report of Dr. Playfair and Mr. Lindley on the Present State of the Irish Potato Crop and on the Prospect of Approaching Scarcity, p. 1, Nov. 15, 1845 [28], p. 1.

37   **blight continues to spread:** Confidential Reports of Constabulary Subinspectors tracking the blight's progress, National Archives of Ireland, Famine Relief Commission papers: RLFC2/Z14344, Oct. 22, 1845; reports for Ennistimon, Clare;

Bagnalstown, Carlow, Tralee, Kerry; Drumlish, Longford, et al., RLFC2/Z14284, Oct. 26, 1845, reports for Cookstown, Tyrone, Mitchelstown, Lowtherstown, Clonakilty, Cork; Elphin, Roscommon, Newport, Thurles, Tipperary. RLFC2/Z14450, Oct. 23, 1845; reports from counties Fermangh, Galway, Leitrim, et al., RLFC2/Z15634, Oct. 11, 1845.

37   **distrust of Irish reports:** Peel, *Memoirs*, part 3, p. 113. On October 13, 1845, Peel told Graham: "There is such a tendency to exaggeration and inaccuracy in Irish reports that delay in acting on them is always desirable."

38   **memories of 1845 harvest:** Roger McHugh, "Famine in Irish Oral Tradition," in *The Great Famine: Studies in Irish History*, Dudley Edwards and T. Desmond Williams, eds. (1956), p. 397; "men wept openly": *The Morning Chronicle*, Sept. 8, 1845; "sprinkled holy water": McHugh, "Famine in Irish Oral Tradition," pp. 397–98. "Demand no rent at present": *Belfast Vindicator*, Oct. 25, 1845.

38   **Prendergast letter:** Oct. 25, 1845. In Prendergast Collection, Boston College.

39   **Corn Law turmoil:** Peel, *Memoirs*, part 3, pp. 185–215; Norman Gash, *Sir Robert Peel* (1972), pp. 562–615; *Hansard*, "The Cheltenham Petition," Mar. 7, 1846, vol. 84, pp. 502–26; Lady Richmond's stuffed rats: Frederick Mount, *Times Literary Supplement*, Aug. 24, 2007.

40   **"England has given us ignorance and bigotry":** *Illustrated London News*, Oct. 15, 1845; "banditti rampage": *The Morning Chronicle*, Oct. 15, 1845, *The Nation*, Oct. 1, 1845.

40–41 **meeting at Drayton Manor:** Peel, *Memoirs*, part 3, Oct. 18, 1845, p. 118. The description of Peel is from a book, *Sir Robert Peel, etude d'histoire contemporain*, Guizot, the French foreign minister, in *Private Letters of Sir Robert Peel*, ed. George Peel (1920), p. 284; Lord Byron's remark and the references to George III and Captain Bligh are drawn from Norman Gash, *Mr. Secretary Peel* (1961), pp. 77–78; visit to Ireland with Wellington: Gash, *Mr. Secretary Peel*, p. 125; Peel's foppishness: Mount, *Times Literary Supplement*, Aug. 24, 2007; Drayton Manor, as an example of deterioration of Victorian taste: Gash, *Sir Robert Peel*, p. 169; Disraeli is quoted by Mount, *Times Literary Supplement*, Aug. 24, 2007; courting Catholic Ireland: Gray, *Famine, Land and Politics*, p. 112.

42   **discussion of treatments to stop blight:** Peel, *Memoirs*, part 3, Peel to Graham, Oct. 18, 1846, p. 118.

42   **"recall a former . . . calamitous failure":** Peel, *Memoirs*, part 3, Monteagle to Peel, p. 135.

43   **"Potato Triumvirate":** *The Times*, Oct. 20, 1845; Playfair, Oct. 24, 1845, expert on atomic volume: *Oxford Dictionary of National Biography*, oxforddnb.com.

43   **Playfair courtier:** Large, *Advance of the Fungi*, p. 26; Kane, *Oxford Dictionary of National Biography*, oxforddnb.com.

43   **shops along Grafton Street and "the equal of Frenchwomen in good taste":** E. Smith, *Irish Journals*, p. 72.

43–44 **Dublin market report:** Peel, *Memoirs*, part 3, Playfair to Peel, Oct. 26, 1845, pp. 138–39.

44   **Potato Triumvirate tours countryside, half the crop destroyed:** Report of Dr. Playfair and Mr. Lindley on the Present State of the Irish Potato Crop [28], Nov. 15, 1845.

44   **Lord Kenyon:** Peel, *Memoirs*, part 3, p. 153; Duke of Norfolk's recipe for curry powder, *The Times*, Dec. 11, 1845.

44 **Playfair, "Pray aid us":** Peel, *Memoirs*, part 3, Playfair to Peel, Oct. 26, 1845, p. 139.

45 **"Advice Concerning the Potato Crop":** "How to Save the Value of Every Bad Potato"; Second Report of Commissioners (Kane, Lindley, Playfair) Appointed by the Government to inquire into the actual condition of the potato crop in Ireland, Nov. 3, 1845, reprinted in *Downpatrick Recorder*, Nov. 8, 1845; *The Belfast Vindicator*, Nov. 19, 1845.

46 **reactions to Potato Commissioners' reports:** *The Times*, Oct. 18, 1845; *The Freeman's Journal*, Nov. 10, 1845.

46 **arrival at Viceregal Lodge:** *The Morning Chronicle*, Nov. 5, 1845; description of Heytesbury's behavior: John O'Rourke, *History of the Great Irish Famine of 1847*, 3rd ed. (1902), pp. 45–46; "They may starve," *The Freeman's Journal*, Nov. 4, 1845; Heytesbury feels exasperated, Peel, *Memoirs*, part 3, Heytesbury to Peel, Oct. 24, 1845, pp. 133–34, Oct. 27, 1845, p. 138.

47 **Peel's plan for averting disaster:** Peel, *Memoirs*, part 3, Cabinet Memorandum, Nov. 1, 1845, 141–48; Cabinet Memorandum, Nov. 6, 1845, p. 158.

47 **Corn Laws will change British society:** G. S. K. Kitson-Clark, "Hunger and Politics in 1842," *Journal of Modern History*, vol. 24 (Dec. 1953), p. 370.

47–48 **"The aristocracy are struggling against":** *The Economist*, Dec. 6, 1845.

Three: "The Irish Can Live on Anything"

49 **Routh biographical information:** Sir Randolph Routh, *Oxford Dictionary of National Biography*, oxforddnb.com; Salt Hill Hotel: Robin Haines, *Charles Trevelyan and the Great Irish Famine*, 2004, p. 120.

50 **"lead the government into unnecessary expenditure":** Haines, *Charles Trevelyan and the Great Irish Famine*. Doubts about appointment of Edward Lucas: Gray, *Famine, Land and Politics*, p. 128. Both Haines and Gray provide a fairly detailed account of the concerns that influenced Home Secretary Graham's selection of Commission members. Gray is especially good in explaining how Routh's "large views" on finance and tendency to "lead the government into unnecessary expense" almost cost him a Commission appointment. See p. 128.

50 **Treasury memo on role of Irish landlords:** C. E. Trevelyan to Sir Randolph Routh, Corr. exp. [735], Jan. 26, 1846, p. 68.

50 **members of Relief Commission:** C. E. Trevelyan, *The Irish Crisis* (1848), p. 104.

50 **Kane:** "He has gained some practical experience": Woodham-Smith, *The Great Hunger*, p. 57.

50 **changing conception of poverty:** Gertrude Himmel Farb, *The Idea of Poverty* (1985), pp. 1–3.

51 **depressed state of Irish peasantry:** Nicholls, *History of Irish Poor Law*, p. 162; size, character, and workings of Irish Poor Law system: ibid., pp. 222–54.

51 **origins of Irish Poor Law system:** Nicholls, *History of Irish Poor Law*, pp. 118–26. Nicholls was the chief architect of the Irish Poor Law system.

53 **"a fearful ordeal by water":** Sinead Collins, *Balrothery Poor Law Union, County Dublin, 1839–1851*, (2005), pp. 28–29.

53 **challenges facing Relief Commission:** Treasury Minutes, Dec. 9, 1845, Corr. exp. [735], p. 2; Routh summation of relief operations also highlight the scale of challenge: Corr. exp. [735] July 31, 1846, pp. 217–23; T. P. O'Neil, "The Organization and Administration of Relief in The Great Famine," *Studies in Irish History* (1957), pp. 212–20.

54   **difficulty in calculating extent of crop losses:** Kinealy, *This Great Calamity*, pp. 41–43; similarities to previous relief plans: ibid., p. 38.

54   **pin factory:** Adam Smith, *An Inquiry into the Nature and Causes of the Wealth of Nations* (1776), Book 1, Ch. 1, 1.3.

55   **Peel plan to buy corn:** Trevelyan to Baring Bros., Corr. exp. [735], Nov. 5–9, 1845, pp. 1–3; same to same, Dec. 29, 1845, p. 4; *Hansard*, vol. 84, Mar. 9, 1846, pp. 781–84; corn employed to regulate prices: Routh to Pine Coffin, Corr. exp., May 15, 1846, p. 137.

55   **"feed a million people for forty days":** Gash, *Sir Robert Peel*, p. 543.

55   **"Wherever [the potato] shall":** Horticultural Society of London's warning about the Irish potato crisis in *Edinburgh Review*, Jan. 1848, p. 235.

55   **degrading aspects of potato:** *Edinburgh Review* (1848), pp. 230–33. The author of the article, Charles Trevelyan, the assistant secretary of the Treasury, included his views on the moral effects of the potato and maize in a little book, *The Irish Crisis*, published later in 1848. Mr. Trevelyan believed grains like maize fostered "thrift," "energy," and a "vast accumulation of capital."

56   **"food for the contented slave":** *The Economist*, Oct. 5, 1845; William Wilde's views on the potato: *Dublin University Magazine*, vol. 43 (1854), pp. 127–28.

56   **"The little industry":** Routh to Trevelyan, Corr. exp. [736], Mar. 6, 1846, pp. 108–9. For Routh's other complaints about the moral effect of the potato, see Corr. exp. [736], Apr. 1, 1846, p. 139, and Apr. 15, 1846, p. 157.

57   **Mr. Ward and purchase of American Corn:** Woodham-Smith, *The Great Hunger*, pp. 56–57.

57   **report of Captain Chads on 1839 crop failure:** "Relief of the People Suffering from Scarcity in Ireland Between the Years 1822 and 1839" [734], pp. 21–22.

57   **"landlord, though he touches":** Beaumont, *Ireland*, vol. 2, p. 289.

58   **differences between Irish and English Poor Law systems:** Nicholls, *History of the Irish Poor Law*, pp. 153–209; Ireland as a giant poorhouse: *Hansard*, vol. 90, Mar. 29, 1847, p. 21.

58   **"locusts will devour the land:"** Graham to Freemantle, December 9, 1845; quoted in Gray, *Famine, Land and Politics*, p. 129.

58–60 **Edinburgh Letter:** *The Morning Chronicle*, Nov. 22, 1845; history of Russell family: John Prest, *Lord John Russell* (1972), pp. 1–7 (Russell's youth); Russell as leader in Reform movement, pp. 38–54; Russell as home secretary, pp. 117–34; "bold man": *Illustrated London News*, Nov. 25, 1845; "straightforward manliness": *The Morning Chronicle*, Nov. 28, 1845. For the political consequences of the Edinburgh Letter, see also F. A. Dreyer, "The Whigs and the Political Crisis of 1845," *English Historical Review*, vol. 80 (1965), pp. 514–37.

60   **Peel government deadlocked over Corn Law reform:** Gash, *Sir Robert Peel*, pp. 540–50.

61   **"Irishmen can live on anything":** Duke of Cambridge's speech extract in *The Nation*, Jan. 24, 1846.

61   **blight as divine punishment for violating the law of free trade:** Gray, *Famine, Land and Politics*, p. 15; "Almighty humbles pride of nations": Peel, *Memoirs*, part 3, Graham to Peel, Oct. 18, 1845, p. 125.

61   **roundelay in governments:** Gash, *Sir Robert Peel*, pp. 554–61.

Four: Want

62   **evictions at Tullycrine:** Letter of Father Martin Meehan, *The Nation*, Jan. 17, 1846; attack on home of Edward Moloney: *The Morning Chronicle*, Nov. 21, 1845.

63   **"The excitement here is daily growing":** *New York Tribune*, Jan. 6, 1846.

63   **Limerick disturbances:** Copy of all communications received by Her Majesty's government relative to the disturbances which took place at Knocksentry, near Limerick, on or about the 10th day of January 1846 [172], Mar. 30, 1846, pp. 4–5; *Limerick Chronicle* report of incident reprinted in *The Times*, Jan. 17, 1846.

64   **reports of deepening hunger:** Counties Sligo, Waterford, *The Times*; Dungarvan, five thousand starving, report from *Cork Examiner* reprinted in *The Times*, Feb. 3, 1846; food situation in other parts of Ireland, The weekly reports of the Scarcity Commission showing the progress of disease in the potato [201], Mar. 1846, Kilfinane, Clare, p. 9, Ballagh, Tipperary, p. 22, Kilglass, Roscommon, Mitchelstown, Cork, p. 19; rise in food prices: Potatoes [Ireland], report of the highest prices of potatoes week ending Jan. 24, 1846, [110], Belfast, p. 1, Galway, pp. 3–4, Howth, p. 3; price of pigs, *The Times*, Feb. 7, 1846.

64   **"With potatoes at their present prices":** E. Smith, *Irish Journals* (1980), p. 90.

65   **priest overwhelmed by distress:** *The Nation*, Feb. 10, 1846.

65   **"Striding nearer every day":** *The Nation*, Mar. 7, 1846.

65   **events in Galway:** *Cork Examiner*, Feb. 7, 1846.

66   **"There are five millions":** Daniel O'Connell, *Hansard*, vol. 83, Feb. 17, 1846, pp. 1050–68.

66   **Prendergrast letter:** Prendergast Collection, Boston College, Oct. 25, 1845.

66   **value of 1845 crops:** O'Grada, *Ireland: A New Economic History*, p. 123.

67   **landlords refuse to underwrite local public works:** Routh to Trevelyan, Corr. exp. [735], Jan. 15, 1846, pp. 9–11; enclosure from minutes of the Relief Commission [meeting] of Feb. 16, 1846, Corr. exp., pp. 40–41; Mr. Griffith, Public Works Commissioner, to Lord Lincoln, Corr. exp., Apr. 18, 1846, p. 110.

67   **Chairman Lucas denounces relief plan as inadequate:** Report of the Commissioners of Inquiry into matters connected with the Failure of the Potato Crop, Feb. 6, 1846 [33], pp. 1–5.

67   **Peel needs help of Irish MPs on Corn Law bill:** Gray, *Famine, Land and Politics*, p. 130.

68   **Mr. Hewetson ordered to Ireland:** Treasury Minutes, Corr. exp. [735], Dec. 23, 1845; Hewetson suggests corn to Peel: Corr. exp., Nov. 5, 1845, p. 1; Peel's thank-you note: Correspondence Exp., Nov. 9, 1845, p. 1.

68   **description of pre-famine Cork:** Inglis, *A Journey through Ireland* (1835), pp. 104–7.

69   **"I am a gentleman traveling on [my] own affairs":** Hewetson to Trevelyan, Corr. exp. [735], Jan. 10, 1846, pp. 6, 7; description of Lee Mills: Hewetson to Trevelyan, Corr. exp., Jan. 13, 1846, p. 7; error on rent, Hewetson to Routh, Corr. exp., Jan. 26, 1846, p. 20.

69   **corn processed in steel mills in South:** E. Margaret Crawford, *Famine: The Irish Experience, 900–1900* (1989), p. 118; advice on potato: Mr. Robertson, Corr. exp. [735], Feb. 11, 1846, pp. 32–33; Captain Maconochie, Feb. 14, 1846, pp. 32, 33; Messrs. Ginnell, Minturn & Co., p. 48.

70   **description of corn processing:** Routh to Trevelyan, Corr. exp. [735], July 31, 1846, p. 218.

70   **"Indian corn . . . cannot be turned out so quickly as wheat":** Hewetson to Trevelyan, Corr. exp. [735], Feb. 18, 1846; difficulty with sacks, Hewetson to Trevelyan, Corr. exp. [735], Feb. 24, 1846, p. 46. Hewetson warns Routh he is falling behind schedule: Corr. exp. [735], Feb. 12, 1846, p. 30; request for outdoor relief refused: Twisleton to Routh, Corr. exp. [735], Feb. 16, 1846, p. 35.

71   **request to purchase food in Ireland:** Routh to Trevelyan, Corr. exp. [735], Feb. 1, 1846, pp. 23–24; denial of request: Trevelyan to Routh, Feb. 4, 1846, p. 26, food supply in military depots: Trevelyan to Routh, Feb. 4, 1846, p. 26.

72   **geography of west:** Routh to Trevelyan, Corr. exp. [735], Mar. 22, 1846, p. 76.

72   *Alban* and *Dee*: Treasury Minute, Corr. exp. [735], Mar. 17, 1846, p. 67.

72   **"Providence had never intended Ireland to be a great nation":** Routh to Hewetson, March 26, 1846, quoted in Woodham-Smith, *The Great Hunger*, p. 67.

Five: The Hanging of Bryan Serry

73–74   **execution of Bryan Serry:** *The Times*, Feb. 17, 1846.

74–75   **rising crime rate:** *Hansard*, Feb. 23, 1846, vol. 83, p. 1349; "It is melancholy to contemplate," *Limerick Chronicle*, reprinted in *The Times*, Jan. 13, 1846; Tuthills: Peel, *Memoirs*, part 3, letter from Col. Sir Charles O'Donnell to Peel, June 8, 1846, pp. 302–3; McElhill girl, Gallaghers of Cavan, *Hansard*, Feb. 23, 1846, vol. 83, p. 1357; Mrs. Bennett, ibid., p. 1354.

75   **lawless condition of Ireland:** Lord Lansdowne: *Hansard*, Feb. 23, 1846, vol. 83; Earl St. German, Feb. 23, p. 1368, Lord Brougham, p. 1371.

75   **"The military uses":** John Mitchel, *The Nation*, Nov. 22, 1845.

75   **rising incidence of disease:** Disease [Ireland] Spring, 1846 [120]; R. M. Tagard, Donegal, p. 2; William Smith O'Brien, *Hansard*, Mar. 13, 1846, vol. 84, p. 987; Josh Lynn, Markethill Infirmary, Disease [Ireland], p. 2; infection rate 1816–1817: Laurence M. Geary, "Famine Fever and Bloody Flux" in *Great Irish Famine*, Cathal Poirteir, ed. (1995), p. 81; Disease [Ireland], Spring 1846 [120]: J. P. Edgar, Ballhooly dispensary, Charles Murphy, Fermoy dispensary, p. 3, and James Adams, Cavan, p. 2.

76–77   **spread of distress:** E. Smith, *Irish Journals*, Feb. 24, 1846, p. 90; Report of Commissioners of Inquiry into matters connected with the failure of the Potato Crop [33], Feb. 1846; Routh to Trevelyan, Corr. exp. [736], July 31, 1846, pp. 217–23 (the Routh letter is a summary of events during the first year of the scarcity, including the appearance and spread of the blight and the government response); Weekly Reports of the Scarcity Commission, showing the progress of disease in potatoes; peasant foraging in field: Susan Campbell Bartoletti, *Black Potatoes* (2001), p. 33.

77   **"Even if we had food land on our shores":** *Belfast Vindicator*, Feb. 4, 1846; formation of relief committees: Instructions to Committees of Relief Districts, 1846 [171], pp. 230–33; "the time has arrived": Routh to Trevelyan, Corr. exp. [735], Feb. 16, 1846, p. 43.

78   **donations to committees:** Corr. exp. [735], p. 235.

78   **reluctant givers:** "The event was coming": Routh to Edward Pine Coffin, Corr. exp. [735], Mar. 21, 1846, p. 70; dealings with Col. Wyndham: Relief Commission letter to Col. Wyndham, Mar. 21, 1846, p. 71.

78–79   **riots in Clonmel:** warning letter from Relief Commission to municipal authorities: Routh to Trevelyan, Corr. exp. [735], Apr. 15, 1846, p. 104; same to same also Apr. 15, p. 150 (in this letter Routh describes the irresponsible attitude of Clonmel authorities); Pine Coffin to Routh, Apr. 16, 1846, Hewetson to Trevelyan, Apr. 19, 1846, Corr. exp. [735], p. 113; description of Clonmel riot: *Belfast Vindicator*, Apr. 18, 1846.

79–80   **landed classes inactive:** Assistant Commissary Officer Dobree to Trevelyan, Corr. exp. [735], Mar. 21, 1846, p. 73. Smith O'Brien's family backgound: William Smith O'Brien, *Oxford Dictionary of National Biography*, oxforddnb.com; "If we could have managed to play our cards well": Daniel O'Connell to William Smith O'Brien, Dec. 22, 1845, *Correspondence of Daniel O'Connell*, vol. 7, p. 353; "If all our exertions": Smith O'Brien to O'Connell in O. Macdonagh, *The Emancipist* (1989), p. 278.

80–82 **Gerrard evictions:** *Hansard*, Lord Brougham, Mar. 23, 1846, vol. 84, pp. 1396–97, Lord Londonderry, Mar. 30, 1846, vol. 85, p. 273, *The Morning Chronicle*, Apr. 3, 1846; *The Nation*, Mar. 28, 31, 1846.

82–83 **St. Patrick's Day at Dublin Castle:** *The Morning Chronicle*, Mar. 25, 1846; Daniel O'Connell on Mrs. Gerrard: Daniel O'Connell, *Hansard*, Apr. 3, 1846, vol. 85, p. 501.

83 **letter of John Mansfield:** RLFC3/1/899. Relief Commission papers, National Archives Ireland, Mar. 23, 1846.

83 **geographic pattern of distress:** Scarcity Commission Report [201], Mar. 1846: Wicklow, Westmeath, p. 5; Galway, Clare, p. 6.

84 **"great risk of our stores being exhausted":** Pine Coffin to Routh, Corr. exp. [735], Mar. 16, 1846, p. 68.

84 **incident at Kilkenny workhouse:** Brendan O'Cathaoir, *Famine Diary* (1999), p. 41.

85 **first starvation death:** Relief Commission papers, National Archives Ireland, RLFC3/1/854, Mar. 21, 1846.

85 **dysfunction in relief committees:** Commissioners of Public Works to Lords of Treasury, Corr. exp. [735], June 5, 1846, pp. 320–22; same to same, July 7, 1846, pp. 332–33 (some of the criticism of the relief committees in the memo was motivated by the commissioners' desire to shift blame away from the failings of the Board of Works); Treasury Minutes, Corr. exp., July 3, p. 331, July 21, 1846, p. 441; members collect "minute reports of circumstances": Instructions to Committees of Relief Districts [171], pp. 230–33.

85–86 **"I believe that the wealthy inhabitants":** *Belfast Vindicator*, Apr. 22, 1846.

86 *Harriet Rockwell* **blown off course:** Corr. exp. [735], Treasury Minute, Mar. 13, 1846, pp. 60–61.

86 **violence on the River Fergus and in Westmeath:** Assistant Commissary Officer Dobree to Trevelyan, Corr. exp. [735], Apr. 24, 1846, p. 123; *Dublin Mail*, reprinted in *The Times*, Apr. 24, 1846.

86–87 **description of opening of Cork depot on March 28, 1846:** *Illustrated London News*, Apr. 4, 1846.

87 **Trevelyan undercurrent:** Darrell Munsell, *The Unfortunate Duke: The Life of Henry Pelham, 5th Duke of Newcastle* (1985), p. 306; Haines, *Charles Trevelyan and the Great Irish Famine*, p. 165.

Six: The Lord of Providence

88–90 **profile of Trevelyan:** For the stained-glass window, see James Hernon, "A Victorian Cromwell: Sir Charles Trevelyan, the Famine and the Age of Improvement," in *Eire-Ireland*, vol. 20 (1987), pp. 15–17. family background: *Oxford Dictionary of National Biography*, oxforddnb.com; "He has no small talk" and "That man is almost always on the right side": Woodham-Smith, *The Great Hunger*, p. 59; as model for Sir Gregory Hardlines: O'Neil, "The Organization and Administration of Relief in The Great Irish Famine," *Studies in Irish History*, p. 214; "Use whatever tool came to hand": Haines, *Charles Trevelyan and the Great Irish Famine*, p. 51; influence of Moralism: Gray, *Famine, Land and Politics*, pp. 16, 24, 163; Boyd Hilton, *The Age of Atonement* (1992), pp. 69–70; Jenifer Hart, "Sir Charles Trevelyan at the Treasury," *English Historical Review*, vol. 75 (1960), pp. 92–110.

91–92 **public works measures:** 9 Vic [Public Works/Acts passed March 5, 1846]; Peel's desire to create works of lasting value: Gray, *Famine, Land and Politics*, pp. 134–35; loan applications from Clare: A. R. G. Griffiths, "The Irish Board of Works in the Famine Years," *Historical Journal*, vol. 13 (1970), pp. 634–52; Lord George Hill and Sir John Bourke apply for grants, Haines, *Charles Trevelyan and the Great Irish Famine*, pp. 174–75; loan applications at about £1 million: Griffiths, "The Irish Board of Works in the Famine Years," *Historical Journal*, p. 638; applications for public works schemes: request for half a million pounds for Great Southern and Western Railroad, George Carr, vice president, the Great Southern and Western Railway (Ireland), to Peel, Corr. exp. [735], May 22, 1846, p. 318; Galway town commissioner for £4,000 for military barracks, Limerick request for £20,000; Mayo request for £15,000, Corr. exp. [735], May 24, 1846, pp. 315–17. See also pp. 287, 292–93, the Galway and Mayo requests are in a chart on pp. 315–17 in [735].

92   **government loan program abounds in fraud and abuse:** Trevelyan to Routh, Corr. Exp. [735], Apr. 15, 1846, pp. 355–56; same to same, Feb. 4, 1846, p. 26. For further information on abuses in public works system, see also: Treasury Minute in Corr. exp. [735], p. 275; "extremely irregular" proprietor behavior: Board of Works to Trevelyan, Corr. exp., Apr. 7, 1846, p. 295. Trevelyan criteria: Treasury Minutes, Corr. exp., pp. 292–93.

93   **disturbances in Carrick-on-Suir:** Routh to Trevelyan, Corr. exp. [735], Apr. 7, 1846, p. 92; *Dublin Mail*, reprinted in *The Times*, Apr. 24, 1846; Elias Thackeray, RLFC3/1/1622.

93   **resistance to Trevelyan's attempts to slow down public works:** Commissioners of Public Works to Pennefeather, Corr. exp. [735], Feb. 9, 1846, pp. 319–20; Thomas Freemantle to Trevelyan, Corr. exp. [735], Feb. 26, 1846, p. 321; Graham to Heytesbury, Apr. 13, 25, and 27, 1846, in Gray, *Famine, Land and Politics*, p. 137; only £70,000 sanctioned for public works projects: Jones to Lincoln, Corr. exp. [735], Apr. 9, 1846, p. 383. By May applications for public works loans had reached £800,000. Woodham-Smith, *The Great Hunger* (1962), p. 80.

93–94   **river travel between Clonmel and Carrick-on-Suir:** *The Times*, Apr. 20, 1846; *The Freeman's Journal* response to Heytesbury, Apr. 15, 1846. For the "thousand human beings . . . taking their departure from here": *The Nation*, May 3, 1846.

94–95   **biography of Henry Pelham:** *Oxford Dictionary of National Biography*, oxforddnb .com; D. Munsell, *The Unfortunate Duke*, pp. 1–20; Peel and Graham urge Lincoln to contain Trevelyan undercurrent: Munsell, *The Unfortunate Duke*, pp. 69–76; Trevelyan's control over staff: Lincoln to Peel, April 9, 1846, May Munsell, *The Unfortunate Duke*, p. 74; chastened Trevelyan: Trevelyan to Routh, Corr. exp. [735], Apr. 20, 1846, p. 113; Trevelyan to Routh, Corr. exp. [735], Feb. 3, 1846, p. 25.

95   **atmosphere at Irish Board of Works:** R. B. McDowell, *Irish Administration* (1964), pp. 198–205; Kinealy, *This Great Calamity*, p. 56, Woodham-Smith, *The Great Hunger*, p. 78.

95   **public works relief plan:** Corr. exp. [735], Board of Works Series, pp. 261–66.

95–96   **overworked board:** "A stranger can form no idea" and "I am without hope": McDowell, *Irish Administration*, p. 211–12.

96   **difficulty recruiting competent board officers:** Griffiths, *The Irish Board of Works*, pp. 634–40; Enclosure C, reprinted in Corr. exp., p. 297.

96   **"We have many":** Commissioners of Public Works to Trevelyan, Corr. exp. [735], Apr. 7, 1846, p. 295.

96–97   **"raining heavily":** weather disrupts food shipments, Corr. exp. [735], Pine Coffin to Trevelyan, Apr. 11, 1846, p. 101.

97   **Brigid Keane:** Bartoletti, *Black Potatoes*, p. 47; James Carrig: O'Cathaoir, *Famine Diary*, p. 52; laborers forcing their way onto work sites: Commissioners of Board of Works to Lords of Treasury, Corr. exp. [735], July 7, 1846, p. 333.

97   **gift for Mr. Pine Coffin:** Trevelyan to Pine Coffin, Corr. exp. [735], Apr. 3, 1846, p. 10.

97   **waiting for depots to open:** Pine Coffin to Routh, May 13, 1846, in Woodham-Smith, *The Great Hunger* (1962), p. 84; Routh to Trevelyan, Corr. exp. [735], May 14, 1846, p. 136.

98   **corn a form of price control:** Pine Coffin to Trevelyan, Corr. exp. [735], June 4, 1846, p. 152.

98   **"It is quite impossible for the government to feed four million people":** Sir Robert Peel, *Hansard*, vol. 85, Apr. 7, 1846, p. 721.

98   **"500 to 600 . . . fishermen":** *The Nation*, May 18, 1846; visit to Cork city relief committee: *Cork Southern Reporter*, May 10, 1846; in Longford, people walked ten Irish miles: Routh to Trevelyan, Corr. exp. [735], June 3, 1846, pp. 149–50; young woman in Galway: *Galway Vindicator*, quoted in O'Cathaoir, *Famine Diary*, pp. 48–49.

99–100 **complaints about Indian corn:** Hewetson to Trevelyan, Corr. exp. [735], Feb. 27, 1846, p. 50. Routh to Trevelyan, Corr. exp. [735], Mar. 6, 1846, pp. 56–57; Pine Coffin to Trevelyan, Corr. exp., Mar. 30, 1846, p. 84.

100   **dispute over number of grindings of corn:** Routh to Trevelyan, Corr. exp. [735], Feb. 14, 15, 1846, pp. 37, 218; Trevelyan to Routh, Corr. exp. [735], Feb. 20, 1846, p. 43.

100   **O'Brien the baker:** Trevelyan to Scott Russell, Corr. exp. [735], June 10, 1846, p. 160.

100   **increase in government corn supply:** Routh to Trevelyan, Corr. exp. [735], July 31, 1846, p. 218; see also: James Donnelly, "Famine and Government Response," in *New History of Ireland*, W. E. Vaughan, ed., vol. 5 (1989), p. 278.

100   **importers alarmed at government intervention:** Hewetson to Trevelyan, Corr. exp. [735], June 20, 1846, p. 177.

101   **Routh ordered to raise price of meal:** Trevelyan to Routh, Corr. exp. [735], June 3, 1846, p. 148; Trevelyan orders food purchases halted: Trevelyan to Routh, Corr. exp., June 13, 1846, p. 161. "Serious food shortages develop": Routh to Trevelyan, Corr. exp. [735], June 20, 1846, p. 169; populace "staggering through the streets": *The Freeman's Journal*, June 5, 1846; people "in tears for want of food": Helpman to Sir James Dombrain, Corr. exp. [735], May 19, 1846, p. 130; in County Wicklow: E. Smith, *Irish Journals*, p. 96.

101–2   **issues of government corn in Cork and Limerick:** Routh to Trevelyan, Corr. exp. [735], June 22, 1846, p. 169, Perceval to Trevelyan, Corr. exp. [735], June 22, 1846, p. 171; Mrs. Smith receives letter: E. Smith, *Irish Journals*, p. 96; "thousands would be dying by the roadside": Pine Coffin to Trevelyan, Corr. exp. [735], June 25, 1846, p. 175.

102   **renewed disagreement over food prices:** Routh to Trevelyan, Corr. exp. [735], June 28, 1846, p. 183; Trevelyan to Routh, Corr. exp. [735], June 29, 1846, p. 184.

102   **Trevelyan shut-down order:** June 25, in Woodham-Smith, *The Great Hunger*, p. 86.

102   **public works wage:** Jones to Trevelyan, Corr. exp. [735], May 9, 1846, p. 314. Jones complains that the "boys"—laborers—expect to be employed at "high wages."

103   **Board of Works overwhelmed by employment applications:** Commissioners of

Board of Works to Lords of Treasury, Corr. exp. [735], June 5, 1846, p. 322; workers from Shannon River project, p. 321; migrant laborers, p. 322; numbers of laborers employed: Commissioners of Public Works to the Treasury, Corr. exp., Aug. 8, 1846, pp. 351–52.

103 **complaints about abuses of public works laborers:** Commissioners of Public Works to Lords of Treasury, Corr. exp., June 5, 1846, pp. 320–23; Mr. Pennefeather to Trevelyan, Corr. exp. [735], June 30, 1846, p. 330.

103 *Waiting for Godot:* William Wilde, *Dublin University Magazine,* vol. 43 (1854), p. 138.

104 **fall of Peel:** description of Bentinck, *Illustrated London News,* Oct. 6, 1845; description of Disraeli's suits, *Cork Southern Reporter,* Jan. 24, 1847; machinations of plot and Peel's reaction to defeat, Gash, *Sir Robert Peel,* pp. 601–22.

105 **"Peel is a true man of old Ireland" ; "God Bless our Queen"; people feel saved:** "We know now what we [would] do": Pole to Trevelyan, Corr. exp. [735], June 3, 1846, p. 150; "A frightful famine has been warded off": Father Mathew to Trevelyan, Corr. exp. [735], June 18, 1846, p. 167; "the state has established": Pole to Trevelyan, Corr. exp. [735], May 11, 1846, p. 134; "The motive of self preservation:" Pine Coffin to Trevelyan, June 4, 1846, p. 152. Major Simmonds to Trevelyan, Corr. exp. [735], July 4, 1846, pp. 191–92; "foresight of Her Majesty's Government": Routh to Trevelyan, Corr. exp. [735], June 13, 1846, p. 162. Routh boasts of the positive press reaction to the relief program in Routh to Trevelyan, Corr. exp. [735], June 17, 1846, p. 167.

105 **scarcity promotes Irish modernization:** Gray, *Famine Land and Politics,* p. 123; see also Routh to Trevelyan, Corr. exp. [735], May 28, 1846, p. 195.

105 **sums raised by local relief committees:** *Dublin Evening Post,* June 6, 1846; public works expenditure: £456,000 for road work, £126,000 on other works of "utility": A statement of total expenditure for the purposes of relief in Ireland [615], p. 477.

105–6 **encounter with Mr. Lucas:** Routh to Trevelyan, Corr. exp. [735], June 17, 1846, p. 167.

Seven: The Great and Glorious Cause of Ireland

107 **The anecdotes of life in Ireland on the eve of the second crop failure are from the *Cork Examiner*:** horticultural exhibit, June 26, 1846; Limerick County Fair, July 9, 1846; victory of the invincible Pill, July 13, 1846; Kingston races, July 6, 1846; Temperance Institute, July 13, 1846; new "Paddy" joke, April 24, 1846.

108 **"The crisis of the struggle":** Routh to Trevelyan, Corr. exp. [735], July 10, 1846, p. 201.

108 **reports of destitution:** Killarney, Saunders to Hewetson, Corr. exp. [735], July 11, 1846, p. 204; Donegal, RLFC 3/2/714; Kilkenny, RLFC 3/1/3351; Skibbereen, Mr. Thomas to Major Beamish, Corr. exp. [761], Commissariat Series (July 1846 to Jan. 1847), Aug. 21, 1846, p. 28.

108–9 **Captain Pole's visitor:** Pole to Trevelyan, Corr. exp. [735], July 13, 1846, pp. 205–6.

109–10 **Constabulary's uniform and posture:** Donal J. O'Sulllivan, *The Irish Constabulary, 1822–1922* (1999), p. 62.

110 **inclement harvest weather:** *The Times,* Aug. 3, 1846; *Belfast News-Letter,* Aug. 2, 1846; *Galway Mercury,* Aug. 10, 1846; *The Nation,* Aug. 15, 1846; Old Deruane, Bartoletti, *Black Potatoes,* p. 53; Routh's warning: O'Cathaoir, *Famine Diary,* p. 59.

111   **crop failure:** Wilde, *Dublin University Magazine*, vol. 43 (1854), p. 134; descriptions of singing farmer, mother and girl, and visit to cabin: *The Nation*, Aug. 22, 1846.

111–12 **reactions to crop losses:** Dobree to Trevelyan, Corr. [761], Commissariat Series, Aug. 19, 1846, p. 16; potatoes not fit for pigs: *Belfast Vindicator*, Aug. 28, 1846; in Cork town: *The Times*, Aug. 27, 1846; John Meagher: RLFC3/1/4398; "Gentlemen, the placards warned": O'Cathaoir, *Famine Diary*, pp. 67–68. Fr. Matthew to Trevelyan, Corr. [761], Commissariat Series, Aug. 7, 1846, p. 3.

113   **75 percent crop loss:** Routh to Trevelyan, Corr. [761], Commissariat Series, Aug. 13, 1846, pp. 7, 8; Trevelyan shut down order: Treasury Minute, Corr. exp. [735], July 21, 1846, pp. 393–94; see also: Corr. exp. [735], June 23, 1846, p. 171; Routh's reaction to shutdown order: Routh to Trevelyan, Corr. exp. [735], June 24, 1846, pp. 173–76; Routh again brings up shut down order in a letter to Trevelyan on July 6, 1846, Corr. exp. [735], pp. 191–92; Archbishop MacHale's reaction: *The Freeman's Journal*, Aug. 8, 1846.

114   **amount of Peel corn purchases:** "A Statement of Total Expenditure for Purposes of Relief in Ireland Since November 1845 . . . 1846" [615], p. 477; Routh to Trevelyan, July 6, 1846, in Haines, *Charles Trevelyan and the Great Irish Famine*, p. 197.

115   **demonstration at Westport House:** description of Westport town, Inglis, *Ireland*, p. 254; demonstration at Lord Sligo's: Perceval to Trevelyan, Corr. [761], Commissariat Series, Aug. 20, 1846, p. 20; same to same, Aug. 22, 1846, pp. 21, 22.

116–20 **confrontation between O'Connell and Young Ireland:** description of Conciliation Hall, Macdonagh, *The Emancipist*, pp. 286–312; social and cultural differences between Old and Young Ireland: J. Donnelly, "A Famine in Irish Politics," in *A New History of Ireland*, vol. 5 (1989), pp. 557–69; events during July 1846 meetings, including speeches of Meagher and Smith O'Brien and reaction of Jane Elgee: Thomas Keneally, *The Great Shame* (2000), pp. 115–21.

120   **William Russell's advice to his older brother John:** Prest, *Lord John Russell*, p. 55; divisions in Russell cabinet: Gray, *Famine, Land and Politics*, pp. 231–36; Mr. Wood, *Oxford Dictionary of National Biography*, oxforddnb.com; note to Trevelyan: Haines, *Charles Trevelyan and the Great Irish Famine*, p. 216; *Punch* cartoons: Prest, *Lord John Russell*, pp. 217, 268.

121   **cost of relief to British ratepayer:** £476,000 on loans for roads, £126,000 for roads, harbors, etc., "Return of all sums of money either granted or advanced from the Exchequer of the United Kingdom on account of distress and famine," 1849 [352], p. 2; £185,492, the exact sum spent on corn: "A statement of total expenditures for purposes of relief in Ireland," 1846 [615], p. 2.

121   **"Alas, the Irish peasant":** *The Times*, Sept. 22, 1846.

122   **dying O'Connell returns to Dublin:** Macdonagh, *The Emancipist*, p. 299.

122   **a season of "terrible emergency":** *The Economist*, Sept. 5, 1846.

122   **"mysterious potato murrain":** *The Morning Chronicle*, Sept. 4, 1846; Sicilian soldiers sweat, alpine ice melts: *The Freeman's Journal*, August 12, 1846; 50 percent rise in Mark Lane and Edinburgh prices: *The Nation*, Aug. 29, 1846; rise in Dublin prices: *The Freeman's Journal*, Aug. 10, 1846; Limerick corn dealer: Routh to Trevelyan, Corr. [761], Commissariat Series, Aug. 15, 1846, p. 12; 1,488,234 tons of Indian corn: Corr. [761], Commissariat Series, Oct. 3, 1846.

122   **continental crop losses:** Eric Vanhaute, Richard Paping, and Cormac O'Grada,

eds., "The European Subsistence Crisis of 1845–1850," in *When the Potato Failed* (2007), p. 22.

124–26 **Russell diary entry:** Prest, *Lord John Russell*, p. 4; Russell, Commons Speech, *Hansard*, vol. 85, Aug. 17, 1846, pp. 767–85.

127 **"I think I see a bright light shining in the distance":** Trevelyan to Lord Monteagle, Oct. 9, 1846, Monteagle papers, National Library of Ireland; high prices beneficial: Trevelyan, *The Irish Crisis*, p. 38; "We shall need iron nerves": Wood to Russell, Sept. 22, 1846, in G. P. Gooch, ed., *The Later Correspondence of Lord John Russell* (1925), p. 147.

127 **revisions in crop losses:** Prest, *Lord John Russell*, p. 240; Cave Hill, Ulster: *The Nation*, Aug. 19, 1846; gombeen men: Pole to Trevelyan, Corr. [761], Commissariat Series, Sept. 15, 1846, pp. 75–76; Father Ryan's letter: O'Cathaoir, *Famine Diary*, p. 60; Major Mahon's tenants: O'Cathaoir, *Famine Diary*, p. 67; visit to Connemara: *The Nation*, Sept. 3, 1846.

128 **Dombrain report:** Sir James Dombrain to Routh, Corr. [761], Commissariat Series, Sept. 5, 1846, p. 49; Treasury Minutes, [761] Commissariat Series, Sept. 8, 1846, p. 50.

128 **Irish exports:** *The Times*, Aug. 28, 1846.

128 **remains of summer food supply:** Corr. [761], Commissariat Series, Aug. 29, 1846, p. 31. (In late August 1846, the British food reserve in Ireland consisted of 241 tons of cornmeal and 241 tons of oatmeal; Government food depots unable to close: Routh to Trevelyan: Corr. [761], Commissariat Series, Aug. 26, 1846, p. 93. Routh mentioned the pressure on the depots in a second letter to Trevelyan on August 26 (also p. 93). Trevelyan's ban on foreign purchases: O'Neil, "The Organization and Administration of Relief in The Great Famine," *Studies in Irish History*, pp. 223–24.

128 **approach to Baring Bros.:** Baring to Trevelyan, Corr. [761], Commissariat Series, Aug. 27, 1846, p. 24.

129 **Mr. Erichsen's purchasing activities:** Trevelyan to Routh, Corr. [761], Commissariat Series, Aug. 28, 1846, p. 25; Trevelyan to Routh [761], Sept. 8, p. 54; Trevelyan to Routh, [761], Sept. 22, pp. 83–84; Erichsen, Returns for August and September 1846, [761], p. 103; little towns along the Rhine: Trevelyan to Routh, Corr. [761], Sept. 8, 1846, p. 54.

130 **Sligo depot under siege:** Donnelly, "The Administration of Relief 1846–47," in *A New History of Ireland*, vol. 5; demand for relief in Cork: *Cork Constitution*, Sept. 29, 1846; "very large orders": Trevelyan to Routh, Corr. [761], Sept. 29, 1846, p. 98; Cork merchants Hall and Murphy: Cormac O'Grada, *Black '47 and Beyond* (2000), pp. 124–46; price tipping point into famine: Donnelly, "Adminstration of Relief," p. 298; Irish importers second rate: Assistant Commissary Officer Milliken to Trevelyan, to Routh, Corr. [761], Dec. 8, 1846, p. 344.

131 **neglected harvest:** Routh to Trevelyan, Corr. [761], Commissariat Series, Sept. 9, 1846, p. 55, Skibbereen demonstration: *The Nation*, Sept. 12, 1846.

131 **relief committee charges for corn:** O'Cathaoir, *Famine Diary*, p. 67; report of Cork Constabulary officer: ibid., p. 68. Eviction of Thomas Brien, *The Nation*, Oct. 10, 1846.

132 **break-in at Cork workhouse:** *Cork Southern Reporter*, Oct. 15, 1846; Fermanagh workhouse: Desmond McCabe and Cormac O'Grada, Destitution and Relief . . . during the Great Famine, unpublished manuscript, p. 10.

132   **"The whole country is expecting miracles":** Routh to Trevelyan, Corr. [761], Commissariat Series, Sept. 17, 1846, p. 79.

132–33   **Mrs. Smith returns home:** E. Smith, *Irish Jounals*, pp. 100–104.

Eight: The Mandate of Heaven

134–36   **voyage of *Skibbereen Perseverance*:** William Makepeace Thackeray, "The Irish Sketchbook," in Cornelius Kelly, ed., *The Grand Tour of Cork* (2003), pp. 122, 126, 127; profile of prefamine southwest Cork: D. McCarthy, "Statement of Present Condition of Skibbereen Poor Law Union," Feb. 1, 1834; Inglis, *Ireland*, p. 29.

136–37   **great distress in southwest Cork:** Beamish to Trevelyan, Thomas letter enclosed, Corr. [761], Commissariat Series, Aug. 24, 1846, p. 28.

137–38   **crisis in Skibbereen in mid-September:** Rev. E. Spring to Hughes, Corr. [761], Commissariat Series, Sept. 18, 1846, p. 86; the relief committee of Kilfaunabeg and Kilacabra to Commissary Hughes, Corr. [761], Commissariat Series, Sept. 18, 1846, p. 87; meetings of same committee at Leap police barracks, Corr. [761], Commissariat Series, Sept. 18, 1846, p. 87; Hughes to Routh, Corr. [761], Sept. 20, 1846, p. 86; Routh to Hughes, Corr. [761], Commissariat Series, Sept. 23, p. 86. "This doomed people": A. M. Sullivan, *New Ireland* (1878), p. 59; "If we go on at this rate": Trevelyan to Routh, Corr. [761], Commissariat Series, Sept. 20, 1846, p. 81; Treasury Minute, Corr. [761], Commissariat Series, Aug. 31, 1846, p. 65.

139–40   **depots under assault:** Routh to Trevelyan, [761], Commissariat Series, Sept. 4, 1846, p. 43; Routh to Trevelyan, Corr. [761], Commissariat Series, Sept. 15, 1846, p. 76; Moore to Inspector General, Coast Guard, Corr. [761], Commissariat Series, Aug. 18, 1846, p. 9.

140   **applications for depots from 15 to 17 October:** Corr. [761], Commissariat Series, p. 179.

141   **"Deaths innumerable":** *The Nation*, Oct. 17, 1846; Clare gunman: copy of letter, postmarked from Six Mile Bridge, printed in *The Freeman's Journal*, Oct. 4, 1846; Earl of Huntingdon: *Cork Southern Reporter*, Sept. 29, 1846.

141   **Lord George Bentinck:** *The Times* covered the fête at the shire in depth, Sept. 28, 1846.

142   **riot in Youghal:** *Cork Examiner*, Sept. 18, 1846.

142   **"Och! Paddy, my honey":** *Punch*, reprinted in *The Times*, Dec. 17, 1846.

143   **Russell orders reinforcements to Ireland:** Gooch, ed., *Later Correspondence of Lord John Russell*, Russell to Viceroy Bessborough, Oct. 15, 1846, p. 154.

143   **Routh warns about inflammatory effect of exports:** Routh to Trevelyan, Corr. [761], Commissariat Series, Sept. 28, 1846, p. 96; Routh issues second warning: Corr. [761], Commissariat Series, Sept. 29, 1846, p. 97; Trevelyan responds to Routh, Corr. [761], Commissariat Series, Oct. 2, 1846, pp. 107–8.

143   **Irish imports and exports:** Austin Bourke, "The Irish Grain Trade," *Irish Historical Studies*, vol. 78 (Sept. 1976), p. 165.

144   **economic errors of Russell government:** Prest, *Lord John Russell*, pp. 246–47.

144–45   **changes in landscape of Castlefarm road:** P. Fitzgerald, *History and Topography of Limerick*, vol. 1 (1827), pp. 404–6.

145–46   **Flight of Mr. Kearney:** Inglis to Walker: Correspondence from July 1846 to January 1847 relating to measures adopted for the relief of distress in Ireland, Board of Works Series [764], Sept. 29, 1846, p. 94 (reader's note: this number designates a new collection of Board correspondence which will heretofore be referred to as the Board Series); same to same, Corr. [764], Board Series, Sept. 30, 1846, p. 95; Kearney to Griffith, Corr. [764], Board Series, Oct. 1, 1846, p. 115.

146   **"Out of a population of 11,000":** *Cork Southern Reporter*, Oct. 12, 1846.

146   **response of Irish press to lack of employment:** Griffiths, "The Irish Board of Works in the Famine Years," p. 645.

146   **personnel situation at Board of Works:** Memorandum from Commissioner of Public Works to Treasury, Corr. [761], Board Series, Oct. 10, 1846, pp. 107–8.

147   **violence in Tralee:** *The Nation*, Oct. 15, 1846; work riot in Dungarvan, *The Freeman's Journal*, Sept. 22, 1846.

147   **increase in public works labor force from end of September to end of October 1846:** Commissioners of Public Works to Lords of Treasury, Corr. [764], Board Series, Nov. 12, 1846, pp. 195, 344.

147   **shortage of implements:** Walker to Trevelyan, Corr. [764], Board Series, Oct. 21, 1846, p. 160. See also Corr. [764], Board Series, pp. 218–20; need for silver, Treasury Minute, Sept. 1, p. 65.

148   **range of pay under the piece-rate system:** To Board of Works officer Joseph S. Walker, Instructions of Task Work and Wages, Corr. [764], Board Series, pp. 139–40.

148   **laborers return home rather than accept piece-rate system:** *Cork Southern Reporter*, Oct. 1, 1846.

148   **"I have a wife and nine children":** *The Nation*, Oct. 3, 1846; Mr. Molloy to Captain Gordon, Corr. [764], Board Series, Aug. 31, 1846, p. 71.

148–49 **"the people are barely able to support life":** *Cork Southern Reporter*, Sept. 29, 1846.

149   **Ennis men dressed in ladies' hats:** Report of John Hill, Corr. [764], Board Series, Oct. 29, 1846, p. 156; Board officer Andrews dragged from horse: Report of George Andrews, Corr. [764], Board Series, Oct. 27, 1846, p. 156.

149   **"No one but a person on the spot":** Jones to Trevelyan, Corr. [764], Board Series, Nov. 3, 1846, p. 162.

149   **"At the hour of half past eight this morning":** Stephens to Walker, Corr. [764], Board Series, Nov. 2, 1846, p. 161. Colonel Jones's publicity campaign: Trevelyan to Jones, Corr. [746], Board Series, Oct. 14, 1846, p. 140; Griffith, "The Irish Board of Works in the Famine Years," *Hansard*, vol. 13 (1970), pp. 645–46.

150   **shilling poll tax:** *The Times*, Aug. 17, 1846.

150–51 **controversy over Labor Rate Act:** Black, *Economic Thought and the Irish Question*, pp. 112–17; Dorothy Howell Smith, *Duncannon* (a biography of Lord Bessborough) (1992), pp. 292–99; Prest, *Lord John Russell*, pp. 241–45; Wood to Monteagle, Sept. 27, 1846; Wood to Monteagle, Oct. 13, 14, 1846, Monteagle Papers, National Library of Ireland; Labouchere to Russell, Gooch, ed., *Later Correspondence of Lord John Russell*, p. 143; petitions of gentry: *Cork Examiner*, Sept. 16, 1846; *The Freeman's Journal*, Sept. 25, 1846.

154   **pervasive influence of Providential thinking:** Hilton, *Age of Atonement: The Influence of Evangelicalism on Social and Economic Thought, 1785–1865* (1988), pp. 1–30.

154   **"The blacks have a proverb":** Bew, *Ireland*, p. 204.

154   **Trevelyan and Wood's view of the blight as a call for "salutary" change:** Gray, *Famine, Land and Politics*, pp. 232–36. The section in this book on the relation-

ship between famine policy and Moralism is based on the work of Professor Gray, who has done a penetrating study of the subject. Notes Gray: "For Wood, Trevelyan and other adherents of moralist discourse alleviating the famine-related sufferings of individuals could never be the prime concern of government, particularly, if it impeded the necessary inducements of self help" (p. 232).

155 **size and influence of *The Times*:** Donald Read, *Peel and the Victorians* (1987), pp. 36–37; Leslie Williams, *Daniel O'Connell, the British Press and the Irish Famine* (2003), pp. 8–10.

155 **"There are times":** *The Times*, Jan. 6, 1847; "An island, a social state, a race is to be changed": *The Times*, Oct. 7, 1846.

156 **role of *The Economist* in famine and motto of founder:** R. D. Edwards, "The Pursuit of Reason," *The Economist, 1843–1993* (1995), pp. 38–45; *The Times*, Jan. 30, 1847.

156 ***The Economist* attacks relief policy and Mr. Hewetson:** Aug. 22, 1846; "before [Smith] wrote": *The Economist*, Sept. 10, 1846.

156–57 **Lord Shaftesbury:** Bew, *Ireland*, p. 183.

158 **applications for public works funds:** Commissioners of Public Works to Lords of the Treasury, Corr. [764], Board Series, pp. 107–8.

Nine: A Sermon for Ireland

159 **description of pre-famine Killorglin:** Inglis, *Ireland in 1834*, p. 133; J. Kohl, *Travels in Ireland* (1843), p. 123; Samuel Lewis, *A Topographical Dictionary of Ireland* (1837), pp. 41, 44, 63, 152.

159–60 **account of Mr. Hewetson's inspection tour:** Hewetson to Trevelyan, Corr. [761], Commissariat Series, Sept. 29, 1846, p. 114.

161 **"Give us food":** *Belfast Vindicator*, Oct. 3, 1846; Jones to Trevelyan, Corr. [764], Board Series, Oct. 28, 1846, p. 154.

161 **crisis in food supply:** For weekly statements of provisions in depots, see Trevelyan to Routh, Corr. [761], Commissariat Series, Oct. 7, 1846, p. 127; Routh to Trevelyan, Oct. 10, 1846; p. 142, Routh to Ibbetson, Oct. 9, 1846, p. 145.

161 **food supplies en route:** Routh to Trevelyan, Corr. [761], Commissariat Series, Oct. 13, 1846, p. 155.

161 **"We foresaw this":** *Cork Southern Reporter*, Sept. 29, 1846.

162 **revenues of Cork merchants:** Hewetson to Trevelyan, Corr. [761], Commissariat Series, Dec. 30, 1846, p. 439.

162 **Mr. Hall purchases maize:** Cormac O'Grada, *Black '47 and Beyond*, p. 144; merchant Russell raises prices: Hewetson to Trevelyan, Corr. [761], Commissariat Series, Nov. 18, 1846, p. 278.

162 **Routh's defense of free trade and attack on him:** *Clare Journal*, reprinted in *The Times*, Oct. 2, 1846; visit of Achill delegation: *The Nation*, Oct. 17, 1846; for Routh's version of the encounter with Monahan, see Routh to Trevelyan, Corr. [761], Commissariat Series, Nov. 18, 1846, pp. 277–78.

163 **rebellion among depot officers:** Mr. Wood in Woodham-Smith, *The Great Hunger*, p. 139; Dobree to Trevelyan, Corr. [761], Commissariat Series, Oct. 12, 1846, pp. 153–54; Routh to Lord Sligo, Oct. 14, 1846, p. 160.

163 **death of McKennedy:** Report of H. A. Gordon, Corr. [764], Board Series, Nov. 9, 1846, 219–20.

163–64 **disturbances in Skibbereen and Galway City:** *The Times*, Oct. 9–10, 1846.

164   **price rise in Cork:** Relief Officer Cummins to Trevelyan, Corr. [761], Commissariat Series, Oct. 28, 1846, p. 206.

164   **demand for depots:** City of Cork to Lords of Treasury, Corr. [761], Commissariat Series, Oct. 6, 1846, p. 128; depot applications Oct. 8 to 10, Oct. 12 to 14, 1846 [761], Commissariat Series, pp 139, 141.

164   **protest of Mr. Johns:** Johns to Routh, Corr. [761], Commissariat Series, Oct. 3, 1846, p. 143.

165   **Mr. Trevelyan leaves home:** Haines, *Charles Trevelyan and the Great Irish Famine*, p. 253.

165   **relief plan flaw:** N. Cummins to Trevelyan, Corr. [761], Commissariat Series, Oct. 26, 1846, p. 199.

165–66   **changes in relief plan:** Treasury Minutes, Corr. [761], Commissariat Series, Aug. 25, 1846, p. 19; Mr. Ward to Trevelyan, Corr. [761], Commissariat Series, Aug. 25, 1846, p. 19; Larcom to Trevelyan, Corr. [761], Commissariat Series, Oct. 6, 1846, p. 122; Dobree to Routh, Corr. [761], Commissariat Series, Oct. 8, 1846, p. 147; Ibbetson to Trevelyan, Corr. [761], Commissariat Series, Nov. 2, 1846, p. 215; Erichsen to Trevelyan, Corr. [761], Commissariat Series, Nov. 3, 1846, p. 224.

167   **recipe for unground corn:** Hewetson to Trevelyan, Corr. [761], Commissariat Series, Oct. 5, 1846, p. 117.

167–68   **hand mills:** Traill to Trevelyan, Corr. [761], Commissariat Series, Oct. 2, 1846, p. 109; Trevelyan to Melvill, Corr. [761], Commissariat Series, Oct. 17, 1846, p. 112; Oct. 9, 1846, p. 111; Henderson to Trevelyan, Corr. [761], Commissariat Series, Oct. 10, 1846, p. 110; Monteagle to Trevelyan, Corr. [761], Commissariat Series, Oct. 10, 1846, p. 110; Trevelyan to Henderson, Corr. [761], Commissariat Series, Oct. 20, 1846, p. 110; Trevelyan to Routh, Corr. [761], Commissariat Series, Nov. 18, 1846, p. 273; Mann to Trevelyan, Corr. [761], Commissariat Series, Nov. 16, 1846, p. 274.

168   **Scotland-first policy:** Trevelyan to Routh, Corr. [761], Commissariat Series, Nov. 5, 1846, p. 226.

168–69   **delivery of food to Ireland:** *The Times*, Nov. 20, 1846; food prices in Cork: Routh to Trevelyan, Corr. [761], Commissariat Series, Dec. 1, 1846, p. 326; demonstration in Cork, *The Nation*, Nov. 28, 1846.

169   **deaths in Skibbereen workhouse:** Woodham-Smith, *The Great Hunger*, pp. 141–42; deaths of Thomas Mollone and Mary Byrne, O'Cathaoir, *Famine Diary*, p. 84; squalid nature of death in Ballina, *The Times*, Dec. 24, 1846.

169–70   **Ireland becomes a bloodlands:** armed men roam countryside, *Tipperary Constitution*, Nov. 15, 1846; slaughter of cattle: *The Times*, Oct. 28, 1846; pillage of bake shops in Kinsale: *Cork Southern Reporter*, reprinted in *The Times*, Nov. 4, 1846; attack on large farmers: *Waterford Chronicle*, reprinted in *The Times*, Oct. 7, 1846; public works laborers on hill cutting: Hill to Walker, Corr. exp. [764], Board Series, Oct. 21, 1846, p. 152; speech of Father Hardiman: *The Times*, Oct. 29, 1846.

170   **collapse of Irish economy:** Transactions of the Central Relief Committee of the Society of Friends during the Famine in Ireland, 1846 and 1847, 1852, National Library of Ireland, p. 53.

171   **lack of planting:** Hughes to Routh, Corr. [761], Commissariat Series, Nov. 8, 1846, p. 186; bank deposits: Douglas to Routh, Corr. [761], Commissariat Series, Nov. 26, 1846, p. 330. Normally, Irish bank deposits averaged £300 a week; in November 1846, Douglas found the rate had doubled, to £600 per week.

171   **increase in public works employment:** Corr. [764], Board of Works Series, p.

486; peasantry still in need of work: *The Freeman's Journal*, Nov. 10, 25, 1846; report of Captain Stirling, Corr. exp., Board Series, Dec. 5, 1846, p. 390.

172   **"The landlords are frightened":** Jones to Trevelyan, Corr. exp. [764], Board of Works Series, Oct. 28, 1846, p. 154.

172   **average wage of public works laborer:** Kinealy, *This Great Calamity*, p. 95.

172–73   **collapse in workhouses during the great famine:** Timothy Guinnane and Cormac O'Grada, Mortality in the North Dublin Workhouse, destitution, human agency and relief... during the great famine, unpublished paper, 2008, p. 12; *The Nation*, Dec. 17, 1845; Desmond McCabe and Cormac O'Grada, Destitution and Relief... during the Great Famine, unpublished manuscript, pp. 12–14.

174–75   **fall of Daniel O'Connell:** Macdonagh, *The Emancipist*, pp. 303–9.

Ten: Snow

176   **morning of November 29:** E. Smith, *Irish Journals*, pp. 106–7.

177   **story of Bridie Sheain:** O'Grada, *Black '47 and Beyond*, p. 201.

177   **coffins:** Des Cowman, *The Famine in Waterford* (1995), pp. 161–63; *The Nation*, Dec. 12, 1846.

178   **breakdown in social fabric:** *Cork Southern Reporter*, Jan. 5, 1847; *Cork Examiner*, Jan. 6, 1847.

178   **public nakedness:** Count de Strzelecki, Report of the British Association Report for the Relief of Extreme Distress... [in] the Remote Parishes of Ireland and Scotland, Appendix A [1849], pp. 92–93; *The Freeman's Journal*, Jan. 26, 1847; shipments of Irish clothing and hair: Robert Scally, *The End of Hidden Ireland: Rebellion, Famine and Emigration* (1995), p. 181.

179   **animal die-offs:** Dobree to Routh, Corr. [796], Commissariat Series, Feb. 13, 1847, p. 122.

179   **two young women and American visitor:** Nicholson, *Annals of the Famine in Ireland* (1851), p. 44.

179   **food supply before depots open:** Routh to Trevelyan, Corr. [761], Commissariat Series, Dec. 16, 1846, p. 379; 8,000 tons consumed in two months: Trevelyan to Routh, Corr. [761], Dec. 18, 1846, p. 381. For discussion of role of Navigation Acts in relief policy, see also Gray, *Famine, Land and Politics*, pp. 250–52.

179–80   **shipping shortage:** Routh to Trevelyan, Corr. [761], Commissariat Series, Dec. 16, 1846, p. 379.

180   **"The people are starving":** Wynne to Walker, Correspondence from January to March 1847 [797], Board Series, Jan. 12, 1847, p. 7.

180   **Hill sells food below market price:** Lord George Hill, RLFC3/2/7; the file contains several of the protests Hill made to the Relief Commission about its market price policy.

180   **workhouse rebellion and subsequent impoverishment:** Kinealy, *This Great Calamity*, pp. 106–9; Patrick Hickey, "Famine in the Skibbereen Poor Law Union," in *Famine* (1997), *The Great Irish Famine*, C. Poirteir, ed. (1997), pp. 186–90; George Nicholls, *A History of the Irish Poor Law* (1854), pp. 323–26.

181   **Twisleton warns Home Office of workhouses failing:** Twisleton to Gray: Copies or Extracts Relating to Union Workhouses [766], Dec. 26, 1846, pp. 17–18.

181   **Circular 38, Board of Works, Relief Department, Dec. 9; Jones to Trevelyan, Corr. [764], Board Series, Dec. 19, 1846, p. 400; "no government could tolerate such a measure":** Gooch, *Later Correspondence of Lord John Russell*: Russell to Bessborough, Dec. 17, 1846, p. 165; "paying a man for the ordinary cultivation

of his own land": Wood to Labouchere, Dec. 16, 1846, quoted in Gray, *Famine, Land and Politics*, p. 250.

182   **Bessborough's indiscretions:** Lincoln to Peel, Sir Robert Peel from His Private Correspondence (1899), C. S. Parker, ed., Nov. 17, 1846, pp. 465–66.

182   **December rise in Board of Works employment:** Commissioners of Public Works to the Lords of Treasury in Corr. [764], Board of Works Series, p. 344.

183   **inquest of James Byrne:** O'Rourke, *History of the Great Irish Famine of 1847* (3rd ed., 1902), pp. 93–94; condition of laborers: *Cork Examiner*, Jan. 1 and Jan. 6, 1847; inadequacy of public works pay: Jones to Trevelyan, Corr. exp. [797], Board of Works Series, Jan. 18, 1847, p. 17; Skibbereen infirmary: *Cork Southern Reporter*, Dec. 8, 1846.

185–87 **Captain Wynne:** Wynne to Secretary of Board of Works, Corr. exp. [764], Board Series, Dec. 5, 1846, p. 308; Wynne Memorandum, [764], Board Series, Dec. 7, 1846, p. 313; Wynne to Jones, [764], Board Series, Dec. 24, 1846, pp. 434–35; Hennessy to Walker [764], Board Series, Dec. 11, 1846, pp. 341–42; Gamble to Griffith, [764], Board Series, Dec. 7, 1846, pp. 313–14; David Fitzpatrick, "Famine, Entitlements and Seduction: Captain Wynne in Ireland, 1846–51," *English Historical Review*, vol. 110 (1995), pp. 196–216.

188   **change in British attitudes:** Eyewitness accounts of Irish suffering, such as Lord Dufferin's "Narrative of a Journey from Oxford to Skibbereen" and William Bennett's "Narrative of a Recent Journey of Six Weeks in Ireland" (1847), had a powerful impact in Britain, as did the writings of Quaker visitors like James Hack Tuke and William Forster. See also Mr. Trevelyan's *The Irish Crisis* for further details on outpouring of sentiment for Ireland.

189–90 **the journey of the Forsters:** *Transactions of Central Relief Committee of the Society of Friends During the Famine*, pp. 96–97, 150, 152, 153, 155; see also Helen Hatton, *The Largest Amount of Good: Quaker Relief in Ireland 1654–1921* (1993), pp. 34–35, 90.

190   **description of Cork city:** Cummins to Trevelyan, Corr. exp. [761], Commissariat Series, Dec. 6, 1846, p. 366; *Fraser's Magazine*, April 1847, pp. 497–99.

191   **description of Skibbereen:** *Cork Examiner*, Dec. 29, 1846; Jan. 1 and 6, 1847; death estimates in Skibbereen: *Cork Examiner*, Jan. 6, 1847; Inglis to Hewetson, Corr. [761], Commissariat Series, Dec. 21, 1846, p. 430; Lord Dufferin, "Narrative of a Journey from Oxford to Skibbereen in the Year of the Famine" (1847). See also Patrick Hickey, "Famine in the Skibbereen Poor Law Union," pp. 187–89.

191–92 **meeting of Skibbereen Board of Guardians:** *Cork Southern Reporter*, Dec. 8, 1846.

192   **Trevelyan reluctant to aid Skibbereen:** Trevelyan to Routh, Corr. [761], Commissariat Series, Dec. 3, 1846, p. 327; same to same [761], Dec. 18, 1846, pp. 378–79; Trevelyan to Jones, Corr. exp. [764], Board Series, Dec. 4. 1846, p. 301; Pinchin to Jones, [764], Board Series, Dec. 10, 1846; Jones to Trevelyan [764], Board Series, Dec. 16, 1846, p. 402; Walker to Redington [764], Board Series, Dec. 15, 1846, p. 401.

192   **value of 1846 money:** measuring worth (of old money); according to the Economic History Association, 10 pounds in 2010 money is worth 1,070 pounds in 1846 money, roughly a multiplier of 100, eh.net.

192–93 **food supply in Skibbereen:** Hickey, "Famine in the Skibbereen Union," p. 188; wealth of Skibbereen gentry: Routh to Trevelyan, Corr. [761], Commissariat Series, Jan. 7, 1847, p. 458.

193 **visit to South Reen:** *The Times*, Dec. 24, 1846.
194 **Trevelyan refuses to supply eastern Ireland:** Trevelyan to Routh, Corr. [761], Commissariat Series, Dec. 22, 1896, p. 403; Trevelyan to Routh [761], Commissariat Series, Dec. 24, 1846, p. 408.
195 **Cummins to Duke of Wellington:** *The Times*, Dec. 24, 1846.
195 **Snow "was falling":** James Joyce, "The Dead," in *Dubliners* (2006), p. 225.

Eleven: The Queen's Speech

196–97 **description of opening day of Parliament:** *Cork Southern Reporter*, Jan. 26, 1847; *The Times*, Jan. 20, 1847.
198 **queen's speech:** Hansard, vol. 89, Jan. 19, 1847, pp. 1–4.
198–99 **Russell outlines new relief plan:** *Hansard*, vol. 89, Jan. 25, 1847, pp. 423–52.
199 **Poor Law Extension Act:** 10th and 11th Vict. Cap. 90; Nicholls, *History of the Irish Poor Law* (1856), pp. 330–33; General Order of the Poor Law Commissioners for Regulating Outdoor Relief, January 1, 1847.
199 **"The locusts will devour the land":** Graham, quoted in Gray, *Famine, Land and Politics*, p. 129.
199 **forgiveness of debt:** J. Russell, *Hansard*, vol. 89, Jan. 25, 1847, p. 437.
199 **"I don't know what will become of us":** E. Smith: *Irish Journals*, Jan. 21, 1847, p. 125.
199–200 **Rotunda meeting of Irish party:** O'Rourke, *History of the Great Irish Famine of 1847* (1902), pp. 27–28.
200 **"Audacious beggars":** *Liverpool Mercury*, Jan. 1, 1847; Butt on Union: Isaac Butt, *Dublin University Magazine*, vol. 29 (April 1847), p. 514.
200–201 **Bentinck plan:** G. Bentinck, *Hansard*, vol. 89, Feb. 4, 1847, pp. 774–79; Roebuck rebuttal, ibid., pp. 810–15.
201 **Daniel O'Connell speech:** *Hansard*, vol. 89, Feb. 4, 1847, pp. 942–48.
201 **"Help yourselves and Heaven will help you":** J. Russell, *Hansard*, vol. 89, Jan. 25, 1847, p. 452.
201–2 **Asenath Nicholson in the Liberties:** Nicholson, *Annals of the Famine in Ireland* (1851), pp. 36, 42–46.
202 **Trevelyan initiates charity drive:** Trevelyan to Routh, Corr. [761], Dec. 5, 1846, Commissariat Series, p. 332; same to same, Dec. 18, 1846, pp. 379–81; Trevelyan, *The Irish Crisis*, pp. 115–22; see also Gray, *Famine, Land and Politics*, pp. 256–59.
203 **Report of the British Association for the Relief of the Extreme Distress, (1849) National Library of Ireland, p. 7; sum of donations:** Trevelyan, *The Irish Crisis*, London (1848), pp. 126–30.
203 **"Our resources are at present far too scanty":** Hewetson to Rev. J. O. Sullivan, Corr. [761], Commissariat Series, Jan. 16, 1847, pp. 124–25; Carrickbeg: Douglas to Routh, Corr. [761], Commissariat Series, Jan. 28, 1847, pp. 41–42.
204 **Count de Strzelecki:** *Australian Dictionary of Biography*, vol. 2, adb.anu.edu.au; "No pen can describe": de Strzelecki, Report of British Association, London, 1849, p. 20.
204 **mother's nipple bitten off:** *Manchester Guardian*, March 14, 1847; "Worse than dead," Nicholson, *Annals of the Famine in Ireland*, p. 179.
204 **"It is difficult to persuade a starving population":** Kevin Nowlan, *The Politics of Repeal* (1975), p. 122.
205–6 **Galway storm:** *The Freeman's Journal*, Jan. 29, 1847.
206 **description of Skull:** Lewis, *A Topographical Dictionary of Ireland*, p. 560,

books.google.com; scenes witnessed by Caffin: Caffin to Hamilton, Corr. [796], Commissariat Series, Feb. 15, 1847, p. 163.

208   **towns overwhelmed by country people:** Hunt to Inspector General, Corr. [796], Commissariat Series, Jan. 7, 1847, p. 10; attack in Cahersiveen: Hewetson to Routh, Corr. [761], Commissariat Series, p. 362.

208   **"Even in the depths of a winter":** *Dublin Evening Post*, Feb. 16, 1847.

208   **Brougham speech on emigration:** *Hansard*, vol. 89, Feb. 1, 1847, pp. 612–13.

208   **"sending men from starving in Skibbereen":** Russell to Bessborough, Dec. 29, 1846; Canada becoming a Catholic country: Colonial Secretary Gray to Russell, Sept. 4, 1848. Both letters are quoted in Prest, *Lord John Russell*, p. 249.

209   **increase in public works employment:** Nicholls, *History of the Irish Poor Law*, p. 316.

209   **relief committees still hiring:** Report of Colonel Douglas, Corr. [797], Board Series, Jan. 28, 1847, p. 41; report of Captain Bull, Corr. [797], Board Series, Feb. 20, 1847, p. 271; report of Captain Layard, Corr. [797], Board Series, Feb. 6, 1847, p. 270; Routh to Trevelyan, Corr. [761], Commissariat Series, Dec. 9, 1846, p. 352; report of Sir Thomas Ross, Corr. [797], Board Series, Feb. 20, 1847.

209–11 **state of workhouses:** Black, *Economic Thought and the Irish Question*, p. 112; First Report of Relief Commissioners [799], pp. 6, 8, 10; Second Report of Relief Commissioners, May 15, 1847 [819], pp. 4–5; report from Skibbereen, Corr. [797], Board Series, Mar. 4, 1847; Erichsen to Trevelyan, Corr. [796], Commissariat Series, Mar. 3, 1847, p. 221; *The Freeman's Journal*, Jan. 16 and 20, 1847; McCabe and O'Grada, "Destitution, Human Agency and Relief," p. 15; Bentinck, *Hansard*, vol. 90, March 11, 1847, p. 1149; Nicholls, *The Irish Poor Law*, p. 329; Colonel Stokes to Trevelyan, Corr. [797], Board Series, Feb. 6, 1847, p. 94; Brown to Pigot, Corr. [796], Commissariat Series, Mar. 1, 1847, p. 222; Hewetson to Trevelyan, Corr. [761], Commissariat Series, Dec. 19, 1846, p. 395.

212–13 **mass evictions:** *The Nation*, Jan. 16, 1847; *Manchester Guardian*, Feb. 1, 1847; Transactions [Quaker report], Richard Bennett, pp. 163–64.

214   **Encumbered Estates Act:** Gray, *Famine, Land and Politics*, pp. 196–201.

214   **change in Highland gentry:** T. M. Devine, *The Great Highland Famine* (1988), pp. 150–52.

Twelve: Pestilence

215   **"fate opened her book":** John Callanan, Appendix to the Fever report on Munster, *Dublin Quarterly Journal of Medical Science* (hereafter, *DQJ*), vol. 7, Feb. and May 1849, p. 270.

215   **mortality in famine of 1740–1741:** Geary, "Famine, Fever and Bloody Flux," p. 77, and David Dickson, "The Other Great Irish Famine," p. 54, in Poirteir, ed., *The Great Irish Famine* (1995). For the epidemiological work of Drs. Cheney and Barker, see Geary, *Famine, Fever and Bloody Flux*, p. 80.

216   **fever facilities in workhouses:** Peter Froggatt, "The Response of the Medical Profession to the Great Famine" in *Famine: The Irish Experience, 900–1900*, ed. Margeret Crawford (1989), p. 137. Nicholls, *The History of the Irish Poor Law*, pp. 125–26.

217   **absence of fever in the summer of 1846:** William MacArthur, "Medical History of the Famine," in *The Great Famine: Studies in Irish History* (1977), ed. R. D. Edwards and T. D. Williams, p. 290; 1846 outbreaks in Cork, Galway, and Leitrim: *DQJ*, vol. 7, pp. 68–70, 355; "Nothing remarkable": *DQJ*, vol. 8, p. 1; "Fate opened her book": *DQJ*, Callanan, p. 270.

217 **study of admissions to Dublin fever hospitals:** MacArthur, "Medical History of the Famine," in *The Great Famine*, p. 290.

217 **Dublin castle relies on "ordinary law":** Henry Labouchere, *Hansard*, vol. 89, Jan. 31, 1847, p. 463.

217 **Elihu Burritt:** *A Journal of a Visit of Three Days to Skibbereen and Its Neighborhood* (1847), pp. 1–23; soup line, ibid., p. 7; visit to cemetery waterhouse, ibid., p. 8, www.gutenberg.org.

218 **spread of fever in winter and spring of 1847:** *DQJ*, vol. 7, pp. 341, 347; *DQJ*, vol. 8, pp. 1, 4, 6, 7, 37, 47, 68, 70.

218 **"Previous to [the] outbreak":** Dr. Roache, *DQJ*, vol. 8, p. 1.

218 **confusion in distinguishing between typhus and relapsing fever:** Two years after the epidemic, Henry Kennedy, a Dublin physician, still believed the two types of famine fever were simply different faces of the same disease. In his *DQJ* questionnaire, Kennedy wrote an exquisitely detailed clinical profile of both diseases: "All my observations go to support the idea that relapsing fever and typhus fever are but part and parcel of the same disease" (*DQJ*, vol. 7, p. 53).

218 **symptoms of typhus:** *DQJ*, vol. 8, pp. 292, 294, 295; Dr. Cavet stricken with typhus: *DQJ*, vol. 8, p. 100.

219 **observations of Dr. Lynch on relapsing fever:** *DQJ*, vol. 8, pp. 305–6.

219 **Dominick John Corrigan and malnutrition theory:** Geary, "Famine, Fever and Bloody Flux," p. 75.

219–20 **Irish physicians find hunger theory insufficient:** Geary, "Famine, Fever, and Bloody Flux," p. 75; Dr. Lalor's observation about the connection between social disorder and epidemic fever: *DQJ*, vol. 8, p. 33.

220 **lice:** National Public Health Pesticide Applicator Training Manual; W. MacArthur, "Medical History of the Famine," in *Great Famine, Studies in Irish History* (1957), R. D. Edwards and T. D. Williams, eds., p. 265.

220 **"gives up the ghost":** Hans Zinsser, *Rats, Lice and History* (1996), p. 168.

220 *Rickettsiae* **gravitate to skin cells:** W. MacArthur, "Medical History of the Famine," in *Great Famine*, p. 265; effect on blood vessels in brain, Dr. Pemberton, *DQJ*, vol. 8, p. 371; *frabhras dubh*, MacArthur, "Medical History of the Famine," p. 266; typhus mortality, Medline Plus (online service); role of *Rickettsia* in relapsing fever: E. B Hayes, D. T. Dennis, "Relapsing Fever," in *Harrison's Principles of Internal Medicine*, D. L. Kasper et al., eds. (2004), pp. 991–95; "Tick Borne Relapsing Fever," U.S. Centers for Disease Control, cdcinfo@cdc.gov.

221 **"Nothing was more common":** Dr. French, *DQJ*, vol. 8, p. 389.

221 **previous outbreaks of relapsing fever:** *DQJ*, vol. 8, p. 43; MacArthur, "Medical History of the Famine," p. 268.

222 **"Each class was liable to a particular form [of fever]":** Thomas Kehoe, *DQJ*, vol. 8, p. 103.

222 **class differences in two types of fever:** Thomas Kehoe, *DQJ*, vol. 8, p. 103.

222 **tax collector Driscoll:** *The Freeman's Journal*, Jan. 21, 1847; mortality rate in Skull: *DQJ*, vol. 8, p. 101.

222 **three deaths connected to Galway gentleman:** *DQJ*, vol. 8, p. 390; peasants take in strangers: *DQJ*, vol. VIII, p. 342.

223 **social breakdown and disease:** Geary, "Famine, Fever and Bloody Flux," pp. 79–80, 82; MacArthur, "Medical History of the Famine," p. 270.

223 **spread of pestilence in Castlebar gaol:** Dr. Dillion, *DQJ*, vol. 8, p. 366.

224 **deaths of caregivers:** *DQJ*, vol. 8, pp. 383, 329, 281; Woodham-Smith, *The Great Hunger*, p. 192.

224 **"I have . . . seen whole families":** Dr. Pemberton, *DQJ*, vol. 8, p. 368.

224 **dysentery:** *DQJ*, vol. 8, p. 348. In his response to the *DQJ* questionnaire Dr. Hunt of County Down noted: "Among the poor dysentery was almost universal and in many instances, most obstinate, often causing ulceration of the intestines, hemorrhage and fatal results."

224–25 **"Patients . . . die by inches":** Dr. Lynch, *DQJ*, vol. 7, p. 401; epidemic dysentery: Dr. Hunter, *DQJ*, vol. 8, pp. 347–49.

225 **most famine death due to disease:** O'Grada, *Ireland's Great Famine*, p. 64.

225 **symptoms of starvation:** "Undernutrition, Symptoms and Signs" in *Merck Manual*, http://www.merckmanuals.com.; edema in Skibbereen: E. Burritt, "A Journal of a Visit of Three Days to Skibbereen and Its Neighborhood," pp. 10–13.

226 **arrival of *Hibernia*:** *New Bedford* (Mass.) *Mercury*, Jan. 20, 1847; description of nineteenth-century Boston: Oscar Handlin, *Boston's Emigrants, 1790–1865* (1941), pp. 1–25.

226 **Archbishop Fitzpatrick's sermon:** *Pilot* (Boston newspaper), Feb. 13, 1847; "The people had known hard times": *History of the Archdiocese of Boston*, by Robert Lord, John Sexton, and Edward Harrington, vol. 2 (1944), pp. 435–36.

227 **Washington rally for Ireland:** *New York Sun*, Feb. 15, 1847.

227–28 **biomedical winter:** *The Morning Chronicle*, Mar. 13, 1847; *DQJ*, vol. 7, pp. 340, 348, 362, 365, 367, 369; *DQJ*, vol. 8, pp. 13, 14n, 270, 280, 281.

228 **"Almost without exception":** Giovanni Boccaccio, *The Decameron*, trans. Rosemary Horrox (2003), pp. 6–9; "painful . . . to observe": de Strzelecki, British Association Report, p. 93; "the instant fever appears": Bishop to Routh, Corr. [796], Commissariat Series, Jan. 27, 1847, p. 39.

228–29 **pestilential state of workhouses :** *DQJ*, vol. 7, pp. 341, 369, 385; vol. 8, pp. 24, 27, 31, 277, 281, 297, 305; MacArthur, "Medical History of the Famine," pp. 294–95.

229 **Board of Health reinstated, construction of 373 fever facilities:** Kinealy, *This Great Calamity*, p. 65.

230 **"Why?" Trevelyan asked:** Woodham-Smith, *The Great Hunger*, p. 201.

230–32 **O'Connell's last days:** Macdonagh, *The Emancipist*, pp. 313–15.

Thirteen: Atonement

233 **Cummins's letter on the state of Ireland:** Cummins to Trevelyan, Corr. [796], Commissariat Series, Feb. 24, 1847, p. 178.

234 **queries about mortality rate:** Smith O'Brien, *Hansard*, vol. 90, Mar. 9, 1847, pp. 1101–3; Mr. Labouchere's reply: *Hansard*, vol. 90, Mar. 11, 1847, p. 1151; Lord George Bentinck: *Hansard*, vol. 91, Mar. 29, 1847, pp. 571–72.

234 **average public works wage of 7½ pence:** Kinealy, *This Great Calamity*, p. 95.

234 **Yankee corn:** Hewetson to Trevelyan, Corr. [796], Commissariat Series, Feb. 7, 1847, p. 97; *The Freeman's Journal*, Mar. 23, 1847.

234 **"Most of the laborers are in debt":** E. Smith, *Irish Journals*, March 9, 1847, p. 132. For a piercing look at the desperate condition of the Irish peasantry in the late winter of 1847, see also Smith's diary entries for Jan. 11, 1847, p. 113, and Jan. 21, 1847, p. 125.

234–36 **biography of General John Burgoyne:** *Oxford Dictionary of National Biography*, oxforddnb.com. Lt. Col. George Wrottsey, *The Life and Correspondence of Field*

Marshal Sir John Burgoyne (1873), pp. 1–80; Labouchere's letter of welcome: Wrottsey, *Life and Correspondence*, p. 453.

236   **Routh says no:** Routh to Trevelyan, Corr. [796], Commissariat Series, Jan. 25, 1847, p. 26; "He consults no one": Richard Griffith to Lord Monteagle, Jan. 6, 1847, Monteagle Papers, National Library of Ireland; "obey any orders": Howell-Smith, *Duncannon*, p. 304. For a fuller catalogue of Routh's failings, see also Woodham-Smith, *The Great Hunger*, p. 173: Bessborough sees Burgoyne as a counterweight to Trevelyan: Howell-Smith, *Duncannon*, pp. 304–6; Trevelyan asks to review Burgoyne's correspondence: Trevelyan to Burgoyne, Corr. [796], Commissariat Series, Mar. 10, 1847, p. 232.

237   **Burgoyne's slowness in establishing soup kitchens:** Donnelly, "The Soup Kitchens," chap. 15, in *The New History of Ireland*, vol. 5 (1989), pp. 308–10.

237   **fourteen tons of documents:** First Report of Relief Commissioners (1847) [799], p. 8; rules governing qualifications for and dispensation of free soup: Appendix to First Report, pp. 12–40.

237–38 **Soyer soup and reactions to it:** Soyer letters to *The Times*, Feb. 10 and 18, 1847; "No Cook," Feb. 22, 1847, Medicus, Feb. 24, 1847; cost of soup and official enthusiasm for Soyer: Julian Strang and Joyce Toomre, "Alexis Soyer and the Irish Famine: Splendid Promises and Abortive Measures," in A. Gribben, ed., *The Great Famine and the Irish Diaspora in America* (1999), p. 72.

239–40 **opening of Soyer soup kitchen on Apr. 5, 1847:** *The Times*, Apr. 7, 1847; *The Morning Chronicle*, Apr. 8, 1847; *The Nation*, Apr. 10, 1847; *The Illustrated London News*, Apr. 17, 1847.

241   **Soyer an artist:** Routh to Trevelyan, Corr. [796], Commissariat Series, Mar. 2, 1847, p. 195.

241   **rise in Irish savings rate:** *The Times*, Mar. 4, 1847.

241   **failure to plant 1847 crops:** Earl of Bessborough to Sir George Grey, Corr. [797], Board Series, Mar. 8, 1847, p. 231; Lieut. Colonel Jones to Trevelyan, Corr. [797], Board Series, Jan. 13, 1847, p. 8; same to same, Jan. 16, 1847; Mr. Griffith to Colonel Jones, Corr. [797], Board Series, Jan. 29, 1847, pp. 30–31; Jones to Trevelyan, Corr. [797], Board Series, Mar. 2, 1847, p. 170; Captain Haymes to Routh, Corr. [796], Commissariat Series, Feb. 9, 1847, pp. 118–19; *The Times*, Mar. 11, 1847; *Manchester Guardian*, Mar. 13, 1847.

241   **increase in public works force:** Commissioners of Public Works to Lords of Treasury, Monthly Report for January (1847), Daily Number of Persons employed on Public Works during week ending 30th January, Corr. [797], Board Series, Feb. 6, 1847, p. 49; same to same, Monthly Report for February (1847), Board Series, Daily Number of Persons employed, etc., Mar. 3, 1847, p. 226. For a full range of employment figures over the 1846–1847 relief season, see Board Series [764], pp. 195, 344, 486.

242   **Mr. Primrose attacked:** Report of W. W. Primrose, Corr. [797], Board Series, Mar. 6, 1847, pp. 217–18.

242   **Russell and the general election:** Prest, *Lord John Russell*, pp. 252–53.

242   **cost of public works employment:** After the first crop failure, £476,000 was spent on job-generating roadwork projects and half the cost was absorbed by the British government. After the second crop failure the public works employment bill rose to £4,848,000 and the borrowers, the Irish gentry, were liable for the entire sum. If the British government had not forgiven half the debt, the entire class could have ended up in the Court of Chancery. That sum amounted to well over a third

of the entire Poor Law valuation of Ireland, 13 million pounds. Kinealy, *This Great Calamity*, p. 91.

242   **March 10 announcement of workforce reduction:** Treasury Minute, 10 March, First Report of Relief Commissioners [799] (1847), pp. 3–5; appeals to not shut down public works, Trevelyan, *The Irish Crisis*, pp. 46–47; only 100 committees in operation by March 26; Routh to Trevelyan, Mar. 10, 1847, in Woodham-Smith, *The Great Hunger*, p. 184; Second Report of Relief Commissioners [819], Mar. 15, 1847, p. 7; overlooked act of kindness: Labouchere, *Hansard*, vol. 91, Mar. 22, 1847, pp. 358–59.

243–44   **Constabulary death report:** O'Cathaoir, *Famine Diary*, p. 108.

244–46   **Armagh's Day of Atonement:** Gray, "National Humiliation and the Great Hunger" in *Irish Historical Studies*, vol. 32 (Nov. 2000), p. 194, "give liberally": ibid., p. 196; Leslie Badham, ibid., p. 202. Observance in Dublin: Gray, *Famine, Land and Politics*, pp. 258–59; Irish churches full: *Dublin Evening News*, Mar. 26, 1846; description of Greenwich, *Daily News*, Mar. 25, 1847; day trippers under London Bridge: *The Morning Chronicle*, Mar. 26, 1847; "Miso-Humbug" and "Not a Fast Man": *The Morning Chronicle*, Mar. 24, 1847; description of ceremonies at London houses of worship: *The Times*, Mar. 25 and 26, 1847. Even by modern standards, *The Times*'s coverage was superb. The March 25 edition of the paper included in-depth reports of the observances held at nearly every major church and synagogue in London.

247   **"One body [is] covered":** *The Freeman's Journal*, July 17, 1847; body parts in Skibbereen graveyard: *The Times*, May 7, 1847; shopkeeper and dead mother: Bartoletti, *Black Potatoes*, p. 68.

247   **English make three promises to themselves:** *Journals of Nassau William Senior, 1860–63*, vol. 1, p. 175.

247   **"the consequence will be a complete revolution in property":** Sir James Graham quoted by Charles Greville in H. Reeve, ed., *The Greville Memoirs: A Journal of the Reign of Queen Victoria*, vol. 3 (1885), pp. 433–34.

247   **Russell's estimate of increase in Irish poor rate:** Prest, *Lord John Russell*, p. 251; divisions in Russell cabinet, lobbying efforts of Irish gentry, and reaction of Lady Palmerston: ibid., p. 252.

248   **"What is to be the End of it?":** *Liverpool Mercury*, Feb. 10, 1847; Irish invasion: *The Times*, Feb. 25, 1847.

248–49   **Mr. Trevelyan explains how Poor Law Extension Act will produce class harmony in Ireland:** Trevelyan, *The Irish Crisis*, pp. 158–59, 162–63, 184–85.

249   **Mr. Labouchere complains that the Poor Law debate keeps going off subject:** *Hansard*, vol. 90, Mar. 8, 1847, p. 1036.

249   **English gentlemen "seemed not to think it beneath them":** Mr. Shaw, *Hansard*, vol. 90, Mar. 12, 1847, pp. 1295–307; Ireland "a monster workhouse": Bateson, *Hansard*, vol. 90, Mar. 12, p. 1285; Gregory clause: Mr. Gregory, *Hansard*, vol. 91, Mar. 29, 1847, pp. 583–86.

250   **52 percent fall in number of small farms:** Miller, *Emigrants and Exiles*, p. 289.

250–51   **Thomas Chalmers and the special Visitation of Providence:** Hilton, *The Age of Atonement*, pp. 109–11.

251   **"commence a salutary revolution":** Trevelyan, *The Irish Crisis*, p. 1; "sometimes harshness is the greatest humanity": *The Times*, Jan. 7, 1847.

251   **farewell party for M. Soyer:** *The Freeman's Journal*, Apr. 17, 1847.

251–52 **further reductions in public works labor force:** On April 10, 1847, the Office of Public Works issued Circular No. 84, ordering a further 10 percent reduction on April 24 and the close of the entire program by May 1, 1847. See Second Report of Relief Commissioners, [819], May 15, 1847, p. 7; County Roscommon relief officer feeding people out of his own pocket: Kinealy, *This Great Calamity*, p. 143.

252 **conditions in workhouses:** Workhouses Ireland [257]; reports made to Board of Health by Medical officers in Cork, Bantry, Lurgan, Mar. 27, 1847, pp. 11, 17, 21.

252 **Smith O'Brien reminds Mr. Labouchere about Lord John's promise:** *Hansard*, vol. 91, Mar. 29, 1847, pp. 583–85.

252–53 **number of soup kitchens established and people served:** Donnelly, "The Soup Kitchens," in *New History of Ireland*, vol. 5, p. 309.

253 **lack of seed and other agricultural supplies:** *The Nation*, Mar. 10, 1847.

Fourteen: "I Shall Arise and Go Now"

254 **state of weather, state of crops:** *The Times*, May 19, 1846.

254 **116,000 emigrated in 1846:.** Macdonagh, "Irish Overseas Emigration During the Famine," in *The Great Famine: Studies in Irish History*, p. 322: emigration in 1847: Miller, *Emigrants and Exiles*, p. 292.

254 **ancient Gaelic-speaking nation flees :** Scally, *The End of Hidden Ireland* (1995), pp. 159–71.

255 **"The Englishman's hand is strong and harsh":** Miller, *Emigrants and Exiles*, p. 251.

255 **"where a mother and father":** *The Nation*, June 13, 1847; "in a few more years": *The Times*, in Miller, *Emigrants and Exiles*, p. 307; "no new light of thought": ibid., p. 299.

255 **landowners send tenants to Canada:** Gerard Moran, *Sending Out Ireland's Poor* (2004), p. 40; Major Mahon: Second Report from the select committee of the House of Lords on colonization from Ireland, [593] (1847–48), p. 202.

256 **James Gormally:** Frank Neal, "Liverpool, the Famine Irish and the Steamship Companies," *Immigrants and Minorities*, vol. 5 (Mar. 1985), p. 36; "beyond all doubt": ibid.

256 **ways emigrants raised fare money:** David Fitzpatrick, "Emigration 1801–70," *New History of Ireland*, vol. 5, pp. 599–600.

256 **"I cannot hold on long":** Annie Prendergast to adult children in Boston, Prendergast papers, Boston College, Dec. 24, 1848; "For the honor of our Lord Jesus Christ": David Fitzpatrick, "Irish Famine Letters to Australia," in *The Hungry Stream*, E. Margaret Crawford, ed. (1997), p. 162; "Pity our hard case": Miller, *Emigrants and Exiles*, p. 298.

256 **decline in Catholic population of Elphin:** Macdonagh, "Irish Emigration During the Famine," p. 321; "Every house on our side": Miller, *Emigrants and Exiles*, p. 300; "Anywhere than here": Macdonagh, "Irish Emigration During the Famine," p. 321; "Every hope is blighted": Miller, *Emigrants and Exiles*, p. 295; "No Tongue can describe": Fr. T. Mathew, Report of select committee of House of Lords on Colonization from Ireland [737] (June 25, 1847), p. 243.

256 **one in three Irishmen die abroad:** Miller, *Emigrants and Exiles*, p. 291.

257 **first sea two out of three Irish emigrants sailed:** Scally, *The End of Hidden Ireland*, p. 184; Liverpool as the bully of the litter, ibid., p. 186; poor quality of Liverpool packets: Neal, "Liverpool, the Famine Irish and the Steamship Companies,"

pp. 28–35; "nine out of ten": ibid., p. 45; voyage of Stewart Redmond: ibid., p. 41; deaths on *Londonderry*, ibid., p. 41.

258–60 **famine-era Liverpool:** Herman Melville, *Redburn* (1849), pp. 200, 211, 223, 238, 256, 260, 288. Though a novel, *Redburn* captures the vivid, rollicking, squalid nature of Liverpool street life in the 1840s better than any nonfiction book I am aware of. Irish emigrants enter Liverpool: ibid., 296, 231; pauper dumping: Select Committee on Poor Removal [396], Testimony of Edward Rushton, p. 358.

261 **"Liverpool perhaps most abounds in":** Melville, *Redburn*, p. 174; scams of dock runners and other land sharks: ibid., pp. 256–60; Macdonagh, *Patterns of Government Growth: Passenger Acts and Their Enforcement* (1961), pp. 22–23, 42–43.

262 **increase in number of Irish on relief in Liverpool:** Neal, "Black '47, Liverpool and the Famine Irish," in *The Hungry Stream*, E. Margaret Crawford, ed., pp. 126–27; "240 from Cork": *Liverpool Mercury*, Mar. 28, 1847.

262–64 **increase in Liverpool poor rate:** Neal, *Sectarian Violence: The Liverpool Experience, 1819–1914* (1988), pp. 126–27; Liverpool death rate: E. Margaret Crawford, "Malignant Maladies," in *The Hungry Stream*, p. 137; "As long as native inhabitants": Neal, "Black '47," in *Hungry Stream*, p. 123; subterranean population, ibid., *Hungry Stream*, p. 123; visit to Vauxhall cellar, Neal, *Sectarian Violence*, p. 84; Lace Street, ibid., Neal, p. 91. "The dead are taken by relatives": *The Times*, Apr. 5, 1847; Bent Street: *Liverpool Mercury*, Mar. 13, 1847; fever morbidity and mortality in Liverpool, Margret Crawford, "Malignant Maladies," in *Hungry Stream*, p. 130.

264 **register general's report on Liverpool:** Neal, *Sectarian Violence*, p. 94; "whose fault is that": *Liverpool Mail*, Nov. 6, 1847.

265–66 **"Liverpool Mirror":** Scally, *The End of Hidden Ireland*, p. 211–16; "in his rags and laughing savagery": Thomas Carlyle, *Chartism* (1839), pp. 28–31; suicide of Patrick Culkin: Neal, *Sectarian Violence*, pp. 92–100.

266 **emigrants' departure from Liverpool:** Edward Laxton, *Famine Ships: The Irish Exodus to America* (1997), p. 236.

267 **"in all the freshness of early summer":** Robert Whyte, *Ocean Plague* (1848), p. 20.

267 **more than 214,000 Irish emigrate to North America in 1847:** Miller, *Emigrants and Exiles*, p. 292.

267 **timber trade and emigrant ships:** William A. Spray, "The Irish Famine Emigrant and the Passenger Trade to North America," in *Fleeing the Famine*, Margaret Mulrooney, ed. (2003), pp. 10–11; "ships of the United States superior": Report of select committee on ship wrecks [567] (1836), p. xi.

268 **testimony of John Griscom and Dudley Mann:** Report of Select Committee of the Senate of the United States on the Sickness and Mortality onboard Emigrant Ships, 33rd Congress, No. 386 (1854), pp. 43, 69.

268 **deaths on the *Sarah and Elizabeth*:** Papers relative to emigration to the British Provinces of North America [50] (1847–48), p. 38.

268 **comparison of Buffalo and Montreal:** Report on the Affairs of North America from the Earl of Durham (1839), vol. 2, pp. 212–13.

269 **Earl Grey assures Parliament that the 1847 emigration season will be a historic success:** *Hansard*, vol. 90, Mar. 15, 1847, pp. 1330–31.

269–70 **entries from Robert Whyte's diary:** Robert Whyte, *Ocean Plague*, pp. 44, 46, 49, 51.

270 **"None of us":** Albert Camus, *The Plague* (1991), p. 181.

271 **"The Black Hole of Calcutta":** Dudley Mann, Select Committee of the Senate of the United States, on the Sickness and Mortality onboard Emigrant Ships. De

Vere testimony; 1854, p. 49. Papers relative to emigration to the British Provinces in North America [932], testimony of S. de Vere, pp. 14–16. The hazards of emigrant travel are particularly well documented in Papers relative to the British Provinces in North America [809] (1847). For further account of perils of emigration, see also First Report: Policy and Operation of Navigation Laws, Select Committee [340], Minutes of House of Lords Evidence, Henry Davidson, Mar. 16, 1848, p. 68; Mark Whitwill, Apr. 7, 1848, p. 241; William Briggs, May 5, 1848, p. 360.

271   **"Stowed away like bales of cotton":** Herman Melville, quoted in Macdonagh, *Patterns of Government Growth*, p. 363.

272   **98,000 to Canada:** Miller, *Emigrants and Exiles*, p. 292.

272   **ice floes in Montreal harbor:** *New York Tribune*, May 6, 1847.

272   **"Next [year], the number of sick":** Dr. George Douglas to Earl of Elgin, Governor General of Canada, Dec. 27, 1847. Douglas was reminding Elgin of a prediction he had made at the end of the 1846 emigration season. The letter appears in a collection of documents and eyewitness accounts of the 1847 season at Grosse Isle, compiled by Marianna O'Gallagher and published as *Eyewitness Grosse Isle* (1995). The Douglas letter is a summary of the 1847 season and will be quoted again in this section. The above quote appears on p. 372 of *Eyewitness Grosse Isle* (referred to hereafter as *Eyewitness*).

272   **Archbishop Joseph Signay:** Circular Letter to All Pastors of the Parishes of Quebec, Feb. 12, 1847 (*Eyewitness*, p. 11).

272   **1832 cholera epidemic:** Donald Mackay, *Flight from Famine* (1991), pp. 135–45.

272–73 *Le Canadien:* April 16, 1847 (*Eyewitness*, p. 15), and Apr. 23, 1847 (*Eyewitness*, p. 25).

273   **"The soldier, the merchant":** *New York Herald*, May 17, 1847.

273   **American restrictions on immigration:** Woodham-Smith, *The Great Hunger*, p. 213.

273   *Le Canadien:* Apr. 28, 1847 (*Eyewitness*, p. 25).

273   **maypole on St. Lawrence:** *New York Tribune*, May 6, 1847.

273   **"With utmost energy [we protest]":** *Le Canadien*, May 12, 1847 (*Eyewitness*, p. 422).

274   **nothing extraordinary being done to prepare Grosse Isle:** Testimony of Dr. Joseph Morin Before the Special Committee to Inquire into the Quarantine Station at Grosse Isle, July 17, 1847 (*Eyewitness*, p. 182); Douglas's medical training: *Eyewitness*, p. 6.

275   **death of Owen Wood:** *Eyewitness*, p. 69.

275   **arrival of ships at Grosse Isle during the early weeks of 1847 emigration season, and morbidity and mortality among passengers:** Papers Relative to Emigration to the British Provinces in North America, 1847–48 [50], Enclosure 1, Dr. Douglas to Earl of Elgin, May 24, 1847, p. 1; Alexander Buchanan (Chief Emigration Agent) to Earl of Elgin, May 29, 1847, pp. 3–4. All citations from enclosure 1 to May 29, 1847, are part of "Papers relative" [50]. Dr. Douglas's Dec. 27, 1847, letter to the Earl of Elgin also provided a detailed account of ship arrivals at Grosse Isle (*Eyewitness*, pp. 373–82).

275–76 **shortages of medical staff and supplies:** Douglas to Elgin, December 27, 1847 (*Eyewitness*, p. 376); Testimony of Captain Boxer, Report of Special Committee to Inquire into the Quarantine Station at Grosse Isle, July 20, 1847 (*Eyewitness*, p. 185); nurses' pay: Testimony of Boxer, *Eyewitness*, p. 185. A report on the shortages on Grosse Isle can also be found in Papers Relative to Emigration to the British Provinces of North America [932] [964] [971] [985], pp. 14–16.

276   **"Water! Water!":** Mackay, *Flight from Famine*, p. 270; if infection does not arise: *Eyewitness*, p. 173.

277   **examining physician visits emigrant ship:** Whyte, *Ocean Plague*, pp. 75–76.

277   **criticism of Dr. Douglas's management at Grosse Isle:** Testimony of Captain Boxer, in Report of Special Committee (*Eyewitness*, p. 186.); complaints of visiting Quebec City Medical Commission: Mackay, *Flight from Famine*, p. 264.

278   **Archbishop Signay issues appeal:** Circular Letter to Catholic Archbishops of Ireland (*Eyewitness*, p. 87).

278   **"Of the 4,000 or 5,000":** Papers Relative to Emigration to the British Provinces in North America [50], June 9, 1847, p. 28.

278   **physical conditions on Grosse Isle, June–July 1847:** Douglas to Elgin, Dec. 27, 1847 (*Eyewitness*, p. 377); on some vessels, a third to a quarter of passengers dead: Douglas to Elgin, Dec. 27, 1847 (*Eyewitness*, p. 377).

279   **conditions in Quebec City:** *Quebec Herald*, reprinted in *New York Herald*, Aug. 7, 1847; *Quebec Gazette*, June 21, 1847, Aug. 20, 1847; Douglas to A. C. Buchanan, Papers Relative to Emigration . . . June 9, 1847 [50]; Mackay, *Flight from Famine*, p. 274.

280   **"pigs upon the deck":** S. de Vere: Papers Relative to Emigration to the British Provinces of North America [932], p. 45.

280   **"Every hour furnishes":** *Montreal Herald*, July 16, 1847.

281   **Mills letter to Queen Victoria:** J. Mills, Papers Relative to Emigration to the British Provinces of North America [50], June 23, 1847, p. 8. See also in same report: Mills to Lord Elgin, June 14, 1847, pp. 8–9; Peter McGill (speaker of Canadian Legislative Assembly) to Queen Victoria, July 6, 1847; Alan MacNab (MP, Canadian Legislative Assembly) to Queen Victoria, June 25, 1847, p. 7.

281   **conditions in Pont St. Charles and Montreal generally:** *Montreal Gazette*, July 8, 1847; *Montreal Herald*, July 16, 1847; July 20, 1847; *Montreal Witness*, Aug. 2, 1847.

282   **spread of disease into Ontario:** Mackay, *Flight from Famine*, p. 273.

282   **"I much fear . . . serious embarrassment":** Elgin to Colonial Secretary Grey: Papers Relative to Emigration to the British Provinces of North America [50], p. 12.

282   **mortality among Irish emigrants to Canada and impact on relations between Canada and Great Britain:** A. B. Hawke, Chief Emigration Agent, Upper Canada, Papers Relative to Emigration to the British Provinces of North America [50], Sept. 20, 1847, p. 19; Hawke to Elgin, Papers Relative to Emigration to the British Provinces of North America, Oct. 16, 1847; Macdonagh, *Patterns of Government Growth*, p. 183; Miller, *Emigrants and Exiles*, p. 313.

283–84 **assisted emigration:** Papers Relative to Emigration to the British provinces of North America [932]: report on arrival of *Aeolus* in St. John's, pp. 47–48, 53–64; the arrival of the *Virginius* is described by Dr. Douglas in his Dec. 27 letter to Elgin. For further information on assisted emigration, see G. Moran, *Sending Out Ireland's Poor*, pp. 94–110. See also Lieutenant Governor Colebrook to Earl Grey [932], July 13, 1847, p. 67; same to same, Aug, 27, 1847, p. 103; same to same, Nov. 11, 1847, p. 149; Earl Grey to Colebrook, Dec. 2, 1847, p. 93.

285   **shooting of Major Mahon:** Scally, *The End of Hidden Ireland*, pp. 38–40.

Fifteen: "Yankee Doodle Dandy"

286   **New York weather in early March 1847:** Document No. 2, Board of Assistant Aldermen . . . Annual report of City Inspector . . . for the year 1847, Mar. 27, 1848, pp. 139–41, www.archive.org. Ebook and Texts Archive, American Libraries.

286   **Staten Island quarantine station:** William Smith, *An Emigrant's Narrative or a Voice from Steerage* (1850), pp. 24–25.

287   **"All Germany is alive":** Report of George Bancroft to Washington, D.C., Feb. 3, 1847, Bancroft Papers, Box 30, National Archives, Washington, D.C.

287   **immigrants "men of health and energy":** *New York Herald*, Apr. 21, 1847; Staten Island's Committee of Safety: *New York Herald*, Aug. 6, 1847; Hubert Street rebels: *New York Herald*, Aug. 6, 1847.

287   **role of Erie Canal in New York's development:** Robert Ernst, *Immigrant Life in New York City* (1949), p. 14.

287–88 **status of pre-famine Irish in New York City:** Paul Gilje, "The Development of the Irish American Community in New York Before the Great Migration," in *The New York Irish*, R. Bayor and T. Meagher, eds. (1997), p. 81.

288   **Charles Dickens:** Dickens, *American Notes* (1883), p. 89; "repulsive to our habits and our taste": quoted by Edward O'Donnell, "The Scattered Debris of the Irish Nation," in *The Hungry Stream*, E. Margaret Crawford, ed. (1997), p. 54.

288–89 **link between immigrant Irish and Democratic party:** Daniel Patrick Moynihan, "The Irish," in *Making the Irish American* (2006), pp. 477–85. Parts of chapter fifteen were deeply influenced by the Moynihan essay, a knowledgeable and stylish examination of the New York Irish.

289   **excitement on approaching New York:** W. Smith. *An Emigrant's Narrative*, pp. 20–23.

289   **famine death toll two million:** Report from Irish press, reprinted in *New York Herald*, May 8, 1847.

289   **death rate on the *India*:** W. Smith, *An Emigrant's Narrative*, p. 24; mortality on British, American, and German vessels: Second Report of the Commissioners of Emigration of the State of New York, Jan. 9, 19, 1949, p. 10, books.google.com.

289–90 **epidemic in New York:** *New York Tribune*, May 18, 1847. Board of Assistant Aldermen, Annual Report of City Inspector, Document No. 21 (1847), pp. 104–7. Some of the report's observations about the outbreak of pestilence in New York sound remarkably like the observations collected by the editors of the *Dublin Quarterly Journal of Medical Science*.

290   **reports of Staten Island Committee of Safety on "low Irish":** *New York Herald*, Aug. 6, 1847.

290   **failure in quarantine system:** Report of Select Committee of New York State Legislature on Quarantine.

290   **comparison of mortality rates in New York and Montreal:** *New York Herald*, Aug. 1, 1847.

290–91 **description of New York harbor life:** Ernst, *Immigrant Life in New York City*, pp. 28–45; chapters three and four of Herman Melville's *Redburn* also give some flavor of harbor life in the 1840s; "the number of boats shooting hither and thither": *New York Herald*, Aug. 23, 1847.

291–92 **character of different boardinghouses:** Thomas Butler Gunn, *The Physiology of New York Boarding Houses* (1857). For English boardinghouses, see pp. 236–45; for German, pp. 255–62; and for Irish, pp. 263–69. See also Ernst, *Immigrant Life in New York City*, p. 28.

292   ***Harper's Weekly* quotation and behavior of dock runners:** Florence Elizabeth Gibson, *The Attitude of the New York Irish Toward State and National Affairs, 1848–1892* (1951), pp. 13, 131; the boardinghouse scams of Irish runners are described in Gunn's *Physiology of New York Boarding Houses*, pp. 263–69; description

of other runner scams: Frederich Knapp, *Immigration and the Commissioners of Emigration of the State of New York* (1870), pp. 55, 67, 80. (This 1870 book authored by Knapp, a German American member, was a summation of the commission's activities during the high tide of emigration, the 1840s through the 1860s.) Scams of running houses: Knapp, *Commissioners of Emigration*, pp. 70–73; Mr. Ahern and bonding system: ibid., pp. 46–50. Tapscott's Private Poor House and Hospital: ibid., pp. 50–53; interviews with poorhouse inmates: ibid., p. 54; provisions of 1847 Passenger Act: ibid., p. 85; criticism of Emigration Commission by *New York Irish-American*.

294   **immigration reforms:** Ernst, *Immigrant Life in New York City*, p. 39; financial provisions of Passenger Act of 1847: Knapp, *Commissioners of Emigration*, p. 98.

294–95   **American barriers to immigration:** *Liverpool Mail*, April 24, 1847; Passenger Act of 1847.

295   **1.8 million emigrants between 1847 and 1851:** Hasia R. Diner, "Most Irish City in the Union," in *The New York Irish* (1997), p. 91; emigration to New York, May to December 1847, and nationalities of emigrants: First Annual Report of Commissioners of Emigration of the State of New York (1847), p. 10, books.google.com; 98,000 Irish arrive in 1848: Second Annual Report of Commissioners of Emigration, pp. 9–10; 112,000 Irish immigrants in 1849: Third Annual Report of Commissioners of Emigration, Jan. 23, 1850, p. 42, books.google.com.

295   **117,000 Irish arrived in U.S. in 1847:** Miller, *Emigrants and Exiles*, p. 292.

295–96   **weather in July 1847:** Board of Assistant Aldermen, Annual Report of City Inspectors 1847 (Mar. 27, 1848), p. 142, www.archive.org. Ebook and Texts Archive, American Libraries.

296   **letter of Biddy Nulty, July 21, 1847:** James Charles Roy, "Letters to and from Galway Emigrants," *Journal of the Galway Archeological and Historical Society*, vol. 56 (2004), pp. 97–98.

296–97   **letters of Patrick Fitzpatrick, Patrick McGoorty, Margaret Collins, and William Burns:** Ruth-Ann Harris and Donald M. Jacobs, eds., *The Search for Missing Friends: Irish Immigrant Advertisements Placed in the Boston Pilot*, vol. 1, 1831–1850 (1999), p. 224 (Fitzpatrick), p. 222 (McGoorty), p. 217 (Collins), p. 215 (Burns and Grady).

298   **Biddy jokes:** Roy, "Letters to and from Galway Emigrants," pp. 90, 100; employment advertisements: Ernst, *Immigrant Life in New York City*, p. 67.

298   **half of all skilled labor in New York being Irish:** Ernst, *Immigrant Life in New York City*, p. 73.

298   **Shakespeare and Duke of Wellington:** The true ethnicity of these two alleged English gentlemen emerged during a father-son exchange in *Long Day's Journey into Night*:

SON: Shakespeare was an Irish Catholic?
FATHER. So he was. The proof is in his plays.
SON: Well, he wasn't and there's no proof of it in his plays except to you!
SON, again: The Duke of Wellington, there was another good Irish Catholic!
FATHER: I never said he was a good one. . . .
SON: Well he wasn't. You just want to believe no one but an Irish Catholic general could beat Napoleon.

299   **"I commenced working":** Miller, *Emigrants and Exiles*, p. 318.

299   **description of Five Points:** Ernst, *Immigrant Life in New York City*, p. 39.

299–300   **"large quantities of manure and garbage":** Annual Report of Board of Assistant Aldermen, Document No. 20, City Inspector (1845), Mar. 22, 1846, p. 683.

300   **"It is but truth to say":** E. O'Donnell, "Scattered Debris of the Irish Nation," in Crawford, *The Hungry Stream*, p. 54; 848,000 Irish immigrate to New York, and a quarter of Brooklyn Irish: Diner, "Most Irish City in the Union," pp. 91–93.

300   **"The Irish":** Thomas Babington Macaulay quoted by Moynihan, "The Irish," p. 489.

300–302   **vocabulary used to describe immigrant Irish:** Dale Kobel, "The Celtic Exodus, the Famine Irish, Ethnic Stereotypes, and the Cultivation of American Racial Nationalism," in *Fleeing the Famine*, Margaret Mulrooney, ed. (2003), pp. 80–81; Irish not taught punctuality, sobriety, etc.: Richard Shaw, *Dagger John: The Unquiet Life and Times of Archbishop John Hughes of New York* (1977), p. 236; incidence of Irish prostitutes, paupers, etc., in New York: O'Donnell, "Scattered Debris," in *Hungry Stream*, p. 54; "senseless machines," *Southern Literary Messenger* quoted by Kobel "The Celtic Exodus' in *Fleeing the Famine*, pp. 82–83; Irish and lack of most desirable racial characteristics: Kobel, p. 88; Irish riots: Diner, "Most Irish City in the Union," p. 97; denunciation in *Presbyterian Quarterly Review* quoted by Kobel, p. 89; Irish 21 percent of population: Diner, "Most Irish City in the Union," p. 92.

302   **burial of John Hughes's sister:** Shaw, *Dagger John*, pp. 8–15; "My lot," Hughes said later": *Dagger John*, pp. 224–25; Hughes created a homeland for the immigrants, p. 225. For an examination of Hughes's leadership style and achievements, see also O'Donnell, "Scattered Debris," p. 55; Moynihan, "The Irish," pp. 485–89.

305–6   **Tammany Hall, its leading characters, and the rise of the Irish in New York political life:** Moynihan, "The Irish," pp. 475–80; differences in sensibility between Yankee elite and Irish: Gibson, *The Attitude of the New York Irish Toward State and National Affairs*, pp. 31–32, 41, 257–64. Miss Gibson, an intelligent but highly impressionable Yankee lady, was deeply shocked by the tribal behavior of the Irish immigrant community.

309   **"England, God damn her":** Moynihan, "The Irish," p. 491.

309–10   **John Mitchel's *Last Conquest of Ireland (Perhaps)*:** relief measures as machinery of destruction, p. 102; grain exported, p. 112; bureaucratic obfuscation, p. 120; Trevelyan's "typhus laboratories," p. 120.

310–11   **influence of John Mitchel and Young Ireland on Irish America:** Miller, *Emigrants and Exiles*, pp. 307–12, 335, 341–42. A mid-nineteenth-century ballad highlights how deeply anti-British feeling permeated the immigrant communities of New York, Boston, and Philadelphia:

The day will come when vengeance loud will call
And we will rise with Erin's boys to rally one and all
I'll be the man to lead the van beneath our flag of green
And loud and high will raise the call "Revenge for Skibbereen."

311   **British spies in Irish emigrant communities:** Gibson, *The Attitude of the New York Irish*, pp. 183–84; Boss Tweed wires fare money home after Irish invasion of Canada: ibid., p. 204.

312   The concluding image in this chapter, Yankee Doodle Dandy, owes a great deal to Senator Moynihan's "The Irish," pp. 492–93.

Sixteen: Catastrophe and Its Consolations

313–15 **description of reaction to O'Connell's death and funeral:** "Hero of Christianity": *The Freeman's Journal*, Aug. 13, 1846; loitering in Dublin harbor, *Liverpool Mercury*, Aug. 6, 1847; "at last the wish of the Irish people": Aug. 4, 1847; day of funeral: reprint of *The Freeman's Journal* article in *Caledonia Mercury*, Aug. 9, 1847.

315 **disquiet about 1847 potato crop:** *Cork Southern Reporter*, May 30, 1847 (it was a correspondent from the *Southern Reporter* who visited the suspect potato field); *The Times*, June 2, 1847.

315–16 **"glorious summer" weather:** Clarendon to Revee, Sept. 18, 1847, in *Life and Letters of George William Frederick, Fourth Earl of Clarendon*, Herbert Maxwell, ed., vol. 1 (1913), p. 280.

316 **2,000 Burgoyne kitchens feed 3,020,712:** Fourth Report of Relief Commissioners [859], 1847, p. 5.

316–17 **arrival of imports:** *Liverpool Albion*, June 7, 1847; fall in food prices, G. R. Porter to Trevelyan, Apr. 15, 1848, in Gray, *Land, Famine and Politics*, p. 186; "time for Ireland's regeneration at hand": Trevelyan, *The Irish Crisis*, p. 199.

317 **three-quarters of a million jobs lost:** Final Report of Board of Works in Ireland, Sept. 1847 [1047], p. 6; Corr. [797], Board Series, pp. 344, 486.

317 **"The majority [of landlords] look for salvation":** *Liverpool Mercury*, Oct. 5, 1847; Mr. *Punch*'s suggestions: reprinted in *The Times*, May 29, 1847.

318 **tax collections 1846 vs. 1847:** Summary of Financial Returns and Workhouses in Ireland, 1848 [919], p. 674.

318 **James Hack Tuke's tour of Ireland:** Tuke, *A Visit to Connaught in the Autumn of 1847* (1848). For conditions in north, east, west of Ireland, pp. 4, 29; visit to village of Keel, pp. 11–12. Cavendish predicts a violent winter: Michael O'Malley, "Local Relief During the Great Famine: The Case of County Mayo," unpublished Ph.D. diss., Loyola University, Chicago (2000), p. 152.

318–19 **Russell's attitude toward financial condition of Irish landed class:** Prest, *Lord John Russell*, p. 269.

319 **British financial crisis:** Gray, *Land, Famine and Politics*, 288–89; role collapse of corn prices played in crisis: Prest, *Lord John Russell*, pp. 265–67; "Every second house to let": Smith, *Irish Journals*, p. 154.

319–20 **emigration to Britain:** Woodham-Smith, *The Great Hunger*, pp. 278–82; incident at St. Marylebone church: *The Observer*, Oct. 18, 1847; England and Scotland use resources for own people, *Preston Guardian*, July 17, 1847; 1847 election results. Gray, *Famine, Land and Politics*, p. 290.

320 **Let Irish die:** Fourth Report . . . on Poor Laws [Ireland] [170] (1849), p. 299.

320–23 **history of Rochdale and Michael Duignan:** Samuel Lewis, *A Topographical Dictionary of England* (1848), pp. 679–86. Michael Duignan's last day: a detailed account emerged from Michael's inquest, which was published in *Manchester Guardian*, Sept. 29, 1847.

324 **"bright light shining":** Albert Camus, *The Plague* (1947), p. 90; "Reason is now able to make herself heard": Trevelyan, *The Irish Crisis*, p. 190.

324–25 **The description of Mayo in autumn 1847:** This is drawn from Asenath Nicholson, *Annals of the Famine*. Seagull eggs, p. 97; search for harvest remains, pp. 297–98; visit to young woman, p. 322.

325 **suicide of Tipperary vicar:** *The Morning Chronicle*, Aug. 20, 1847; deaths continue to increase: Rev. E. L. Moore, *Manchester Guardian*, Sept. 5, 1847.

326   **"This must . . . end":** Wood to Clarendon, Aug. 15, 1847, quoted in Gray, *Famine, Land and Politics,* p. 292.

326   **"Les beaux jours":** Clarendon to Russell, Sept. 18, 1847, *Life and Letters of George William Frederick, Fourth Earl of Clarendon,* p. 280.

326   **Michael Bradley:** James Donnelly, "The Administration of Relief, 1847–1851," in *New History of Ireland,* vol. 5, p. 325.

327   **eviction in Mullagrobe:** Tuke, *A Visit to Connaught in the Autumn of 1847,* pp. 63–64.

327   **unpaid balance of £854,049:** Nicholls, *A History of the Irish Poor Law,* p. 345; experience of tax collector Patrick Martin: Papers Relating to the . . . Distressed Unions in the West of Ireland [1010] (1849), p. 139; "troublous" Captain Wynne: *Erne Packet,* reprinted in *The Times,* Dec. 6, 1847; Distressed Unions, pp. 113–15.

327–28 **appointment of Mr. Twisleton:** *Dublin Evening Mail,* Feb. 2, 1847.

328   **poor rates in Mayo and Clare:** Donnelly, "Administration of Relief, 1847–1851," p. 327.

328   **"Ireland cannot be left to her own resources":** Clarendon to Russell, Aug. 28, 1847, quoted in Prest, *Lord John Russell,* p. 270.

328   **Burgoyne letter to *The Times*:** Oct. 12, 1847.

328   **clergy protest Queen's Letter:** Wood to Clarendon, Oct. 18, 1847, quoted in Woodham-Smith, *The Great Hunger,* p. 306.

329   **selection and rules governing distressed unions:** Papers Relating to the Relief of Distress and the State of the Unions and Workhouses in Ireland [896], pp. 15–20.

329   **Trevelyan letter:** *The Times,* Oct. 12, 1847.

329–30 **Elphin history and geography:** Lewis, *Topographical Dictionary of Ireland,* pp. 520–21; assassination of Lloyd: *The Times,* Dec. 2, 1847; assassination of Baley: *The Times,* Nov. 24, 1847; assassination of Peter Nash, *The Times,* Dec. 30, 1847.

330–31 **rise of land question:** T. P. O'Neil, "The Irish Land Question," *Irish Historical Studies,* vol. 34 (1955), pp. 330–40; Clarendon to Russell, Nov. 10, 1847; same to same, Nov. 17, 1847; same to same, Nov. 15, 1847, all in *Life and Letters of George William Frederick, Fourth Earl of Clarendon,* pp. 281–83.

332–33 **eviction of John Costello:** Papers Relating to Relief of Distress [896], pp. 466–67.

Afterword

335   **"perfect engine":** J. O'Rourke, *History of the Great Irish Famine* (1902), p. 171.

335   **eviction rate rose by nearly 1,000%:** Donnelly, "Mass Evictions and the Great Famine," in C. Poirteir, ed., *The Great Irish Famine,* p. 156.

335   **numbers on relief:** Nicholls, *History of the Irish Poor Law,* p. 346.

336   **poor rates at confiscatory levels:** Kinealy, *This Great Calamity,* pp. 189–90.

336   **Young Ireland uprising:** Woodham-Smith, *The Great Hunger,* pp. 358–59.

336   **wave of evictions in August 1848:** Donnelly, "Mass Evictions and the Great Irish Famine," pp. 164–65.

337   **resistance to the Poor Law:** Kinealy, "The Role of the Poor Law During the Great Famine," in *The Great Irish Famine,* pp. 116–21.

337   **memorial on evictions to Queen Victoria:** Donnelly, "Mass Evictions and the Great Irish Famine," p. 168.

337   **British emergency assistance:** Kinealy, "The Role of the Poor Law," p. 119.

337 **Russell willing to provide more assistance:** Black, *Economic Thought and the Irish Question* (1960), p. 127; Ireland in the 1850s, ibid., p. 44.

338 **number of small farms on eve of World War I:** Diarmaid Ferriter, *Transformation of Ireland* (2004), pp. 62–63.

338 **famine mortality and emigration rate:** Donnelly, "Excess Mortality and Emigration," in *New History of Ireland*, vol. 5, pp. 350–54.

Acknowledgments

I am indebted to several historians for their guidance and assistance. I would like to thank Cormac O'Grada, Professor, University College Dublin, School of Economics; James Donnelly, Professor emeritus, Irish and British History, University of Wisconsin, Madison; Robert Scally, Professor of History (emeritus), Irish Studies, New York University; J. Joseph Lee, Glucksman Chair of Irish Studies, New York University; Joel Mokyr, Professor of Economic History, Northwestern University; and Stephen Morse, Professor of Clinical Epidemiology, Mailman School of Public Health, Columbia University. I also owe a debt of gratitude to the staff at the National Archives and National Library in Dublin and the staff at Butler Library at Columbia University.

There are four people I would particularly like to thank, my agent, Ellen Levine, my editor, Marjorie Braman, and most especially my wife, Sheila Weller Kelly. Sheila's unfailing support, inexhaustible patience, and shrewd editorial judgment eased the difficulties of writing a challenging book. I would also like to thank my son, Jonathan Kelly, for his assistance in fact-checking the book.

Index

Page numbers in *italics* refer to illustrations.

About the Author

JOHN KELLY is the author of nine previous books about science, medicine, and human behavior, among them a history of the Black Death, *The Great Mortality* (2005), and *Three on the Edge* (1999). Kelly lives in New York City and Sandisfield, Massachusetts.